A Reef in Time

A Reef in Time

THE GREAT BARRIER REEF
FROM BEGINNING TO END

J. E. N. Veron

THE BELKNAP PRESS OF
HARVARD UNIVERSITY PRESS
Cambridge, Massachusetts
London, England

First Harvard University Press paperback edition, 2009

Library of Congress Cataloging-in-Publication Data

Veron, J. E. N. (John Edward Norwood)
A reef in time : the Great Barrier Reef from beginning to end / J.E.N. Veron.
p.   cm.
Includes bibliographical references and index.
ISBN 978-0-674-02679-7 (cloth : alk. paper)
ISBN 978-0-674-03497-6 (pbk.)
1. Great Barrier Reef (Qld.)
2. Climatic changes—Australia—Great Barrier Reef (Qld.)
3. Coral reef conservation—Australia—Great Barrier Reef (Qld.)
4. Environmental responsibility—Australia—Great Barrier Reef (Qld.)
5. Environmental protection—Australia—Great Barrier Reef (Qld.)
I. Title
QE566.G7V47   2008
578.77′8909943—dc22   2007011253

Contents

Preface *vii*

1   The Big Picture   *1*

2   The Great Barrier Reef: An Overview   *12*

3   Corals and Reefs: Controls and Processes   *26*

4   The State of the Great Barrier Reef   *46*

5   Mass Extinctions and Reef Gaps   *66*

6   Messages from Deep Time   *89*

7   The Cenozoic Roller Coaster   *113*

8   Australia Adrift   *126*

9   The Ice Ages   *134*

10   The Last Glacial Cycle   *150*

11   Many Origins   *161*

12   Stone Age Utopia   *174*

13   An Enhanced Greenhouse World   *183*

14   Temperature and Mass Bleaching   *200*

15   Ocean Acidity and Coralline Osteoporosis   *212*

16   The Ocean's Canary   *221*

Notes   *235*

Glossary   *265*

Acknowledgments   *273*

Index   *277*

Color illustrations follow page 100

Preface

I will admit, as some colleagues have noticed, to having become an "armchair scientist," for I do indeed spend a great deal of time secluded behind a wall of literature, much of it having something to do with coral reefs. Nevertheless, I have also been privileged to have worked in every major coral reef region in the world, sometimes revisiting the same country year after year. And I enjoy talking—at meetings, in pubs, on field trips, wherever. Be it armchair or wetsuit talk, a lab discovery or a new book, reef science remains for me one of the world's most interesting frontiers of discovery. Of course I have my biases—one of them being conservation, indisputably the main focus of reef science today—and my passions—including one of the most wonderful places on Earth, Australia's Great Barrier Reef.

The Great Barrier Reef (GBR) is an icon of primordial wilderness, a place of grandeur to be cherished when so many other of our Earth's great showplaces have been diminished within the span of a single human life. Surely the GBR, owned by a prosperous country and accorded much of the protection it deserves, will not go the way of the Amazon rainforest or the parklands of Africa; it will endure forever. That is what I once thought. But I think it no longer, which is why I have written this book.

Certainly the GBR claims center stage in most of these chapters, and I occasionally wax lyrical because if the question "Why should we care?" has no clear answer, then the rest of the book has no clear purpose. Nevertheless there are many hundreds of popular books, articles, guides, and television documentaries about the GBR and the life it contains, and the number of scientific articles on subjects relevant to it has long numbered in the tens of thousands. This extraordinary coverage has no equal anywhere in the ocean realm, and it undeniably demonstrates a lot of caring. I draw heavily on that reservoir of knowledge when delving into the seemingly remote subjects covered here, for otherwise—were this book to do justice to the full breadth of its subject matter—it would need to be the size of an encyclopedia.

My work on coral reefs has motivated me to write several books, but not this one. This book was prompted by warnings that the Earth's climate could be changing—a remote subject as far as I was concerned, until I saw for my-self the devastation that elevated sea temperatures can inflict on corals. Since then, like many others, I have followed the debates about where our climate might be headed in the future. Initially I was skeptical of some of the claims being made concerning climate change—a view long since gone.

What finally goaded me to embark on this book was a sense of frustration in continually seeing disputes with two root causes: walls between scientific disciplines, which seem to have become increasingly impervious, and fail-ures of understanding surrounding that most elusive of subjects, time. The word *time,* together with the many adjectives that qualify it, is used to de-scribe intervals that often have nothing to do with each other. Human, biological, evolutionary, and geological time frames are all described using the same words—a practice that seldom fails to create confusion in texts that move through very different time intervals, as this book does. I offer no apologies for being pedantic about this issue. It first arises in Chapter 1 and remains a mantra through to the end of the book.

For most of my life I have been absorbed by corals: their taxonomy, bio-geography, and evolution, and when given the chance, their paleontology, ecology, and genetics as well. It is this combination of approaches that per-petually causes me to see time from very different perspectives. There is nothing new for me here. In 1995 I published *Corals in Space and Time,* which touched on all of these subjects and attempted to integrate them. Yet this book is not another along that line. Here I put genuine geological skep-tics, conservation alarmists, and biological pragmatists into the same boat, throw in a healthy dose of climate science, and set it on its course. Few spe-cialists will enjoy this company, and fewer still will appreciate my avoidance of their specialized terminology. I seek the big picture, and technical jargon just gets in the way.

Prediction is by far the most difficult aspect of time, yet there are mes-sages about the future lurking everywhere in the past—and some of them arise from the most unlikely sources. Nevertheless, the point of reference to which I keep coming back is the GBR, not just because I am biased, but because it allows me to bring into play the full range of subjects that put time—past, present, and future—into meaningful perspective.

Put simply, we are running out of time—human time—to stop climate change from destroying coral reefs. This book explains why.

A Reef in Time

— 1 —

The Big Picture

The Great Barrier Reef, Nature's pinnacle of achievement in the ocean realm, is the embodiment of wilderness, of remoteness—a place of endless beauty that has endured when so many other places on Earth, cherished by generations past, no longer engender strong emotions or else have been altered beyond all recognition. A truly cohesive account of how the Great Barrier Reef has changed in the geological past and will change in the human-controlled future must embrace concepts of time, the linking of disparate scientific disciplines, and the human takeover of climate control. As we turn from past to future in this book, we delve into scientific advances that are still in their infancy and that often go unappreciated because they are viewed in isolation rather than as part of a bigger picture.

What an extraordinary experience it must have been for the pioneering astronauts to have seen the Great Barrier Reef (GBR) from space. When they first looked down on the blue planet, the GBR was readily recognizable, for it is the largest construction of living organisms anywhere on Earth. Unfortunately, not many of us are privileged to see it from this vantage point. Even a bird's-eye view of the GBR during surveys using long-range aircraft cannot convey the same sense of size. As the plane flies on, hour after hour, the senses become overloaded, and when we review the flight path afterward we are always reminded that we saw just a fraction of the GBR's total area.

Diving on the reef is a completely different matter, for reefs create feelings of limitless size, unlike anything on land. Only the best movie photographers can capture the ambience of truly pristine reefs surrounded by a profusion of animal life: corals, fish, anemones, urchins, starfish, shellfish, and small creatures everywhere—a diversity rarely seen on land, not even in rainforests. Then there are the vertical cliff faces and the ceilings of caverns, all ablaze with the color of filter feeders: ascidians, sponges, sea fans, crinoids, and nonreef hard and soft corals. A healthy reef has an amazing wealth of life, most of it still beyond the knowledge of science.

Diving at night is to enter yet another world, for the diver's light reveals tiny animals by the thousands: clouds of plankton of all shapes, sizes, and colors, swimming frantically, lured by the light. Corals, opening their tentacles to catch these frenetic little swimmers, transform themselves into beautiful anemone-like creatures, quite different from their daytime guises. At night large predators move through the distant darkness: sharks that roam unceasingly, in the hundreds, around all the great reefs of the world—at least those few remaining reefs where these sleek marauders have not yet been decimated. Day and night, corals are home to thousands of smaller animals that live within the protection of their stony branches.

Good photographs sometimes capture these scenes, but they can never convey the emotions of those of us fortunate enough to have actually looked upon this world. The greatest reefs of the GBR instill awe and wonder—but also fear, especially the less well-known reefs in the remote far north. The sight of large animals—whale sharks, manta rays, giant groupers, big ocean-going silver fish, and even the occasional whale—never fails to thrill, and all such sightings are added to the already prodigious collection of tales, to be retold (usually with embellishments) by the thousands of divers who have explored the reef.

Then there is the ever-present threat of depth, for clear-water reefs that plunge down into deep ocean can be deceptive, and all too often become a fatal attraction for an enthusiastic diver who wants to get just a little more out of the trip of a lifetime.

Electronic navigation and satellite imagery have virtually put an end to the GBR's long-held reputation of being one of the world's most dangerous places for ships. Today tropical cyclones are more feared than reefs, but there was a time when the GBR had more shipwrecks than the rest of Australia combined. A glance at any chart shows why, for within it reefs of all sizes—hiding just below the surface and enveloped by strong tidal currents—form a maze of many thousands of square kilometers.

Although I have worked on all the major reef regions of the world, most of the exceptionable dives of my life have been somewhere on the GBR. Of the truly great places on our planet that those first astronauts looked down upon, the GBR is surely one.

A Special Place: Tijou Reef

Tijou Reef, in the northern GBR, illustrates topics that arise in several of the following chapters. I remember my first dive down its outer face; as far as I know, it was the first time anyone had dived down the outer face of any ribbon reef. We made the dive specifically to see how close the Queensland Trough came to the face, which was not shown on the charts of the time. The question was answered quickly enough: as the depth contour on the accompanying aerial photograph shows, the outer face *was* the edge of the trough. With the water crystal clear and the reef sloping steeply, at 50 meters the face looks much as it did at 10 meters—a death trap for divers, for it gives no sense of depth. Divers do, however, experience a distinct fear, for the face is patrolled by hundreds of sharks, mostly harmless reef sharks and many 2-meter-long "silver-tips"; nevertheless, every ten minutes or so one spots a larger one, a bull shark or a tiger shark. Tiger sharks are not so much dangerous—they tend to ignore divers—as simply *big*. Certainly they remind divers to stick close to the reef—as well they may, given that the life there is vivid beyond description.

The reef face is a wall of coral: thick, solid colonies in the shallows, where the turbulence is strongest (see Plate 22), giving way to branching growth forms at greater depths. The profusion of life everywhere gives divers pause—to stop, to rest, to think, and to marvel about the life around them, to wonder about eons past when this face was dry land, or to speculate about what it was like when humans may have walked where the deepest corals now grow. These can only be fleeting thoughts, however, for divers must never give in to the reef's siren call: they can afford only a short time to muse before they must head back up the face to a decompression stop or a waiting boat.

Emerging Science: Its Guises and Gaps

Looking back, I think that this book had its beginnings while I was on a dive on Tijou Reef during the summer of 1973. I remember thinking then that the reefs we were visiting must be very old, for surely they had piggybacked on Australia's coast as she drifted north from Antarctica. But then I wondered if it would not have been too cold for corals at such times. If so, where did the corals come from, and why did they bother to build such enormous ramparts that apparently serve no purpose? Did fish and all other reef life

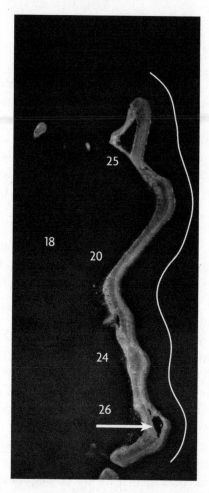

Figure 1.1 Tijou Reef, a ribbon reef mostly 1 kilometer wide. The white line along the eastern side is the 1,000-meter depth contour; the numbers to the left are depths in meters. The arrow indicates the position of Walker's Caves, described in Chapter 12 and illustrated in Plate 42. (Aerial collage by Geoscience Australia, Commonwealth of Australia.)

come and go with the corals? How is it that most reefs are planed off at pre-cisely the same level, even though sea level has apparently always been ris-ing and falling? What did this immense area look like when there was no ocean covering it? I found it hard to accept the idea that people had proba-bly once lived in caves that were now submerged far below me.

Coral reefs tend to engender these kinds of thoughts, and theories about them abound, some branching in the most unlikely directions. Even back in the 1970s I had a feeling that, despite its grandiose proportions and seeming indestructibility, the GBR was really a puppet on a string, at the mercy of events in other parts of the world. I soon learned that extraterrestrial forces, such as eccentricities of the Earth's orbit around the sun, might have had a hand in its history, and that great events in the geological past had repeatedly brought reef-building corals close to extinction. But how?

The beginnings of this book had been written in notebooks by the late 1970s. Had I turned those scribbles into something readable back then, some parts of that book would indeed have been similar to what appears in these pages. The GBR was the same place of tantalizing beauty and mystery then as it is today. We would have marveled then, as we do now, at the myriad of ecological interactions, interdependencies, and fascinating life histories of so many of its inhabitants. We would have examined the significance of each biological, geological, or oceanographic discovery—the sediments, the water chemistry, and the revelations of drilling projects. Much of that book would also have focused on the remote past—but it would have been followed by a rather different version of the birth and history of what we see today.

Certainly the relationship between humans and the reef would have been described very differently. In the 1970s, conservation issues might have accounted for only a page or two of my book, for the GBR seemed more than big enough to look after itself, and what few issues there were seemed to fall easily within the scope of the newly constituted marine park authority. The only real cloud on the horizon was that ever-present menace, the crown-of-thorns starfish. Of all the negative impacts we are aware of today, it—and perhaps it alone—has remained unchanged over the decades.

So, despite the similarities, a 1970s version of this book would have had a very different emphasis and range of subject matter, for much of today's science and many of our current concerns were wholly unknown—even unimaginable—back then. In the 1970s I might have ended the book with a heartwarming bromide: "And now we can rest assured that future generations will treasure this great wilderness area for all time." Today, as we are coming to grips with the influence that humans are having on the world's environments, it will come as no surprise that I am unable to write anything remotely like that ending.

Before 1980, El Niño events and enhanced (meaning human-induced) greenhouse warming seemingly had little to do with coral reefs. Then, in

1982, I saw for myself the aftermath of a mass bleaching event. Since then it has become increasingly clear that the implications of climate change cannot be fully understood without integrating the findings of many scientific and political disciplines, spanning such wide-ranging and sometimes unlikely subjects as sunspots, carbonate buffers, bolides, oxygen radicals, the Ocean Conveyor, Cretaceous CO_2, Paleocene methane, the human population explosion, and international politics.

Whirlwind Tours, Links, and Syntheses

This book, therefore, is not simply an exposé of reef science as applied to the GBR. What I offer here is a much broader view that takes in aspects of general biology, oceanography, evolutionary theory, paleontology, reef geology, and ocean chemistry and combines them with what we know of ancient climates and current concepts of climate change. The fabric of our knowledge can be likened to a fishing net that, though often mended, is nonetheless still full of holes. The netting itself is woven from the many strands of science—at least the strands that seem to me to matter—and the mends are the spots where I have taken patches from one set of scientific findings and used them to fix holes in another. To fashion these patches I have made do with the best information at hand, occasionally improvising where the science is altogether missing. In such instances, I have endeavored to make a clear distinction between what is science and what is improvisation. My aim throughout is to make the big picture as accurate and as clear as possible, looking toward the future with the advantage of hindsight.

Inevitably, this book takes whirlwind tours through many different sciences. I do not visit these in isolation, for my purpose can only be served by linking them together to form a cohesive whole. This has been no small task, for every discipline comes with a massive literature and a unique jargon. Not surprisingly, several readers of the manuscript asked me why I wrote this book by myself. Why didn't I leave parts to others? Jared Diamond, facing the same problem in *Guns, Germs and Steel*, offers an explanation: "These requirements [the many fields of science considered] seem at first to demand a multi-author work. Yet that approach would be doomed at the outset, because the essence of the problem is to develop a unified synthesis. That consideration dictates single authorship, despite all the difficulties that it poses. Inevitably, that single author will have to sweat copiously in order to assimilate material from many disciplines, and will require guidance from many colleagues."[1]

And so we come to the inadequacies of language—of words that have very different meanings across discipline boundaries. In everyday language we use the strongest of terms—"disasters," "catastrophes"—to describe the impact on humans of natural events such as earthquakes, volcanoes, tsunamis, droughts, and forest fires. Yet in a geological context these events are insignificant trivia. In fact there have been no natural events in all of written human history that rate any mention on the scale of our planet's history. Not so for the natural events that coral reefs have survived, and thus the problem for me is inescapable unless I resort to technical terms—jargon, words that have a clear meaning for those who have expertise in a particular subject yet are meaningless to everybody else. A couple of examples relevant to humans make the point. Mass extinctions are universally described as "events," yet all have taken longer to occur than our species, *Homo sapiens,* has existed. Many sea-level fluctuations of the distant past described as "rapid" have taken longer to occur than the total span of human civilization.

Many terms in this book can be ambiguous, even such basic words as "limestone," "reef," "coral reef," and "coral" as well as many marine terms, such as "plankton" and "substrate." These are explained either in the text when they are first used or else in the glossary. Unavoidably, I must use a few technical terms like "thermohaline circulation," "El Niño event," and "orbital forcing," as there are no alternatives. I also use the names of geological intervals without reservation, although I am aware that these have little meaning for nonspecialists. To help put such terms into context, explanatory time-line diagrams have been added to relevant chapters, and time intervals expressed in millions of years ago (mya) are sprinkled liberally throughout the text—a convention helpful to many if irritating to some. Yet problems that surround the concept of time are in a class of their own.

Time in Context

We use the same array of adjectives—"abrupt," "rapid," "gradual," "constant," and so on—to describe all manner of time intervals, no matter what the context—geological, evolutionary, biological, or human. Nevertheless, as in the previous examples, an event seen as major in one time frame may be irrelevant in another. These distinctions really *do* matter. For example, throughout this book I provide diagrams to depict changes in various phys-ical environmental factors such as atmospheric CO_2 levels or global tem-peratures. Each serves a purpose in its temporal context—yet other dia-grams of the same factors set in different time intervals would appear to tell a very different story. (I have, for instance, used four such diagrams to de-pict atmospheric CO_2 levels.) Context is everything, and the miscommuni-cations created when context is not appreciated continue to plague us.

Time on a geological scale, like distance in space, is easily read or written about. Geological intervals have names (like "Triassic") for easy reference, and if one prefers to express those names in years (like "251,000,000 to 206,000,000 years ago") it is easy to look them up or memorize them: the numbers are mostly zeroes anyway. It is thus a simple matter to be precise about time. It is, however, never possible to understand what all those zeroes actually mean in terms of reality, for geological time is not comprehensible to humans—not if we try to relate it to any form of personal experience or knowledge. Some innovative authors and documentary filmmakers have tried to illustrate this point by analogy. If we imagine the Earth to be just one year old, the "Mesozoic covers only two weeks of the last month of the year, from December 11 to 26, when the Cenozoic begins. The human race appears at 2 P.M. on December 31; the pyramids were built 30 seconds to midnight."[2] Or, going marine: "If the ultimate historians, geologists, were to show the full history of Earth vertically on a scale as long as the depth of the deepest sea, all human history, about ten thousand years, would fit nicely into the upper-most inch—about the depth of the depression made by a seagull lightly rid-ing on the surface."[3]

The time frames of major events in the history of reefs and in human his-tory are indeed very different, and it is this difference that leads some who deal in geological time to dismiss current climate changes as simply another blip in the history of the world's climate, a matter of little long-term conse-quence. However, our knowledge of the geological events of the past, if seen with the benefit of the biological and environmental knowledge of the pres-ent, helps to put these views into a human context. The long time frames of major geological events and the shorter ones of human influence on the Earth's history are beginning to overlap, and they are doing so with increas-ing relevance to the contemporary world. The overlap does not reveal itself in the geological chapters of this book, for the events described there are set in time intervals so vast that they have no meaning for humans. However, the events themselves do have meaning, for they provide us with some sort of perspective on what *can* happen when climates change; they also provide a basis for pondering what might be a "normal" world and what might be truly unprecedented. Past events may therefore be useful in anticipating what might happen in the future.

The Structure of This Book

I start with three chapters giving the essential preliminaries. Chapter 2 looks at the GBR in relation to other coral reefs globally and its setting on the east Australian coastline. Chapter 3 is concerned with the relationship between corals and reefs, focusing on points that are sometimes not well understood, and Chapter 4 is a synopsis of the current state of the GBR from a big picture perspective.

I then leave today's GBR to delve into the past—the past not only of the GBR, but of all reefs, as they are all affected by the same global climates. In Chapter 5 I journey to the very remote past to reflect on the great extinction events that wiped out much of the life on our planet. It is seen that these extinctions have some aspects in common and that they are all linked to deterioration of tropical oceans. Reefs appear to have been the hardest hit during such extinctions, and after every episode it took millions of years for them to recover. Chapter 6 examines the real causes of mass extinction of corals, through a mix of the biological and geological sciences. I discuss the carbon cycle in general and greenhouse gases in particular, two subjects that haunt the rest of the book. It is apparent that CO_2, along with methane (natural gas), has again and again played a hand in mass extinctions, not just by creating greenhouse conditions but by changing the chemistry of the oceans—a frightening scenario that could easily be repeated, even during the present century.

Chapters 7 and 8 are both about our own era, the Cenozoic. Chapter 7 is a continuation of the saga of environmental upheavals—their causes and consequences as far as coral reefs are concerned—and the familiar role of greenhouse gases in modifying global climates. It is in this chapter that we enter the time frame of the origins of the GBR. Chapter 8 is specifically about Australia and her journey from Antarctica toward the equator, experiencing the great climatic events just mentioned, yet following a unique geographic and biological history.

In Chapter 9 I return to climates, as the Earth plunges into the Ice Ages. The GBR, along with all the other coral reefs in the world as we see them today, is destroyed, recovers, and is destroyed again, over and over. After each of these episodes, the GBR seems to flourish as if nothing had happened. But appearances are deceptive. Much did happen during these cycles; to see precisely what, I focus in Chapter 10 on the last great glacial cycle and describe major climate change in action. In this chapter we are still in geological time, although just barely.

In Chapter 11 I turn back the clock to address a quandary. The age of the GBR as I depict it, the age most reef geologists believe it to be, and its biological age are three time intervals that have little in common. Why? Questions such as this have attracted the attention of scholars since the earliest maritime explorations. I go on to consider the sorts of questions that I remember pondering in 1973, including whether the original human occupants of this ancient land might have lived in caves that are now deep under the reefs. I advance the case for this argument in Chapter 12.

I then leave the past and turn to the present and the immediate future. Chapters 13 to 15 describe how greenhouse conditions can warm and acidify the oceans. You may well ask why, when this book is about a coral reef, so much space is devoted to matters of climate. My answer is the same as my reason for including so much geology in the earlier chapters. The GBR has not been self-determined in the past, and it will certainly not be in the future. We are now entering concertinaed time, for human influences are compressing geological time out of all recognition. Incredibly, today's reefs are facing a future that will be determined within the lifetime of people already alive or their immediate descendants. In Chapter 13 I turn to enhanced greenhouse warming, and in doing so reflect on what the fuss we encounter daily in the press is really all about.

Having established the factors most important to reef health and survival in geological time, in Chapter 14 I take a close look at ocean warming and the mass bleaching and subsequent death of corals that it causes. Chapter 15 moves on to that most serious of all subjects—ocean acidification. Earlier, in Chapter 6, I discussed how the carbon cycle in general and CO_2 in particular were implicated in past mass extinctions: Chapter 15 shows how these same processes are active today.

The material concerning the carbon cycle and the role of CO_2 in acidifying the oceans (Chapter 15) may seem to contain the kind of detail that I have been carefully avoiding, but I offer no apologies for this. We have come to the point where the critical issues are indeed matters of detail. Perhaps in the century to come scientists will be able look back on these details and see them in context; however, this is a luxury we do not have today. I have provided a path through these details for nonscientists: if detail is needed for explanation it is included in these chapters, but, for broad understanding of the issues, chemical equations and the like can be skipped with impunity.

Chapter 16 draws the essential threads of the book together, tying them into summaries as specific as current knowledge allows. Climate change is happening too quickly and in steps that are too erratic for detailed timelines. There are no tidy endpoints in this chapter, but instead expressions of hope—a hope that lies in technology, awareness, and political persuasion. Chapter 16 and the earlier material on which it draws stress that the production of greenhouse gases must be curbed as a matter of great urgency if we are to have any chance of avoiding another coral reef–led marine extinction. And this will not be *just* a coral reef extinction—it will be an extinction event the likes of which the Earth has not experienced for many tens of millions of years.

— 2 —

The Great Barrier Reef:
An Overview

The GBR, the largest World Heritage reef area on Earth, forms the southern border of the global center of reef biodiversity that straddles the equator. The ecology of the GBR is dominated by a strong east-west environmental gradient from clearwater offshore reefs to a wide range of coastal reefs supporting diverse communities. Substrate depth defines the southern limit of the GBR, but currents have dispersed corals beyond this boundary to form the southernmost reefs in the world. All of these reefs are under the aegis of comprehensive management practices.

Most but not all of the GBR is within the Great Barrier Reef Marine Park—an area of 345,500 square kilometers (larger than the United Kingdom or New Zealand), which accounts for 70 percent of the world's designated World Heritage reef area. The area covered by the reefs themselves is rather less—26,000 square kilometers, representing 10 percent of all the coral reefs in the world and second in size only to the reefs of Indonesia.[1] The variety of reefs—3,650 all told—is greater than in any other place on Earth, largely because the GBR is set on a wide, flat continental shelf with well-defined environmental gradients extending both across its width and down its 1,800-kilometer length. As a result, sediment-tolerant corals populate shallow inshore reefs along the GBR's western margin and blue-water corals occur to great depths on the wave-hammered outer reefs of the eastern edge. Contrary to general belief, these inshore reefs have more coral species than their better-known (and more photogenic) offshore blue-water counterparts,[2] which is the main reason that the cross-shelf (east-west) gradient dominates the region's ecology: most environmental variation, and thus most habitat variation, occurs *across* the GBR, not down its length.[3] I make repeated reference throughout this book to the difference between the inshore and offshore reefs, for these vast zones have little in common. Moreover, they account for most of the biological characteristics of the GBR, including ranges of variation seldom found in the reefs of other countries.

Zones across the Reef

Throughout most of the GBR province a wide coastal zone is dominated by nutrient-rich brown mud discharged by rivers. As all rivers opening onto the GBR are strongly seasonal according to the "wet" and "dry" seasons (in summer and winter, respectively) and have high rates of flow during peak rainfall, they have a major influence on nearshore seabed communities, including those dominated by coral. In fact they are a major reason why most of the well-formed GBR reefs are situated several tens of kilometers offshore. Corals that are commonly found in inshore muddy waters (such as *Alveopora*, *Heliofungia*, and *Goniopora*, the former two illustrated in Plates 16 and 20) live on food particles (detritus) in the sediment rather than on plankton in the water column, so they do not have batteries of stinging cells on their tentacles to capture prey. Nor do they retract their tentacles during the day. Corals of one group (*Pachyseris*) are so completely adapted to absorbing nutrients from the water that they have no tentacles at all. However, as I describe later, all reef corals, whether detritus feeders or plankton eaters, obtain a large part of their nutrient requirements from sunlight via the photosynthesis of symbiotic algae living in their tissues.

The GBR is riddled with islands—either cays or high islands. Cays, which are particularly common in the south and far north, are composed entirely of sand, rubble, and beach rock, all originally derived from coral and coralline algae debris. The debris is accumulated by wave action into platforms that may be many hectares in extent, yet are seldom more than 2 meters above high-tide level. High islands, which commonly form extensive archipelagos, are distinct from cays: they are simply chunks of continental shelf that project above the water. Thus they vary greatly in area and height; Hinchinbrook Island in the central GBR has the second highest mountain in Queensland.

Both types of islands are found mostly in inshore and midshelf regions. Looking like chains of one "island paradise" after another, both are alluring. However, if the truth be known, all of the many hundreds of cays are pretty much the same—some are covered with scrub or trees, others not. However, they all have a profusion of bird life seldom found on other coral cays of the world, no doubt the result of an Australian tradition of protecting birds, as well as close regulation of the number of visitors allowed on the islands. High islands, on the other hand, are usually very unlike each other. Underwater, they are even less alike, for each embayment offers an individual, almost unique, set of environmental conditions: different exposure to waves and an endless mixture of different sediment compositions, depth, water clarity, and substrate type. In general, the more convoluted the coastline, the greater the range of the marine habitats. This is the main reason why high islands have the greatest diversity of corals (and probably most other marine invertebrates), even though most colonies do not grow on anything that can be described as a reef. They do, however, form fringing reefs where the water is not too turbid, and often these fringing reefs enclose wide mud platforms, which may have extensive mangrove communities. Another reason these islands have such great biodiversity is the presence in the water of nutrients, which come either directly from the island or from the adjacent mainland. A further reason is the reluctance of crown-of-thorns starfish to invade turbid water.

Farther offshore from the nearshore zone, much of the GBR is devoid of reefs. This is an area variously referred to as the "lagoon" (not to be confused with the lagoons of individual reefs) or the "steamer channel," as it is the only shipping lane that hugs the northern Queensland coast. The absence of reefs in this area is due partly to the depth of the water (20–40 meters), which results in low light levels on the lagoon floor, and partly to the periodic influx of river water during wet season floods. However, neither low light nor low salinity can account for the full extent of the GBR lagoon. For this explanation we have to turn the clock back and see what the GBR was like thousands of years ago. When we do this, we find that at frequent intervals it was much narrower than at present, that today's outer reefs were the only reefs, and that today's lagoon was part of the terrestrial coastal zone, probably looking much like the equivalent coastal zone of today.

This is a large and intriguing subject, which we turn to later (see Chapters 9–12). However, life on the seabed of today's lagoon is oblivious to the area's past: the lagoon floor supports another great diversity of life—so-called soft-bottom communities. As with so many of the smaller reef organisms, we know less about this life than we should; even many of the most common organisms—sea pens, crinoids, endless kinds of crustaceans and molluscs, and even some fish—are virtually unknown to science. Although this area is part of the Great Barrier Reef Marine Park, much of it has been destroyed by decades of bottom trawling, a victim of the "out-of-sight, out-of-mind" syndrome that now afflicts so much of the world's great marine habitats.

The outer reefs are much better known to most visitors, for they are exceptionally photogenic, in or out of the water. The ocean around the outer reefs (those beyond the lagoon) is clear because it is well beyond the reach of river mud, and the sand there is white. This is calcareous sand, derived entirely from organisms—mostly corals and coralline algae—that have calcareous skeletons. The combination of calcareous sand and clear water makes for a range of habitats unlike any found along the coastal zone or around inshore islands. Nutrient levels are low and light levels are high, so reef life is highly dependent, directly or indirectly, on photosynthesis.

There are other major differences: offshore currents are relatively strong and wave energy is high. Wind-driven waves, especially those created by the southeast trade winds that blow most of the year, make the waters of the GBR choppier than those of most equatorial reefs, but the outer reefs protect the coastline from any impact of deep-ocean swell. Not so for the outer reefs themselves, which are exposed to large waves that build up over the reef front and break onto the outer flat. This wave action creates well-defined zones; the outermost coral zone is illustrated in Plate 22. Behind this zone wave-hammered corals become so flat that they resemble a stone pavement, the stones being individual coral colonies. The pavement they form is so uniform that an aircraft could almost use it as a runway at low tide. Farther behind these—in the part of the reef that takes the full brunt of the biggest waves—the reef flat often has no corals at all, just hard limestone cemented by coralline algae. Although these are the zones that exist today, they are not normal for reefs but are a geologically recent phenomenon, the product of an unusually long period—about 6,000 years—of stable sea level.

Ribbon and Deltaic Reefs of the Shelf Edge

In many ways the GBR is not a single reef province at all, but a coalition of several provinces that happen to be located together. Thus the region as a whole, as extensive as it is, has a wide range of tidal regimes, currents, temperatures, and weather conditions. For example, the tidal regime of one part of the GBR may be very different from that of another only a few hundred kilometers away, and a cyclone may batter one part while another is as calm as a lake. Little wonder that scientists who work on the GBR can become rather parochial in their thinking, as much of what they generally observe has a range of variation and size simply not found in other countries. Nevertheless, there are many types of reefs and reef environments that are not found on the GBR, such as reefs without any tidal range, reefs growing next to deserts, reefs with a sedimentary environment created by black volcanic ash, or reefs fringing continental margins that plunge abruptly to abyssal depths. Perhaps the one aspect of the GBR that makes it truly unique on Earth is encapsulated in the word "wilderness"—for by any standards much of the GBR is still just such a place.

There have been many attempts to classify reefs, but there is a lack of general agreement because there are always gradations from one reef type to another. Moreover, reefs can also be classified according to their geological history, their shape, their position relative to landmasses, and the nature of the material of which they are made. In essence, reefs can be merged into four broad categories: fringing reefs, barrier reefs, atolls, and platform reefs. The first three are Charles Darwin's original groups, while the last is a convenient name used for most of the other kinds of reef. All of these reef types are found on the GBR except atolls, for atolls can form only on a subsiding seafloor, and most of the GBR rests on an unusually stable foundation. However, this is not the case in the far north and at various places along the eastern margin, where shelf edges have flexed by tens of meters at different times. In addition, flooding owing to sea-level changes has caused the inner reefs to rise and the shelf-edge reefs to subside by 6 meters or more. Faulting off Townsville in the central region and the Pompey Complex in the south has caused substantial subsidence, even drowning, of some of the reefs.[4]

I do not delve here into details of the reef types of the GBR, for that is a subject that has little relevance to the purpose of this book. Yet a word must be said about the two most distinctive reef types of all—the ribbon reefs in the north (one being Tijou, which I introduced in Chapter 1) and the deltaic reefs of the far north and far south.

Ribbon reefs, which form a 550-kilometer-long wall that looks like a ribbon from the air, make up the eastern edge of the northern and far northern GBR. The inner (western) face of a ribbon reef like Tijou rises to the surface from a shallow lagoon floor, whereas its outer (eastern) face plunges so steeply into the Queensland Trough that it resembles a giant dam wall. This juxtaposition of reef edge and deep ocean clearly has a dynamic history, if only because it is so abrupt and so extensive. We know that the ribbon reefs have not kept their positions by growing ever thicker on a subsiding seafloor, like atolls growing on subsiding mountains. The logical alternative explanation is that they formed when the continental shelf was scrubbed clean during periods of low sea levels (see Chapter 11) and have grown incrementally since then.

Currents are responsible for the patterns looking like river deltas in "deltaic" reefs, which occur north of the northern end of the ribbon reefs (illustrated below),[5] and in the Pompey Complex in the south.[6] The patterns are produced by tidal currents moving rubble back and forth, grinding the reef away. The channels, which are often over 40 meters deep in the reefs illustrated in the accompanying figure, and twice that depth in the Pompey Complex, have vertical walls and horizontal floors, devoid of coral or any other form of life.

Where Corals and Coral Reefs Grow: A Global View

Give a coral biogeographer a map of any coastline and he or she will make a reasonably good guess about what corals occur there and on what type of reefs they are found—provided the map includes detailed information about the environment. This suggests that the corals themselves determine where they grow, but that is not the case. Corals grow anywhere their long-journeying larvae can reach, provided that the environment on arrival is suitable for their growth. Reefs, as I explain later, have further constraints, forming only within narrow environmental boundaries. When we try to predict or explain anything about reefs—as I do many times in this book—we are always constrained by these boundaries.

A wealth of information, from experiments as well as studies of genetics, taxonomy, and biogeography, suggests that coral larvae (illustrated in Plate 11), one way or another, are able to make very long ocean voyages, enduring weeks, even months, on the sea surface before settling.[7] That is not to say that all corals can reach every destination that is suitable for reef building: the larvae are always at the mercy of the currents that carry them, and most are lost at sea. But occasionally a few survive long journeys and arrive at distant locations suitable for settlement. Then, perhaps, a few live on to form a new colony. The shorter the journey, the greater the chance of survival and of population increase, whereas the longer the journey, the wider the dispersal. For these reasons, the number of coral species in any particu-

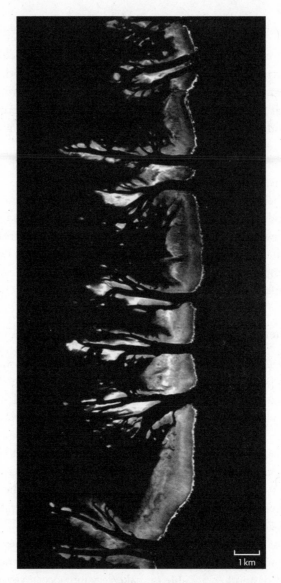

1 km

Figure 2.1 Deltaic channels of far northern outer reefs. The white parts of this reef line look like muddy deltas but are actually solid limestone; the dark "rivers" are channels cut by tidal currents. The channels have vertical sides and horizontal floors up to 40 meters deep cut by currents that reach 4 meters per second (7 knots) on outgoing tides. The Pompey Complex of the southern GBR has channels reaching 80 meters. (Aerial collage by Geoscience Australia, Commonwealth of Australia.)

lar place depends on the proximity of other reefs in the region and on the direction of the currents. It is no accident that extensive reef complexes, notably in the island archipelagos of Indonesia and the Philippines, have the most species and that this diversity is streamed out to other regions by the great boundary currents that hug the continental coastlines.

If, against long odds, a larva should arrive at a place potentially suitable for settlement, its geographic journey might be over—but its life journey will have only just begun. Now the chances of survival are even less: it must be within a suitable temperature range, have a substrate suitably clear of mud, have adequate sunlight, and be beyond the reach of fresh water from rivers. Only when all of these conditions have been met is the coral able to grow enough to produce another generation and continue to disperse and to evolve.

That last point needs qualification. Evolution in corals is exceedingly slow, whereas long-distance dispersal can be rapid—even within the span of a single generation. The two processes are only tentatively linked, because genetic pathways are constantly being changed by the vagaries of ocean currents, and opportunities for evolutionary change via natural selection are generally restricted to the rare occasions when species are isolated in space as well as time (see Chapter 3 and Plate 9 for further explanation).

Australian Reefs in a Global Context

The accompanying map shows the global diversity (species richness) of the coral regions of the world. The center of diversity, nicknamed the "Coral Triangle," contains more species than anywhere else on Earth—nearly 600 at its center. Moving east from the Coral Triangle across the South Pacific, the diversity progressively drops off, as is shown on the map, whereas moving west there is a relatively uniform diversity across the Indian Ocean and into the southern Red Sea. There is also a drop-off in species numbers north from the Coral Triangle to Japan and south down both the east and west coastlines of Australia. The far eastern Pacific has a very small number of species, most if not all having crossed the emptiness of the eastern Pacific since the last Ice Age. The region of the Caribbean was once—during an earlier part of our era (around 30 mya)—the world's center of coral diversity, but now contains fewer species (about 60) than are usually found on any small patch of reef of the GBR. There are many biogeographic and evolutionary explanations for these patterns,[8] the most important of which are the following: (1) There are no regions within the dispersal range of corals where environmental conditions are suitable for growth that do *not* have corals. (2) Latitudinal change in diversity north and south from the Coral Triangle is due primarily to dispersal, not evolution. (3) The longitudinal change around the tropics is largely an evolutionary outcome created over tens of millions of years of continental drift. I discuss these points in greater detail further in Chapters 3 and 11, as they help to explain the history and faunal composition of the GBR.

Corals and Reefs of Eastern Australia

The corals of the GBR are not particularly distinctive from those of other regions of the central Indo-Pacific, and most species are shared with other regions, especially southern Papua New Guinea and Vanuatu. On the other hand, the corals of the north coast of Papua New Guinea have more in common with Indonesian corals than with their Australian neighbors to the south.

Biogeographically, the coastline of southern Papua New Guinea (that is, the southeastern coast of the island of New Guinea) is almost a continuation of the GBR, for these reefs form a line shaped like a walking stick with a curved handle. The fact that the walking stick is now broken at the handle by the Fly River is a relatively transient matter in the long history of the corals.

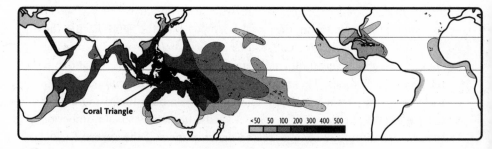

Figure 2.2 Contours of coral diversity (species richness). Species disperse over long distances from regions of high diversity, notably the Coral Triangle, to other Indo-Pacific regions, owing to the endurance of coral larvae. Many regions of the world, including most of the Atlantic (but not the Caribbean) and far eastern Pacific, have few if any corals and no reefs. However, over distances of 1,000 kilometers, the occurrence of both corals and reefs is highly predictable.

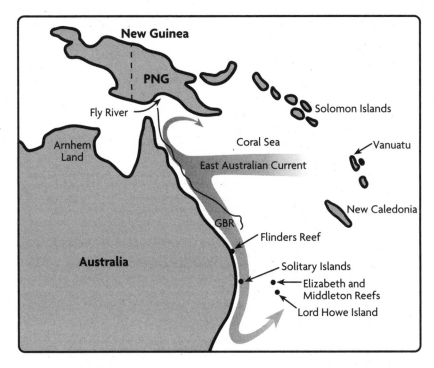

Figure 2.3   Place names, currents, and reefs referred to in the text.

Corals are also distributed south down the eastern coast of Australia, re-ducing in number of species as they go. This distribution occurs in an or-derly dropout sequence, as the number of tropical species gradually dimin-ishes and they are not replaced by subtropical counterparts.[9] This sequence is caused primarily by a decrease in the variety of habitat types in the south-ern GBR and farther south, as much as by decreasing temperature. It is also due to the southward flow of the East Australian Current, which carries lar-vae south, on nonreturn journeys, to the southernmost reefs in the world. Similar patterns are found along the coast of western Australia, where the Leeuwin Current carries larvae south to the southernmost reefs of the In-dian Ocean, and along the east coast of Asia to mainland Japan, where the Kuroshio carries larvae north to the world's northernmost reefs.

Contrary to popular belief, the southern limit of the GBR is not deter-mined by temperature (the 18°C limit explained in the next chapter), but rather by a lack of substrates suitable for coral growth.[10] The 200-meter depth contour south of the GBR hugs the shoreline all the way down the east

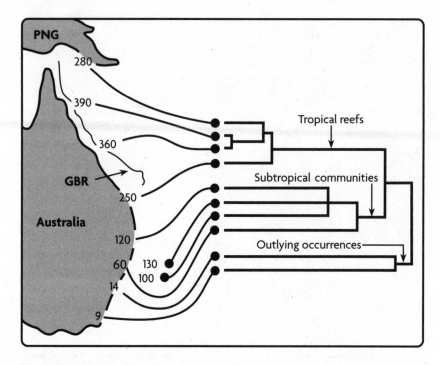

Figure 2.4   The number of species of corals occurring down the eastern
Australian coast and a measure of how much the corals in these localities differ
from one another. The longer the prongs of the dendrogram, the greater the
difference between the populations. Thus tropical reefs have more uniform species
assemblages than those of subtropical localities. This "dropout" sequence has most
likely been active for the geological duration of eastern Australian corals; however,
it probably changes periodically in response to alterations in sea temperature or
currents.

Australian coast. The seafloor is mostly rubble and sand except for a few
shallow rocky outcrops (Flinders "Reef"—made of sandstone—off Brisbane) and occasional high islands (including the Solitary Islands, farther
south). These sites all have coral communities.[11] There are also several sites
of fossil reef communities that have been uplifted and are now exposed to
the air.[12]

None of these southern coastal locations has any reef limestone, but there
are well-formed reefs far to the south of the GBR. The southernmost (the
most southern coral reef in the world) is the fringing reef of Lord Howe

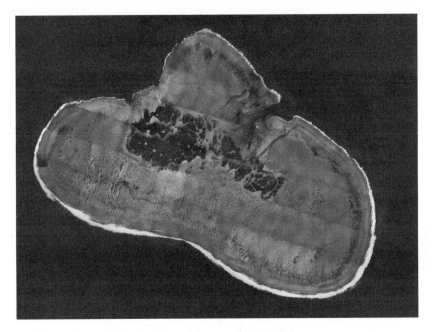

Figure 2.5 Aerial mosaic of Elizabeth Reef, about 10 kilometers in east-west diameter, showing concentric coral zones and the central lagoon (see also the aerial photograph of Middleton Reef, Plate 3). If suitable shallow substrates were available in the intervening region, these reefs would be part of the GBR, extending it 1,300 kilometers to the south. Both Elizabeth and Middleton reefs may have atoll-like origins, as they formed on seamounts of the Lord Howe Island Rise. (Aerial collage by Geoscience Australia, Commonwealth of Australia.)

Island (illustrated in Plate 2), complete with lagoons, beaches of limestone sand, and flourishing coral communities,[13] surrounded by bedrock of the Middle Pleistocene (1.7 mya) or older. A second region just to the north of Lord Howe Island has two platform reefs about 10 kilometers in diameter— Elizabeth and Middleton reefs (illustrated in the accompanying figure and in Plate 3). Both have central sandy lagoons and wave-washed outer slopes of poorly consolidated limestone[14] and extensive coral communities. These reefs are 1,300 kilometers southeast of the southern end of the GBR, yet they have about half the coral diversity of the southern GBR.[15] If suitable offshore seafloors were available, the GBR would no doubt be 1,300 kilometers longer than it is now.

The Western Coral Sea

The accompanying map shows two extensive limestone platforms lying to the east of the GBR, the Marion and Queensland plateaus, separated by the Townsville Trough. The Marion Plateau, 100–1,000 meters deep, lies to the east of the southern GBR, effectively forming an extension of the continental shelf. The Queensland Plateau is much deeper, mostly 1,000–2,000

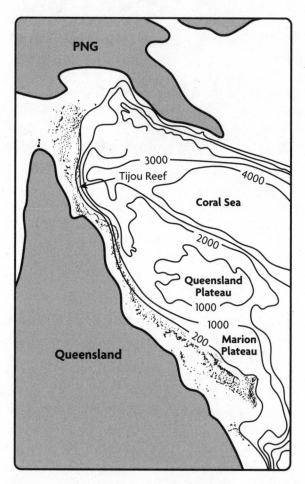

Figure 2.6   Depth contours of the main features of the western Coral Sea. We return to the features of this map several times, especially in Chapters 8 and 11, in connection with the geological history of the GBR.

meters. Both have occasional small reefs reaching to the surface that are well populated with corals.

The region of the far north is more complex. To the east, beyond the northernmost reefs, lies a series of relatively small troughs and plateaus aligned east-west along the southern coast of Papua New Guinea. The coastline itself is fringed by extensive reefs that would, as previously mentioned, geographically form an extension of the GBR were the reefs not cut by the Fly River. The Coral Sea Basin, mostly more than 4,000 meters deep, separates the reefs and plateaus of southern Papua New Guinea from the Queensland Plateau.

We return later to various subjects touched on in this all-too-brief chapter. In the meantime we must hasten on, for the "big-picture" geography of this chapter reveals little of the inner workings of a coral reef, let alone an entire province the size of the GBR. I now turn to an array of "how?" and "why?" questions about the various processes that control coral reefs and that allow them to exist the way they do today. Reef scientists have long pondered some of these questions; others arise anew because later chapters of this book demand answers to them.

— 3 —

Corals and Reefs:
Controls and Processes

Corals are ancient organisms superbly designed to build reefs. Their success can be attributed to their colonial lifestyle, skeletal plasticity, and symbiosis with photosynthetic algae. Ecological and environmental constraints on corals and reefs interact in complex and sometimes divergent ways, which may allow corals to thrive when reef growth is inhibited. These controls are considered individually and then within the broader context of ecological interactions and outcomes.

Scleractinian corals (the true stony corals alive today) have been building coral reefs for 250 million years—reefs that are the largest structures ever made by living organisms. Yet corals have a simple structure. Their bodies are saclike polyps that usually grow together to form colonies. They have a body wall with only two cell layers and a skeleton made of calcium carbonate, which is actually outside the body so that the living polyp grows *on* its skeleton (see Plate 5). This simple structure allows most corals to form complex colonies that are readily modified to suit a wide range of environments.

What Are Reefs?

The term "reef" can mean different things, or conjure up different images, for different people. To most geologists and paleontologists reefs are rock formations—massive ramparts of limestone—that have been built by organisms in the distant past but may no longer be animate. To the biologist a reef is a veneer of living organisms forming ecosystems that are as complex and fragile as any on Earth. These two concepts of reefs can seem as remote from one another as forests are from coal deposits, yet they share a common past. Reefs, the geological structures, are the direct products of living ecosystems, and as such their formation has always been controlled by the kinds of events that control other ecosystems, both marine and terrestrial.

Even within each scientific discipline, the term "reef" can have a wide range of meanings, a range that has to be narrowed down to be meaningful in the context of this book. Ancient reefs must be distinguished from the coral reefs of today. Corals are not the principal builders of all reefs. Many ancient reefs, especially those of the Paleozoic (490–251 mya), were not built by corals alone, but by a wide array of other organisms, including algae, sponges, and molluscs. Sponges rather than corals were the dominant builders in many Paleozoic reefs, and the same role was played by molluscs in some late Mesozoic reefs. We will meet some of these animals in Chapter 5.

Even modern reefs are not necessarily coral dominated. Some, forming intertidal structures in the Caribbean and Bermuda, are made by vermetid "worms" (molluscs). There are also widespread subtidal structures dominated by serpulid worms (annelids) and odd reefs everywhere that owe their existence to other organisms, especially oysters. However, the reefs dominated by organisms other than scleractinian corals and their allies (including a few minor taxa such as the blue coral *Heliopora* and the fire coral *Millepora*) are insignificant in extent and have little in common with coral reefs other than the material of which they are made. Such structures excluded, we still have to narrow down the term "coral reef" even further. Some deep-ocean corals form extensive structures built by one type of coral (*Lophelia*) that are commonly called reefs. However, these have none of the characteristics of coral reefs as geological structures (they do not form solid limestone) or as biological structures (they do not depend on photosynthesis, nor are they biologically diverse). Thus they warrant a separate name.

Before we move on, we need one further clarification, for although coral reefs are principally made of calcium carbonate derived from coral, corals are incapable of building reefs on their own. Coral skeletons must be cemented into solid rock, a job undertaken by coralline algae. Although such algae generally have a wider distribution range than corals, the ones that cement coral debris into reefs flourish in shallow, turbulent, well-lit environments. Thus it is coralline algae as much as corals that determine where highly consolidated reefs grow best and that may also have a dominant influence on how fast they grow or if they grow at all in deeper water. What is good for coral growth and what is good for reef growth are often very different matters.

Reef Carbonates in Context

Although 90–95 percent of terrestrial limestone is derived from reefs built by a variety of animals in shallow marine environments, this by no means reflects the principal source of carbonates on Earth. Around 90 percent of all today's marine carbonates are deep-sea sediments derived primarily from plankton (mostly foraminifera and coccoliths). Owing to their deepwater location these are rarely uplifted to form geological rock formations on land; rather (over immense geological intervals), they are either dissolved in the oceans or subducted into the Earth's mantle. Another 5 percent of carbonates are of mixed composition and are found on continental slopes. In a few regions these carbonates have been consolidated and uplifted or otherwise exposed on land.

Perhaps surprisingly, a total of only 5 percent of all carbonates today are of coral reef origin, although this small proportion includes vast tracts of mountain slopes like the calcareous reefs of Austria, which can be traced back to millions of years of coral reef growth. The proportion of total carbonates represented by living reefs is much less than 1 percent. Nevertheless, as far as humans and many other living organisms are concerned, this small proportion is all-important.

Why Do Corals Build Reefs?

If corals grow in sufficient quantity and the rate of both skeleton production (calcification) and algal cementation exceeds that of erosion, the resulting accumulation of calcium carbonate can form limestone reefs. The success of the process depends very much on speed, which is why reef-building corals enlist symbiotic algae (simple plants called zooxanthellae) to harness the energy of the sun to power the process. However, the question remains: Why do these organisms go to so much trouble? After all, in all of Earth's history no other ecosystem has put nearly so much metabolic energy, or such evolutionary focus, into building something that is dead.

To answer this intriguing question we first have to compare the Cnidaria (the phylum to which all types of corals belong) that have skeletons with those that do not. If we set aside jellyfish and sea wasps (which live in the water column), it is clear that only Cnidaria that have skeletons form large, three-dimensional structures capable of resisting the physical impact of waves. This has been achieved by removing the limitations of individuals and replacing them with the wider range of options offered by the formation of colonies—groups of individuals formed asexually that grow in unison (see Plate 15). The implication is that skeletons are needed to form colonies and that colonies are needed to build large, wave-resistant structures.

The two evolutionary innovations of colony formation and algal symbiosis clearly go together, and it is very likely that they evolved together. Indeed all living Cnidaria that reap the advantages of reef building are both colonial and symbiotic. The two major groups of extinct reef-building corals (rugose and tabulate corals) are also colonial, but whether or not they were symbiotic remains a much-debated point.

Coral reefs, like rainforests, are ecosystems—not just aggregations of individual species competing with each other for survival, but rather groups of species living cooperatively for joint survival. Certainly individual species compete; however, with reefs and rainforests alike, there is a level of selection that is higher than the selection of species. From a Darwinian perspective, this might be called "selection for survival of the fittest ecosystem" as opposed to selection for the fittest species. To see how this might work, imagine a well-established symbiosis between two species: any advantage (or disadvantage) that affects one of the pair will have an effect on both. Darwinian selection is no longer working on just the genetic composition of a single species but on the partnership. Imagine this two-way interdependence magnified to the multiple interdependencies of a coral reef and you begin to see how this process might result in complex coevolution of, at first, subcomponents and then, later, entire ecosystems.

Rainforests, for example, must have canopy trees in order to exist, but these trees can grow only if they are supported by an ecosystem that preserves the environmental conditions they require. This is the concept of guilds, where each guild is a functional unit whose task is undertaken by a group of species or individuals (the term "guild," appropriately enough, coming from functional units in human society).[1] Reefs certainly have guilds: corals to produce building blocks, coralline algae to cement the blocks together, herbivores to prevent macroalgae from taking over, and, critically, photosynthetic algae to provide food. It is easy to imagine guilds forming a hierarchy, from those just mentioned on down to less prominent guilds that handle such relatively inconspicuous tasks as parasite control, sediment mixing, and nutrient cycling.

Guilds are functional units that are selected for because they perform their functions efficiently. It matters little which species perform the function, only that they do it with the necessary speed. Corals are the most prominent reef builders today because, owing to their zooxanthellae, they can harness the energy of the sun to make building blocks sufficiently quickly that the rate of reef accretion outstrips that of erosion. That is not to say that all zooxanthellate corals contribute to reef building. Perhaps half of all species make no significant contribution to reefs at all. Either they do not inhabit environments suitable for reef growth—especially where the water is too turbid or too cold or where there is limited hard substrate—or their skeletons are fragile and easily removed by wave action.

Why corals build reefs thus has as much to do with the environment as with organisms: it is a matter of ecology. A complicated diagram might explain the interactions of light, temperature, substrate, depth, and turbulence on the rates of growth of corals and reefs. However, I take a pragmatic approach, examining these constraints separately and then focusing on how they act, either separately or in combination, in ecological contexts.

Light

Like trees, reef-building corals depend on photosynthesis, using the unlimited resources of solar energy and air to produce food. To reinforce this point, note that about half of all Scleractinia, the azooxanthellate species, do not have symbiotic algae. Some azooxanthellate corals live on coral reefs, especially under overhangs or in caves (see the illustration of *Tubastrea*, Plate 14). However, with the exception of a few species that are both symbiotic and nonsymbiotic, all zooxanthellate corals need light, and it is only these sun-loving species that build reefs. As a result, reefs are restricted to shallow sunlit waters. Azooxanthellate corals are not limited by light, nor are they confined to shallow sunlit water; they live in the vast expanse of the ocean depths, where there is less competition for space. The downside is that they cannot build reefs and must live without photosynthesis, existing solely on the chance capture of passing plankton.

ALGAL SYMBIOSIS.   Symbiosis, the interdependence of different organisms for the benefit of one or both participants, is much more prevalent in the oceans than on land. Within the spectrum of symbioses, zooxanthellae clearly have a special place. They are not found just in Scleractinia; they occur in other cnidarians (soft corals, anemones, and their allies) as well as in an assortment of other animals, encompassing single-celled ciliated protists, sponges, flatworms, and molluscs, including giant clams. Once thought to

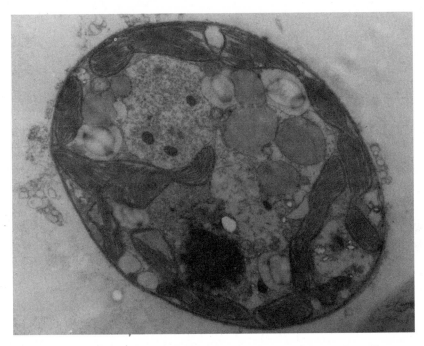

Figure 3.1   An electron microscope image of a zooxanthella. This tiny cell, 0.01 millimeters (10 microns) in diameter, has all the structural components of a typical algal cell. See also Plate 12. (Electron microscope image by Ove Hoegh-Guldberg.)

be a single species, zooxanthellae have been found to be genetically diverse (consisting of many genetic types or clades),[2] but under a microscope they all look much the same (see below and Plate 12). They can all live independently, although not in such concentrated numbers nor with the same long-term security as in the tissues of hosts. In the case of corals (but not clams), they live inside the cells of the host organisms—in the innermost (gastrodermal) layer of the two-cell-layer body wall (see Plate 5). All zooxanthellae are tiny, around 0.01 mm in diameter, but only one to four of them occur within each coral cell.

Zooxanthellae photosynthesize, as do other green plants, but up to 95 percent of the nutrients they produce are leaked directly to the host organism.[3] This is an interesting arrangement because most corals are voracious feeders on zooplankton and thus have two very different sources of food. Nevertheless, many if not most corals that are kept in darkness (so that their zooxanthellae cannot photosynthesize) start to die after a few months, no matter how much food they have. Somehow, the zooxanthellae have made themselves indispensable, but just how or why remains unresolved.

In brief, important points about algal symbiosis are as follows.[4] Corals acquire their zooxanthellae either directly from the parent colony or through infection of free-swimming or newly settled larvae. Uptake of non-parental zooxanthellae in early life may be by random chance, giving different advantages to different colonies: some colonies might be infected with temperature-tolerant symbionts, others with more productive ones (this hypothesis has yet to be confirmed). Zooxanthellae readily change in abundance depending on conditions such as season, position on the coral, and light level. More than one genetic type of zooxanthellae can occupy a single colony. The abundance of genetic types varies geographically on any scale,[5] and some genetic types facilitate a faster growth rate than others.[6]

WATER DEPTH, TURBIDITY, AND LATITUDE.   Any factors that alter light in the marine environment will have a significant effect on calcification rates and reef development. It can be hard for a diver to appreciate the extent to which light decreases with depth because the human eye adjusts to reducing levels of light. Even so, the depth to which zooxanthellate corals can grow has been greatly understated in most of the literature because corals extend below depths accessible to scuba divers. Nevertheless, only a few zooxanthellate corals live below 100 meters, even where the water is very clear and the substrate does not slope so steeply that it is shaded. *Leptoseris* commonly forms extensive beds to at least 160 meters in the Red Sea and Hawaii, and there are several records of moderately diverse coral communities at depths of over 100 meters elsewhere, including the outermost reef faces of the GBR.

Turbidity plays a dominant role in controlling light levels in all except clear-water habitats. Where the water is not very clear, as is the case with most reefs near major landmasses, including all but the outer reefs of the GBR, coral diversity drops off sharply at depths below about 50 meters. Where the water is particularly muddy, such as along much of the coastal zone of the GBR, the depth limit for any coral can be as little as 5 meters. Turbidity, especially that caused by fine clay particles that are easily resuspended by wave action, has other effects on corals besides reducing light. Nevertheless, its key role in controlling the nature and extent of coral communities throughout the nearshore (western) zone of the GBR is largely the result of its effect on water clarity.

Latitude also has an effect on light availability, one that is much more pronounced in the ocean than on land owing to the refraction of sunlight as it enters water. The higher the latitude, the shallower coral communities must be in order to have adequate light. Yet this factor is of less consequence today than in past geological intervals, when waters were warm enough for reef building to occur even to the latitudes of the Arctic and Antarctic circles.

EXCESS LIGHT. Corals growing in very shallow water such as reef flats have chemical agents in their tissues, called sunscreens, to reduce the amount of light reaching their zooxanthellae. If incident light is not controlled, the zooxanthellae can produce harmful amounts of oxygen. We return to this subject in the next chapter, where we see that a combination of excess light and high temperature is now causing widespread coral death by "mass bleaching," a direct result of oxygen toxicity.

Temperature

The subject of temperature, like greenhouse gases and concepts of time, is ubiquitous in this book. We will see that temperature, at its lower limits, may have determined the time of the GBR's origin and now, at its upper limits, threatens its future. Temperature, in synergy to some extent with light, sets limits on the latitudinal spread of *corals* throughout the world, but a different temperature constrains the spread of *reefs*. Because it is so widely misinterpreted, the difference between the constraints on corals and those on reefs has created havoc in paleoclimatic reconstructions of past reef environments as well as in studies of reef growth.

Animals that can adjust their body temperature are able to control the rate at which all their metabolic processes take place. Corals have no such control; thus they must widen their temperature tolerance—accommodating thermal ups and downs—if they are to survive. For GBR corals, all metabolic activities (including photosynthesis and calcification) progress at an optimal rate at a temperature of around 27°C. If the temperature is higher than that, the rate of these metabolic activities is accelerated in an increasingly uncontrolled way—a critical subject that I pursue in Chapters 4 and 14.

LOW-TEMPERATURE LIMITS TO REEF GROWTH. It has been known for decades that reefs do not form where the ocean temperature regularly goes below 18°C for intervals of weeks to months. Reef geologists concerned with the history of reefs refer to this well-established fact, yet in so doing they often assume that lower temperatures kill corals. This is seldom the case.

We have seen that reef building allows entire ecosystems to exist, largely because the rampant growth of macroalgae is held in check.[7] This requires a great deal of uninterrupted energy, which is why reef-building corals are so dependent on symbiotic algae. We have also seen that this symbiosis needs exposure to sunlight, which requires that corals live in shallow water. At around 18°C corals are able to produce calcium carbonate fast enough to fulfill their guild role as producers of building materials. They are able to do this not by growing faster than algae, but by creating three-dimensional habitats where herbivores, especially fish, can control algae for them (see Plate 18). At lower temperatures algae usually get the upper hand, but the corals themselves are not affected by temperatures lower than 18°C. This is best seen along the Ryukyu Islands of Japan, where the southern islands have extensive reefs. Farther north, however, the sea temperature progressively decreases until it reaches the critical point, 18°C. It is there that reef development fails, but the corals themselves do not. Nearly half of all coral species regularly tolerate prolonged exposure to 14°C,[8] and a few even tolerate 12°C, although seldom less (azooxanthellate corals excepted).

It was once believed that corals in cold high-latitude regions have an ephemeral existence, neither reproducing nor growing like their tropical counterparts, but this is not so. Corals at the Houtman Abrolhos Islands (the southernmost reef of western Australia) reproduce normally, and those of Lord Howe Island (the southernmost reef of eastern Australia; see Plates 2 and 19) produce spawn as abundantly as their tropical counterparts and have normal recruitment of young. There are some taxonomic variations in this pattern, including the massive colonies of *Porites*, the most important of all reef builders, which seldom do well in temperate waters. Some other taxa, notably fungiid (mushroom) corals, likewise do not flourish, but it is not known why.

Surface waters of the GBR seldom go below 22°C except during periods of prolonged wind chill during cold winter months. However, they regularly go as low as 18°C in the reef lagoon of Lord Howe Island without harming the corals.

HIGH-TEMPERATURE LIMITS TO REEF AND CORAL GROWTH.   Low- and high-temperature limits do not mirror each other. Oceans can cool until they freeze, yet they cannot warm much beyond the peak temperatures we see today because evaporation holds the upper temperature limit in check, at least for extensive areas of ocean. As far as the GBR is concerned, the Western Pacific Thermal Cap (around 31°C) has been in place throughout its entire existence. As we will see in later chapters, this is a temperature that corals have evolved to depend on. Smaller bodies of water are less constrained; thus the GBR lagoon can get warmer than this, and small reef lagoons may be as much as 5°C warmer. Similar comparisons apply to other areas of the world and to other intervals in geological time.

Nevertheless, high temperature per se has little direct negative effect on corals, at least not unless it is pushed to extreme limits. The warmer the water, the faster most metabolic processes become and the faster calcification could become if it were not for its effect on zooxanthellae. Faster metabolic rates for zooxanthellae mean faster photosynthesis, which in turn can result in oxygen being produced at rates where it becomes toxic. This is the reason corals are forced to expel their increasingly poisonous zooxanthellae and "bleach": it is a response to temperature and light acting in synergy.

When it comes to high-temperature limits, coral growth and reef growth share more or less the same upper limit, which is linked to the upper limit of ocean warming. This link is an evolutionary one; it has apparently always existed, for there is no interval in geological time when high temperature has excluded reefs from equatorial regions.

The Coral Triangle (see Figure 2.2) is in an equatorial position, but the region's high diversity is probably not due solely to high temperature. As similar high diversity is not seen in other tropical regions, we conclude that other factors, including habitat diversity and the close interlinking of surface currents, play a role. Higher temperatures also lead to higher coral growth rates, up to the point where oxygen toxicity becomes an issue. These higher rates are normally associated with weaker skeletons, as if the coral tissue outgrows its ability to form its own skeleton. Moreover, there seems to be no good correlation between temperature and the rate of *reef* growth. It might be that the higher rate of production of skeletal calcium carbonate is offset by the production of weaker skeletons (which are more quickly eroded), but this issue is sufficiently complex that such a theory cannot have unqualified support.

Substrate, Turbulence, and Mechanical Effects of Turbidity

In Chapter 2 we saw that there is a strong ecological gradient across the GBR, from a muddy inshore coastal zone to a clear-water offshore reef zone. Substrate type and water clarity are always closely linked, especially when depth and turbulence are factored in. White calcareous sand, although typically coarse grained, is light, so it is readily moved around by wave action; if it is suspended in sufficient quantity, it can bury corals. However, it is clay from rivers, even in small amounts, that is most harmful to corals: not only does it attenuate light, it also necessitates cleaning. Corals clean using a variety of methods, including reliance on tiny hairlike cilia on their tentacles, and cleaning is relatively costly in terms of metabolic energy.

Substrate is also of paramount importance to settling larvae, for these are fussy in their choice of a home. They will not settle on sand of any sort or on substrates that are coated with bacterial slime, as commonly develops on highly degraded reefs.

One very obvious effect of turbulence on coral skeleton formation is that wave action produces dense skeletons. The corals illustrated in Plate 22, typical of those on high-energy reef fronts, have extremely hard, dense skeletons, whereas those in protected lagoons, as illustrated in Plate 25, have light, brittle skeletons. This is partly because of the differences in the species that occupy these habitats, yet even within the same species (such as the *Pocillopora damicornis* colonies illustrated in the figure shown below), this effect is pronounced.

Water Quality

The term "water quality" is commonly used in connection with the health of the marine environment. Water quality that is good for particular coral reefs or coral communities is assumed to have tolerable levels of sediments, nutrients, and environmental contaminants. The term is therefore largely used in the context of the health of reefs and possible degradations of that health caused by human activities, a subject pursued in the next chapter. Otherwise, it is used as a descriptor of "normal" environmental conditions. In this context, "normal" does not mean permanent, for there are no baselines for coral reefs, only intervals of time over which the environment *appears* not to change.

Salinity is an aspect of water quality that has not been adequately studied. Corals appear to be sufficiently tolerant of high salinity that lethal levels seldom, if ever, occur naturally on the GBR. The opposite commonly applies to low salinities, for these play a significant role in creating areas where there is little or no coral or reef growth, such as in estuaries or in parts of the GBR lagoon. Interestingly, corals commonly grow in and around mangrove areas, either because of a tolerance of low salinities or because these places have no freshwater input other than directly from rain, which remains on the ocean surface until removed by wind or tide.

Other environmental controls on reef building, bound up in the complexities of water chemistry, may not overtly limit reef distribution today but may have been important in the geological past and are destined to reemerge in the near future. The chemical composition of the oceans is something we take for granted. Oceans are normally so well buffered that chemical changes are infinitesimally slow, providing plenty of time for organisms to evolve adaptations to any alteration. However, sometimes the rate of change exceeds physical or biological thresholds, and the resulting conditions cannot be tolerated by any but the most specialized organisms. This can happen when large tracts of ocean become anoxic, hydrogen sulfide concentrations reach toxic levels, pH alters beyond tolerable limits for calcification, or other contaminants make the water uninhabitable. These are all factors we will encounter again during our travels through geological time in later chapters.

Corals and Reefs in Environmental Contexts

SPEED AND COMPETITION: MIXES OF SUCCESS.   Speed and competition are nebulous matters in nature, yet they are the factors that have the most impact on both coral survival and reef building, once the basic environmental needs described earlier are satisfied. Speed is critical to reef building, which demands a combination of corals and coralline algae that can build reefs fast enough to outstrip the rate of erosion. Competition is also largely a matter of speed—for corals on reefs, like trees in a rainforest, must compete not only with other organisms but also with each other for light. In order to do this successfully, some have developed skeletal architectures unequaled in the animal kingdom. The *Acropora* illustrated in Plate 15 shows how thousands of individuals can combine to produce structures that not only capture the most light per unit of building material but also allow them to overgrow other corals. This is a matter of strategy—and it is a highly successful one, for *Acropora* now dominate most actively growing reef faces. Other corals have opted for long-term survival by being more durable: they can survive whatever wave energy the oceans throw at them and will still be

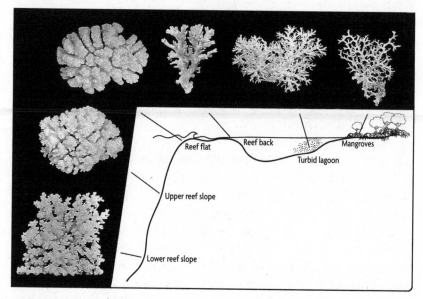

Figure 3.2 One of the reasons for the success of the Scleractinia is their capacity to modify their growth forms to suit different environments. This is the range of growth forms of a single species, *Pocillopora damicornis,* which occurs in habitats ranging from reef flats exposed to strong wave action to muddy mangroves. (Photographs by the author.)

there when the fast-growing colonies are destroyed—the coralline equivalents of fast-growing weeds versus long-lived trees.

Competition has also led to the selection of zooxanthellae that maximize the return of food per measure of light. Light and temperature on the scale of an ecosystem regulate both coral and reef growth—the warmer and lighter the better, provided that the right zooxanthellae are there to exploit the prevailing conditions and that temperature does not become excessive. Selecting the right type of zooxanthellae is a strategy that has worked well for millions of years, because the ocean temperature for most regions has had a dependable upper limit.

SKELETAL PLASTICITY: STRATEGIES THAT WORK. The Scleractinia have been successful through our own era because the simplicity of their body design allows them to form colonies and exhibit an array of skeletal architectures, each designed to exploit the particular environmental conditions in which they grow. Even a single species, as illustrated below, can have many different growth forms, each tailored to a particular habitat. This flexibility is fundamental, for it has enabled the Scleractinia to survive the many environmental catastrophes that, as we will see, are their lot in life.

CORALS DO NOT NEED REEFS.   It is certainly true that without corals there can be no coral reefs, yet it is not true that without reefs there are no corals. Rather the opposite: there are at least as many corals (excluding azooxanthellate species) growing in environments that will not support reef development as there are in environments that will. Temperature, light availability, sediment load, depth, and lack of turbulence may all act independently or in various combinations to prevent reef growth. These environmental constraints clearly operate together to produce habitats in which corals might flourish yet cannot produce skeletons quickly enough to beat erosion or in which encrusting coralline algae do not grow. Without the cementing action of these algae, coral debris remains unconsolidated. For example, the sea off the northern coast of Arnhem Land (600 kilometers west of Torres Strait in the far northern GBR; see Figure 2.3) is shallow and moderately turbid. The coastline is rocky, and the rocks usually give way to sand at a depth of less than 10 meters. There are no reefs, yet 60 percent of all GBR corals grow there, some forming colonies as big and healthy as those on any reef. Long-term ecological issues aside, almost all species of Indo-Pacific corals grow as well in nonreef habitats as they do on reefs.

REEFS DO NOT NEED CORAL DIVERSITY.   That reef growth is somehow dependent on coral diversity is a widely held misconception, which becomes important in reconstructions of the geological history of reefs (at times when global biodiversity was low) as well as in today's conservation debates (when the goal is to conserve biodiversity). This notion probably comes from the rather obvious observation that most reefs occur where coral diversity is at least moderately high. There are no contrary examples in Australian waters, as all reefs there have at least a hundred coral species. However, all reefs of the Caribbean have a lower diversity than this, and well-formed reefs of the Abrolhos Islands of Brazil have fewer than 20 species. Clipperton Atoll in the far eastern Pacific clinches the issue, for it has actively growing reefs that provide significant habitat diversity, yet only seven species of coral occur there, just three of which contribute to reef building.[9]

CORALS NEED HERBIVOROUS FISH.   The notion that corals build reefs
in order to have shallow substrates where they can outcompete macroalgae
correctly implies that corals are the key structural components of reefs.
However, herbivorous fish that eat these algae are the critical functional
components. Corals give fish the habitat they need to exist in sufficient numbers to keep the algae in check, especially during seasonal growth spurts.
This effect is so dramatic that, if the fish were removed from most reefs for
just a few years, the corals would be smothered by algae and die. It is probably true that corals need fish just as much as fish need corals; in any event,
neither is ultimately dependent on the presence of reefs.

Rates of Growth and Erosion

The growth rates of coral colonies and of reefs—two very different subjects—are both important to paleoclimatic reconstructions. All corals can
grow much faster than any reef. There are three basic reasons for this:
(1) Reefs are made of a much denser material than coral skeletons, so that
the latter must be chemically and physically compacted to make limestone,
a process known as diagenesis. (2) There are gaps between coral colonies
that must be filled in to make solid limestone. (3) Reef accretion is the rate
of growth minus the rate of erosion; as erosion is commonly greater than
accretion, especially in marginal habitats, reefs do not always form where
coral grows.

CORAL GROWTH RATES.   The much-studied coral *Porites* forms large hemi-
spherical colonies and typically grows (radially) at a rate of around 1 cen-
timeter a year, as determined by X-rays of thin slices like the one shown in
the figure. Some more heavily calcified colonies of other corals grow at
slower rates than this, although most are faster. Staghorn *Acropora* readily
grows (linearly) up to about 30 centimeters a year. Plate-forming *Acropora*,
such as the colony illustrated in Plate 15, also grows up to about 30 centimeters a year in diameter.

RATES OF REEF GROWTH.   Rates of reef growth (accretion) can be measured directly from cores taken from reefs or by a wide range of indirect
measures of carbonate production.[10] Normally the maximum rate of reef
growth is about 0.6 meters per century,[11] although rates under optimal conditions may reach three times this figure.[12] These optimal conditions only

—— 100mm ——

Figure 3.3 Growth bands in corals such as those seen in this X-ray of a slice of *Porites,* are the marine equivalent of growth rings in trees. They not only allow detailed measurements of growth rates but can also reveal much about the environment in which the coral grew, including temperature and salinity. (X-ray image by Janice Lough.)

occur where the water is shallow and clear and currents are strong—the probable reason why continuous areas of reefs (where there is more reef than open ocean) occur only where the tidal range is great and the ocean floor is shallow. These environments provide high light levels combined with continuous flushing and nutrient transport. Such conditions are notably found in the Pompey reefs of the southern GBR and in the reef complexes of the far north.

RATES OF REEF EROSION. Reef erosion is a much neglected subject. Yet it is critical because rates of erosion determine the appearance, and indeed the very existence, of reefs every bit as much as rates of growth—simply because accretion must outstrip erosion for any reef to form in the first place. This is important when considering the origin of the GBR (Chapter 11), and it may become increasingly crucial to the future of reefs if today's human influences continue to tilt the balance in favor of erosion.

There are no reliable estimates of rates of reef erosion because the process is too slow to be directly measurable. Best estimates suggest that around 90 percent of all calcium carbonate produced by coral calcification is removed by erosion.

There are four main mechanisms of reef erosion: physical erosion, enhanced chemical erosion, bioerosion, and rainwater dissolution. The first three occur only when reefs are submerged, whereas the fourth happens only when reefs are exposed to the air, either by an uplift of the land or by a fall in sea level.

As illustrated in Plate 23, physical erosion leads to the formation of the grooves seen in most reefs, which are due to the action of waves moving rubble back and forth. As these channels are ground deeper, they typically produce spur-and-groove structures, especially common along reef fronts exposed to strong wave action. On a larger scale, erosion caused by tidal currents has produced some of the most dramatic reef structures of the GBR, notably the deltaic patterns described and illustrated earlier.

Changes in ocean chemistry that affect the stability of skeletal material can have a significant effect on the balance between reef accretion and erosion, a process I discuss in more detail in Chapters 6 and 15.

Bioerosion is a seriously underrecognized process, but it can be very active in shallow water, where it not only erodes the limestone surface but also prevents the growth of newly recruited corals and coralline algae on available substrates. Over thousands of years, the actions of many types of bioeroders, such as the urchins illustrated in Plates 39 and 40, would probably keep pace with slow sea-level falls or successions of slow falls, thus leaving no reef exposed as water receded. (This is a subject that is very relevant to the discussion of the age of the GBR in Chapter 11.) There are many studies of the rate at which different organisms—such as sponges, urchins, limpets, chitons, and parrot fish—ingest limestone, typically up to 18 cubic centimeters per animal per year for intertidal invertebrates such as sea urchins. But these figures cannot be reliably translated into rates at which these animals might plane off whole reef surfaces.

Rainwater dissolution commonly results in rill weathering, a process that creates interlocking knifelike edges on the surface of limestone outcrops.

Depending on the chemical composition of the limestone, some aerially exposed reefs last much longer than others, as evidenced by the ancient reefs illustrated in Plates 33–35.

Surface Currents, Coral Reproduction, and Reticulate Evolution

The idea that species appear (evolve) or disappear (go extinct) according to Darwinian notions of natural selection and survival of the fittest is one of the most fundamental concepts of all biology. The underlying implication is that species are units that can be changed in evolutionary time as well as in geographic space at different points in time. Evidence for such notions is indeed all around us, including the endless array of exquisite adaptations animals have evolved to enable them to survive in a competitive world.

Nevertheless, there is increasing evidence from an array of both terrestrial plants (such as eucalypts) and marine animals that the concept of a species unit, with a unique suite of genes and that cannot hybridize with other recognizably different units, is too simplistic. For example, two GBR coral "species" may be reproductively isolated and form two distinct taxonomic units. However, if a third "species" that can hybridize with both GBR species should emigrate from a remote region (say, the Solomon Islands), a biological meltdown would soon result. All three original species would become one species on the GBR, with blurred affinities with the original Solomon Islands species. The real world, of course, is seldom that simple: this process perpetually involves hundreds of "species," all of which manifest different types of genetic and morphological variations on all scales of space and time. These genetic and morphological patterns are the result of surface ocean current patterns, and not just the currents of the present but also those that existed when the ancestors of today's species evolved. To understand this process better, we need to take a closer look at the way in which corals reproduce and disperse.

On the GBR most corals release their gametes with an extraordinary degree of synchrony—within a couple of hours, a few hours after dark, a few days after the full moon, in October and/or November. This is an astonishing sight underwater: masses of small egg and sperm bundles, released synchronously from thousands of corals, turn the water column pink and form slicks on the surface hundreds of meters in length (see Plate 10).[13] Such massive aggregations allow eggs from one colony to be fertilized by sperm from another; they also allow species to cross-fertilize if they can. The resulting larvae, whatever their genetic composition, are then distributed far and wide by ocean surface currents. Over many generations, the distance traveled can be vast; the majority of GBR species occur throughout the Coral Triangle and many are even recognizable as far away as the Red Sea.

The relative strength and direction of the currents and the endurance of the larvae are the keys to these spatial patterns—not just the patterns of today, but also those of times past, for as long as these species have existed. Today currents are relatively stable and move in predictable directions. However, over geological time, the currents—their strengths, their directions, and the barriers they encounter—have all changed dramatically, and with those changes have come opportunities for larval dispersal and genetic mixing. The result has been an interlocking or reticulate pattern over geological time, which is illustrated in the diagram in Plate 9. There is little change in genetic information from the bottom of the diagram to the top, yet at different time intervals (imaginary horizontal lines across the diagram) the number of taxonomic units (be they called species, subspecies, hybrids, or whatever) changes considerably.[14]

The reticulate patterns thus formed are the basis for much of the complexity of coral taxonomy, genetics, and evolutionary reconstructions. For the purposes of this book, we must bear in mind that species are not unique units. They are instead sections of genetic continua that have no time or place of origin and are not necessarily genetically isolated from other such units. Evolution occurs through genetic changes within groups of species, which means that, even if individual species may appear to go extinct, their genes persist in other species. It is also true that evolution in corals and most other marine invertebrates is not necessarily a path of improvement. It is rather one of change, as seen most readily when comparing the morphology of very ancient organisms like crinoids and trilobites of different ages: the younger forms are not necessarily better, just different. During times when surface currents are relatively strong, corals undergo extensive genetic mixing, resulting in relatively few species all of which have with wide distribution ranges. When currents are relatively weak (such as they are today), there is more genetic isolation, offering a better chance for species to form relatively distinct units with narrower ranges.

Much would have to be added to this chapter to make it a comprehensive overview of all the controls and processes that govern the growth of today's corals and coral reefs. Nature is never simple, and there are always exceptions to any general statement or conclusion, some of which I have had to bypass. We must move on—to today's GBR, to examine its present state of health and to compare it with reefs in other parts of the world, many of which, in terms of human impacts, are not doing so well.

— 4 —

The State of the Great Barrier Reef

The GBR is reviewed against the background of other major coral reefs of the world. We observe how it has changed over past decades, then consider current issues, including the crown-of-thorns starfish, water quality, bottom trawling, and genetic dwarfing. Although important matters today, these threats and others like them are seen to be of little consequence in comparison with the impending impact of global climate change.

Today there are headlines every time a ship goes aground on the GBR, especially if the accident involves an oil spill. We also hear much about the possible consequences of global climate change—seemingly in the same context: "damage to The Reef." Yet these two matters have nothing in common: one is local with short-term consequences, whereas the other is global and chronic. They are worlds apart.

Local short-term impacts in an area the size of the GBR, such as the grounding of a ship, are trivial as far as the reef itself is concerned. Chronic impacts are another matter. In this chapter I single out the impacts and threats to the GBR that seem most important: the recurring damage from crown-of-thorns starfish outbreaks, the cumulative effects of changes in water quality, the degradation of inter-reef areas caused by bottom trawling, and possible long-term consequences of genetic dwarfing. This leads me to a discussion of mass bleaching—currently the most serious observable threat to the GBR resulting from global climate change. I grapple with the future consequences of climate change later in the book (see Chapters 13–15), when they can be seen in the context of the geological past of the GBR and of coral reefs in general.

Impacts on the GBR (and there are many others that I have not mentioned) are the concern of the Great Barrier Reef Marine Park Authority (GBRMPA), an Australian government organization that, with a staff of 170, is by far the largest reef management organization of its kind in the world. For Australia and Australians, the GBR is a national treasure, and any threat to it soon becomes a matter of widespread publicity and national concern—even though many Australians never see it for themselves.

Regrettably, the *global* impacts that the GBR is about to experience through climate change—which utterly trivialize all others, both short- and long-term—are beyond the control of both GBRMPA and Australia. The effects of global climate change are in a category of their own. They dominate the big picture and are thus the central concern of the rest of this book. In this chapter, however, I begin with local issues, putting the GBR into context in comparison with other reef regions of the world and then examining how human impacts may have already changed it.[1]

The GBR and Other Reefs of the World Compared

The question of how the GBR compares with other major reef regions from a human point of view will become increasingly important as the number of tourists rises. Travelers who want to see marine megafauna, or even fauna that is not so mega, would (with two isolated exceptions) be ill advised to visit anywhere in Asia. Large marine animals of any kind, except for occasional oceangoing fish and the odd turtle or crocodile, are seldom seen in this part of the world. In fact, in most parts of Asia, including the reefs of Japan, one can dive for days without seeing a single large shark or big fish of any sort. The same is pretty much true for most of the coastal reefs of the Indian Ocean. It is only in some of the more inaccessible areas of the Pacific and the protected reefs of Australia that the megafaunal population is anything like it used to be.

If travelers are looking for scenic beauty they should avoid most of the Asian and coastal Indian Ocean reefs, simply because the water has become too turbid over the past few decades for panoramic views. Such scenery is only to be found in areas remote from the river-dominated influence of major landmasses, such as the coral cays of the Seychelles in the Indian Ocean, parts of the Red Sea, and the oceanic reefs of the southern and western Pacific. However, the state of any of these reefs is likely to change quickly. The Global Coral Reef Monitoring Network reports on the state of the world's reefs every few years, because it can change significantly even over this short span of time.[2] Except for forests specifically targeted for destruction, few, if any, other large ecosystems are as ephemeral as coral reefs.

If travelers, be they scientists or photographers, seek marine faunal diversity, they need a different destination. I would direct them to the Coral Triangle, which is the global high point for both diversity (species numbers) and endemism (species found nowhere else). This distinction applies to reef fish as well as corals and probably to most other major groups of marine animals as well. The epicenter of it all is eastern Indonesia. The diversity of life on the reefs in this area is truly wonderful, yet it is threatened because the region has no comprehensive, enforced land or marine management practices and because the rate of human population increase is among the highest in the world. Many areas along the north coast of New Guinea and the Solomon Islands have extensive areas of reef, with coral and most other invertebrate life apparently flourishing despite the absence of large fish. However, owing to political or social instability and, in some places, lack of suitable infrastructure, these reefs are not major destinations for divers.

In terms of the combined criteria just mentioned—megafauna, scenic beauty, and diversity—the GBR is rivaled by the Solomon Islands, which have a higher diversity and comparable scenery. New Caledonia, as yet relatively unknown, ranks high in all of these attributes, largely because, like northeast Australia, the population density is low and most of the country remains sufficiently well forested to guard against excessive sedimentation from river discharge. The most recent surveys of reef fish show that eastern Indonesia has 1,686 species, the Solomon Islands have 1,365, and New Caledonia is similar to the GBR with around 1,100.[3] Eastern Indonesia has 535 species of coral, the Solomon Islands have 485 species, and New Caledonia is again similar to the GBR with around 390 species.[4] Depending on what the tourist considers most important, I believe that these three locations (with the inclusion of parts of the southern Red Sea) stand out from all others.

Accuse me of bias if you wish, but, on the basis of these three attributes, the GBR deserves its reputation as the greatest coral reef region in the world. This is partly a result of a history of good management, low population density, and the remoteness of most of the reefs. Even so, only the far north deserves the descriptor "pristine." Damage from the crown-of-thorns starfish continues unabated, with control measures as ineffective today as they were 40 years ago. Issues of water quality are looming, although they are minor compared with the predicted effects of coral bleaching. Bottom trawling, despite recent restrictions and greatly improved methods, still inflicts a level of damage that is strikingly at odds with professed conservation goals. As reef tourism becomes increasingly popular and less-well-managed reefs of many neighboring countries deteriorate, tourism pressure on the GBR will increase, especially with the influx of sophisticated travelers constantly in search of the unusual or the best. The northern GBR, in particular, remains one of the great wilderness regions of the world. The challenge over the next few decades will be to see that it remains so—for ultimately there may come a day when it is the last refuge of much of the world's coral reef fauna.

How the GBR Used to Be

There is a good reason why the outer reefs of the GBR, especially reefs like Tijou in the far north, were almost never visited by tourists until about 20 years ago: they could only be reached after a sea voyage of several days. For the most part this changed with the advent of fast multihulled boats, although the northern GBR, which is still beyond the range of such boats, has seen little rise in the number of visitors. Nevertheless, many well-traveled divers believe that even this part of the GBR is not as it used to be.[5]

We all suffer from landscape (or, in this case, seascape) amnesia, tending to forget how a place used to be, or remembering it as better than it actually was. Memory deceives. Yet I, and others of my ancient generation, remember early days on the GBR, when we saw sharks and other big fish by the dozens if not hundreds during *every* dive on *any* outer reef. It would be useful to have a reliable record of those sightings now, but there is none: in those days a census would have been considered pointless. The photograph in Plate 27, taken in 1960 on the beach in front of the Heron Island Research Station during a spearfishing competition, shows how it used to be. Today there are few places left in the world where such a catch would be theoretically possible—and they are all places where protection laws *are* enforced. The megafauna of reefs, like so many of its terrestrial counterparts, now depends on human protection from human predators, a subject to which I return in the last chapter.

Yet there were particular events for which recollection need not depend solely on memory. In 1989, at a conference in Okinawa, a few scientists (myself included) asserted on a widely broadcast television program that 70 percent of the world's reefs were showing signs of human-induced degradation. To me that seemed a reasonable estimate, although some of my colleagues thought it an exaggeration. Today—less than 20 years later—such a claim would be an absurd understatement, especially considering the comparisons I have just made between the GBR and other Indo-Pacific regions. The plight of most Caribbean reefs is also at least as grave as that of the reefs of Asia.

The main causes of this degradation vary from country to country. Overfishing—as evidenced by the almost total removal of the top predator, sharks, from the coast of Asia—will create ecological imbalances that may take decades to become apparent. Fishing using primitive explosives—practiced in many of the poorer countries of the tropical world, which own the majority of the world's coral reefs—has a more obvious impact. So do the collection of live fish for the aquarium trade using cyanide and the physical destruction of shelter-providing coral. However, the impacts of environmental degradation—pollution and sedimentation resulting from land clearing and coastal construction—create the most important changes, mainly because they are much harder to counter or to reverse. These issues are about the here and now, not the remote past or the immediate future. Yet despite the outcries, not much is changing: the rate of reef destruction throughout most of the world remains unchanged because the root cause is increasing human population pressure.

The threats to reefs I have just outlined have generated a widespread response. By mid-2004, some 691 initiatives (involving 451 nongovernmental organizations and 14 international networks and agreements) had been established to conserve coral reefs, and the list keeps growing.[6] Many scientists have been quick to respond, with the majority of research proposals addressing a component of the reef degradation issue. Most recent newspaper articles and virtually all of the television programs about coral reefs highlight the need for conservation. That need has now become a matter of general public awareness. The call has certainly been heard—yet some appear unconvinced that anything abnormal is afoot, and others believe, perhaps with climate change in mind, that it is already a case of too little too late.

The Crown-of-Thorns Starfish

During the 1960s and 1970s there were really only two burning questions about the GBR: Is the crown-of-thorns starfish going to destroy the reef? And should it be drilled for oil? The starfish (*Acanthaster planci*, illustrated in Plate 29) was heralded as the greatest threat to coral reefs the world had ever seen. Throughout the 1970s, under the slogan "Save the Barrier Reef," the GBR became the subject of the biggest conservation movement in Australian history, spurred on by such influential books as Patricia Clare's *The Struggle for the GBR*, Theo Brown's *Crown of Thorns: The Death of the GBR?*, Peter James's *Requiem for the Reef*, and Judith Wright's *The Coral Battleground*.[7]

Since then the vexing starfish problem has not diminished at all. It was originally thought that a major cause of the outbreaks was the collecting of one of the starfish's natural predators, the giant triton (*Charonia tritonis*). This theory can now be ruled out: the key to the cause of the outbreaks clearly lies with survival of the larvae and juveniles, not the adults. Scientists have tackled the crown-of-thorns starfish problem in earnest, and more than a hundred scientific articles have been published about it. Yet, despite these efforts, the list of possible causes still remains largely unchanged. Runoff of agricultural nutrients has commonly been blamed, although repeated outbreaks have occurred from the Maldives to French Polynesia, including northwestern Australia and other regions where there is very little agriculture. Whether or not human activities have created the conditions for major outbreaks remains unknown. As is so often the case, immediate management needs may seem crucial when a threat first arises, yet they soon fade when seemingly more important matters loom. The starfish threat has not diminished, nor is it fully understood, yet it has been moved onto a back burner. This is most unfortunate, as coral communities that are weakened by repeated mass bleaching and other stresses from climate changes in the future will be less able to recover from starfish outbreaks, whenever and wherever they occur.

Water Quality: An Issue for the GBR?

One of GBRMPA's main concerns today is water quality—effectively the state of the GBR's physical environment.[8] The reason may not be clear if one looks at the GBR in isolation; however, water quality is the dominant management issue in other parts of the world, where reefs are exposed to high levels of sedimentation and many forms of pollution, including high nutrient loads and pesticides. Reefs that once flourished near major cities such as Singapore, Hong Kong, and Jakarta are extreme examples of what happens when water quality declines: there is nothing left of them now. On a global scale, the reefs most at risk are those exposed to terrestrial runoff from land clearing, which is currently denuding 1 percent of the Earth's existing forest each year. Human population increases and migration to coastal regions, which are themselves increasingly urbanized, are having a dramatic influence on many reefs in the Coral Triangle,[9] as well as on those of Madagascar and most of the coastal reefs of East Africa.[10]

When it comes to water quality, the GBR has a particular problem not seen in other major reef regions of the world: it is so wide that almost all the sediment that enters the region stays there, creating the cross-shelf gradient I referred to in Chapter 2. This sedimentation has been going on ever since the GBR flooded after the last Ice Age, which ended only 6,000 years ago. Ever since that time, rivers have been transporting sediment from the land onto the reef, a process initially helped by the burning of vulnerable forests by Aboriginal people—an impact older than the biological reefs themselves. Over the past 150 years this process has gathered speed through the extensive clearing of forests, especially lowland rainforests and wetlands, for sugarcane, as well as dryland forests, for cattle.[11] The last process, in particular, creates sheet erosion, in which the nutrient-rich uppermost layer of topsoil is washed into rivers during heavy rain, a phenomenon exacerbated by the introduction of drought-resistant breeds of cattle that are capable of grazing grassland to dust during the dry season.

The harm caused by this transport of sediments and nutrients onto the GBR is the subject of some debate. Many studies show that most of the volume of river-borne sediment remains in nearshore embayments, where it has accumulated since the last great sea-level rise to form a layer up to 20 meters thick. This process is of little natural consequence for corals, perhaps because the few that occupy these areas have been there for thousands of years and are clearly able to tolerate high levels of sedimentation. In terms of physical composition, it is the clay part of the sediment that does the harm, partly because it chokes corals and other bottom-dwelling organisms and partly because it increases turbidity, which in turn reduces light levels. Sand is relatively harmless unless it is moved around in excessive amounts, such as by tropical cyclones, so measures of sediment volume are not good indicators of its potential impact on reefs. The chemical composition of sediments, however, is a rather more complicated issue.

There is a widely held myth that corals cannot tolerate high nutrient levels, probably stemming from the long-held image of corals thriving in the "nutrient deserts" of blue-water ocean. Actually, most corals grow well in places where nutrient levels are high, even artificially high, such as in aquaria or near sewage outlets. What corals cannot tolerate are the ecological changes that can be caused by high nutrient levels. Such conditions are rare in Australia but commonplace elsewhere, where raw sewage is discharged directly into the ocean. The effect varies considerably according to local conditions, but in most cases excess nutrients cause an imbalance between corals and algae, one that is checked by the success or failure of herbivores. Importantly, the presence of abnormal nutrient levels diminishes the ability of reefs to recover from the kinds of degradation created by cyclones, crown-of-thorns starfish, disease, or mass bleaching, whether acting individually or in synergy.

There are many aspects to the effects of terrestrial runoff.[12] Dissolved inorganic nutrients are quickly extracted from seawater by phytoplankton, bacteria, and the food webs of bottom-dwelling organisms and are not likely to have widespread major effects. Although chronically high levels of nitrates and phosphates might decrease the rate at which corals calcify, their main potential harm is in creating algal blooms, which, if they coincide with a release of crown-of-thorns larvae, could greatly enhance the survival of the larvae. Should this happen, the place where the larvae finally settle may not be clearly linked to the place where the nutrient enrichment occurred.

Particulate organic matter is generally good for most corals, except where coral competitors, particularly algae and bacterial slime, receive greater advantage. Particulate nutrients are also a direct food source for crown-of-thorns larvae.

Nutrient imbalances can effectively turn reef environments into estuarine environments. Aggregations of "marine snow"—the name given to the flocculation of sediment particles by bacteria—is one such effect. It can lead to the smothering of small bottom-dwelling organisms, including newly settled larvae.[13]

Reduced light availability and the lack of hard substrates are the main reasons why reefs are not found in shallow coastal areas that are exposed to the discharge of extensive sediment-laden rivers. In areas where river discharge is relatively clear, such as along the Daintree coast, unconsolidated coastal reefs are often extensive.

Coral larvae are readily killed by low salinity associated with floods. However, mass spawning, which typically occurs around October and November on the GBR, is unlikely to coincide with very heavy monsoonal rainfall, which occurs during the summer wet season from December to March. Cyclonic conditions creating floods are another matter, for early cyclones have the potential to destroy all larvae from a mass-spawning event.

About 50 species of coral habitually survive high sediment loads. These are mostly detritus feeders (they have no stinging cells for capturing zoo-plankton), can readily rid themselves of sediment of all sizes, and have light skeletons that allow rapid upward growth when need be. *Alveopora catalai*, illustrated in Plate 16, is just such a coral.

I conclude that problems of water quality are less important for the GBR than they are for the majority of other major reef regions of the world. In many countries water deterioration is clearly the root cause of extensive reef destruction. More specifically, and with conservation of biodiversity in mind, the issue of water quality is not anywhere near as serious on the GBR as it is for most of the reefs of the Coral Triangle, or indeed most of the other major reefs near large landmasses. In a majority of such regions, water qual-ity currently rivals uncontrolled fishing, damage from crown-of-thorns starfish, and mass bleaching as the most significant impact. Nevertheless, if it were possible to compare the GBR of today with that of a century ago, such a comparison would likely show that a substantial proportion of reefs in the coastal zone have suffered significantly as a result of degraded water quality. It would also show that this has come about primarily through reduced re-silience to other impacts. There is certainly no reason to be complacent about water quality on the GBR today, for the situations in other countries show clearly how dangerous such complacency can be.

Bottom Trawling

The vast areas of flat seafloor between the reefs of the GBR have a rich di-versity of life, much of it unknown to science. Unfortunately most inter-reef areas suitable for bottom trawling have been fished for decades, with un-known consequences for both the inter-reef fauna itself and the soft-bottom ecosystems that provide biological connections between reefs and serve as nursery grounds. The management issues are not so much about the species that are targets of the trawling—prawns and bottom-dwelling fish. Rather, they are about the physical damage trawling does to the seafloor and its ef-fect on a wide range of bottom-dwelling life (the so-called by-catch, illus-trated in Plate 28), which dies and is dumped back into the ocean.

Recent modifications to trawling equipment, together with restrictions on the areas where trawling is permitted, have reduced both the quantity and the diversity of by-catch; nevertheless it can be argued that the extent of the damage still caused by trawling in a World Heritage marine park is at odds with the park's primary mandate for long-term conservation. Bottom trawling has a highly variable impact on different creatures: some species are almost unaffected, whereas others show no short-term recovery. The essential conservation issue is that trawling damages habitat, whereas other forms of fishing, if managed appropriately, affect only the target species.

Nor can commercial trawling be justified on financial grounds. Approximately 24,000 metric tons of seafood valued at US$100 million per year are harvested commercially, whereas recreational charter fishing harvests 3,500–4,300 metric tons and, with its associated tourism, attracts a regional income of US$3.4 billion annually.[14] Total abolition, or at least more severe restriction, of trawling is clearly an option that must be considered to conserve the GBR's financial value and at the same time provide as much protection as possible from the environmental dangers that lie ahead.

Genetic Dwarfing:
A Darwinian Debt

Curiously, the long-term consequences of major disruption to ecosystems that have taken millennia to evolve can remain hidden from scientists and wildlife managers alike. A case in point, as yet poorly studied, is the genetic dwarfing of fish and perhaps a wide range of other reef fauna, caused by the selective harvesting of large individuals. This is clearly happening with most fishing practices; it is the result of management protocols intended to protect immature individuals. This selection process—survival of the smallest—would have only a weak influence on GBR fauna *if* the fauna were genetically isolated from other countries. However, most reef fauna of the GBR is not isolated; it participates in genetic exchange with fauna in other countries that is fished intensively.

The consequences of this will depend on the amount of gene flow between the GBR and neighboring countries where fishing pressure is heavy. This in turn varies among different species depending on their individual larval behaviors. There is good reason to believe that humans have become the world's greatest evolutionary force and that genetic dwarfing will ultimately affect all commercial fisheries.[15]

Local Impacts, Global Impacts, and the Future

How does abrupt global climate change fit into the overall scale of impacts I have just outlined? It does not: it is in a different league altogether. Local issues might seem important today—and by today's standards they may indeed be important—but they are not going to stay that way long. The proverbial deck chairs on the *Titanic* will seem far less important when the looming iceberg ahead becomes visible to all.

For the remainder of this book I leave lesser local concerns behind. Climate change is affecting the whole planet, and the GBR is no exception. Rather the opposite: the most thoroughly studied and best managed of all marine showpieces will point to the future well ahead of most of the world's other great ecosystems. The ocean's canary has already sounded the alarm, and it will do so with increasing persistence in the decades to come.

Bleaching

Coral tissue that has turned white or pale is described as "bleached." Bleaching is not in itself a disease; rather it is a symptom of stress in the coral, the coral's zooxanthellae, or both. It can occur in small patches of individual colonies or across whole tracts of reefs. Much of the natural patchy bleaching occasionally seen in otherwise healthy corals is unimportant, as it causes little or no long-term problems for a colony. Such patches may be due to a temporary loss of photosynthetic pigment from the zooxanthellae, predators of many sorts, or attacks from neighboring colonies in the battle for growing space. Colonywide bleaching is clearly of more concern, as it can result in the death of the coral. Such bleaching has a number of causes, including disease, lowered salinity, high temperature, or increased light (as a result of a decrease in turbidity), all of which indicate that tissue integrity has been compromised. Although any of these conditions can result in widespread mortality, by far the most common and most conspicuous cause is a combination of strong light and elevated temperature. When entire reef tracts are affected, the phenomenon is known as "mass bleaching," and it often leads to mass death.

Such temperature- and light-induced bleaching normally begins with excessively elevated levels of photosynthesis, which lead zooxanthellae to produce toxic levels of oxygen. This occurs most commonly in shallow reef waters, where corals are exposed to a combination of high seawater temperatures and high levels of sunlight; corals can regulate the quantity of zooxanthellae in their tissues, but not the rate at which these produce oxygen. Under conditions of high temperature and excess light, zooxanthellae become poisonous, actually deactivating the sunscreens corals produce to protect themselves.

After studying this process in detail, coral physiologists have discovered it to be a general phenomenon found in terrestrial plants as a mechanism for protecting leaf tissue from excess oxygen through overexposure to sunlight.[16] In corals exposed to extreme levels of solar radiation and high water temperatures, zooxanthellae produce oxygen four to eight times faster than the coral host can take it up. When this happens, some oxygen ceases to play a normal role in photosynthesis and becomes chemically active in other ways, as oxygen radicals, causing cellular distress. As oxygen radicals become toxic, the zooxanthellae that produce them are expelled by the corals, even though this action also puts their lives at risk.[17]

Expulsion most commonly takes place by sloughing off the gastrodermal cells in which the algae live, but there are other mechanisms, such as resorption and tissue death. Such discoveries explain why bleaching is light as well as temperature dependent. They also account for a host of experimental variations correlated with environment, colony characteristics (including shape and species), and the place and depth where experimental corals were originally collected.[18] Moreover, they help explain why some corals die after they bleach: even when other nutrients are present and there is plenty of food in the form of zooplankton, they may simply not have enough gastrodermal cells left to function.

The temperature and light conditions that cause corals to expel their zooxanthellae are normally not localized but commonly affect a significant portion of the reef. This can result in widespread mass bleaching of coral colonies, particularly at shallow depths.

Mass Bleaching

Mass bleaching was first recorded in early 1980 in the Caribbean and surrounding seas (notably in Jamaica and the Bahamas), in the far eastern Pacific (Panama and the Galápagos Islands), and in isolated instances in the Pacific (notably French Polynesia and Thailand), as well as the GBR.[19]

There have been seven major bleaching events to date on the GBR, the three spanning the summer seasons of 1981/1982, 1997/1998, and 2001/2002 being the most widespread. However, it was the 1981/1982 event that really drew attention to the connection between ocean temperature and bleaching.[20]

Reports of mass bleaching on the GBR in the summer of 1981/1982 were largely confined to the central sector, because the more remote regions of the southeast and far north were (and still are) seldom visited, and there were few adequate techniques for surveying the vast areas involved. Even being towed behind a boat using a manta board—a technique particularly useful for large areas—clearly has major limitations for divers confronted by thousands of kilometers of reef edge. Surveys from aircraft can help, but the depth that can be surveyed is limited and the results are difficult to quantify. Nevertheless, in 1998 some 654 reefs out of the GBR's total of 3,650 were surveyed from aircraft skimming 160 meters over the ocean surface. The results obtained were followed up by semiquantitative "ground-truth" surveys by divers at selected spots. Reefs of all types were covered—no mean feat given that 26,000 square kilometers of reefs had to be sampled. Not unexpectedly, the divers reported significantly more damage than was seen from the air. Even more unhappily, over 60 anecdotal yet reliable reports from tour group operators and scientists in other fields confirmed that the bleaching was indeed worse than the aerial reports indicated. One particularly beautiful embayment of Orpheus Island (near Townsville, where I worked extensively during the 1970s) was devastated: 60–80 percent of all the corals of the reef flat, including 90–95 percent of all *Acropora*, had died within nine weeks of the onset of bleaching. This level of destruction has to be seen to be appreciated. In all, about two-thirds of the inshore reefs and 14 percent of the offshore reefs suffered moderate to high levels of bleaching, that is, had bleaching with a widespread and obvious impact.[21]

This 1997/1998 mass bleaching event—the second of the three great worldwide events to date—was extraordinarily widespread, affecting reefs in over 50 countries throughout the Pacific and Indian Oceans, the Red Sea, and the Caribbean, and even corals in higher latitudes, including those of the Persian/Arabian Gulf. On the GBR, this mass bleaching coincided with the highest sea surface temperatures ever recorded.[22] It was also at this time that 500-year-old corals died (see Plate 47)—strong evidence that mass bleaching is a recent, anthropogenic phenomenon.

The third major mass bleaching event took place in 2001/2002, again affecting reefs in many countries.[23] By this time it had become clear that there was a causal link between the periodicity of global bleaching and changes in ocean-temperature-associated El Niño Southern Oscillation cycles (described later). The gap between such events appears to be closing as the difference between El Niño years and non–El Niño years diminishes, a process that is destined to persist into this century. Significantly, although 2006 was not an El Niño year, there was nevertheless significant mass bleaching of corals on the GBR. Extensive mass bleaching occurred in waters off several countries of the Caribbean in both 2005 and 2006. Present indications are that increases in global temperatures will lead to mass bleaching *every* year by 2030.

Mass Bleaching and the Environment

Mass bleaching is caused by the inability of corals to process all the oxygen from light produced by photosynthesis. This occurs only in corals that are exposed to strong sunlight and where the water becomes abnormally warm. What matters is the degree of heating above normal limits rather than absolute temperature, and this varies geographically. Moreover, short periods of high temperature may be more stressful than longer periods of a slightly lower temperature, but bleaching stress is basically cumulative over periods of weeks to months.

Bleaching (but probably not mass bleaching) can be caused by stresses other than temperature and light in combination, including increased ultraviolet radiation, lack of water movement around the colonies, low salinity after floods, bacterial infection, sudden chilling, and chemical pollutants. However, it is the combination of high temperature and high solar radiation that causes maximum bleaching.

Geographic variation in mass bleaching has several important aspects. Corals growing on equatorial reefs are, not surprisingly, more tolerant of heat than those growing at higher latitudes.[24] Corals bleach at lower temperatures on the southern GBR than in the north, which indicates the importance of temperature thresholds. Moreover, bleaching can also occur in higher-latitude coral reefs, including those of the Northern Hemisphere off Hawaii and Bermuda.[25] Local geographic variation in the extent of bleaching has been found within the same species,[26] and to a significant extent susceptibility is a function of the history (experience) of the individual coral colony.[27]

Some groups of corals—taxa and communities—are more susceptible than others. The families Acroporidae and Pocilloporidae are commonly the most affected, as is the hydrocoral *Millepora*. The least affected are the corals with massive growth forms, notably the faviids. There are, however, many reported differences in detail among studies of different taxa. Several imaginative explanations for these differences have been put forward, one being that the least affected species belong to the oldest families, another that the faster-growing corals are the most susceptible, and still another that it is mostly a matter of tissue thickness and associated densities of zooxanthellae. However, all corals with zooxanthellae will bleach if conditions become severe enough for long enough.

Mass bleaching is most common and most severe in shallow communities, but it is not restricted to the shallows, and it has been recorded to depths of more than 25 meters on the GBR and 30 meters on Scott Reef, Western Australia. It is sometimes prevalent in intertidal pools, but normally corals that are aerially exposed at low tides are the most heat- and light-tolerant of all and often do not bleach when those in nearby deeper water do. On the GBR it is more common in inshore communities, but even within the same region it is occasionally more severe offshore.

The effects of bleaching are still unfolding. We already know that it inhibits coral growth. However, the effect is temporary if the stresses are removed and normal levels of zooxanthellae return. It can disrupt the reproductive cycle—an outcome that has the potential to inhibit recovery of some coral species and thus change their relative abundance. Lower energy reserves caused by repeated bleaching may have contributed to the outbreaks of disease that have greatly affected the corals of Florida and the Caribbean, and are now being seen increasingly on the GBR. For healthy reefs, including those of most of the GBR, there are many accounts of recovery of bleached corals, and this may occur in as short a time as several months. Even completely white corals sometimes recover, but recovery of coral communities in which most of the corals have died requires the settlement and growth of new colonies and normally takes a decade or more, depending on larval supply, algal takeover after bleaching, and other local factors.

Significantly, several recent studies indicate that some genetic types of zooxanthellae appear more resistant to high levels of light and/or temperature (up to 1–1.5°C) than others, although this remains controversial.[28]

High Temperature: The Big Issue Today

As we have seen, mass bleaching is normally initiated by a combination of high light and high temperature. Since overall light energy does not change materially, we must investigate the possible sources of increasing temperature to explain mass bleaching events.

SEA SURFACE TEMPERATURE.   There are hundreds of books and articles showing sea surface temperature patterns obtained from satellite images, such as the illustration in Plate 53. In a world full of environmental complications, the implicit assumption is that temperature is the one variable that is easily measured. Unfortunately that is not the case.

For good reason we depend heavily on satellite images for temperature data, but what satellites actually see is a surface layer that is thinner than the paper these words are printed on. One does not have to be a physicist to understand why this can be deceptive. Any large body of water kept under a cloudless tropical sun for even a day without a breeze will acquire a warm surface layer. As time passes, this layer will continue to get warmer until it reaches a point at which further heating is held in check by evaporative cooling and the conduction of heat to deeper water. As warm days turn into hot weeks (as happens in the Doldrums), the warm layer gets thicker rather than warmer. The arrival of a breeze can change these conditions in a matter of hours, partly through increasing the rate of evaporation, but mainly through the mixing of the warm layer with deeper water by wave turbulence. Divers working in the summer tropics regularly experience this phenomenon: the temperature of the water of a reef slope (say, at a depth of 10 meters) may be tolerable enough even in a full wetsuit; yet once that diver surfaces, that few meters of surface can be oppressively warm. A light wind will change these conditions, but what the diver does not experience is the mixing, as far down as 100 meters, that even a light wind will cause.

The importance of this warm surface water to a coral reef is easy to imagine. A body of water that has a warm but thin surface layer may float harmlessly over a well-submerged reef. However, if the layer comes into contact with corals, its impact will vary not only with its temperature and thickness, but with the tidal regime as well. Where the tidal range is great, the thin warm layer might have only a brief contact with the coral, perhaps only at low tide. Where the tidal range is small, the coral may remain within the warm layer for as long as that layer endures. If there has been some mixing and the warm surface is thick, all the corals in its path, irrespective of tide, may broil for weeks.

Thus the system is not simply two-dimensional, as represented on a map or in a satellite image. Rather, it is multidimensional, affected by time and tide as well as temperature. More to the point, El Niño conditions (described later) generally create a thin layer of warm water in summer and a cooler-than-normal layer in winter. When it comes to bleaching, small wonder that some corals seem to be affected by different oceanic conditions, and still less wonder that these effects vary greatly with depth.

THE WESTERN PACIFIC WARM POOL AND THERMAL CAP.   The Western Pacific Warm Pool (indicated by white patches in the diagrams in the next section) is a highly mobile, changing mass of water that varies in size with both season and year. It also varies in depth within a matter of hours (depending on wind-driven mixing) and in width within weeks (depending on currents). The changes in depth and width do not change the total heat content of the ocean, which is held in check by inertia, but they do redistribute it. Although there are many scales operating here, it is easy to imagine how the pool affects the GBR. During the earlier part of the last century, warm surface ocean water from the warm pool would have controlled the temperature of the outer reefs, except where there was upwelling. When tidal currents moved this water into the GBR lagoon it languished under the summer sun, gradually warming further, for the area is too small to have any upper thermal limit. At that time this warming did no harm to the corals because the water never exceeded their thermal tolerance; however, this has now changed.

Although few people have even heard of it, the Western Pacific Thermal Cap—the maximum temperature the open water of the western Pacific can reach—is of great importance to the GBR. Owing to the evaporative cooling I have just described, the surface temperature of this huge region has an upper limit (thermal cap) of 31°C.[29] It is thus no coincidence that this happens to be the upper temperature tolerance limit for the corals of the area. However, it is important to remember that this thermal cap only applies to very large areas of ocean. Higher temperatures are commonly recorded in more enclosed areas, including the GBR's lagoon, and temperatures higher than 36°C may occur annually in smaller semienclosed seas with poor circulation, notably in the southern Red Sea and Persian/Arabian Gulf.

The El Niño Southern Oscillation

The El Niño Southern Oscillation (ENSO) is a coupled ocean-atmosphere climate system of great importance to the coral reefs of the Pacific, including the GBR. It delivers pulses of warm water from the Western Pacific Warm

Pool to coastal and island regions throughout the whole tropical western Pacific. ENSO can be explained with the help of the accompanying diagram and the satellite imagery in Plate 53.

In "normal" years (the accompanying diagram on the left), easterly trade winds along the equator push surface waters westward in the South Equatorial Current. This current piles surface water heated by the tropical sun in the eastern Pacific up in the western Pacific, increasing sea level there by about 0.6 meter. As part of this process, the thermocline (the depth where warm surface water meets cold deep-ocean water) is depressed in the west and raised in the east. The shallow thermocline in the east allows upwelling of cool, deep-ocean water to the surface, and the resulting cold water tongue typically extends from the coast of South America to the International Date Line. This east-to-west (cold-to-warm) surface water temperature gradient reinforces the surface easterly trade wind circulation. As the trade winds move west they accumulate moisture from the warm ocean, and the warm humid air mass ascends over the Western Pacific Warm Pool, causing heavy rainfall. This air then returns eastward at higher atmospheric levels to complete the so-called Walker Circulation.

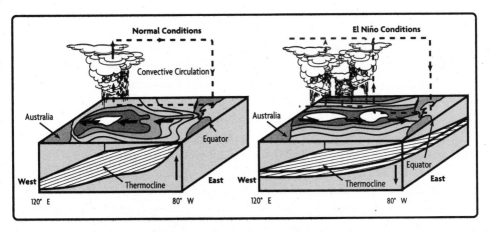

Figure 4.1 Normal and El Niño atmospheric and water circulations: the Walker Circulation (see the satellite imagery in Plate 53). Concentric rings represent areas of water with a similar temperature, the white central section being the warmest. During normal years (left diagram) equatorial surface water is pushed westward by easterly trade winds. The warmest pool of water does not affect the GBR. During El Niño years these trade winds weaken and the surface direction of the temperature anomaly reverses. El Niño conditions affect the GBR late in the cycle as the western Coral Sea reaches its thermal cap.

During an El Niño event, the trade winds along the equator weaken as atmospheric pressure rises in the west and falls in the east. As a result of the weaker trade winds, the Western Pacific Warm Pool remains relatively un-moved and thus continues to warm. The temperature anomaly created (but not necessarily the water itself) moves eastward. The thermocline also flat-tens across the equatorial Pacific. Sea surface temperatures increase in the central and eastern equatorial Pacific owing to the deeper thermocline sup-pressing upwelling. This results in an eastward shift in the center of the deepwater convection and rainfall, creating the ascending branch of the atmospheric part of the Walker Circulation as illustrated. El Niño condi-tions also leave their mark on the global carbon cycle (see Chapter 15), as reduced upwelling along the South American coast reduces the release of dissolved CO_2 into the atmosphere.

La Niña events, the opposite of El Niño events, are characterized by stronger than normal trade winds, cooler sea surface temperatures, and heav-ier rainfall in the tropical western Pacific. Fluctuations between the two ex-tremes, El Niño and La Niña, typically occur every 3–7 years, and each event evolves and decays over about 12–18 months. ENSO events are associated with typical patterns of atmospheric and oceanic anomalies throughout the tropics, which also extend their influence to climates at higher latitudes. The majority of coral reefs are most at risk from higher than normal sea surface temperatures, conditions conducive to coral bleaching, during El Niño events. La Niña events can, however, lead to unusually warm sea surface temperatures in the region of the South Pacific Convergence Zone of the western Pacific, which can expose reefs in Fiji, French Polynesia, and the Cook Islands to conditions that can lead to coral bleaching.[30]

Although not normally as extreme or extensive as in the Pacific, warm surface water can occur across the Indian Ocean concurrently with the Western Pacific Warm Pool. This pattern typically causes widespread drought in Australia, across Southeast Asia, and from India to North Africa. These tropical phenomena are further transmitted to high latitudes and the Caribbean Sea, giving ENSO events a near-global impact.

Today's Changes in Perspective

Under normal circumstances, corals and reefs would be able to recover from a mass bleaching event more or less as they do from crown-of-thorns starfish attacks. However, as is usual for so many subjects covered in this book, the significance of ENSO events is a matter of time—in this case the return times of damaging heat pulses. Spatial expansion and deepening of the Western Pacific Warm Pool as a result of climate change will progressively diminish the impact of El Niño events until they are irrelevant, at least to the GBR. Put another way, when this happens, as far as surface temperature is concerned, every year will effectively become an El Niño year. The day I became convinced that this would happen is the day that I started the research that led to this book.

Climate change, like a snowball rolling down a mountain slope, is increasing in scope and speed. Some scientists have been watching the snowball for decades, gradually coming to recognize it for what it is. Others have been taking longer, yet now it is there for all to see—at least for those who want to take the trouble to look. The snowball has now passed the point at which it can easily be stopped, and it is fast approaching the point at which it could—and many believe will—become an avalanche.

In the next chapters I take a look at avalanches of the past to see what sort of damage they did and what such avalanches might be capable of doing in the future. As we move closer to the present, we will start picking out the details of our particular snowball, if only to predict what sort of avalanche it could become and what we might be able to do to contain it.

I am not advocating dropping today's research and management priorities to concentrate exclusively on those of an uncertain future. My point of view does not make today's priorities any less real. However, it is essential that we look in earnest toward the long-term future, a future that is rapidly becoming more immediate. Good management is needed now more than at any time in the past, as impacts on coral reefs increase with human and environmental pressure and as we face a world of increasing uncertainty.

— 5 —

Mass Extinctions and Reef Gaps

The fossil record indicates that mass extinction events have affected reefs as much as or more than any other major ecosystem on Earth. These events, five in total, were all due to global environmental upheavals that have been linked to a wide range of causes. Reefs took an immense interval of time—many millions of years—to recover from each of these great extinctions.

Someone (I forget who, but it could only be a geologist) once said that the farther back in time you look the farther ahead you see. Maybe so. Certainly a glance back at the major upheavals of the ancient world makes it easier to understand why some skeptics view the climate changes of the present as being so trivial that they are hardly distinguishable from background noise in the Earth's climate history. As we progress through ancient worlds, one of our goals will be to evaluate this point of view and to determine whether the changes the world is now experiencing are indeed part of a greater natural variability.

On five different occasions during its existence, conditions on Earth have not simply changed but have gone berserk, and the Earth's biota has been plunged into a mass extinction event. These events certainly put present concerns into context. More to the point, in all five cases shallow tropical oceans in general and reefs in particular appear to have been hit extraordinarily hard, and the effects on them appear to have lasted many millions of years. We will see, in this chapter and the next, that a variety of causes, or rather various combinations of causes, have been blamed for the different extinctions.

In this chapter I look first at mass extinction events and the causes that paleontologists and paleoclimatologists have attributed to them, a broad-spectrum review that does not focus only on reefs. I then move on to a topic peculiar to reefs: reef gaps, the extraordinary amount of time reefs have taken to recover from mass extinctions. Both these subjects are relevant to the world of today, and especially to what could happen in the future. The combination of the geology and paleontology of the past with the biology and climatology of the future makes for a highly informative mixture.

Mass Extinctions and Coral Reefs

Mass extinction events are characterized by fundamental changes in plant and animal diversity, where many high-level taxonomic groups go extinct at about the same time over a period of 1–2 million years. They are also characterized by very slow recovery, led by the *evolution* of new species rather than *recolonization* by survivors.

The five great mass extinction events (commonly referred to as "the big five") occurred at widely spaced intervals, all but one marking a major division in the Earth's history.[1] Of these, one at the end of the Permian (251

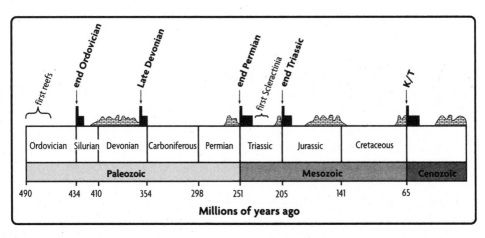

Figure 5.1   Timeline of events described in this chapter. The five named vertical bars indicate mass extinction events. Black rectangles represent global reef gaps (unimaginably long periods largely devoid of reefs) and brick-pattern shapes show times of prolific reef growth. At other times reef growth appears to have been between these extremes, although there were many gaps not associated with mass extinctions and there were intervals of prolific growth in limited geographic regions not indicated here. The oldest (tabulate) coral fossils, as opposed to reefs, go back to the Cambrian (the period immediately before the Ordovician) and are over 500 million years old.

mya) and one at the end of the Cretaceous (65 mya) were so profound that
they, respectively, designate the end of the Paleozoic and Mesozoic eras—
time intervals so fundamental to the paleontological record that they have
been used as the basic divisions in the Earth's history since the middle of the
nineteenth century. Although only the last mass extinction (the end of the
Cretaceous) occurred when Australia (let alone the GBR) even existed, they
all have relevance for modern coral reefs, not because of their geological
timing but rather because they show beyond a doubt what *can* happen when
the environment undergoes a massive upheaval. Mass extinction events in
this context represent worst-case scenarios.

There is a popular misconception that mass extinctions were dramatic
catastrophes inflicted on an otherwise peaceful Earth, but that was not the
case. There were actually many minor or background extinction events at
other times that left clear marks in the fossil record—no fewer than 27, according to a particularly detailed study.[2] Although not global, some of these
extinctions were just as catastrophic as mass extinctions for particular
ecosystems or particular places, and many had major impacts on coral reefs.
In Chapter 7, I note the occurrence of background extinctions in our own
era, because they played a major role in determining the diversity and distribution of today's coral reefs; but I have bypassed the earlier ones.

Hundreds of examples illustrate the difference between mass extinctions
and other types of extinctions in the fossil record. I select just one: a 25-
million-year-old rock sequence in North America formed during the
Carboniferous (around 330 mya, a period when glacial cycles repeatedly
changed the sea level). This sequence contains some ten marine strata al-
ternating with ten layers of coal of terrestrial origin. These strata clearly represent ten separate total extinction events in the region. However, as each
terrestrial coal layer was formed from similar plants, the sequence contains
no evidence of any mass extinction: the same plants simply reinvaded each
time the sea level fell. In contrast, fossil communities subsequent to mass
extinction events show evidence of major taxonomic change—genera, families, classes, and sometimes even complete phyla never reappear after the
extinction.

Reefs, more than any other major type of ecosystem, leave a geological
record that tracks such events. On an Earth history scale, this record does
not show a process of gradual evolutionary development or improvement,
but rather a stop-start response to a succession of environmental upheavals.
The vulnerability of reefs to these upheavals is demonstrated many times in

the fossil record, although the paleoclimatic record provides only uncertain glimpses of it—narrow windows separated by immense walls of time.

How Reliable Is the Coral Fossil Record?

Given that most coral reefs are made primarily of corals, in total volume they account for more fossils than all other animal life combined. However, the record (reconstructed for Scleractinia in Plate 8)[3] is not as good as it seems to be. There are two fundamental reasons for this: (1) Modern corals can be studied in situ and in the laboratory, allowing an almost unlimited amount of information (both morphological and molecular) to be gathered about them, as well as about the environments in which they grow. In contrast, the fossil record depends on rare discoveries and thus our knowledge of it, inevitably fragmented in both time and space, becomes a matter of accumulated individual opinions. (2) Paleozoic corals (rugose and tabulate corals) have skeletons made of calcite, a highly stable form of calcium carbonate in which skeletal details are often well preserved (illustrated in Figure 5.4). Mesozoic and Cenozoic corals (Scleractinia), on the other hand, have skeletons originally built of aragonite, an unstable form of calcium carbonate that recrystallizes to calcite, a process that obliterates skeletal details.

Some glimpses of how easily misinterpretations of the fossil record can distort our view of the past are afforded by the growth forms of living *Pocillopora damicornis,* illustrated in Figure 3.2. These sorts of variations in growth forms can readily be traced underwater, seen in single large colonies, studied in microscopic detail, and separated from similar variations in another species where two or more species grow together. However, before the advent of scuba diving, which paved the way for most of these kinds of studies, as many as 27 different names had been given to a single species by different coral taxonomists at different times in different countries. We can easily imagine how this might be reflected in the fossil record. If the sequence of specimens of a species such as *Pocillopora damicornis* had been studied as individually isolated fossils (as they typically would be), they would probably have been classified into several different genera. Similarly, a local change in sea level would likely have altered the (depth-dependent) sequence of growth forms, which would look like an evolutionary sequence in a fossil record.

Moreover, a major change in sea level might suggest that global extinctions had occurred in some of the supposed species, whereas the change had in fact only narrowed the morphological range of this single species. Any environmental change that removed part of a growth range (such as the infilling of a lagoon or a change in exposure to wave action) would likely suggest a local extinction of species or even genera in the fossil record. To further complicate the matter, fine skeletal details of individual polyps occurring on a branch tip are often very different from those of older polyps at branch bases, so much so that different parts of a single colony of a modern species (e.g., *Pavona maldivensis*) were once put into two different genera. Such details have been studied in some common fossil colonies, but opportunities for doing so are rare. Sometimes fossil studies have led to an explosion of different names for what could have been one and the same species (such as *Retiophyllia*, the branching coral on the right of the Triassic reconstruction in Plate 36).

As I noted earlier, reticulate evolution suggests that morphology (of both fossil and living corals) may not be an accurate indicator of genetic diversity. This effectively means that, at lower taxonomic levels, corals may survive extinctions more effectively than their fossil record indicates.

Azooxanthellate corals are in a category of their own, as most do not form colonies. For this reason and because they occupy relatively uniform environments, they do not have a wide range of growth forms. One all-important issue (which arises later in conjunction with mass extinction events) is the distinction between zooxanthellate and azooxanthellate corals in the fossil record. With exceptions, these distinctions can be made with some reliability at the time of the end Cretaceous mass extinction (65 mya), but not for earlier ones. If the matrix in which the fossil is embedded is reef limestone, it clearly suggests that the coral grew in a reef environment; however, as about half of all zooxanthellate coral colonies are not associated with reefs (see Chapter 3), the converse is not necessarily true.

In the light of these observations and later discussions in Chapter 6, I believe that the taxonomy of modern corals tells us the following about the fossil record: (1) Scleractinian *species* are seldom if ever recognizable in the fossil record. (2) Unless the fossils have direct affinities with modern species, most fossil genera cannot be placed with certainty into families. (3) The relationship among families cannot be reliably ascertained unless they have extant descendants, in which case their affinities can be investigated using molecular methods. These are not cries of despair: we must use the information we have—but we must also do so realistically, especially where our conclusions may have broad repercussions.

Key Environmental Indicators:
How Good Are They?

Several chapters of this book reflect on environmental conditions of the remote past. One may well ask how these past environmental reconstructions are made and how realistic they are. Leaving specifics to a later discussion, I note here that the most central of all the issues are those created by changes in sea level and (as I conclude in Chapter 6) atmospheric CO_2 levels and temperature.

Sea-level changes can be divided into long-term, major changes that result from plate tectonics, which reshape ocean basins, and much more rapid changes driven by glacial cycles, which move ice between land and ocean. The former are not known in any detail, as they can only be reconstructed through informed guesswork about the geography of a succession of ancient worlds. The latter, at least for the last glacial cycle, are known in great detail. The two are, in fact, quite different matters.

Atmospheric CO_2 levels are much more problematic, as they can vary greatly on all the time scales I use in this book. For this reason, several diagrams are used to illustrate CO_2 fluctuations over specific time intervals. Unlike sea-level changes, CO_2 levels have probably fluctuated over intervals as short as a few hundred thousand years throughout the entire existence of coral reefs. This means that any specific statement about atmospheric CO_2 levels—like "they fell abruptly in the Late Devonian"—must be highly questionable: the statement may be true for many thousands of years but false for many other intervals over that amount of time. Conclusions about atmospheric CO_2 concentrations also vary considerably with the investigative techniques used. These include carbon mass modeling, isotopic measurements of fossil soils (paleosols), study of the concentration of breathing pores (stomata) in the leaves of plants, and measurement of boron isotope concentrations in calcium carbonate skeletons of shallow-water Foraminifera.[4] Not all of these measurement methods necessarily have a direct bearing on the level of CO_2 in the ocean.

As I noted in Chapter 3, temperature is even more variable than CO_2, primarily because the atmosphere, oceans, and ice masses have very different inertias (lag times) when it comes to change. This also means that, unlike sea levels and atmospheric CO_2 concentrations, temperature can be geographically variable. Ice core records (see Chapter 9) provide details of atmospheric temperatures not seen in other sources, yet long-term records come primarily from analyses of deep-ocean sediments. The differences between these types of measurements can be misleading. Mean global temperatures, such as those commonly referred to in this book, are dominated by mean ocean temperatures, as the oceans are the principal containers and transporters of heat on the Earth. During the last glacial cycle, for example, the global average temperature changed approximately 7°C over thousands of years, whereas snap *atmospheric* reductions of 8°C or more have occurred frequently over as little as a century (see Chapter 13).

Mass Extinctions in Paleozoic Reefs and Ancient Corals

Three of the five great mass extinction events occurred during the Paleozoic Era (490–251 mya). Before delving into the fate of the corals and reefs, I must reemphasize that the term "reefs" used throughout this enormous expanse of time does not necessarily mean coral reefs as we know them today. Giant stromatoporoid sponges (illustrated in Plate 32) as well as several animal groups other than corals were often the dominant reef builders. Nevertheless, although we cannot always use the term "coral reef" to describe these structures, the term "reef" is certainly applicable, for they were sometimes of immense size, as illustrated in Plate 33.

THE END ORDOVICIAN MASS EXTINCTION, 434 MYA.   The first great mass extinction "event" took place at the end of the Ordovician, a time when, according to the fossil record, 26 percent of all families and 60 percent of all genera of both terrestrial and marine life worldwide were exterminated.[5] This extinction occurred at the end of a period of high mean global temperatures, caused perhaps by global greenhouse stability, a condition that seemed to have prevailed since the end of the Cambrian 70 million years earlier. The extinction, however, was not just one "event." It took place over a very long time span—perhaps several million years—and appears to have been the cumulative outcome of a succession of disasters. Possible causes suggested by paleontologists include major fluctuations in sea level, multiple short-lived polar glaciations, and changes in ocean temperature, circulation, and chemistry—all rather vague. The extinction occurred at a time when Australia did not even exist (see the accompanying figure) and would have little relevance for this book were it not for the fact that it was particularly disastrous and long lasting for reefs.[6] Although some individual rugose and tabulate coral taxa hung on, living reefs disappeared from the face of the

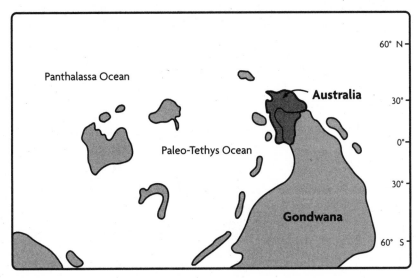

Figure 5.2 The Ordovician world, showing the position of Australia, which at that time was mostly submerged and thus did not exist as a recognizable entity.

Earth and did not reappear for another 4–6 million years, long after the climate had returned to preextinction conditions. This is the first true "reef gap," meaning a gap in the geological record of reefs. In the case of the Ordovician mass extinction, when reefs did reappear, they did so only sporadically.

THE LATE DEVONIAN MASS EXTINCTION, 360 MYA.   The Late Silurian to Late Devonian (425–350 mya) period—a further 75 million years or so dominated by global greenhouse conditions of high temperatures set between ice ages—probably included all-time peaks of Paleozoic reef development.[7] Sea levels were mostly high, so that seas flooded extensive areas of continents, forming so-called epicontinental seas. However, despite the apparent proliferation of reefs, their development was intermittent, with major periods of worldwide expansion, especially during the Middle Silurian to Late Devonian (a time that included at least two Northern Hemisphere reef systems that were larger than the GBR is today) interspersed with periods of apparent collapse.[8] This is a pattern that repeats itself throughout the history of reefs: even these "good" times for reefs were transitory intervals of widespread development separated by multiple short-lived downturns of one form or another.

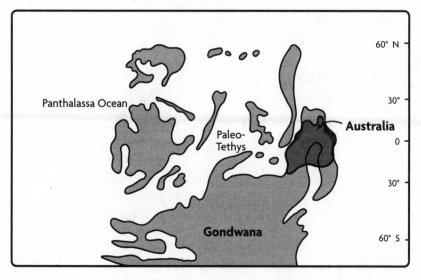

Figure 5.3   The Devonian world, showing the position of Australia and the location of the two reef outcrops, on the northeast and northwest coasts, that exist today.

Devonian reefs are particularly widespread in Australia, where the south and center of the continent were at the time flooded by an epicontinental sea. The oldest reefs to have grown anywhere near today's GBR are a little-known group of limestone outcrops about 150 kilometers inland from Townsville in the central region of the GBR. The outcrops, collectively called the Big Bend Reefs,[9] are each about the size of an average to small modern-day coral reef, yet they are part of a reef line that may well have been longer than the GBR is today. Despite their age the corals of Big Bend are sometimes so well preserved that even microscopic details of their skeletal structures remain visible (see Figure 5.4)—a legacy of their formation from calcitic rather than aragonitic varieties of calcium carbonate.

Of course this reef has nothing to do with today's GBR, and even calling it Australian is an anachronism, for when it was alive the part of the Earth's crust that we now call Australia hardly existed, as illustrated in the map above. The Big Bend Reefs, and their bigger brothers at the time, the Canning Basin Reefs of northwest Australia[10] (illustrated in Plate 34), were formed in the Middle Devonian, some 380 mya—long before the supercontinent of Gondwana, which eventually gave birth to Australia, even ex-

Figure 5.4   A 25-mm-wide rugose coral from one of the Big Bend Reefs. Despite the age of this specimen (360 million years), details of its structure are still preserved in microscopic detail because the original skeleton was composed of calcite, which was not altered by subsequent chemical changes. Very few fossil Scleractinia are this well preserved because their original aragonite skeletons have been recrystallized into calcite, losing detail in the process. (Photograph by the author.)

isted. When these reefs were alive they were close to the equator in a world in which no modern continents are recognizable. This is truly time beyond comprehension.

Any link between the Big Bend Reefs and living reefs of today is tenuous indeed. Yet therein lies another message, for the world's Devonian reefs may have been every bit as well formed and biologically diverse as today's reefs and—with an estimated area of 5 million square kilometers including inter-reef areas—may have been as much as twice as extensive.[11] However, dur-

ing the Late Devonian (360 mya) something happened; the environment
that had clearly nurtured reefs the world over for at least 13 million years
turned hostile. The corals, the giant sponges, and all the other organisms
that had built these reefs started dying en masse. For the second time in the
history of reefs, the world was plunged into a mass extinction event.

The Late Devonian mass extinction, like that at the end of the Ordovician, has also been linked to multiple causes. A bolide (a large exploding
asteroid, several of which have periodically struck the Earth with enormous
force)[12] may have occurred around this time, although most paleontologists
no longer seriously consider this to be a likely cause of the extinction. A pre-
cipitous drop in atmospheric CO_2 (blamed on uptake by vascular plants),
low global temperatures, and wildly fluctuating sea levels have all been
blamed.[13] The extinctions appear to have varied geographically, although
they primarily affected marine life: reef development ceased almost completely. Some reefs, including those of the Canning Basin, may have persisted
as microbe-dominated platforms of some sort; however, they ceased to be
functional "reefs" by any description. Some isolated corals and stromatoporoid sponges lived on in other Devonian reefs, but there was no recovery
of the coral-sponge reef communities anywhere in the world.

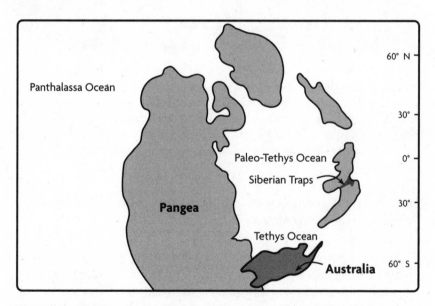

Figure 5.5   The Permian world, showing the position of Australia, which at that
time was mostly land.

Reefs—although still not structures comparable to today's coral reefs—existed sporadically during much of the Carboniferous and Permian (350–251 mya)—through times of oscillating temperatures and sea levels, including the periodic development of polar ice caps. By the Permian, most continental plates had coalesced into one gigantic supercontinent, as illustrated in Figure 5.5, and reefs developed around many of its tropical and subtropical coastlines. Some of these reefs, especially those of the Late Permian (around 260 mya), were very extensive. Their fossil content indicates that they were exceptionally diverse relative to their forebears, for they contained extensive arrays of all of the major marine groups, especially molluscs, echinoderms, and crustaceans, as well as rugose and tabulate corals. This fauna was in fact part of the massive biological buildup, both marine and terrestrial, that awaited the greatest extinction event of all time—the end Permian.

THE END PERMIAN MASS EXTINCTION, 251 MYA. The fossil record of the end Permian mass extinction reveals a staggering loss of life: 82 percent of all genera and perhaps 80–95 percent of all marine species died.[14] All rugose and tabulate corals and most other calcifying organisms went extinct. Why? This was one of the foremost questions in paleontology a century ago, and it remains so today. Paleontologists have not been able to ascertain the cause of this mass extinction with any degree of certainty. At one point or another wildly fluctuating temperatures in response to sharp increases in atmospheric CO_2, acid rain, and lack of oxygen in shallow waters after protracted times of plenty have all been held responsible. The oceans are widely believed to have turned anoxic and to have contained free hydrogen sulfide;[15] another study suggests that a sudden release of methane occurred at this time.[16] Whatever the cause, the impact on reefs was sudden by geological standards and devastating. Some members of most marine phyla survived, yet reefs did not reappear for about 10 million years, an unimaginable amount of time and the greatest hiatus in reef building in all of the Earth's history.

Mesozoic Reefs and Modern Corals

No rugose or tabulate coral of any kind survived the end Permian mass extinction. What emerged after the reef gap in the Middle Triassic (around 230 mya) was a new group of reef builders, the Scleractinia.

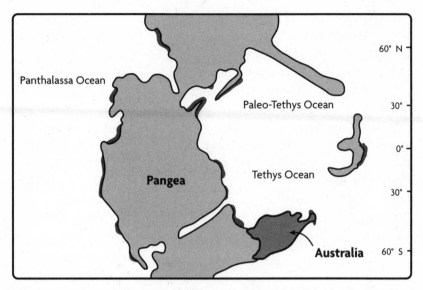

Figure 5.6 The Triassic world, showing the position of Australia. The dark areas indicate the approximate position of the remains of reefs found today.

There has long been debate about the relationship between Paleozoic corals and the Scleractinia, although it now seems clear that the Scleractinia did not evolve from either of the two Paleozoic groups of corals. Rather, they probably evolved from soft-bodied anemone-like survivors of the end Permian mass extinction, filling the ecological void created by the demise of their reef-building precursors. Through two more mass extinctions, this extraordinary group of animals has endured to provide a history, written in many billions of tons of limestone spread from New Zealand to Alaska and throughout all the oceans of the world.[17]

There is much in common between the ancient reefs of the mid-Paleozoic and the first scleractinian reefs that took their place, not so much in the animals that built them but in the stop-start nature of their intervals of growth, their biodiversity, and the sheer size of the structures they formed. Perhaps stop-start intervals occurred in all ecosystems and we just see them in reefs because reefs leave such a lasting legacy in the paleontological record. It is more likely that the starts are the result of an immense capacity for growth when times are good and the stops are the result of the exceptional vulnerability of reefs to hostile environments. We see this with increasing clarity as we get closer to more recent times.

THE END TRIASSIC MASS EXTINCTION, 205 MYA.   For many millions of years Triassic scleractinian corals, in concert with calcifying sponges and algae, went on to build some of the most spectacular reefs of all time, the Late Triassic calcareous alps of Germany and Austria (215–205 mya, illustrated in Plate 35). There was another substantial extinction of corals early in the Late Triassic, followed by a brief interval of dramatic recovery. Then, once again, the Earth plunged into a full-scale mass extinction. The end Triassic mass extinction—the fourth in the history of reefs[18]—is estimated to have claimed about half of all marine invertebrates. The main taxa affected were conodonts (tiny fishlike primitive vertebrates that went completely extinct), ammonites (almost all), and bivalves and gastropods (over half of all species). One-third of all scleractinian families went extinct, and fewer than 25 percent of all genera are known to have survived.[19] Nevertheless, this mass extinction, like its predecessors, was not only marine; perhaps 80 percent of all land quadrupeds also went extinct. The cause, again, has been much debated without a clear outcome.[20] Atmospheric CO_2 reached extreme levels for the Mesozoic (at least eight times today's level[21]), and high greenhouse temperatures certainly resulted. Short-term sea-level fluctuations and various changes in ocean chemistry have been implicated by several paleontologists, although none gives convincing evidence. The extinction was relatively abrupt (in geological time), making the reason for it

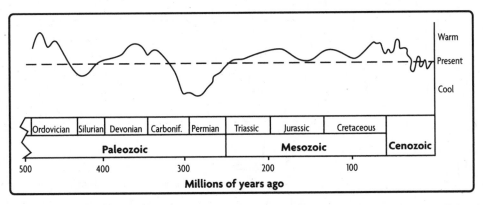

Figure 5.7   Smoothed estimates of mean global temperature of the Earth over the time of the existence of reefs. These are relative temperatures only, but they do not indicate any correlation between temperature and mass extinction events. At this scale, short intervals of cold during the Ice Ages are not visible, but they are described and illustrated for the Cenozoic in Chapters 7 and 9.

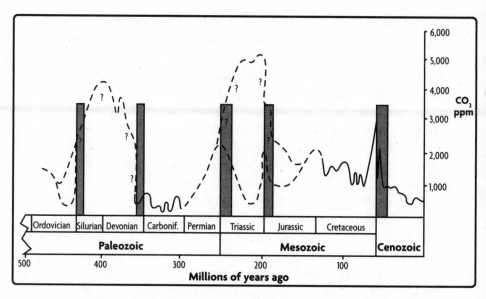

Figure 5.8 Atmospheric CO_2 levels in parts per million (ppm) over the time of the existence of reefs. The vertical bars are the intervals of reef gaps following the five great mass extinction events. All of these, with the likely exception of the Late Devonian, are probably associated with rapidly increasing or high CO_2 levels.

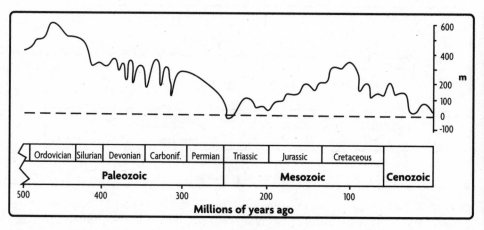

Figure 5.9 Sea levels over geological time. As with the previous diagrams, this line has been smoothed, showing only long-term continental movements rather than abrupt glacial cycles. Nevertheless, there is no correlation between sea levels and mass extinction events.

particularly obscure. Whatever the cause, reefs again remained rare or absent throughout the world for a vast amount of time, perhaps 6–8 million years.[22]

Fortunately for the future of reefs, the coral fauna that did survive, though few in numbers of genera, retained much of the diversity, at higher taxonomic levels, of the Late Triassic (215–205 mya). It was this diversity that eventually led to the greatest proliferation of reefs of the entire Mesozoic and perhaps the greatest diversity of Scleractinia of all time. By the Late Jurassic (160 mya), reefs were again dominating the shorelines of the tropical world. The corals that built them formed distinct biogeographic provinces not unlike those of the present, with only the vast expanse of the Panthalassa Ocean being a major barrier to dispersal, much as its modern equivalent, the Pacific, is today.[23]

The Best Known of All Global Catastrophes: K/T

About 65 million years ago, at the close of the Mesozoic Era, the dinosaurs went extinct—about 15 families in all: herbivores, carnivores, and scavengers of all shapes and sizes. This heralded the fifth and most recent mass extinction event: the end Cretaceous or, as it is commonly called, K/T. (The abbreviation refers to the Cretaceous/Tertiary boundary, the K coming from the German word for chalk.)

K/T has been extensively studied and not just because of the demise of the dinosaurs. Reconstructing the causes of K/T has almost the same level of importance today as understanding what caused the Ice Ages. These two climatic events, the greatest of our era, are the key to the mechanisms that control our environment—or rather the consequences that can ensue when those controls go awry. Now, with our current concerns about climate change, what was once scientific curiosity has given way to a pressing need for enlightened insight.

Many well-known animal groups besides the dinosaurs went extinct at the K/T boundary, including those magnificent flying reptiles, the pterosaurs, as well as almost all marsupials. Virtually no large land animals survived. Plants were also greatly affected, although this is less clearly documented: records of pollen, which was very abundant, indicate extensive regional devastation yet remarkably little extinction at higher taxonomic levels. Once again tropical marine life was decimated, including plesiosaurs, ichthyosaurs, and mosasaurs, as well as an extraordinarily high proportion of calcifying organisms. All remaining ammonites and belemnites (cuttle-fish-like molluscs) went extinct, as did a high percentage of bivalves, gastropods, and echinoids, as well as almost all Foraminifera. Many other unicellular organisms including radiolarians were also severely affected. Curiously, most other major taxa—including freshwater fish, amphibians, turtles, crocodiles, snakes, and lizards—appear to have been almost unaffected, as were placental mammals. There are indeed many parallels with the end Triassic mass extinction (205 mya).

Scleractinian corals were high on the list of K/T casualties; they appear to have just barely hung on: one-third of all families and 70 percent of all genera went completely extinct. Of the surviving families, one (the Faviidae) retained six of its original sixteen genera; the others retained only one or two. Taxonomic detail in the fossil record is somewhat lacking,[24] partly because sea levels were high during most of the Cretaceous (141–65 mya), and reefs were eroded away as the seas receded. Nevertheless, no branching corals appear to have survived, with the consequence that the habitats maintained by this important group—those that provide shelter for algae-grazing fish (see Chapter 3)—would have completely disappeared.

Crucially, as we shall see, deepwater azooxanthellate corals were affected to the same degree as zooxanthellate reef corals. The most diverse azooxanthellate family (Caryophylliidae) lost half of its 27 genera; another family (Rhizangiidae) survived by three, and each of the other thirteen families survived by only one or two.[25]

Yet it was not the great diversity of the reefs of the Jurassic (205–141 mya) that was finally destroyed by K/T, for corals had been declining in abundance, and perhaps diversity, throughout the Early to Middle Cretaceous (141–100 mya). Presumably this decline had environmental causes. It also resulted from the displacement of corals as dominant reef builders by a bizarre group of bivalve molluscs, mostly growing on stalks like large-stalked barnacles, known as rudists. Some corals grew alongside rudists, although most occupied separate habitats.[26] Few rudist reefs would have looked like any modern reef: although rudists sometimes formed massive wave-resistant structures, most of their reefs are called "meadows" by paleontologists owing to their flat contours.[27] By the Late Cretaceous (80 mya), rudists with aragonite skeletons had been largely replaced by those with calcite skeletons,[28] which might have given them a competitive advantage over corals during times of challenging ocean chemistry. Mass extinctions are not to blame for all the changes of fortune in the history of corals. It was only

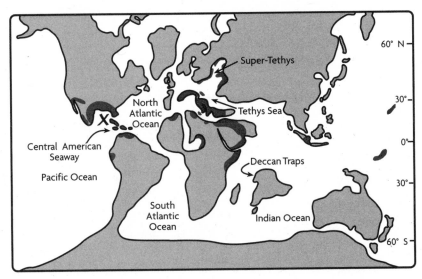

Figure 5.10   Positions of the continents during the Late Cretaceous, showing surviving reef limestone. Epicontinental seas were extensive during this time, especially over Europe and North Africa. X marks the impact site of the K/T bolide in the Gulf of Mexico.

after the rudists themselves had been greatly reduced in number and diversity during the Late Cretaceous that corals returned to their dominant place in reef building.

The Middle Cretaceous (around 100 mya) was a time of great environmental upheaval. Sea levels reached over 300 meters above present levels, an all-time high for the Mesozoic. The oceans flooded up to 40 percent of the continents, leaving only 18 percent of the Earth's surface as land (compared with 28 percent today). The largest of these seas was the Super-Tethys, an epicontinental sea that covered much of Europe and the Middle East, as shown in the accompanying map.

Globally averaged atmospheric temperatures have been estimated to be 6–14°C higher than at present,[29] ranging from a few degrees' difference at the equator to as much as 20–40°C at the poles.[30] Just what that would have meant for reefs is uncertain, as the surface temperature of the largest oceans would have been capped then much as it is today.

Estimates of CO_2 levels vary greatly, as indicated in the reconstruction shown in Figure 5.8; however, the data for K/T are more reliable than those for more ancient extinctions. By the end Cretaceous it seems that peak CO_2 levels were at least five times, and perhaps as much as ten times, those of to-day.[31] The Late Cretaceous was very much a greenhouse world.

Proposed Explanations for K/T

Most people believe they know what caused the K/T mass extinction. In 1980 Luis and Walter Alvarez, a father-son team, and their colleagues published an article asserting that K/T was the result of a devastating bolide impact.[32] Their account received newspaper coverage like no other discovery in the history of geology. The bolide is generally thought to have been about 20 kilometers in diameter; the impact site, off the Yucatán Peninsula of southeast Mexico, would have been gigantic—around 40 kilometers deep and several hundred kilometers wide. Traces of the impact, synchronous the world over, are seen in an instantaneous peak in the concentration of irid-ium (a very rare heavy metal almost entirely derived from extraterrestrial sources) and occurrences of shocked quartz (quartz grains microscopically restructured by the passage of shock waves).

The sensational discovery by the Alvarez team conjures up images of un-bridled devastation—of a "nuclear winter"—and has captured the minds and imagination of people of all ages, nationalities, and professions. This is hardly surprising—after all, it is hard to get a similar thrill out of fluctuating greenhouse gas concentrations or slowly creeping sea levels. Their theory, however, remains highly controversial: over 2,000 books and articles were published about it within a decade of the original publication.[33]

There is no doubt that the bolide impact would have sent shock waves around the Earth, creating tsunamis of immense size and triggering wide-spread volcanic activity. The impact itself and the outpourings of the shock-induced volcanoes are widely believed to have created a stratospheric dust cloud that would indeed have plunged the whole of the Earth into a cold, interminable night. Certainly acid rain (including nitric acid generated from heat-induced fusion of nitrogen and oxygen), high levels of CO_2 re-leased from the impact site and from volcanic eruptions everywhere, and high concentrations of methane released from continental slopes would have combined to create intense greenhouse warming. However, the timing of the ultimate extinction of different animal groups, the time taken for many to go extinct, and the age of the bolide debris do not correlate well. Some animal taxa became extinct within an apparently brief period, whereas others, including the dinosaurs, took longer (hundreds of thousands of years), and their decline started long before the bolide's impact. The debate goes on, yet the tide has certainly turned against the idea that the bolide was the dominant cause of K/T.[34]

Perhaps just as important as the bolide, and bracketing it in time, was a massive outpouring of volcanic lava, one of the largest in the history of the Earth, covering an area of India (then an island) radiating 300–500 kilometers out from what is now Bombay to a depth of over 2,000 meters.[35] This volume of basalt is over 1,000 times that of Krakatoa, the best-known volcanic eruption in modern history. This immense structure, known as the Deccan Traps, was extruded over a period of about 500,000 years. Carbon dioxide levels—already at an all-time high since the Early Jurassic and now augmented by volcanic activity from the rapid seafloor spreading of the North Atlantic—would have reached extreme levels.

The conclusion argued by the biogeographer Jack Briggs is that the K/T extinction was a stepwise event largely confined to the marine tropics and closely associated with CO_2 levels and sea-level fluctuations in response to seafloor spreading.[36] The plight of the dinosaurs may have been a largely independent matter, perhaps the result of displacement by placental mammals that ate dinosaur eggs. The dinosaurs appear to have departed with a whimper rather than a bang, as one paleontologist recently observed. I review these conclusions in the next chapter as I examine the cause of extinctions from the point of view of corals and reefs.

Some corals survived K/T, yet the hiatus in reef growth, although not absolute, was so long that extensive reefs, comparable to those of the Cretaceous before the extinction, did not appear again until the Middle to Late Eocene, at least 10 million years later. Even then all reefs had a low level of diversity. Unfortunately, the fossil record for the corals of this recovery period is poor and so far few details have been gleaned from it.[37]

K/T's Legacy: A Reconstructed World

Toward the end of the Cretaceous, the Earth was not a pleasant place. For many hundreds of thousands, if not millions, of years the environment had been deteriorating. The air was stiflingly hot. Dense, black, water-laden clouds often masked the sun; thunder clapped and lightning flashed day and night. Violent storms—cyclones and tornadoes—were constant, and acid rain deluged the land. Huge tracts of the Earth's surface repeatedly alternated between land and sea, although the salinity of these shallow epicontinental seas was so low that the sea was hardly distinguishable from neighboring lakes. When the sea flooded the land, vegetation, peat, and coal rotted, leaving the water's edge smelling of hydrogen sulfide. Vast areas of tropical seas were largely devoid of life, for the water chemistry was unlike anything seen today, lethally acidified and lacking in oxygen. The surface layers of the deeper ocean had a chemical composition unknown in any ocean today, and, as in the waters of the shallow coastlines, there was a nearly total absence of life. The deepest oceans were entirely anoxic.

The remains of limestone reefs abounded everywhere, but these were not biological reefs, for they had neither corals nor fish nor any of the great diversity of life that had once populated them. Corals struggled on, perhaps in lagoons isolated from low salinity and protected from strong wave action where there was enough limestone rock to counter ocean acidity. Nevertheless, coral reefs as we know them today—marine bastions of biodiversity—virtually ceased to exist. So it remained throughout most of the world, with patchy exceptions, for around 10 million years.

Between then and now, most Cretaceous reef limestone that was in the ocean has been subducted (slid under the continents) as the seafloor has spread or dissolved in the ocean depths. The outcrops that remained on land when the oceans retreated were eroded or chemically altered, the latter process destroying the telltale fossils they had once contained.

I have taken plenty of license with this reconstruction of the end of the Cretaceous, adding patches to our scientific knowledge in several places. I have had no choice, for little of that world remains today.

Unique Events or Common Threads?

It is impossible to fully appreciate the vast amount of time separating the five mass extinction events I have just described. Each event took place in a world substantially different from the one preceding it. Nevertheless, there are certain fundamental physical properties of our planet that all of its inhabitants have evolved to exploit or to survive. A change in a property that has been constant for millions of years could cause great loss of life among the organisms that have come to rely on that constancy. One may well ask if there were any commonalities among the mass extinction events that might suggest a common cause. Or was each unique?

Contrary to the implication of the word "event," all of the mass extinctions appear to have taken place over periods of at least a million years—a series of disasters, rather than a single catastrophe. Thus each extinction spans intervals of major physical changes to the Earth, not just climate changes in the sense of temperature, atmospheric conditions, acid rains, and seawater chemistry, but geographic changes produced by sea-level changes and plate tectonics. In each case there was a major loss of life ranging from species to (occasionally) phyla, leading to a significant shift from one group of biota to a less diverse group. At the time of the first mass extinction event, the end Ordovician (434 mya), most terrestrial plant life and all large land animals had yet to evolve, so it is hardly surprising that the shallow marine world appeared to suffer most. Yet once these groups *had* evolved, the shallow marine environment appears to have remained the most targeted by subsequent mass extinctions. Studies of CO_2 suggest that, with the possible exception of the Late Devonian, CO_2 levels were high or rising significantly prior to each extinction. Various authors have also linked bolides or traps to all mass extinctions.

Interestingly—especially to us on our quest to follow their fate—corals and reefs have an important story to tell. Almost all reef-dwelling animals were decimated in all cases. The existence of reef gaps is a prominent feature of the aftermath of all five extinction events—immense gaps in time varying from 4 million years for the end Ordovician mass extinction (434 mya) to at least 10 million years for the end Permian (251 mya).

Reef Gaps:
Where Biological Recovery Takes Millions of Years

The loss of diversity from extinction events, especially mass extinction events, tells us much about the vulnerability of reefs to environmental change. There is, however, an equally important lesson to be learned from reefs of the past, stemming from reef gaps. Gaps in the fossil record of anything are commonplace and require little explanation beyond the vagaries of chance. However, reef gaps are dependent not on the presence or absence of fossils per se, but rather on the presence or absence of limestone slabs over immense intervals of time. If the rate of growth of modern reefs—0.6 meter per century—is taken as a benchmark (see Chapter 3), the shortest reef gap, 4 million years, is enough time to grow a slab of reef limestone 24 kilometers thick. This, of course, is something that could never happen,

but it demonstrates that the total absence of reef limestone is not the equivalent of the total absence of a fossil sequence. Can the existence of reef gaps
be attributed to chance? It is true that there are other long intervals of time
in the geological record from which no reef limestone remains today—
intervals when reefs simply did not grow, or did grow but were destroyed by
erosion or subduction at continental plate boundaries. However, given that
vast tracts of reef limestone remain today from *before* all mass extinction
events except the first, their absence *after* all mass extinctions seems rather
more than coincidence.

The question is, what actually mattered at these times—the terrestrial climate, the sea levels, the ocean chemistry? This question cannot be addressed
by studying all the environmental variables over all the intervals of a mass
extinction. That would simply result in a series of lists of causes. But the
question can be addressed by examining how each variable *might* affect a
coral reef and, by a process of elimination, narrowing the list to those
changes that were really important. In fact this is not the difficult process it
might at first seem, as we see in the next chapter.

— 6 —

Messages from Deep Time

Many causes of mass extinction events proposed from studies of paleontology and paleoclimatology can be discounted when examined in the light of our knowledge of living corals. Coral reef science argues that carbon dioxide and its chemical associates must carry a large part of the blame. Acidification of the oceans resulting from the long-term buildup of CO_2 and an eventual breakdown of ocean buffers emerges as the principal causal mechanism of reef gaps and scleractinian demise, as well as the collapse of other marine ecosystems.

All accounts of ancient reefs have a monotonous inevitability: reefs spread around the tropical world, they are destroyed, and then they spread again. This cycle recurs over and over. They are wiped out by what we call mass extinction events, but these are not events at all; they just seem so because the intervals over which they are spread are compressed, from our point of view, by the enormity of geological time.

The wax and wane of reefs can be seen continuously in the geological record, strongly punctuated at the mass extinctions but also notable at the lesser extinctions and more generally with changing environmental conditions. However, it is the mass extinctions that cause such catastrophic change that reef building ceases for millions of years. Many theories have been postulated to explain these "reef gaps," ranging from the eminently plausible to the somewhat far-fetched. Unfortunately, the vast time scales over which both extinctions and reef gaps occur make our knowledge of the environmental conditions of those times very sketchy, and consequently our understanding of their causes has been unreliable.

Looking Back from the Present

In this account I evaluate the various explanations given for mass extinctions and reef gaps in the light of today's knowledge of coral biology, something about which we can be much more certain. Extrapolations to past environments must, of course, be cautiously made, as the Scleractinia of today
have been in existence for only the past two mass extinctions (the end Triassic, 205 mya, and K/T, 65 mya). However, just as a number of physical parameters have remained constant throughout the life of our planet, some
physiological processes, while they may vary in detail over time, would in
general have been applicable to the Scleractinia throughout their existence.
Since our knowledge of the K/T mass extinction is far better than that of any
other, I focus on this period before considering to what extent today's biology can be extrapolated back in time.

Scleractinian corals are a particularly good group of organisms for this
purpose. They, or their Paleozoic ecological equivalents, have existed
throughout most of the time span of the complex life forms that we recognize today. Unlike most other animal groups, they offer us two different
records of the geological past: from the direct fossil record of individual
colonies and from the consolidated limestone platforms they form. The
latter are not always rich in fossils, for these usually become so altered by
diagenesis that all structure is obliterated. In terms of quantity, however, this
record of the past is as good as it gets, for indeed most marine fossils are
corals, and these leave a record in limestone comparable only to the record
tropical plants leave in coal. Both ancient and modern coral skeletons dis-
play growth layers that can be interrogated, much like the growth rings of
trees (illustrated in Figure 3.3), revealing many aspects of the environment
in which the corals grew.

The previous chapter showed that, despite the uncertainty of much of the
information surrounding mass extinction events, some statements about
reefs and the organisms that built them can be made with a reasonable degree of confidence. In summary, the four most important aspects are:
(1) Reefs were severely affected by all five mass extinction events. (2) Reef
gaps of 4–10 million years existed after all of these events. (3) A high proportion of reef-building species went extinct at every mass extinction event,
and at the end Permian all reef-building corals were exterminated. (4) The
K/T mass extinction affected deepwater azooxanthellate corals just as much
as reef corals. It is not known whether equivalent impacts occurred to

azooxanthellate species during earlier mass extinctions, largely because a different suite of corals was involved, and less is known about the environments in which they lived.

Mass Extinctions from a
Biological Perspective

What conditions in today's world could lead to a reef gap, major extinctions of reef-building species, and simultaneous extinctions of azooxanthellate species?

As previously described, reef development has three prerequisites: (1) corals (and/or other calcifying organisms) must exist in environments that are favorable for calcification, (2) the resulting calcium carbonate must be consolidated into reefs, and (3) the rate of erosion must be less than the rate of accretion. Reef gaps, then, might occur whenever calcification is decreased or entirely inhibited, or there is a breakdown in the mechanisms of consolidation, or there are factors that greatly increase the erosion or dissolution of calcium carbonate. In fact, there are many combinations of factors that might cause this kind of imbalance without necessarily causing extinction of coral species. In order to have such an imbalance as well as simultaneous extinction of both zooxanthellate and azooxanthellate coral species, we must be looking for global-scale changes in conditions that span not only broad spatial scales, but also wide depth ranges.

To address this issue, we take a look at the various explanations that have been offered for mass extinctions in general and the K/T event in particular, from the point of view of coral and reef biology. Each is initially examined in isolation to evaluate its possible contribution as the *primary* factor in extinction events. However, synergistic effects of multiple causes and stresses must not be underestimated. It is common for ecosystems and organisms to be able to withstand extremes of single environmental factors but to succumb to lesser extremes of multiple factors working in concert. Such synergisms are discussed later in this chapter.

DIRECT PHYSICAL DESTRUCTION FROM BOLIDES.   As I noted in Chapter 5, at one time or another bolides have been proposed as *the* explanation for most extinctions. Certainly huge bolides would have caused massive physical destruction of low-lying terrestrial ecosystems by producing tsunamis— fast-moving shock waves having little in common with the ocean waves with which we are all familiar.[1] There are, however, physical limits to the size of tsunamis, especially their height, which is dependent on local ocean depth. A bolide many kilometers across could possibly cause massive destruction of reefs along the exposed side of an area the size of a continent; however, it beggars belief that such an effect, from a single point source, could affect the whole Earth. Furthermore, tsunamis would have a relatively small impact on the lee side of large landmasses with mountain ranges. Nor is there any way that azooxanthellate species would be equally affected or that surviving reef corals would take millions of years to recommence reef building. Be that as it may, the Earth has several large and well-known craters (13 of which date to the early Mesozoic or later),[2] and many studies, motivated by the discovery of the K/T bolide, have sought to establish bolides as the primary cause of other extinction events. Yet credible links have not emerged.[3] In the case of K/T, however, there is little doubt that secondary effects of the bolide may have had significant influences on the extinction event.

"NUCLEAR WINTERS" INDUCED BY DUST CLOUDS. Bolides are certainly capable of creating dust clouds orders of magnitude greater than humans have ever witnessed—dense clouds that may have enveloped the Earth for weeks or months, creating devastating darkness and cold. Traps—massive lava floods, the largest volcanic products on Earth—typically form plates of basalt thousands of meters thick, with characteristically terraced or stairlike margins like a layered cake. Such traps, like the Deccan Traps of India, as well as the Siberian traps that coincided with the end Permian mass extinction, might have the capacity to envelop the Earth in some sort of dust cloud for hundreds of thousands of years, although not one remotely comparable in opacity to that caused by a bolide. Supervolcanoes can also produce global dust clouds, but, like those from bolides, they are short-lived. Nevertheless, bolides, traps, and perhaps supervolcanoes must all be considered as possible causes of adversely low light levels.

The dust cloud created by a large bolide would also cause atmospheric temperatures to plunge, but only for as long as the cloud persisted. The thermal inertia of the oceans would protect marine environments from significant temperature change. Longer-term temperature fluctuations from other causes are considered below.

LIGHT. Looking at what is known of today's corals, how would the Scleractinia have coped with low-light conditions from dust clouds or other causes? As a result of their dependence on zooxanthellae, zooxanthellate corals go semisenescent in the absence or near absence of light, with greatly reduced growth and calcification. Most eventually die, despite the fact that all can actively feed on plankton or detritus as alternative food sources. Survival estimates for corals in very low light vary from a few weeks to six months or more, depending on the species. It is significant, however, that—except for two or three species—no extant zooxanthellate corals are found naturally in conditions of very low light (such as in caves, under overhangs, or at depths where human vision is significantly diminished). The implication is that, if today's reef-building species were suddenly subjected to conditions of very low light for periods of years rather than weeks or months, we would lose 99 percent of them. In fact the K/T extinction of corals was nowhere near as severe as this; at least some representatives of most major families survived. This strongly suggests that there was no single interval of prolonged darkness.

Between upper and lower thresholds, calcification of today's reef-building corals is correlated with light levels. Thus, low light (as opposed to the absence of light) can significantly reduce both calcification and photosynthesis, a process that decreases competitiveness and engages a raft of negative ecological consequences. At the K/T extinction, low light could have adversely affected the balance between the erosion and accretion of reefs for as long as it persisted, and this would have continued to inhibit reef growth if reef builders had been lost. However, the proportion of reef-building corals that went extinct is not on its own sufficient to explain the demise of reefs for such an extended period. Many taxa that survived (including members of the Poritidae and Faviidae) are among the best reef builders. Once light levels and other environmental conditions became more favorable, these corals would have recommenced reef building.

Of particular importance to the evaluation of low light as the primary cause of extinctions at K/T is the fact that it was not only reef-building corals that were lost; azooxanthellate taxa were also decimated, and these would not have been affected by a reduction of light, as most live in total darkness. It is significant, too, that the K/T mass extinction caused a much higher rate of extinction in corals than in many other photosynthetic organisms, notably terrestrial vascular plants, which would have been more vulnerable to prolonged darkness.

From a biological point of view, I conclude that very low light, even if maintained for months, is exceedingly unlikely to have been the principal cause of the K/T mass extinction event.

SEA-LEVEL CHANGES.   The major sea-level changes throughout Earth's history have been due to plate tectonics—movements of the Earth's crust that change the shape of the ocean basins. These are very different from the sea-level changes that occurred during the Ice Ages, primarily in being much slower and of immensely longer duration.

The effect of increasing and decreasing sea levels on reef growth depends on the rate at which the changes occur. Slowly decreasing sea levels may allow biological forces to completely erode reef limestone, leaving no evidence of past reefs. Faster decreases expose the limestone to the slower-acting effects of atmospheric weathering. Similarly, slowly increasing levels can allow reef growth to keep up with sea-level changes and build thick reef ramparts, whereas faster increases eventually drown a reef, as the water over it becomes too deep for corals to survive in that location. However, corals can disperse long distances in a single generation, and these generation times are less than a decade. As sea levels rise or fall, corals simply relocate. Sea level would have to change (up or down) by several meters within a decade to have any significant effect on extinction rates, and such a rate of change is more than an order of magnitude greater than the fastest sea-level change in known geological history (approximately 1.5 meters per century during the Ice Ages; see Chapter 9).

There is also a specific message from the last glacial cycle, when the sea dropped 130 meters (see Chapter 10). Importantly, this fall was more than the depth range of all zooxanthellate corals except for deepwater species, which means that almost all corals were forced to relocate. During the Ice Ages, such falls were repeated many times, yet only about 10 percent of all corals went extinct over this entire interval. Ten percent over approximately 1.6 million years is no more than a background extinction rate. Thus sea-level changes of any kind, let alone those resulting from tectonic movements—which are immensely slow—can be ruled out as a primary cause of coral species extinctions.

LOSS OF AREA DURING SEA-LEVEL REGRESSION.   Loss of reef area during sea-level changes of the past has been suggested as a significant cause of coral extinctions, but a look at modern corals offers a number of arguments against such a case. There were major losses of reef area during the last glacial cycle, including most of the area of the GBR and the Philippine/Indonesian island archipelago, the two most extensive reef areas on Earth. These great changes left no significant mark on today's coral diversity. At the opposite extreme, restricted areas, such as some bays of the Palm or Whitsunday Island archipelagos in the central GBR, have most of the species complement of the entire province. The great dispersal capabilities of corals mean that recolonization can take place relatively swiftly from just a few surviving niches. Area loss is thus unlikely to have been a primary cause of any major extinction. Furthermore, azooxanthellate species would have been unaffected by a loss of reef area.

LOSS OF BIODIVERSITY AS A CAUSE OF REEF GAPS.   I noted in Chapter 3 that reef building does not depend on high species diversity. Many of the corals that survived K/T belonged to genera (notably *Porites*, illustrated in Plate 17, and faviids) well able to build reefs in the absence of any other coral species. Loss of biodiversity as a primary cause of reef gaps can therefore be discounted.

It has also been suggested that reefs do not reestablish until peak evolution rates of new species are reached.[4] With regard to corals, this is highly improbable and was certainly not the case after K/T, as coral diversity remained low long after extensive reef building had been reestablished.

LOW TEMPERATURES.   Corals today can exist within a temperature range of approximately 2–36°C, the lower limit being tolerated by azooxanthellate corals and the upper limit by zooxanthellate corals in particular locations (see Chapter 3). Both low and high temperatures have been postulated as potential causes of mass extinctions.

Both calcification and photosynthesis by today's reef-building corals are positively correlated with temperature up to threshold limits, above which temperature, combined with light, becomes lethal. These threshold limits are variable, affected by acclimatization and genetic adaptation by individual species. Along continental coastlines today, there is a progression from well-developed reefs at low latitudes to marginal reef growth at higher latitudes, to nonreef coral communities and isolated colonies at still higher latitudes. These changes are accompanied by attenuation in species diversity. Although light also decreases along latitudinal gradients (owing to refraction and the sun's elevation), it can be dismissed as the major factor in changes due to latitude for several reasons: (1) During the Miocene (around 20 mya), well-developed reefs occurred on the north coast of New Zealand, which had a latitude at that time of approximately 45° S, a higher latitude than any reef existing today. (2) Diverse coral communities (but not reefs) occurred 5,000–6,000 years ago near Tokyo, Japan, a response to higher ocean temperatures, not light. (3) Some corals (including *Acropora japonica*) are found in much lower-light conditions at a depth of 35 meters elsewhere in mainland Japan. These facts, together with a wide range of experimental evidence, make it clear that light is not the principal limitation to coral or reef growth at high latitudes. Likewise, ocean chemistry has not been the factor limiting latitudinal attenuation of reefs (at least not yet), as there has been no evidence of carbonate deficiency in the skeletal structure of high-latitude corals. The alternative explanation, as discussed in Chapter 3, is that the overriding environmental factor is low temperature—currently around 14°C for corals and 18°C for reefs.

Conceptually, therefore, low temperatures could explain reef gaps and zooxanthellate coral extinctions, but the data available for global temperatures give no credence to this. During the K/T extinction, ocean temperatures were at or above, rather than below, present levels. Furthermore, the suite of reef-building genera that survived indicates no selection for cold tolerance. Nor does low temperature explain why azooxanthellate species were lost. In fact, even during a full glacial cycle, the world's oceans cooled only around 6°C, and much less than this at the equator (see Chapter 9). Although temperature reductions of this extent would certainly be enough to contract the latitudinal range of species today, such a decrease could not have initiated extinctions in equatorial regions on the scale of K/T or any other mass extinction event. Further evidence that cold had little global effect on corals comes from the fact that neither the glaciations of the Ice Ages (starting 2.6 mya; see Chapter 9) nor those of the Carboniferous (354–298 mya) are associated with mass extinction events. This strongly supports the view that polar glaciations per se are exceedingly unlikely to have been a cause of mass extinctions of tropical corals. Only the first mass extinction event, the end Ordovician (434 mya), is associated with glacial cycles.

HIGH TEMPERATURES.   We saw in Chapter 3 that increasing temperature promotes calcification up to an optimal level of around 27°C for a majority of corals and reaches a lethal limit of around 31°C for most GBR corals. These numbers may have been slightly different in the past, just as they vary geographically today (see Chapters 3 and 4); however, the mechanism that allows symbiosis to enhance calcification would always have had an optimal temperature as well as an upper limit. The latter is unlikely to have been significantly different from today's limit, owing to the thermal cap of large oceans (around 31°C; see Chapter 4).

It is also clear (see Chapter 4) that elevated temperatures can cause mass bleaching of corals and, as discussed further in Chapter 14, can create widespread devastation when reef ecosystems become so degraded that they are taken over by macroalgae. However, even in a warmer world there would have been safe havens. Deep ocean temperatures would have remained well below surface temperatures in past geological times just as they do today, and there would inevitably have been regions of upwelling. The temperature maximum of the Pacific of the past, and the Panthalassa before then, would have been subject to a similar thermal cap. This is an equatorial maximum, and a mass extinction would have required the stressful temperatures to extend to high latitudes, which would not have been possible, even under the most extreme conditions. Furthermore, under such a temperature regime we would expect the surviving coral taxa to be biased toward those that thrive in relatively deep water, especially those exposed to deep oceanic water. In fact, the groups that survived K/T are rarely, if ever, found in such regions. They are shallow-water species (typically occurring down to 20 meters), most commonly occurring in sheltered habitats.

Through bleaching and general stress effects, elevated temperatures could have significant impacts on reef development, including regional extinction of reef-building species. Even so, high temperatures cannot explain the extent or global nature of mass extinction events, nor the suite of K/T survivors. Neither can temperature explain the loss of azooxanthellate species, which would not have been exposed to significant temperature change.

SALINITY.   Corals, and by extension reefs, are adversely affected by low salinity (see Chapter 4), and this may well have been a major cause of regional extinctions at various times, especially in partly landlocked regions such as the epicontinental seas of the Super-Tethys and North Africa during the Cretaceous (100 mya). However, it is inconceivable that any continental landmass could hold enough fresh water to cause a global mass extinction. High-salinity crises, such as occurred when the Mediterranean and Red seas became landlocked during a protracted interval of low sea levels, could cause total regional extinctions, but the consequences could not have been global.

DISEASE AND TOXINS.   There is strong evidence today that stresses such as mass bleaching, low salinity influxes, and a wide range of other ecological imbalances can greatly increase the incidence of diseases in corals. Combinations of stresses from high temperature, high light levels, and disease might lead to major regional losses of corals for as long as those stresses persist. However, it is hard to imagine how azooxanthellate corals could be similarly affected, nor, conversely, how the particular suite of zooxanthellate corals that survived K/T managed to do so. The same arguments apply to toxins. These would have to be very widespread and affect deepwater and nearshore corals equally. The Earth has no toxins in such quantities, nor any that can exist both on land and in the oceans.

I know of no credible case that supports the argument that mass extinctions had a biological cause. A rampant virus, far beyond anything known to science, might conceivably have caused the loss of life at the end Permian mass extinction, as that was so extreme that all life on Earth came close to extermination. However, the same cannot be said for any other mass extinction event, for none had anywhere near the same extent, or the same uniformity, across all forms of life, both marine and terrestrial.

EXTRATERRESTRIAL EVENTS.   Extraterrestrial events apart from bolides have commonly been suggested as causal factors in extinctions. Episodes of ultraviolet or cosmic radiation from solar flares, from supernovas, or from reversals in the Earth's magnetic field (which may be capable of stripping away the ozone layer, allowing high levels of ultraviolet radiation to reach terrestrial life) can be ruled out as causes of mass extinctions because the deep ocean would have shielded bottom-dwelling communities, and these were not spared. There is also evidence that background extinctions are increased on a 26-million-year supercycle.[5] Although interesting, plausible control mechanisms are lacking and there are no correlations specifically with mass extinctions.

The Carbon Cycle: An Introduction

If the above causes of mass extinctions and reef gaps are discounted as primary factors, as I believe they can be, we are left with an array of further possibilities that have one aspect in common: they are either part of the carbon cycle or closely linked to it. The critical point is that the carbon cycle is the only player in the game big enough to inflict mass destruction on all of the Earth's terrestrial and marine life simultaneously.

The carbon cycle is by far the most important of all the great matter cycles on Earth. Or rather carbon *cycles*, for there are many of these, each moving semi-independently through everything from rocks to humans. All are interlinked in complex and varied ways.

In principle, there are four reservoirs of carbon: the atmosphere, the biosphere (which includes soils), the oceans, and the geosphere (which includes fossil fuels). The most important exchange between compartments as far as reefs are concerned is the uptake of CO_2 from the atmosphere by the oceans—the pathway by which excess atmospheric CO_2 gets into the ocean.

Carbon naturally moves from rock reservoirs deep inside the Earth's mantle to the surface as CO_2 gas expelled by volcanoes. This occurs mostly in subduction zones (where CO_2 is typically released into the atmosphere) and at diverging plate margins (where CO_2 is released into the oceans). There are other major geological sources of CO_2, including volcanic hotspots, which typically occur within the interior of rigid plates. These are all outcomes of plate tectonics—of continental drift.

Over very long time scales—millions of years—atmospheric CO_2 levels are primarily controlled by a balance between the rate of volcanic release from the Earth's interior and the rate of extraction through photosynthesis and the chemical weathering of rocks at the Earth's surface, according to the equation $CaSiO_3 + CO_2 \rightarrow CaCO_3 + SiO_2$.

Over time scales relevant to ocean chemistry, photosynthesis and calcification by phytoplankton rapidly convert CO_2 into organic carbon and skeletons of both calcium carbonate and silica. Over geological time scales these skeletons accumulate as marine sediments, eventually forming sedimentary rocks. Over even longer intervals of time, most of these rocks are eventually returned to the Earth's mantle at subduction zones (see Chapter 8). The former process (the formation of marine carbonates and silicates) is clearly far more rapid than the latter (the formation and burying of rocks), which is as slow as seafloor spreading itself. The cycle that converts silicate rocks to plankton skeletons, both carbonate and silicate, is summarized in the equation above—it is the same chemical path that absorbs CO_2 through the weathering of rock. If these marine sediments are then returned to the Earth's interior by subduction, they re-form into silicate rocks and CO_2 under heat and pressure, the reverse of this equation. Of course, the carbon that moves back and forth through all living things is also a major part of the carbon cycle.

It is important to keep in mind that carbon moves between reservoirs at very different rates. Over the time scales of orbital cycles (23,000–100,000 years), geological processes are minor, for they are much too slow to explain,

for example, the close relationship between atmospheric CO_2 and the glacial cycles of the Ice Ages (see Chapters 9 and 10). Ultimately there are only
two places where atmospheric CO_2 can be stored effectively over thousand-
year time scales: in the biosphere and in the oceans, the Earth's two great
"short-term" carbon reservoirs.

Surface water in open-ocean ecosystems dominates the latter process. The
sinking or mixing of surface water that has equilibrated its CO_2 with the atmosphere is one aspect: 15–20 percent of all organic carbon from photosynthesis is transported to the deep ocean by sinking plankton—the
biological pump—to accumulate as sediment or to be converted into CO_2
or methane by organisms. Over decades to millennia, carbon from this
source is returned to the surface through upwelling, the net effect being to
move CO_2 from the atmosphere to the deep ocean and return it to the surface as both CO_2 and bicarbonate ions.

The Carbon Cycle and Mass Extinctions

The chemical cycles discussed in this section, all directly or indirectly linked
to the carbon cycle, could be implicated, entirely or in part, in a mass extinction event. Several may be secondary outcomes of bolide impacts, traps,
and supervolcanoes. However, the slower processes mentioned above—the
vast quantities of gases released from volcanic chains as a result of seafloor
spreading and other tectonic movements—might indeed be potential
causes of relatively abrupt mass extinction events through their cumulative
effect or through synergies.

The discussion of bleaching in Chapter 4 introduced the idea that very
small changes in the concentration of gases in the atmosphere can lead to
major changes in global environments, potentially affecting both marine
and terrestrial life. These gases include major components of our atmosphere, notably oxygen and water vapor, as well as those that are present only
in trace amounts. The latter include a few that are critically important as
climate regulators, as they have an influence far out of proportion to their
concentrations. These are the gases that control the atmosphere's greenhouse warming, CO_2 and methane being the most important. Such gases
will attract most of our attention here because they not only control greenhouse warming but also exert a major influence on ocean pH (a measure of
the concentration of hydrogen ions). First I consider the more peripheral
links to the carbon cycle.

Plate 1 Ribbon reefs of the GBR today. Their appearance is an artifact of an unusually prolonged constant sea level (see Chapter 2). (Photograph by the author.)

Plate 2 The coral reef of Lord Howe Island, the southernmost coral reef in the world. Coral growth here is extensive and shows no signs of thermal stress, although the temperature in the lagoon commonly goes down to 18°C (see Chapter 2). (Photograph by the author.)

Plate 3 Middleton Reef, situated just north of Lord Howe Island, the southernmost platform reef in the world. This reef and neighboring Elizabeth Reef are located 1,300 kilometers southeast of the southern end of the GBR (see Chapter 2). (Photograph by David Doubilet.)

Plate 4 One of the blue holes of the Pompey Complex of the southern GBR. These are all that are left of collapsed caverns that would once have been part of an extensive cave system (see Chapter 12). (Photograph by the author.)

Plate 5   The structure of a coral. Note that the living polyp is attached to the outside of its skeleton and that the polyps grow together to form colonies (see Chapter 3). (Painting by Geoff Kelly.)

Plate 6   A polyp of *Cynarina lacrymalis* living in an aquarium without a skeleton. Such occurrences are rare, but they demonstrate the great versatility of corals (see Chapter 3). (Photograph by Phil Alderslade.)

Plate 7   A polyp of *Cynarina lacrymalis* as it normally occurs with a skeleton. (The white structure is visible through the polyp tissue.) (Photograph by Len Zell.)

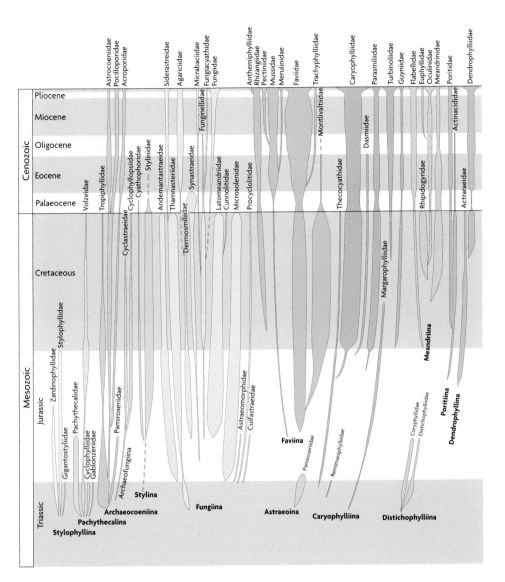

Plate 8 A Family Tree of Scleractinia. The width of the branches indicates overall abundance for whole eras, not variations within them, so the branches do not indicate extinction events unless entire families went extinct. Many of these branches would be joined at their base if the fossil record had adequate information, but they remain separate where this information is missing. (From the author's *Corals of the World.*)

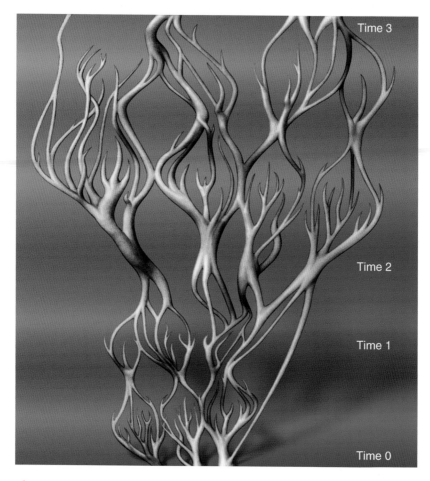

Plate 9 A hypothetical view of reticulate evolution in an evolutionary tree of species. At the bottom of the diagram, the group consists of three species, all of which are widely dispersed by strong currents. At time (1) the currents weaken and the tree is broken up into many small semidistinct species. At times (2) and (3) the genetic content of the original three species is repeatedly repackaged by changing currents. The fossil record of these "species" would suggest a series of extinctions, as well as intervals of rapid evolutionary change, where in fact there was mostly genetic continuity (see Chapter 3). (From the author's *Corals in Space and Time*.)

Plate 10   Egg and sperm masses floating over reefs of the GBR. This is mostly an annual event and provides an opportunity for genetic mixing among related species (see Chapter 3). (Photograph by Bette Willis.)

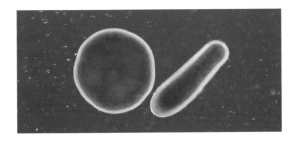

Plate 11   Coral larvae. Larvae typically change shape as they mature. These larvae can float on the ocean surface for weeks and make long journeys (see Chapter 3). (Photograph by Bette Willis.)

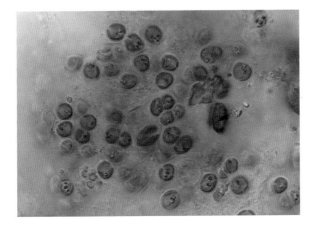

Plate 12   Zooxanthellae in the squashed tip of a tentacle (see Chapter 3). (Photograph by Ove Hoegh-Guldberg.)

Plate 13 *Duncanopsammia axifuga.* This and the *Tubastrea* species (Plate 14) are both part of the same family, which has both zooxanthellate and azooxanthellate members. Algal symbiosis has reevolved many times in unrelated families (see Chapter 3). (Photograph by Clay Bryce.)

Plate 14 *Tubastrea,* an azooxanthellate coral in the same family as *Duncanopsammia,* commonly found in caverns and on vertical faces (see Chapter 3). (Photograph by Patrick Colin.)

Plate 15   A modern *Acropora* colony composed of about 800,000 individual polyps. This type of intricate architecture is the highest level of evolutionary innovation ever achieved by the Scleractinia (see Chapter 3). Engineering masterpieces such as these, unknown in any coral before the Cenozoic Era (see Chapter 7) or in any azooxanthellate coral, capture a maximum amount of sunlight per unit weight of skeleton. This coral can increase its diameter by a massive 30 centimeters a year—but at a price, for it is highly vulnerable to destruction by storm waves. (Photograph by Valerie Taylor.)

Plate 16   *Alveopora catalai* growing on unconsolidated rubble. This coral, although it grows in a highly diverse community, will make little contribution to reef building (see Chapters 2 and 3). (Photograph by the author.)

Plate 17 Corals of Clipperton Atoll, situated in the far eastern Pacific. This atoll is well formed and actively growing, yet it has only seven species of coral, of which only three contribute to reef building (see Chapter 3). Two of these are *Porites*, a genus that overwhelmingly dominated the reefs of the Miocene Tethys Ocean (see Chapter 7). (Photograph by the author.)

Plate 18 An *Acropora* housing about a hundred damselfish (*Dascyllus reticulatus*). If a predator approaches, the fish dart into the protective branches of the coral. Without the coral the fish would have no protection. Conversely, without the fish the coral would be overgrown by algae (see Chapter 3). (Photograph by Gerry Allen.)

Plate 19 Corals and algae battle it out at Lord Howe Island, the southernmost reef of eastern Australia. In most places on this reef there is a well-defined demarcation zone between coral-dominated and algae-dominated communities. Here the bubblelike branching alga *Caulerpa* and some filamentous algae are overgrowing a plate *Acropora* (see Chapter 3). (Photograph by Geoff Kelly.)

Plate 20 The mushroom coral *Heliofungia actiniformis* commonly carpets the seafloor of inshore embayments exposed to extreme sedimentation (see Chapter 2). This coral occurs as solitary individuals that are not attached to the substrate, so it easily rises above sediment by inflating soft tissues with water. As in many inshore corals, the tentacles have no stinging cells and are not retracted during the day. Despite its preference for shallow, muddy water, which might have been a scarce commodity during intervals of low sea level, this species survived the Ice Ages unchanged. (Photograph by the author.)

Plate 21 Only a few species worldwide are found solely in intertidal habitats. All of these, including the *Acropora papillare* shown here, have short generation times and are readily able to relocate when the sea level changes (see Chapter 10). (Photograph by the author.)

Plate 22 The reef front of a ribbon reef today at a depth of 8 meters. This slope continues down to unknown depths (see Chapters 2 and 3). (Photograph by the author.)

Plate 23 Groove formation owing to wave action on rubble (see Chapter 3). The physical erosion of reefs in shallow water is caused by rubble being moved back and forth by wave turbulence. This process stops coral or algal growth from protecting the reef limestone and results in grooves that gradually deepen. The grooves develop to depths of 15 meters on exposed reef fronts, where they are commonly called spur-and-groove formations. (Photograph by the author.)

Plate 24 A reef flat coral community protected from strong wave action but very exposed to temperature-induced bleaching. These communities will be among the first to be destroyed by mass bleaching and sea-level rise (see Chapter 14). (Photograph by the author.)

Plate 25 A coral garden in a protected inshore lagoon at a depth of 5 meters, photographed in 2005 (see Chapter 3). This community was destroyed by Cyclone Ingrid (see Plate 31), but it has the capacity to recover rapidly, provided it is not subject to mass bleaching over the next few years. (Photograph by Katharina Fabricius.)

Plate 26 The dwarf minke whale (*Balaenoptera acutorostrata*) in the northern GBR. The GBR is a place of refuge for all such megafauna and plays a vital role in their conservation (see Chapters 4 and 16). (Photograph by Alastair Birtles.)

Plate 27 One catch from a spear-fishing competition in 1960, on the beach in front of the Heron Island Research Station (see Chapter 4). The only places left in the world where such a catch would now be possible have enforced protection laws. Even so, such a catch would probably not be possible at Heron Island today. (Photograph by Valerie Taylor.)

Plate 28 By-catch on the sorting tray of a fishing trawler (see Chapter 4). Only the prawns will be removed from this catch. The rest will be dumped. Recent modifications to trawling equipment have greatly reduced this level of carnage, yet the damage caused to soft-bottom communities remains significant. (Photograph by Dan Moore, Great Barrier Reef Marine Park Authority.)

Plate 29 The coral-eating crown-of-thorns starfish (*Acanthaster planci*). This individual is 35 centimeters in diameter and can produce hundreds of thousands of gametes in a single spawning, enough to cause a major outbreak should sufficient plankton be available to support mass survival (see Chapter 4). (Photograph by John Keesing.)

Plate 30   Raine Island, situated on the outer reef line of the far northern GBR, will probably not survive predicted sea-level increases, as its small reef will be unable to supply the coral rubble needed to maintain the island (see Chapter 13). This historic photograph, taken in 1973, shows female green turtles starting to climb the beach at dusk to lay their eggs. By the time it was dark, this beach was covered by thousands of turtles—a world record. The hatchlings from that period will be among the last turtles to use this island for egg laying over their full life span. (Photograph by Len Zell.)

Plate 31   Cyclone Ingrid, which struck Tijou Reef in February 2005. The number and severity of cyclones is set to increase (see Chapter 13). The most powerful cyclone to strike the GBR in living memory, Cyclone Larry, hit in March 2006; it was one of three cyclones of the highest category recorded that year. (Satellite image courtesy of the Bureau of Meteorology; originally obtained from the geostationary meteorological satellite MTSAT-1R of the Japan Meteorological Agency.)

Plate 32 Stromatoporoid sponges at the Big Bend Reefs today. Reefs built by these giant calcifying sponges as well as by corals do not resemble any modern coral reef. It is not known if Paleozoic reefs depended on some form of algal symbiosis, but it is highly likely that they did (see Chapter 5). Changes in water chemistry leading to ocean acidification may well have caused extinction of these sponges, as they were probably mostly aragonitic. (Photograph by Clive Wilkinson.)

Plate 33 Silurian reefs were abundant and diverse (see Chapter 5). They also reached impressive sizes, as this reef in Greenland shows. (Photograph by Paul Copper.)

Plate 34   The remains of a massive Devonian reef in the Canning Basin, northwestern Australia. All but microbial life went extinct on this reef during the Late Devonian mass extinction event (see Chapter 5). (Photograph by the author.)

Plate 35 Late Triassic mountains of Austria. The remains of this ancient reef are still up to 1,500 meters thick, formed because they grew on a sinking seafloor. The reefs at the time of formation would have been much thicker than this. Most of the organisms that built these reefs went extinct during the end Triassic mass extinction event (see Chapter 5). (Photograph by Harald Krenn.)

Plate 36 Early scleractinian coral communities did not look like any modern community. This reconstruction shows the most common families, with the branching colony on the right (*Retiophyllia*) overwhelmingly dominant (see Chapter 5). Not all of these corals actually occurred together at the same time and place. (Painting by Geoff Kelly.)

Plate 37 What the outer face of ribbon reefs like Tijou might have looked like 15,000 years ago, when the sea level was 100 meters lower than at present. Like this uplifted reef (in Thailand), the face would have been undercut by waves, making it steeper than it is today. Today's reefs have an additional (Holocene) layer above this Pleistocene substrate, and a different shape as a result. Today this reef would look like those illustrated in Plate 1, but when humans first occupied Australia, Tijou Reef looked like this (see Chapters 10 and 12). (Photograph by Emre Turak.)

Plate 38 What the outermost reefs of today's central region of the GBR might have looked like 10,000 years ago—looking west from the Coral Sea, when the sea level was 50 meters lower than at present (see Chapter 10). The wave-cut notches at sea level (visible in these Indonesian islands) result from the unusually prolonged constant sea level we are experiencing now; they would not have developed on an Ice Age reef. Today's reef would have an additional (Holocene) layer above the Pleistocene substrate, as represented by these islands, which would have given any reef growing today a surface shape that may not closely reflect the shape of the top of these islands. (Photograph by Roger Steene.)

Plate 39 Sea urchins eroding grooves into a hard intertidal reef surface in the Ryukyu Islands. (Photograph by Moritaka Nishihira.)

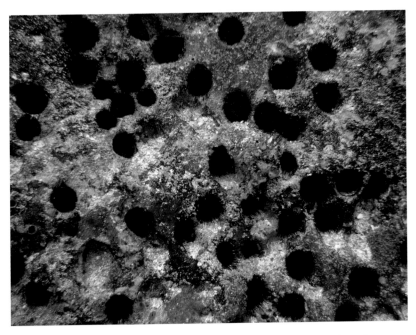

Plate 40 Urchins eating away at a reef face. This form of erosion takes place to depths of about 5 meters. Over geological time, bioerosion can contribute greatly to the planing off of reefs *if* the sea level does not fall too quickly (see Chapter 11). (Photograph by Emre Turak.)

Plate 41 A microatoll of *Porites*. Microatolls are accurate recorders of sea level because their upward growth is stopped at low-tide level. As seen here the inner parts of these colonies are typically eroded by urchins (see Chapter 8). (Photograph by Moritaka Nishihira.)

Plate 42 The inside of one of Walker's Caves at Tijou Reef, looking toward a partly closed-off entrance (see Chapter 12). Caves like this sometimes have stalactites hanging from the ceiling or adorning the walls. (Photograph by Len Zell.)

Plate 43 A fish trap photographed in 1982 near Broome, northwest Australia, with fish splashing in the foreground (see Chapter 12). Several people have seen what appear to be traps like this well below present sea level in eastern Torres Strait, where they have probably remained, undisturbed by cyclones, since before the last glacial sea level rise. (Photograph by Moya Smith.)

Plate 44   Of all corals, Acroporidae bleach the most readily. Here the two main coral genera of coral reefs, *Acropora* and *Montipora*, are completely bleached and will soon be covered with algae (see Chapter 14). (Photograph by Katharina Fabricius.)

Plate 45   A bleached coral garden. The corals that have retained some color are likely to recover; those that have turned completely white are more likely to die. Blue colonies (center) may also be completely bleached (see Chapter 14). (Photograph by Ray Berkelmans.)

Plate 46 This *Goniopora* may recover, at least in part. The white bleached polyps are already smaller than the pale brown polyps, which still have some of their zooxanthellae (see Chapter 14). (Photograph by Katharina Fabricius.)

Plate 47 A bleached *Porites* colony several hundred years old. The death of old colonies such as this (especially of *Porites*, which is relatively resistant to bleaching) suggests that bleaching is a recent phenomenon (see Chapter 14). (Photograph by Katharina Fabricius.)

Plate 48   Luxuriant coral communities such as this one look permanent but may be only a decade old. If this coral community is destroyed, it could regrow in that time if coral larvae are in good supply, if environmental conditions are suitable, and if herbivores keep algae under control. Most corals in this community are *Acropora*, species that grow like weeds but are among the most affected by bleaching. At night, a myriad of life emerges from the coral, for a community such as this is home to the greatest diversity of life in the ocean, if not the whole world. Crown-of-thorns starfish, cyclones, and bleaching can reduce a community like this to one like that shown in the next plate in just a few months. (Photograph by the author.)

Plate 49   After corals are killed by crown-of-thorns starfish, cyclones, or bleaching, the result rapidly becomes a flat rubble substrate devoid of protection for herbivorous fish. At the present time, most areas of the GBR damaged in this way remain within the feeding range of fish, which can thus still inhibit the growth of macroalgae. This particular community will probably undergo rapid recovery, once again looking like the one in the previous plate within a decade. (Photograph by Katharina Fabricius.)

Plate 50   Reef faces such as this in an overfished reef of Papua New Guinea are semipermanent if exposed to repeated denudation from bleaching. The green alga, a rapid colonizer, is neptune's necklace (*Halimeda*). (Photograph by the author.)

Plate 51   If herbivorous fish cannot maintain control, the rubble substrate may become covered with algae within a few months. This alga (*Padina*) is an early colonizer, especially in nutrient-rich water. There are some areas of the Philippines today where algal communities like this have persisted unchanged for a decade or more. (Photograph by Scott Burgess.)

Plate 52 Tall perennial algae like *Sargassum* normally take over once the substrate becomes stable and if herbivores do not hold them in check. If greenhouse warming is not contained, most reefs of the GBR will look something like this from bleaching alone by the middle or end of the present century. (Photograph by Katharina Fabricius.)

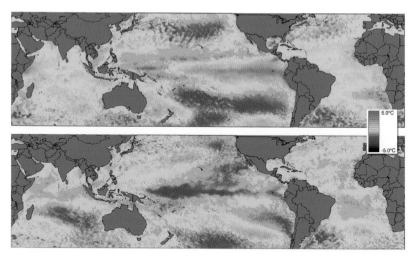

Plate 53 Sea surface temperature anomalies (deviation from long-term normal levels) as determined by satellite during an El Niño year (1998; above) and a La Niña year (1999; below). Note that, during the El Niño year, the greatest anomaly appears in the east and moves west, the reverse of the easterly movement of the warm pool (see the diagram in Chapter 4). Note that anomalously warm water also appears in the Indian and Atlantic oceans as the great oceans are teleconnected. (Computer image from NOAA.)

Plate 54 A reef of the future? Five years after all the corals on this reef in Papua New Guinea were killed by a mass bleaching event, there are no signs of recovery. The coral skeletons are covered by a layer of filamentous blue-green cyanobacteria (which appear reddish). The few living corals nearby are diseased. (Photograph by Emre Turak.)

Plate 55 A reef face dominated by slime. There are no living corals; however, the green alga *Halimeda* is starting to form some sort of three-dimensional habitat. (Photograph by Emre Turak.)

Plate 56   White band disease is common on reefs that have been severely degraded. (Photograph by Emre Turak.)

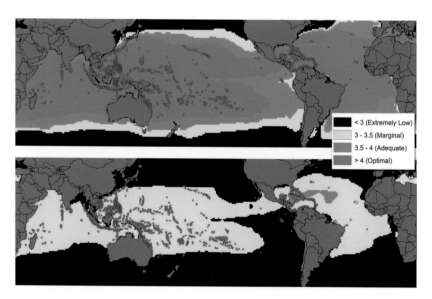

< 3 (Extremely Low)
3 - 3.5 (Marginal)
3.5 - 4 (Adequate)
> 4 (Optimal)

Plate 57   Calculated aragonite saturation state of surface waters (see Chapter 15), the top diagram at a preindustrial CO_2 level of 275 ppm and the bottom diagram at a widely predicted mid-twenty-first-century level of 560 ppm. At the latter concentration, all reefs in the world are affected by acidification. The red dots represent principal reef regions and coral communities. (Computer image by John Guinotte.)

ACID RAIN.   High levels of atmospheric CO_2 produce carbonic acid, and high levels of sulfur dioxide (SO_2) produce sulfuric acid. These substances, together with nitrous oxide (N_2O) from industry and the draining of tropical marshlands, are the main sources of acid rain today. Carbon dioxide and sulfur dioxide are released in massive amounts from some volcanoes, traps (in almost equal amounts), and other sources, both terrestrial and marine. These acid-forming gases are ultimately neutralized by ocean buffers. Although sulfur dioxide and nitrous oxide do not contain carbon, by the time their products reach the oceans they do, and thus they are inextricably linked to the carbon cycle. It is not quantitatively possible for acid rain to be a sole or even primary cause of a mass extinction event; however, acid rain may well have acted in synergy with other causes to promote environmental degradation.

HYDROGEN SULFIDE.   Hydrogen sulfide (H_2S, commonly known as rotten egg gas) is another gas released in large quantities into the oceans and atmosphere from volcanoes or from sulfur-rich geysers and the like. It also has biological origins (from anaerobic bacteria), which is why it regularly occurs in anoxic waters of all types, ranging from aquaria and atoll lagoons to deep ocean basins. As with sulfur dioxide, although it does not contain carbon, it is inextricably linked to the carbon cycle and could, in terms of quantity, have contributed to an environmental upheaval synergistically with other gases and with supranoxic events.

OXYGEN AND ANOXIA.   We all appreciate the role of oxygen in sustaining animal life, yet two points about it are less well known. The first is that oxygen comes from green plants as a by-product of photosynthesis, so it is held in check by the availability of CO_2, the source of photosynthetic carbon. The second is that, above an atmospheric concentration of around 30%, oxygen starts to become toxic, and at still higher concentrations it becomes lethal to almost all life. It follows that most terrestrial organisms can exist only because of the diluting effect of atmospheric nitrogen and a feedback mechanism that links oxygen concentration to the biosphere.

In a nitrogen-dominated atmosphere, oxygen and CO_2 normally have a linked relationship, an increase or decrease of the one creating a parallel effect on the other, all else being equal. However, all else may sometimes not be equal. It is possible that low oxygen (anoxia), resulting from changes in atmospheric CO_2, may have contributed to more than one of the mass extinction events. Low levels of atmospheric CO_2 could inhibit photosynthesis, leading to reduced production of oxygen and eventually to some level of ocean anoxia. This might have been a factor in the Late Devonian mass extinction event; the evidence is inconclusive.

At the other end of the scale, high levels of atmospheric CO_2 can promote ocean acidification (see later). If severe enough, this would impede oxygen production by calcifying phytoplankton, which could also result in some degree of ocean anoxia. It is possible that this contributed to the end Permian and perhaps K/T mass extinctions.

Whether either of these scenarios actually happened in the past is unknown, but deep-ocean anoxia probably continued independently of oxygen concentrations in surface waters, as there is no evidence that the latter went globally anoxic, a process that would have exterminated virtually all marine life including all reef corals.

Deep-ocean anoxia must have been very prolonged and widespread during the time of the formation of the world's great oil fields. Today's crude oil comes mainly from marine sources, having accumulated on the seabed in severely anoxic environments from the Early Jurassic to Middle Cretaceous (around 200–100 mya). During those times, high greenhouse levels of atmospheric CO_2 would have created high surface productivity, especially of phytoplankton, and these organisms would, through sinking, have fed the anoxic environments of the ocean depths. The process must have been very protracted to have allowed oil to be produced in the quantities that have survived to modern times.

During the Mesozoic (intervals of extinctions excepted), azooxanthellate corals may have been little affected by deep-ocean anoxia as the depth of hydrogen sulfide-rich anoxic water would have been far greater than the depth at which aragonite saturation (see later) would have been limiting. It was probably the formation of the Ocean Conveyor (which resulted in greater mixing of ocean layers, described in Chapter 7) that finally obliterated most deep-ocean anoxic environments, allowing a wide variety of biota, including azooxanthellate corals, to invade some of the Earth's deepest ocean basins.

METHANE.   Methane from geological sources, plant respiration, and animal life (especially livestock and termites today) exists in minute amounts in the atmosphere (currently 1.8 ppm). However, it occurs in much greater quantities in permafrost and tropical marshlands, and in vast quantities as icelike solids (variously called clathrates or hydrates) that are stable only under pressure and at low temperatures on continental shelves. The volume of these solids is unknown, although it is of the same order of magnitude as the Earth's total quantity of fossil fuels. Methane leaks into the ocean and atmosphere naturally, for example, as marsh gas. However, if it were released into the atmosphere in substantial quantities, perhaps induced by a bolide impact or a buoyancy change in the methane ice (for which there are many possible causes), there would be serious consequences. It would have a major greenhouse effect (methane has 22 times the potency of an equal volume of CO_2) and would also be converted to CO_2 by microbes and chemical oxidization, causing the same adverse effects characteristic of high levels of CO_2. As far as the oceans are concerned, methane ice need not reach the atmosphere to have negative effects. If it mixes with shallow water it will change to gas, oxidize to CO_2, and directly attack carbonate buffers.

The potential dangers of methane have only recently come to be appreciated, and they are significant. In the next chapter we encounter what was probably a methane-induced extinction event—the extinctions of the Late Paleocene Thermal Maximum. Methane may well have played a major role in other extinction events, but because it so readily converts to CO_2 it easily hides behind CO_2 in paleoclimatic records. After all, with these gases, we are dealing with nothing other than mixtures of carbon and water, natural elements found in almost everything.

CARBON DIOXIDE.   Both increasing and decreasing CO_2 levels have been proposed as major contributors to mass extinction events in the past. Over geological time scales, CO_2 has varied from levels much lower than the 375 ppm of today up to perhaps ten times today's level (depending on the reliability of studies of a small number of fossil soils and whether or not results from single points in time are representative of longer time intervals). High levels of atmospheric CO_2 enhance natural greenhouse warming and, as a direct result, increase ocean temperatures. However, changes in ocean chemistry and pH are a much more sinister consequence of increasing CO_2 as far as marine life is concerned. The extreme importance of this has only been recognized relatively recently and warrants discussion in further detail here.

OCEAN CHEMISTRY AND pH.   We saw in Chapter 3 that coral calcification can be described in a simplified way by the equation $Ca^{2+} + 2HCO_3^- \rightarrow CaCO_3\downarrow + H_2O + CO_2$. The balance between the two sides of this equation is significantly affected by pH; as pH decreases (becomes less alkaline), the equation is pushed to the left, making it more difficult to precipitate calcium carbonate ($CaCO_3$). The process of decreasing pH is known as acidification. (All seawater is alkaline, so it is important to note that when we talk about acidification we mean that the ocean becomes less alkaline, not that it actually becomes acidic.) Owing to corals extracting carbonates from the surrounding water (one way of measuring the rate of calcification), pH can vary slightly around reefs, and it is *the* primary control on the depth range of deepwater organisms that form calcium carbonate skeletons (including azooxanthellate corals). Change in pH is, nevertheless, an extremely slow process because of the buffering of any acidifying influences by ocean chemistry. But over geological time scales there are mechanisms by which acidification of the oceans can occur, and the most important of these is due to increasing levels of CO_2 in the atmosphere.

To be more specific, higher atmospheric CO_2 leads to greater amounts of the gas dissolving in the oceans, which directly reduces pH. This, in turn, alters the proportions of different forms of inorganic carbon (especially carbonate and bicarbonate) in the ocean, which affects $\Omega_{aragonite}$ (the "saturation state" of aragonite) and thus the capacity of calcifying organisms to form skeletons.[6] This can be explained as follows: when CO_2 dissolves in the ocean, it forms a weak acid, carbonic acid (H_2CO_3). This acid forms bicarbonate (HCO_3^-) and carbonate (CO_3^{2-}) ions. Thus inorganic carbon can exist in the ocean in four main forms: CO_2, H_2CO_3, HCO_3^-, and CO_3^{2-}. Increasing the concentration of CO_2 in the ocean increases acidity, which in turn alters the proportion of the other three forms of carbon. Calcifying organisms use carbonate and/or bicarbonate ions to build skeletons, and thus a decrease in their availability slows the calcification process. The proportions of each of these carbon components are sensitive to temperature and pressure, and thus to latitude and depth.

It is important to consider the interactions between acidification of surface waters, where zooxanthellate corals grow, and layers of deeper water, which is where most azooxanthellate corals grow. The former are potentially sensitive to the aragonite saturation of surface water; the latter are sensitive to having their depth range reduced by a decrease in the aragonite saturation depth. These surface and deep layers directly influence each other at high latitudes, where ocean temperatures are relatively uniform and mixing occurs relatively easily. They are, however, well separated in the warm tropics and interact primarily via the sinking of carbonate skeletons of surface-dwelling plankton—the biological pump (the main mechanism by which CO_2 is extracted from the atmosphere by the oceans).

Shallow oceans are currently supersaturated with carbonates, allowing zooxanthellate corals to calcify. However, as the level of saturation ($\Omega_{aragonite}$) decreases, this process requires increasing amounts of energy. The same applies to azooxanthellate corals, although here the process depends on the depth of $\Omega_{aragonite}$, which, in turn, varies with temperature as well as water chemistry. As changes in temperature and/or water chemistry cause the horizon to rise, the maximum depth at which azooxanthellate corals can grow must rise accordingly.

ACIDIFICATION.   What might happen to reefs, reef-building corals, and azooxanthellate corals if the efficiency of the calcification mechanism were to be diminished by changing pH? This is an important question.

The dependence of calcareous algae on high-magnesium calcite, the most soluble of all calcium carbonate skeletons, would make them early casualties of decreasing pH. Since these algae are critical to reef consolidation, their demise would seriously threaten reef growth, even before reduced calcification became a significant issue for corals. With further decrease in pH, aragonitic organisms (including corals) would become increasingly affected, further tipping the balance in favor of reef erosion. Since acidification from elevated atmospheric CO_2 affects oceans on a global scale, the effects on reefs would be worldwide, although influences from temperature and surface water mixing would create local variations both geographically and with depth.

As far as corals are concerned, the first impact would be on azooxanthellate taxa, which would become increasingly displaced from deeper oceans as the aragonite saturation depth decreased, starting at high latitudes. In equatorial regions, reef corals would be affected soon after, depending on the degree of mixing between the warm, shallow, CO_2-enriched surface layers and the buffers of cool, deeper ocean water.

Just what form the specific influence on skeletal structure would take is far from clear. Lowered calcification rates might result in slower-growing yet similarly dense skeletons, or they might result in more lightly calcified, weaker skeletons growing at normal rates. To some extent these differences would be taxon specific, dependent on the ability of individual species to actively control the calcification process. However, as inhibition of calcification progressed, all corals would become increasingly fragile and more readily broken by wave action. Not only would this affect the rate at which they grow, but it would also lower their resistance to predators and disease, as well as their capacity to make three-dimensional habitats for other reef organisms. Fast-growing branching species (especially *Acropora* and its ecological equivalents) would likely be most affected. These are the very species that currently make reefs so resilient to physical damage by recovering rapidly from tropical cyclones or damage from crown-of-thorns starfish and by providing protective habitats for grazing reef organisms to control competition from macroalgae.

The corals likely to resist the effects of acidification the longest would probably have some or all of the following characteristics: (1) They would have massive (or low-profile) growth forms that could remain relatively resistant to wave action even when skeletal density fell. (2) They would be long-lived; by inference these taxa would already be tolerant of environmental variations over their long life spans. (3) They would have relatively well-developed, active control of calcification and therefore be less affected by lowered carbonate availability. (4) They would be less likely to live in habitats where synergistic stresses could exacerbate the effects of acidification.

Is this what happened at K/T? The evidence points strongly toward acidification as the primary cause of coral extinctions and the reef gap, despite deficiencies in the fossil record. Unlike the alternative mechanisms already explored—those resulting from changes in light, temperature, or salinity; disease; toxins; direct destruction; cosmic and solar variability; and so on— acidification can explain why both azooxanthellate and zooxanthellate species were affected. It can also explain the loss of reefs both locally and globally, as well as account for the existence of long-lasting reef gaps. Although acidification may be difficult to initiate because of the buffering action of seawater, once achieved, it will persist as long as atmospheric CO_2 remains high (which in past geological time may have been the case for millions of years). Furthermore, the oceans would remain acidified long after CO_2 levels had declined, as vast time periods are required for the ocean's normal alkalinity to be restored through natural weathering and dissolution processes. Under such scenarios, together with their evolutionary consequences, reef gaps of millions of years would be a plausible outcome.

Ocean chemistry leaves no doubt that increasing atmospheric CO_2 levels, particularly if accumulated rapidly, can overwhelm ocean buffers and lead to acidification on a scale that would initiate global reef degradation.

Although there is uncertainty about atmospheric CO_2 levels in all pre-K/T mass extinctions (most extreme records coming from a single source—fossil soils), in the case of K/T we can be much more confident that background atmospheric CO_2 levels were increasing and reached a high around the start of the extinctions. A gradual buildup of atmospheric CO_2 would take longer to overcome ocean buffers than abrupt increases, and until this point is reached photosynthesis and calcification might well actually increase. The crunch could come when levels become so high that even gradual increases fail to be accommodated any more, or when an abrupt CO_2 spike occurs on top of an already CO_2-rich atmosphere, as probably happened in the case of K/T.

If we examine what we know of K/T, the hypothesis that acidification may have arisen from increasing atmospheric CO_2—primarily from tectonic sources like the widening of the North Atlantic, and secondarily from the additive effects of the infamous bolide and the Deccan Traps—is certainly plausible. This is a more persuasive hypothesis than any of the others discussed earlier. Acidification also provides a *mechanism* to explain both coral extinctions *and* reef gaps.

The fossil record of zooxanthellate corals indicates that the Faviidae were the least affected by the K/T extinction event: 6 out of 16 genera survived. In other families, *Astreopora, Porites* (referred to in the paleontological literature under a variety of names), *Siderastrea, Cycloseris* (perhaps), *Dichocoenia,* and *Hydnophora* survived. All of these corals formed low-profile colonies; the fossil record of survivors of K/T is devoid of branching forms. Today's members of these genera are relatively long-lived: *Porites* is one of the toughest and longest-lived of all Scleractinia, surviving wide-ranging environmental perturbations over its lifetime of many centuries. None is exclusively found either in very shallow water (where they would be likely to suffer synergistic stresses from high temperature, high light, mass bleaching, and low salinity) or in deeper water (where low light and possibly lower temperature could act synergistically with acidification to reduce calcification to sublethal or lethal levels). Indeed, *Porites* has been shown to be tolerant of relatively variable pH from 7.9–8.2 without a significant change in growth rate,[7] probably reflecting a high degree of active control of calcification.

Of course corals were not the only victims of the K/T extinction. Increasing acidification of the ocean would have profoundly affected calcifying organisms of all sorts, as well as all life that was dependent on reef habitats. This would lead to the extinction of large predators ultimately dependent on these organisms unless there were alternative food sources. At K/T we see this. All large air-breathing marine reptiles except turtles (which eat virtually anything) were wiped out. It is not known whether specific groups of sharks and other large fish suffered a similar fate, but they would have been less restricted to surface waters than the reptiles and could have exploited deeper oceanic food sources.

Extinctions on land cannot, of course, have been caused by acidification. However, CO_2 buildup can still be fingered as a major culprit. The oceans provide the dominant means of controlling atmospheric CO_2 concentrations: how would collapse of this control have affected atmospheric conditions at the time of K/T? A wide gamut of adverse environmental responses would have kicked in, such as are being predicted today, but also including very high levels of atmospheric oxygen. These conditions would have been in place at the time of the bolide impact, the effects of which would have created a raft of overloads.

ACIDIFICATION AND EARLIER EXTINCTIONS. Looking further back in time to earlier mass extinctions, we have much less-detailed information to work with. As seen in Chapter 5, with the exception of the Late Devonian mass extinction, preextinction CO_2 levels were high or increasing, conditions that could have led to deteriorating ocean chemistry. For at least one of the earlier extinctions (the end Permian, 251 mya), there is overlap with the formation of the Siberian traps, which would have caused a CO_2 spike. (A further five traps have overlaps with lesser extinctions, which may or may not be coincidental.) Although not conclusive, there is no equally persuasive alternative to acidification (or acidification and anoxia combined) as a *mechanism* for explaining both mass extinctions in the ocean and subsequent reef gaps.

The aragonitic skeletons of Mesozoic and modern scleractinians would have less resistance to increased acidity than the calcitic skeletons of rugose and tabulate corals in Paleozoic oceans. Nevertheless, high acidity would eventually cause major imbalances for all calcifying organisms, including species with calcitic skeletons.

The role of zooxanthellae in the past is uncertain. Marine organisms with zooxanthellae inside their cells (including Scleractinia) would have had greater control of their symbionts than organisms with zooxanthellae outside their cells (such as giant clams). The fate of rudist bivalves may have been linked to this characteristic; if they had symbionts (which is likely), their zooxanthellae were probably extracellular, like those of their modern molluscan relatives. As CO_2 increased in the Late Cretaceous, rudists began making skeletons of calcite, yet still went almost extinct at a time when aragonitic scleractinians, with their intracellular zooxanthellae, continued to proliferate. Looking further back, rugose and tabulate corals of the Paleozoic may also have had symbionts of one form or another (again, perhaps likely), but with no clear links to modern equivalents, little can be inferred about such remote relationships. It is clear that when comparing the ancient past with the more recent past and present, we are not always comparing apples with apples.

There is also the possibility that specialized corals of any of the ancient and modern groups may have existed for unknown intervals of time without skeletons when CO_2 levels were high. This notion is supported by recent observations that certain Scleractinia kept in artificially acidified aquaria can grow without skeletons and, furthermore, can resume skeleton building when acidity is returned to normal.[8]

In ancient oceans the role of reef consolidator may have been undertaken by a different group of organisms from today's coralline algae—perhaps a group less dependent on high-magnesium calcite skeletons and therefore less susceptible to acidity. Nevertheless, as acidification became more severe it would have affected the reef-building role of all calcifying consolidators, and they would have remained affected until the ocean chemistry allowed them to resume their job, perhaps by reevolving new taxa. The ravages of reefs during the Cretaceous might well be attributable to environmental impacts on coralline algae as much as on corals. However, loss of consolidators cannot have been a total explanation during mass extinctions in general because so many corals that occur independently of reefs went extinct.

REEFS DURING CARBON DIOXIDE HIGHS? The foregoing discussions argue that acidification as a *mechanism* explains the observations at K/T well and is not incompatible with information about other mass extinctions. However, studies of ancient environments also suggest that high atmospheric CO_2 levels may have occurred at times when reefs did not decline and may even have proliferated (illustrated in Figures 5.1 and 5.8). There are two main explanations for these apparently opposing observations.

One explanation may lie in the interpretation of information from such ancient times. The first diagram just referred to shows that CO_2 data are very uncertain for most early geological intervals: the data we have are based on a small number of point samples from widely different time periods. When this diagram is compared to those for shorter intervals (Figures 7.4 and 9.3), it is clear that substantial variability is present, which is only seen at finer scales. Two possibilities present themselves: (1) Reefs may not have proliferated at all during CO_2 highs; they may just appear to have survived because they were able to resume growth when levels fell. (2) Extreme CO_2 levels of ancient times may be an artifact of a lack of data. Paleoclimatology desperately awaits more study in this area.

Further explanation is based on the nonlinear nature of the relationship between acidification and atmospheric CO_2 discussed previously. The longer time frame of gradual increases in CO_2 allows mixing and buffering of surface layers by deep ocean sinks as well as adaptation to new environmental conditions by marine organisms. In contrast, when atmospheric CO_2 increases abruptly, its effects are intensified in shallow waters owing to a lack of mixing, giving marine life little time to adapt. An added complication is that the degree of ocean mixing has altered over geological time. The physical surface of the Earth—the geographic positions of the continents, prevailing climate regimes, and the pathways of ocean currents—is such that it is not possible to directly compare one period of the Earth's history directly with another when they are separated by long geological intervals. Threshold conditions for acidification may have varied with tectonic movements, associated changes in current patterns, and deep ocean exchange, and these may all have had influences on the time available for biological adaptation. If, indeed, reef builders and consolidators have been able to adapt to slowly increasing CO_2 levels in the past, it would be more than interesting to know what those physiological adaptations were.

Bottom Lines

Given the right conditions, reefs as geological structures can endure for hundreds of millions of years, through the greatest mass extinctions of corals, or their reef-building equivalents, and beyond. Yet an interesting paradox arises. It is strikingly clear from the foregoing accounts that reef accretion is much more vulnerable to changes in environmental conditions than are the coral taxa from which the reefs are built. Some changing environmental conditions, such as raising or lowering of sea levels, may have little or no impact on survival of coral species and yet can prevent reef accretion altogether, even removing all traces of consolidated reef limestone. Many of the influences that reduce calcification can have a significant effect on net reef accretion long before they might cause significant extinctions of taxa. The dependence of consolidating coralline algae on high-magnesium calcite also adds to reef vulnerability. We should therefore not be surprised at any short-term or local hiatus in reef building observed in the geological record—unfavorable conditions for reef accretion must often have been sufficiently protracted for reef growth to cease and significant erosion to take place. It is the exceptionally long reef gaps of millions of years and the coincident loss of most reef-building taxa that so comprehensively single out mass extinctions from other downturns.

The causes of mass extinctions and those of reef gaps appear to be linked, but the mechanisms involved in prolonging the latter may be somewhat different in each case. The Late Devonian mass extinction may have been caused by extremely low levels of photosynthesis resulting in anoxia of the both the oceans and the atmosphere. The remaining extinctions are most likely to have been caused principally by combinations of acidification and anoxia resulting from increased concentrations of atmospheric CO_2. The reef gap after the end Permian was extended by the need to reevolve a new reef-building fauna, the Scleractinia, but no such cause for prolonging reef gaps is associated with any other extinction. At least this is so for corals; coralline algae are another matter. Either way, acidification, probably combined with anoxia, remains the most likely dominant cause for four of the five mass extinctions and reef gaps. In each case, the carbon cycle was sufficiently out of kilter to create conditions leading to a generalized reduction in the calcifying capacity of marine life.

SYNERGIES, SPIKES, AND LAST STRAWS.   Although the evidence leads to a focus on acidification, it would be misleading to consider this as a cause in isolation. Indeed, most if not all mass extinctions appear to be the outcome of several different influences acting synergistically. Today's biology keeps reminding us that ecology responds to the environment in complex ways. Acidification may well have been a primary mechanism by which marine organisms and their ecosystems were affected; however, low light, bleaching, deteriorating water quality owing to acid rain or anoxia in shallow water, mechanical damage, and disease may all have played their parts. Although the time frames of bolides do not always fit the facts as a singular cause of extinction, bolides or traps or volcanic chains may have created short intervals of extremely adverse conditions that became the straw that broke the camel's back.

LOOKING TO THE FUTURE. K/T finished off the much-beloved dinosaurs and many other life forms besides, but by far the worst repercussion relevant to the modern world was its effect on marine life. CO_2, in the absence of a defensible alternative, must be held to blame, this time in its worst guise: dissolved in the oceans in quantities that changed the chemistry of the water, causing natural buffers to collapse and the biological pump to fail.

Could this happen again? The answer is unquestionably *yes,* for the Earth *does* have the resources, in the form of fossil fuels and methane ice, for a repeat performance. This process has some particularly disturbing aspects: the lag time of the ocean will make acidification a fait accompli before it has barely started, the pH-maintaining action of ocean carbonate buffers will cause acidification to be abrupt when the buffers are eventually overwhelmed, and—at least as far as humans are concerned—it will be for keeps. We must keep in mind what happened at the K/T boundary, for blaming bolides exclusively for mass extinctions, rather than climate change, as some climate change skeptics still do, is science fiction with most of the science missing. The climate upheavals of our own era, to which we now turn, have no mass extinctions, yet climatic changes continue to play a dominant role in the formation and fate of coral reefs. This time, those reefs include the GBR.

— 7 —

The Cenozoic Roller Coaster

Greenhouse conditions persisted long into the Cenozoic Era. Continental movements then dominated climates through the formation of the Antarctic Circumpolar Current, the progressive glaciation of Antarctica, and the establishment of strong poleward ocean temperature gradients. As the Tethys Sea gradually closed, the global center of coral diversity moved from the Tethys Sea and Central American Seaway to the Central Indo-Pacific. Closure of these two seaways established the oceanic template of contemporary climates. Through the latter half of our era decreasing levels of CO_2 gradually set the stage for the Ice Ages.

During our own era the Earth's climate changed from greenhouse to ice-house conditions, an immensely slow process that profoundly affected all living creatures—coral reefs included. We have now seen five mass extinctions in the very remote past against a background of more frequent minor extinctions in a long succession of boom-to-bust changes of fortune. From K/T (65 mya) on, the term "mass extinction" is not appropriate for, although reefs continued to be destroyed the world over by upheavals in global climates, most of the major groups of corals did not go extinct, nor did most other reef fauna. However, of the 27 background extinctions that occurred over the time that reefs have been in existence, three happened in our era, and they all significantly affected coral reefs.

After the oceans made their slow recovery from K/T, it was temperature, not water quality, that governed the fate of most reefs. There are two curious twists to this tale. The first, as I explain later, is that temperature came under the control of continental plate movements more than of atmospheric CO_2 levels, so we cannot view the fate of terrestrial fauna and flora

in the same light as that of coral reefs. What may be good for the one—
CO_2-loving plants and the animals that eat them—usually turns out to be
anything but good for the other. The second was the opening of Drake Passage between South America and the Antarctic Peninsula. This seemingly
minor development was destined to have a greater effect on the formation
of Australian coral reefs than any other single factor of our era at least until
the time that the sea-level oscillations of the Ice Ages became overwhelming.

When considering the fortunes of any reef throughout most of the Cenozoic, we still see that they are dependent on events that took place in remote
parts of the world. It is no mistake that this chapter has more to say about
Antarctica than about Australia, but it is not an account of global Cenozoic
climates as such. Rather it is a description of the climatic impacts that drastically affected coral reefs one way or another the world over and their causes.

Cenozoic Greenhouse

We have seen that the climate of the Cretaceous (141–65 mya) was generally characterized by a warm atmosphere and warm oceans. These condi-

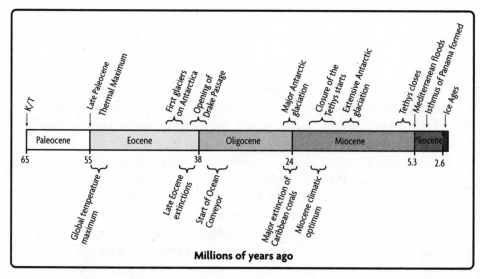

Figure 7.1 The Cenozoic Era, showing the geological settings of events described in this
chapter.

tions, created and maintained by high levels of greenhouse gases, continued through the K/T boundary (65 mya) and on into the Paleocene (65–55 mya).[1] The Earth then was a greenhouse garden: broadleaf forests proliferated everywhere, paving the way for a great diversification of large mammals now released from the dominion of the dinosaurs. Coral reefs, as we have seen, were conspicuously absent or rare around most of the globe.

Greenhouse conditions peaked toward the end of the Paleocene in an event known as the Late Paleocene Thermal Maximum (55 mya).[2] At that time, for reasons unknown, over 1,000 gigatons of carbon, probably from methane (which readily oxidizes to CO_2), was released into the atmosphere, or more probably the ocean, in less than a thousand years.[3] Although this release is nothing like the amount or rate of anthropogenic greenhouse gas emissions of today, it caused deep ocean temperatures, recorded in ocean

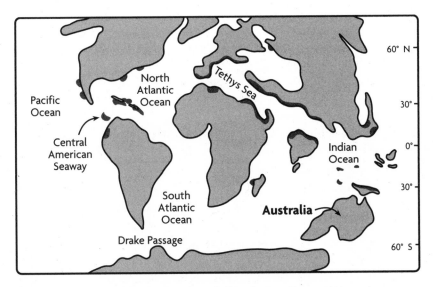

Figure 7.2   Positions of the continents during the Late Eocene (40 mya). Extensive reef remains are found scattered over much of Papua New Guinea and Indonesia (such as it was then), as these islands were (and remain) tectonically active. There are, however, few reef remains from any part of the Cenozoic on the Australian continent—not because Australia did not have reefs at this time, but rather because there has been very little uplift. With the exception of the far northern GBR, what coastal reefs there were remained in place until they were eventually eroded by the ocean.

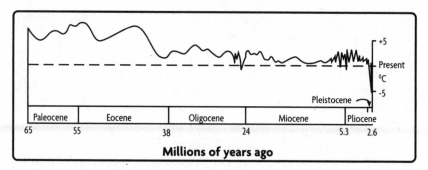

Figure 7.3   Mean global temperatures of the Cenozoic. This is a smoothed curve obtained from different sources. It may not reflect all events specific to the oceans, nor (because of continental drift) to individual countries (including Australia). Note that the minimum mean global temperature during the Pleistocene Ice Ages was only 6°C below that of today.

sediments, to rise by 5–7°C (a rate of at least 0.5°C per century). Not surprisingly, this led to a substantial extinction of bottom-dwelling organisms.[4] However, if one looks at this as a rehearsal for what is occurring today, the concern is that some of this carbon lingered for perhaps as long as 60,000 years, a finding broadly in keeping with model projections of today's atmospheric CO_2 (see Chapter 13).

This methane burp aside, global temperatures probably reached a peak during the Early Eocene (50 mya). Only a few patches of what may be Early Eocene reefs now exist, and those that do have only a few coral species in them. Middle to Late Eocene (45–40 mya) reef remains, seen in surface limestone, boreholes, and fossils, occur mostly around the shorelines of the ancient Tethys and the Central American Seaway. (Interestingly, the fossil record of corals suggested the presence of hostile early Cenozoic environments long before it was confirmed by any paleoclimatic discovery.)[5]

Global cooling probably started after the Middle Eocene (ca. 45 mya), although tropical sea surface temperatures remained as high, or higher, than those of today.[6] By the Late Eocene (ca. 40 mya), the pH of the tropical Pacific was roughly similar to that of today.[7] (Such results vary enormously with the investigative technique used to compile them. Relatively reliable results come from boron isotope ratios in fossil forams—if suitable material is adequately preserved—which are used to estimate the pH of surface seawater and, in turn, to reconstruct atmospheric CO_2 concentrations.) More-

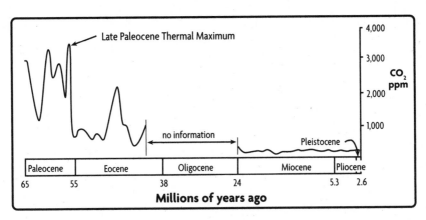

Figure 7.4 Global CO_2 levels (in ppm) of the Cenozoic. The major peaks of the Paleocene and Eocene, especially their duration, are based on little solid information. Very high levels at these times do not necessarily mean that the oceans were as acidic as today's predictions suggest, because the accumulation of high levels of CO_2 was not rapid (in a geological sense). As a result, surface ocean waters would have been buffered by deep-ocean water and carbonate rock. Furthermore, high CO_2 levels over prolonged intervals dissolve terrestrial limestone, a process that would have raised ocean alkalinity.

over, by the Late Eocene, the first cycles of cooling were clearly established, the first glaciers had formed on Antarctica, and deep ocean temperatures had dropped substantially. There are, however, numerous information gaps. Temperatures at this time are poorly known,[8] creating a hiatus in our knowledge of the width of the tropics. CO_2 levels are unknown after the Late Eocene until earliest Miocene (24 mya), yet we do know that from that time to the present day they have remained below 500 ppm, with most estimates between 200 and 300 ppm[9]—near to or well below today's rapidly rising level of 375 ppm.

The end of the Eocene (38 mya) is marked by a global marine extinction that has been blamed (unreasonably, as we saw in the last chapter) on sea-level changes induced by seafloor spreading rather than on temperature, for sea levels peaked at this time, causing much of Europe and some of northeast Africa to be gradually flooded (see Figure 7.2). This extinction was of largely unknown severity (and, in my view, unknown cause); nevertheless, as usual it had a substantial impact on reefs.[10] Subsequently the sea level rapidly declined owing to Antarctic ice accumulation, which, it has been suggested, may in turn have caused some sort of unspecified degradation in ocean chemistry.[11] Nevertheless, recovery appears to have been rapid (geologically speaking), for by the end of the Eocene and throughout the Oligocene (38–24 mya) greenhouse conditions continued to dominate the Earth's climate, and sea levels, as far as we know, remained high.

The Oligocene may have been an interval of stable climes over much of the world, which appears to have remained largely free of major environmental upheavals. Coral diversity around the Central American Seaway reached a peak at this time,[12] and there was extensive reef development throughout the central Indo-West Pacific, now clearly distinct from the Tethys. Antarctica and Australia were both forested. Temperatures were initially higher than those of today,[13] but they decreased as the Oligocene progressed. By the Middle Oligocene (30 mya), forests had thinned out over much of Australia,[14] and ocean temperatures, even in the north, had dropped substantially[15]—a significant matter for coral reefs, as we shall see in the next chapter.

At the end of the Oligocene (24 mya) there was a severe Antarctic glacial cycle followed by several smaller cycles. These geologically brief yet major climate changes—often called "excursions" because they represented sudden departures from global norms—indeed show that the Earth's climate can change abruptly for no apparent reason.[16] The end Oligocene glaciation resulted in another extinction of corals in the Caribbean region,[17] which by then appears to have become almost as vulnerable to glacial cycles as it was later in the Pleistocene (2.6 mya).

When the CO_2 record becomes clear in the Miocene (24 mya), levels are uniformly low and so are most measures of global temperatures, with downward excursions starting to increase in frequency.

The Antarctic Circumpolar Current Takes Control

At the start of the Cenozoic, Antarctica, being ice free, had adjacent oceans with an average temperature as high as 18°C.[18] Ocean circulation then was dominated by a circum-global equatorial path via the Tethys Sea and Central American Seaway (see Figure 5.10). There was no circulation around Antarctica, or rather what was by then left of Gondwana. The oceans were warm and sluggish, and there were no strong latitudinal temperature gradients such as we have today.

This pattern of ocean circulation largely dominated the world's climate until South America finally rifted free of Antarctica during the Late Eocene or Early Oligocene (40–35 mya) and Drake Passage opened. Then, for the first time since Gondwana formed, the Southern Ocean could circulate around Antarctica, moving eastward in response to the direction of the Earth's rotation and checked only by the coastlines of the three southern continents.

The formation of the Antarctic Circumpolar Current was, in my view, *the* most critical event in the history of the Cenozoic because, ever since its formation, it has largely controlled the distribution of heat in all three southern oceans. Put simply, where the three continents (South America, Africa, and, to a lesser extent, Australia) project into its path, cold water is peeled off, turned north, and transported along the western margin of each continent. It then moves westward in the tropics and warms up. On the return journey, this warm water is transported south toward the pole along the eastern side of each continent. These three counterclockwise circulations of the Southern Hemisphere oceans are in turn linked to clockwise circulations in the Northern Hemisphere, much as one gear wheel drives another, in gigantic latitudinally zoned circles. On smaller scales, the great circulations can be modified by other currents. The most important modification relevant to Australia is that of the Leeuwin Current of Western Australia, where water flowing through the Indonesian archipelago from the Pacific continues southward down the western Australian coast, displacing the northward-flowing current described earlier away from the coast.

In effect, the opening of Drake Passage allowed the sluggish tropical circulations of the early Cenozoic to be replaced with stronger circulations, powered by the Antarctic Circumpolar Current, creating the latitudinal temperature gradients of today. In so doing, this current also formed an insulating blanket around Antarctica. There are two important points in this regard. The first is that, being terrestrial, we may see the atmosphere as being primarily responsible for the heat distributions and changes we experience during seasonal cycles. But this is not so—it is the oceans that are the real movers of heat. The second point is that Antarctica—nearly twice the size of Australia and carrying 26 million cubic kilometers of ice, all wrapped in an insulating ocean blanket—is an imperturbable deep freeze, an anchor of all Earthly climates.

When it formed that insulating blanket, the Antarctic Circumpolar Current caused the surface temperature of the Southern Ocean to plunge dramatically, by 10–15°C,[19] thus hastening the freezing of Antarctica and presumably creating cold conditions along the southern and western coasts of all the southern continents, including Australia. Tropical oceans today have a surface layer, only a few hundred meters thick, of warm, low-density water floating on the cold, dense water that makes up most of the bulk of our oceans. At high latitudes there is no such temperature gradient with depth, so water near the poles is relatively easily mixed, which was not the case before the formation of the Antarctic Circumpolar Current. During the entire interval of high CO_2 (perhaps up to the Late Eocene, 40 mya), most

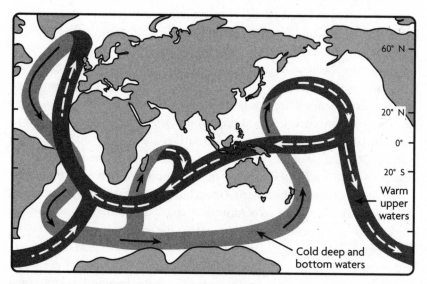

Figure 7.5 Pathways of the Ocean Conveyor today. The Ocean Conveyor is a two-layered system, linked by several points of upwelling and downwelling, which meanders through all three great oceans in both hemispheres. The Conveyor is powered by thermohaline convection. Deep currents are generated by the downwelling of cold (– 2°C), dense, saline water (brine) left behind by the freezing of sea ice, which has a low salinity. This sinking cold water (in both the North Atlantic and the Southern Ocean) must be replaced, and this happens by the drawing in of warmer, less saline surface water from lower latitudes. Thermohaline forcing is assisted by surface wind-driven circulations; nevertheless, surface circulation takes a different path over most deep-ocean water. At today's rate it takes about 1,000 years for a given body of water to complete a full cycle of the Ocean Conveyor. This process is responsible for much of the lag time in the ocean's response to surface chemical changes.

of the Earth had a shallow, slowly moving, and largely isolated surface layer that allowed, among other things, heat to be exported from the tropics. Moreover, there was no ice on Antarctica, nor any Ocean Conveyor. These are some of several major complications that arise when comparing the physics and chemistry of today's oceans with those of the early Cenozoic and before.

The Death of the Tethys and
Birth of the Ocean Conveyor

During the Oligocene (38–24 mya) two major modifications to the circulation pattern I have just described took place, and they prevailed for most of the latter half of the Cenozoic.[20] First, the North Atlantic was much narrower then and did not regulate global climates via the Ocean Conveyor as it does now. Second, the east-west circulation through the Tethys Sea would have had a dampening influence on north-south heat transport. The Tethys, the evolutionary cradle of most tropical marine life, waxed and waned throughout this time, depending on continental movements and sea-level changes, to be finally choked off during the Late Miocene (10 mya). This, finally, severed all tropical connection between the Atlantic and Indian oceans.

The Oligocene marked the beginning of the Ocean Conveyor (see the accompanying figure), an eternal counterforce to the formation of closed circulations within single-ocean basins and one of the major controlling mechanisms of today's climate. We return to the Ocean Conveyor and the thermohaline circulation that powers it in later chapters.[21]

The Global Stage of the Early GBR

The GBR did not form in isolation from the geological history of Australia, nor is that history isolated from the geological history of the rest of the world. Here we look at the global events, and in Chapter 8 we turn to Australia's local history.

The Miocene, spanning nearly 20 million years, is a catchall term for a progression of environmental changes effectively starting from the greenhouse conditions of the Oligocene (38–24 mya) and ending with the onset of icehouse Earth. During the Oligocene and on into the Miocene, CO_2 was being used up—by the world's vast forests and in carbonic acid reactions with rock—faster than it was being produced, and what little volcanism

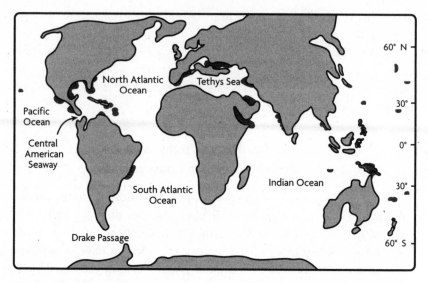

Figure 7.6 Positions of the continents during the Middle Miocene (around 15 mya). Extensive reef remains are scattered around the world and as far south as New Zealand. The lack of records for the South Pacific is an artifact of an incomplete geological record due to the lack of surface limestone. There would almost certainly have been reef regions in the South Pacific similar to those of today.

there was did not replenish it. Yet the Miocene was anything but a time of gradual cooling. Toward its end and on into the Pliocene (5.3 mya), the climatic roller coaster went into a series of fearful dives. There were warm phases lasting hundreds of thousands of years intermixed with relatively sudden intervals of cold,[22] causing repeated changes in the distribution of tropical and subtropical forests around the world and repeated destruction of Antarctica's temperate forests. Importantly as far as reefs are concerned, these upheavals were not linked to CO_2 levels, which remained low.

Early Miocene (ca. 20 mya) reefs had much the same distribution that reefs have today, with the major exception of the Tethys Sea, which, as the accompanying map shows, was held open only by only a narrow passage connecting the Indian Ocean with the proto-Mediterranean. Just what the diversity of corals was at this time is unknown; however, by then the Indo-West Pacific had inherited much of the diversity that had originally evolved in the Tethys and the Caribbean. This was indeed fortunate for the subsequent history of corals, for the Tethys—the birthplace of at least half of all

Cenozoic coral genera—was being choked to death by the northward drift of the former Gondwana continents. By the end Miocene (5.3 mya), the Tethys had been all but squeezed out of existence, and only about five coral genera were left, *Porites* hanging on to the last.

The Miocene Climatic Optimum

By the Middle Miocene (15 mya), Antarctica had turned into the coldest and driest continent on Earth, and Australia may have become the hottest and second driest.[23] At some point during this interval there was a sharp drop in mean ocean temperature as a result of intensified polar glaciation,[24] but as this was accompanied by a rise in pole-to-equator surface temperature gradients it probably had only minor effects on the tropics. There was also a short warm phase during the Miocene, the Miocene Climatic Optimum (17–14.5 mya), which may have been the warmest time for 35 million years, with midlatitude atmospheric temperatures reaching as high as 6°C above the present norms. CO_2 levels throughout the Miocene were low (around 180–290 ppm) and ocean pH was similar to that of today. This may be related to oceanographic changes resulting from the opening of Drake Passage, closure of the Tethys, or both. Yet, whatever the cause, this interval, among others less dramatic, shows conclusively that significant global warming can take place independently of CO_2 levels.[25]

The Miocene Climatic Optimum was followed by a geologically rapid end Miocene increase in glaciation that caused sea levels to fall by as much as 40–50 meters. This is a well-known time, for it resulted in the isolation of the Mediterranean and the Red Sea, both eventually to become vast evaporative basins of extraordinary depth, with the Mediterranean completely drying up for most of its area, the lowest level of any landlocked sea ever known.[26] With environments rivaling that of the Dead Sea today, all marine life in the Mediterranean and the Red Sea was exterminated. That is how the Miocene ended, with the extinction of the last remnants of the ancient fauna of the Tethys. No trace of Miocene reefs now remains over much of the South Pacific, except for northern New Zealand, which had reefs dominated by coral genera that are common on the GBR today.[27]

The reflooding of the Mediterranean—perhaps the most spectacular waterfall of all time—heralded a return to milder climates and the beginning of the Pliocene (5.3 mya). However, the remainder of the Pliocene was a time of further cooling—stepwise and with reversals—correlated with the onset of Northern Hemisphere glaciation, soon to dominate the climate changes of the Ice Ages.

The End of the Central American Seaway and the Isolation of the Caribbean

There was one final event crucial to ocean circulation before ice age cycles took control—the formation of the Isthmus of Panama in place of the old Central American Seaway. This gradual process was finally completed 3.4 million years ago.[28] Deepwater flow of the Ocean Conveyor to the North Atlantic, so important in climate regulation today, would have had much less effect before this closure,[29] as would any precursor of today's ENSO cycles.

Corals had yet to undergo one more major change in their global pattern of diversity. Throughout much of the Miocene (24–5.3 mya), but certainly by the Late Miocene, the eastern Atlantic had become too cold for reef corals, as a result of the cold current plying northward up the western African coast.[30] The Atlantic thus became an isolating barrier where once it had been a corridor, now separating the Caribbean from the dying Tethys. Caribbean corals were also largely separated—for as much as 10 million years—from the Indo-West Pacific center of diversity by the vast empty expanse of the eastern Pacific. The consequences of this for the corals of the region during the Pleistocene (2.6 mya) were substantial indeed, for most if not all corals on the Pacific side of the Isthmus of Panama, including many species that had spread as far as the Gulf of California, were exterminated by cold at this time. Today there are no coral species in common between the Atlantic and the Pacific, and only a dozen or so species occur at all in the far eastern Pacific.

Lessons from the Ancient Cenozoic

It is clear enough, and consistent with most of what we saw in the Mesozoic, that during the early Cenozoic, high levels of CO_2, aided by methane, were the major cause of long-term greenhouse conditions, as well as shorter-term fluctuations in ocean acidity.

Throughout the later Cenozoic we have seen that the Earth is capable of climate changes that are both rapid (geologically speaking) and severe. There were temperature excursions in both directions, although downward excursions appear not to have occurred during the early Cenozoic when CO_2 levels were high.

We cannot be certain that the high levels of greenhouse gases that persisted after K/T caused the reef gap that extended through the Paleocene (65–55 mya) and on into the Early Eocene (50 mya). Nevertheless, it is more than coincidental that widespread reefs did not start forming until after CO_2 started declining in the Late Eocene (40 mya). No doubt the sudden release of methane responsible for the Late Paleocene Thermal Maximum would have helped the delay.

Mid-Cenozoic climates show that global warming can take place without high levels of (and probably without an increase in) greenhouse gases. Present CO_2 levels appear not to have occurred since the earliest Miocene (ca. 25 mya), yet there have been major intervals of warming during this time, the most dramatic being the Miocene Climatic Optimum and, as we shall see, the interglacial intervals of the Ice Ages.

In summary, the history of Cenozoic climates is not one of gradual change from greenhouse to icehouse. Deep ocean sediment cores, our best archives of ancient climate swings, show that, throughout the whole Cenozoic, the Earth was incapable of achieving long-lasting stability. Ultimately, change was due to plate tectonics—seafloor spreading—and its associated climatic repercussions, notably the release of CO_2 from volcanoes and methane from the ocean at the margins of the moving continents. However, these ultraslow processes were continually punctuated by shorter-term events (measured in thousands rather than millions of years) of many kinds, biological as well as geological. We see such events much more clearly during the Ice Ages, when they came to dominate all aspects of global climate. The Cenozoic also shows us that the climatic stability we humans have so far enjoyed during our brief occupation of the Earth has given us a false sense of security. No such illusion has ever existed for a coral reef. We now follow the path of Australia along the Cenozoic roller coaster and in so doing, track the climatic and geographic changes that initiated the formation of the GBR.

— 8 —

Australia Adrift

Australia was close to Antarctica at the time of K/T. During the Cenozoic, Australia's journey north took her through a progression of climates of both global and regional origin, the latter largely due to decreasing latitude. The main structural features of the Coral Sea developed early on this journey. Most of the northern coastline had coral reefs of some sort, except perhaps during the mid-Cenozoic, when the Antarctic Circumpolar Current formed and Antarctica froze. For the latter half of the era, northern Australia has been mostly tropical and part of the global center of coral diversity.

At this point, we return to the formation of that part of the world that is now called the GBR to put this region into its climate-controlled biological context. We have seen that K/T brought corals to near-extinction the world over, and those that survived may have had to battle on in a world largely devoid of reefs for many millions of years. At that time, as now, not all parts of the world fared equally. Why this is so today is abundantly clear, but why it was so for reefs during the early part of our era is not at all apparent, because not enough limestone remains to tell the story. Nor are there adequate records, terrestrial or marine, to provide a clear track of climates during Australia's journey.

At the beginning of the Cenozoic, Australia was snuggled close to Antarctica; yet it was warm, so the continent may have had whatever corals (as opposed to reefs) were in existence at that time. What happened between then and now is mostly a matter of continental drift, coral biogeography, and climate.

When we look at drifting Australia, moving from Antarctica to her present location, we see that the country itself remained remarkably unchanged—so much so that the shape of most of Australia's shoreline can be recognized, with a little imagination, almost back to the early Cenozoic. No, the GBR did not form then and move north to where it is now, clinging to Australia's starboard bow: only some of the world's oldest mountain ranges and deepest ocean trenches have been in existence that long. Nevertheless, this was the journey that largely decided the fate of most of Australia's terrestrial and marine life. As Australia came within migratory range of Asia, most terrestrial biota formed frontiers with Indonesia—biogeographic demarcations that remained virtually intact until Europeans set about dismantling them only two centuries ago. Australia's marine life tells a different story—one far more ancient, because for it the ocean was a bridge, not a barrier. Coral reefs, once again, are Nature's historians of this epic journey, piecemeal though their account may be.

The Journey North

The Late Cretaceous (80 mya), with its climatic upheavals and devastating finale, was not just an interesting time for the world's biota in general;[1] it was an especially important time for the continent of Greater Australia (Australia and New Guinea combined, as they have been for most of the Cenozoic). By that time, the forces of seafloor spreading had long placed the ancient supercontinent of Gondwana under intolerable stress. By the Middle Cretaceous (100 mya), Africa, Madagascar, and India were well free of Antarctica, and India had started its dash for the equator. Greater Australia had also started to dawdle along her journey.

Around the time of the K/T extinction, Greater Australia had a highly distinctive fauna that included giant labyrinthodont amphibians; both orders of dinosaurs, plesiosaurs, ichythyosaurs, and mosasaurs; ancestors of modern Australian amphibians, reptiles and birds (presumably, for the fossil record of birds is almost nonexistent); monotreme mammals, most of the world's marsupial mammals (again presumed, as the fossil record is poor), and perhaps placental mammals (the fossil record is almost nonexistent). In addition, there were abundant forests of *Nothofagus* trees (still abundant in Australia today) and broadleaf deciduous trees that have no modern equivalent.[2] Imagine, if you can, forests growing on a rugged landscape that had the same seasonal daylight regimes that Antarctica has today.

Australia was isolated from immigration from the north far more then than it is now, an isolation that allowed its little marsupials to proliferate and its monotremes to survive, both safe from any large placental predator. This isolation, however, gave no protection from the K/T mass extinction—convincing evidence of its universal impact. Fortunately for the monotremes and the primitive marsupials, the dinosaurs and most placental mammals (if any of the latter were actually present) died in Australia just as they did everywhere else, turning Greater Australia into a lifeboat that carried its strange flora and fauna northward toward the equator at a speed of about 6 centimeters a year. The journey became a race against time as the Earth started its erratic yet relentless decline toward glacial mode and Antarctica froze, extinguishing all of its once great subtropical diversity.

This is a well-known story. However, its marine equivalent has remained untold, for only corals and reefs have much to say about it. As with terrestrial life, we turn to the fossil record and the biota we find living today to reconstruct it, but we also get help from the limestone remains that past reefs have left behind. Corals and coral reefs are a primary information source concerning sea levels, ice volume, and temperature because of the isotope records kept in uplifted reefs and in the growth layers of individual colonies (illustrated in Figure 3.3). In addition, fine-grained colonies (especially *Porites*) form doughnut-shaped microatolls (illustrated in Plate 41) in intertidal habitats because their upward growth is truncated precisely at low-tide level. Thus they mark the level of the sea at the time of growth with great precision.

Formation of the Western Coral Sea

The process of seafloor spreading that separated Australia and Antarctica is likely to have started in the Early Cretaceous (130 mya) and was well established around the time of K/T. (Estimated times for the separation of Australia and Antarctica vary considerably because the rifting was initially very gradual and did not speed up until the Late Eocene, 40 mya.)[3]

By the Late Cretaceous (80 mya) the Queensland and Marion plateaus had formed, and so had a series of ocean basins, including the precursor of the Coral Sea Basin of today (see the contour map, Figure 2.6). The latter subsequently took shape as the Papuan Peninsula rotated counterclockwise away from northeastern Australia in the Paleocene (65–55 mya). The Queensland Trough, along which the ribbon reefs of today's northern GBR are aligned, dates from that time.

Except in the far north, where further seafloor spreading took place into the Late Oligocene (27 mya),[4] the main structural features of northeastern

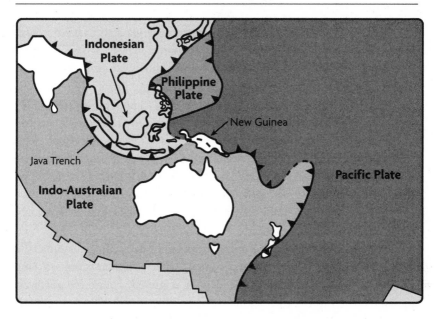

Figure 8.1 The positions of continental plates and subduction zones. During subduction the rim of one continental plate slides (is subducted) beneath the rim of another—a significant process in the geological history of all Australian reefs. In the case of the collision between Greater Australia and the Indonesian plate, it was (and still is) the Indo-Australian plate that became subducted. This lifted the rim of Indonesia to create the Java Trench and the semicircular island arc that extends from Sumatra to New Guinea. In the case of the collision with the Pacific plate, it was (and still is) the Pacific plate that became subducted, creating the Owen Stanley mountain chain of New Guinea. (This is a simplified description: New Guinea and Indonesia are actually composed of at least five semi-independent, rotating subplates and have a more complex recent history.)

Australia and the Coral Sea were established by the Early Eocene (50 mya),[5] a time when Australia was still close to Antarctica. Just as India was destined to hit the continent of Eurasia, pushing up the Tibetan Plateau, Greater Australia collided with the continental plates of Indonesia and the Pacific, which blocked her northward path. This collision started in the Miocene and remains active today. Some remnants of the northern shorelines of Cretaceous Gondwana are still preserved as uplifted reef remnants in Papua New Guinea; however, most reefs have long since been submerged in deep ocean or have slid under the continental plate boundaries, as illustrated in the accompanying figure. This process has affected the western, northern, and eastern coasts of Greater Australia very differently.

In the northwest of Australia, seismic profiles show that reefs once formed extensive platforms, the ages of which are as yet unknown.[6] Many oil exploration bores have been sunk through reefs of the northwest shelf, reefs that are clearly visible in these profiles. However, the drillers were heading for much deeper strata. As far as they were concerned, the reefs were only unwanted overburden, so the drilling extract was not retained for dating. Most of the reefs that once grew along the northwest coast (extensions of those now seen in seismic profiles) either drowned as their basement subsided or were subducted under the Indonesian plate. Today only a few widely spaced reefs reach the surface.[7]

The reverse happened along the northern coast of Greater Australia (the northern coast of modern New Guinea), where uplifted reefs are now preserved as limestone outcrops of all ages, scattered around the northern highlands. Even to the most casual observer, the island of New Guinea is geologically young and active, in stark contrast to its larger senescent neighbor to the south.

Northeastern Australia has another, very different, history. Except in the far north, the ancient continent was not troubled by the events of the Miocene. Most of the GBR grows along one of the most stable coastlines in the world.

The Journey of the Corals

With a little filling in of the gaps, we can reconstruct the journey of the corals. During the Late Cretaceous (80 mya), as Australia was rifting free of Gondwana, reefs may have developed when and where temperature and ocean chemistry permitted. If they did, they would not have closely resembled any reef of today. Most corals, fish, and other life would have been unfamiliar— the reefs might even have had some lingering rudists and perhaps the occasional plesiosaur. This fauna was gradually depleted as the oceans became increasingly acidic and devoid of oxygen until, by the time of K/T, any reefs that had formed would have become little more than meadows of algae and would have remained so for millions of years (or else would have eroded completely away), during which period the gap between Antarctica and Australia gradually widened. If reefs made a comeback, the CO_2 peak at the Late Paleocene Thermal Maximum (55 mya) would probably have snuffed them out, so it was not until the Middle to Late Eocene (45–38 mya) that wide-scale reef development might have recommenced. If it did, this recovery would also have been short-lived, for the end Eocene extinction (38 mya), a minor extinction globally, seems to have affected reefs all over the Earth. Be that as it may, the event of greatest importance—at first just for the region but later for the rest of the world—was the start of the separation of South America from Antarctica. As we have seen, this allowed the Antarctic Circumpolar Current, moving through the deeps of Drake Passage, to begin its domination of the Southern Ocean.

As the Antarctic Circumpolar Current grew in influence during the Oligocene (38–24 mya), ocean temperatures may have reached an all-time low for Australia, for the continent was only halfway along its journey by this time. However, recent results from the Ocean Drilling Program suggest that the Coral Sea may not have been as cold during the Oligocene as was formerly thought, and may well have been warm enough to permit coral reef development. Whether this was so or not, the end Oligocene extinction (24 mya) would probably have stopped all reef development, for it was severe enough to have had a major impact on the reefs of the Central American Seaway, even though these were not far north of the equator.

It was during the Early Oligocene that corals, and probably most other marine fauna, finally enjoyed an uninterrupted immigration path to Australia from the north. At last the emigrating larvae, carried by warm southward-flowing currents, had a permanent highway. Northern Australia had finally broken its ties with Antarctica, at least as far as marine life was concerned.

Although Oligocene reef limestone abounds in Indonesia and Papua New Guinea, the fossil corals it contains are not sufficiently well preserved or dated to reveal details about their affinities. (The Late Oligocene to Middle Miocene Daril limestone bed of northern Papua New Guinea is an immense structure, up to 1,000 meters thick in some places.) Nevertheless, the diversity of the corals can be estimated by combining our knowledge of their present distribution with their geological longevity. When this is done it is clear that both the ancient Tethys and the Caribbean region had been displaced as the global center of coral diversity. By the Early Miocene (20 mya) or earlier, that distinction belonged to the Central Indo-Pacific, as can be seen in the accompanying map, Figure 8.2.[8]

By the Early Miocene, Australia still had some way to go before she was close enough for contact with Asia as far as most terrestrial life was concerned; yet for marine life, the journey was effectively over. Major ocean

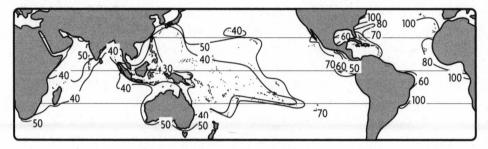

Figure 8.2 Contours showing the average age of extant reef coral genera (in millions of years). This pattern is due to the Indo-Pacific inheriting most genera of the Tethys and also having many younger genera found nowhere else. Reefs enclosed by the 30-million-year contour indicate the area where the most recent evolution took place—the Indo-Pacific center of diversity, the equatorial part of which has been dubbed the Coral Triangle (see Figure 2.2).

currents were similar to those of today, so that the northern and eastern Australian coastlines were downstream of equatorial currents, as they are now. At least 60 percent of all modern genera had evolved by then, and many modern species, or their immediate ancestors, date back to this time.[9] These corals would have had dispersal capabilities and habitat tolerances com-

Figure 8.3 *Duncanopsammia axifuga* in situ in the Pleistocene Era Beds west of Port Moresby, Papua New Guinea. There are no differences between this specimen and skeletons of the same species alive today. The living coral is illustrated in Plate 13. (Photograph by the author.)

parable to those of today. They would have colonized shorelines anywhere that their long-journeying larvae could have reached, provided that there were suitable places to grow and adequate water quality. Where corals grew and the temperature was normally above 18°C, reefs of one sort or another would have formed.

We have only one detailed glimpse of Indo-Pacific corals before the onset of the Ice Ages—at the Era Beds on the south coast of Papua New Guinea, 300 kilometers east of the far northern GBR (see Figure 8.3). This tiny outcrop, which was sealed in mud sufficiently well to prevent diagenesis from destroying the skeletal detail of the corals, has the world's most diverse fossil coral assemblage, probably Early Pleistocene (ca. 2 mya) in age. Here 78 percent of coral species are virtually identical to their living counterparts. Only 10 percent of them went extinct during the Ice Ages.[10]

This raises the question of just when the GBR originated, a matter to which I turn in Chapter 11. Before that, however, we must continue our journey through time, for we have reached that part of global geological history when almost the entire GBR was repeatedly destroyed, as the world plunged into the traumas of the Ice Ages.

— 9 —

The Ice Ages

Ice Age cycles have affected the GBR more than anything else in its history. Understanding the nature of Ice Age climate changes is crucial to this history, so we examine interactions among the cycles, events, flips and flickers of the time and their influence on sea level, temperature, and CO_2. Although the GBR underwent immense change during Ice Age upheavals—the reefs we see today were repeatedly destroyed—these changes had only minor consequences for the continuing survival of the corals themselves.

Long before the beginning of the Ice Ages, Australia had successfully escaped the clutches of the frozen continent of Antarctica to the south and forged new biological alliances with the equatorial regions farther north. The GBR province became the southern border of the global center of reef biodiversity, but the roller coaster climate changes of the Cenozoic continued to exert their effects on Australian corals and reefs. Antarctica, now in collusion with the Arctic, had another card to play, one that could cause havoc for every coral reef in the world. That card was sea-level change—not the gradual changes caused by seafloor spreading in the remote past, but far more rapid changes produced by the movement of frozen water back and forth between land and ocean.

Sea-level change, temperature, and acidification are the three primary long-term constraints on reef development. During the Ice Ages, the first two were intimately linked with each other at the poles in cause-and-effect cycles. However, it was sea-level change that reached out from the poles to totally devastate reefs around the world. This happened again and again over the 2 million years of the Ice Ages, devastating all reefs that we have today, stripping them of marine life, and leaving them to whatever use terrestrial plants and

animals had for them. Yet the displaced marine biota was extraordinarily unaffected. Whole communities moved, as shifting sea levels closed doors on one
habitat after another, even as they opened other doors in different places. Marine life of all shapes and sizes kept finding new temporary dwellings. Ultimately most of the life forms we associate with coral reefs today carried on
through these cycles with little modification, for there was not much time for
evolutionary change between the cycles. The continuity of life through extreme changes makes for convincing evidence of coral reefs' immense powers
of recovery when times are good, and their endurance when they are not.

Carbon Dioxide and the Great Barrier Reef

Once again, CO_2 comes to the fore, enclosing as it does the three climatic
adversaries of reefs—sea-level change, temperature, and acidification—in
that prophetic envelope we have seen so often in the remote past. Today we
call that envelope climate change, created by too much CO_2; during the Ice
Ages it was sea-level change, caused by too little CO_2. I offer an explanatory
account of these observations and delve into the mechanisms that controlled ice age climates, which in turn controlled the fortunes—or rather the
misfortunes—of the GBR.

In this chapter we enter a time that, according to many reef geologists,
corresponds to the GBR's origin. Thus we now need further clarity about
what the name "Great Barrier Reef" actually means. I define it as an area
that is (1) a region of coral reefs similar to today's reefs or (2) a province of
dry land occupying the same geographic position or (3) various combinations of (1) and (2), but located at different latitudes, depending on the
northward drift of Australia. Clearly these are descriptions of very differ-
ent-looking places, making the GBR province a highly changeable and
slowly drifting, yet generally discrete, geographic region. In effect we have
to put an imaginary fence around it and call it "the GBR" or "the GBR
province" whether it is a coral reef or not. For *most* of the past 2 million
years or so, the region we know as the GBR would in fact have looked more
like a modern-day cattle station—kangaroo country—than a coral reef.
This is the area to which we now return, having left it adrift in the Miocene.
The previous chapter and this one are preludes to a discussion of the origins of the GBR, the subject of Chapter 11.

Understanding the Ice Ages—what happened and why—has long been
the Holy Grail of global climate science. Over the past few decades there has

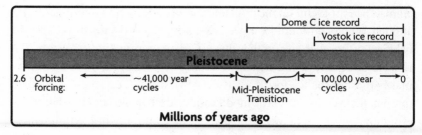

Figure 9.1 The Pleistocene. Its currently accepted beginning, 2.6 mya, is a recent revision from a previously accepted time of 1.8 mya. The ice records (Dome C and Vostok) are those of Antarctica, referred to in the text. The geological settings of orbital cycles are events that are also referred to in the text. Note that the Holocene, our current geological time interval, which began only 11,800 years ago, is not visible at this scale.

been a proliferation of theories as to how our present climate is changing and where it is heading. Yet all such speculations are ultimately held in check by the Ice Ages—by the undeniable fact of their existence and by the staggering severity of the climate swings involved. If those swings were well understood, current concerns about global warming could be put into broad context—albeit a context that does not factor-in the antics of humans.

Ice Age Cycles

We have seen that the Earth's climate from the Late Eocene to the Late Pliocene (40–3 mya) was dominated by a long and erratic decline in temperature. From that point onward, when the Ice Ages began, climate descriptions take on a different terminology, no longer employing the concept of progressive change. Rather we have the concept of cycles, which are of several types, each of different duration and each superimposed on other cycles.

> Big cycles have little cycles upon their backs to bite 'em,
> Little cycles have lesser cycles and so ad infinitum.

Of course "ad infinitum" is an exaggeration. Yet considering the tidal, lunar, and seasonal cycles we all observe, the climate "swings" recorded in human history, the array of El Niño and similar "oscillations" of the Holocene, the cycles peculiar to the Ice Ages described below, and finally the permanent orbital cycles also described below, this hijacked couplet seems applicable enough. All things considered, climate cycles can get confusing. Each *may* cause changes in ocean temperature, sea level, chemistry, and circulation, and these *may* have parallel changes in the atmosphere—but not necessarily. Some general observations may help us to understand why.

Antarctica is a continent surrounded by ocean, whereas the Arctic is an area of ocean surrounded by land. This difference, together with the blanket-forming Antarctic Circumpolar Current (see Chapter 7), is the main reason why the two poles had very different climatic histories through most of the Cenozoic. Permanent ice formed in the Arctic as much as 40 million years

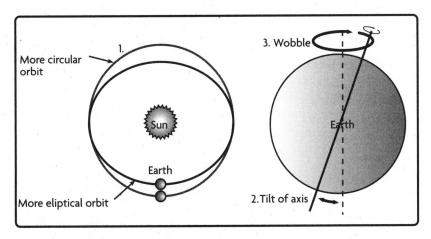

Figure 9.2 Orbital forcing, commonly called Milankovitch cycles, is due to three types of variation in the Earth's orbit around the sun: (1) variations in the shape of the orbital ellipse, a 100,000-year cycle; (2) variations in the tilt of the Earth on its axis, a 41,000-year cycle; and (3) variations in the seasons when the Earth is closest to, and farthest from, the sun (the precession of the equinoxes), a 23,000-year cycle. As orbital forcing is an aspect of planetary motion, it might be expected that these cycles would take the form of perfect sinusoidal curves, like sound waves. Not so. They interact with each other and with other planetary movements, with the result that their wavelengths commonly vary by 30 percent or more, which is one reason why curves depicting climate cycles are always irregular. It should also be remembered that orbital cycles are not new to Earth history—they have always existed; they only *seem* to belong to the Ice Ages because it was at that time that the Earth became exposed to their influence—or rather lost its capacity to resist their dictates.

after it first appeared on Antarctica. However, during the Pleistocene (2.6 million to 11,800 years ago), both poles remained frozen, and neither played a dominant role in regulating climate cycles, including sea-level changes. That job was taken over by the Arctic perimeter rather than the pole itself, for the perimeter is a mixture of land and ocean, and as such it is vulnerable to climate forcing—amplifying or driving changes and reacting rapidly to them by facilitating the formation and destruction of ice shelves. Even without any external forcing, polar ice caps have an internal cycle of expansion and regression—of formation and self-destruction. This internal cycle interacts with external forces, especially orbital changes in the Earth's rotation around the sun.

The intrinsic cycles of ice masses and the effects of orbital forces upon them are only first-order (superficial) explanations of the complications of climate cycles. The atmosphere, the oceans, solid earth, and polar ice caps all have very different time frames for heat storage and transport; that is, they have different lag times. In these (second-order) matters, Antarctica becomes the dominant player, for the continent is too big and too cold to be easily pulled around. Perhaps the Arctic perimeter can be likened to a puppy on a leash, tugging this way and that, whereas Antarctica, its master, is moved from its path only with great reluctance. At least this is the case until the puppy experiences a growth spurt and becomes strong enough to get its own way.

Exactly when and how climate behavior became overtly cyclical is unclear. The geological record has been overwritten many times, and in any case it was very different for the two poles, let alone for the rest of the world. However, as our account approaches the present, the nature of each type of cycle, its specific cause and effect, becomes increasingly distinct in both form and detail. In the 1970s it was generally believed that the Ice Ages—meaning the Pleistocene (then thought to be 1.8 million to 11,800 years ago)—consisted of four short glacial intervals (stadials) separated by long interglacial (interstadial) intervals with climates roughly similar to those of today. It is now clear that it was the other way around: the warm stable interglacials, such as we have had since the end of the Pleistocene, are the exception, not the norm. It is these warm intervals that are short-lived, accounting for only about 10 percent of a complete cycle.

There are several very different sources for information about climate cycles, but a particularly revealing one is temperature records derived from oxygen isotope ratios in the skeletons of Foraminifera. Forams that live in the ocean have shells (tests) made of calcite that contain two isotopes of oxygen (^{18}O and ^{16}O) taken directly from seawater. For each 4.2°C increase in temperature the ^{18}O component of this calcite decreases by 0.1 percent. There are both planktonic and bottom-dwelling species of forams; thus, when their shells are recovered from ocean sediment layers, they can provide details about temperature and, through extrapolations, ice volume. Foram assemblages in deep ocean cores indicate that there may have been over 40 glacial cycles throughout the Ice Ages.[1] Ice core records confirm that there have been eight major cycles during the past 740,000 years.[2] They also suggest that interglacial intervals created sea levels that may have gone well above the present level, as ice volumes fell to levels well below those of today.

Prior to about 800,000 years ago, sediment cores indicate that glacial cycles generally lasted around 41,000 years (the second cycle illustrated above). Starting about 500,000 years ago, they had a dominant periodicity of about 100,000 years (the first cycle), whereas during the intermediate period (the Mid-Pleistocene Transition) they exhibited both periodicities, with smaller amplitudes. Although the reason for these changes is not well understood, their existence—seen in both ice core and marine sediment records as well as in records of pollen and other sources—has been well substantiated.[3] They have also been faithfully reproduced by computer models.[4]

Again we return to the all-important subject of CO_2. Marine sediment records do not reveal levels of greenhouse gases, but these are preserved with astonishing resolution in ice cores. CO_2 is preserved in these cores (which are up to 4 kilometers long) because bubbles of air are entrapped when snow coalesces (sinters) into ice. These bubbles are released for analysis and dating by crushing the ice in a vacuum. Cores from Antarctica are particularly informative because of their age and their low average temperature (−55°C), which has kept deeper ice from melting. Ice cores taken from Greenland go back 100,000 years; those from two sites in Antarctica, Vostok and Dome C, date back 430,000 and 740,000 years, respectively. These samples reveal a complex of glaciation patterns centered on the two orbital periodicities of 41,000 and 100,000 years referred to earlier.

Greenhouse gases and polar temperatures change with broadly similar periodicities, suggesting a simple (and often-cited) cause-and-effect mechanism. However, the reality is not that simple: an increase in atmospheric CO_2 causes warming, but the complement is also true—warming increases atmospheric CO_2.[5] During glacial intervals, the level of CO_2 typically falls

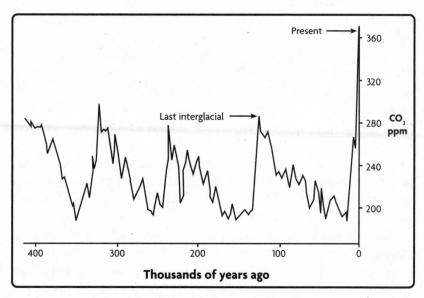

Figure 9.3   Approximate variation in CO_2 levels (in ppm) at the end of the Pleistocene, as determined from the Vostok Antarctic ice cores.

to about 180 ppm. During interglacials it rises to about 300 ppm, taking 200–1,000 years *after* the onset of warming to do so.[6] This is best seen in Dome C ice core records, which reveal increases of 75–100 ppm during each of the past four warming intervals (see the accompanying illustration). It is not clear why this increase occurs.[7] There may be several mechanisms controlling it, including methane release (see below) and the simple fact that the solubility of CO_2 in the ocean decreases as temperature increases. Reefs also play a significant role: at the top of each cycle, when continental margins are flooded and reefs proliferate, 20 percent of the biological increase in atmospheric CO_2 comes from coral growth,[8] with the gas released as coral skeletons form. This occurs because CO_2 is generated by calcification and respiration at a faster rate than it is consumed by photosynthesis.

Methane also shows cyclical behavior, linked to the monsoonal flooding of tropical marshlands and the seasonal thawing of the northern tundra.[9] One authority in this field has even suggested that methane-driven anthropogenic warming may have begun 8,000 years ago as a result of early agriculture, not 200 years ago as a result of industrialization.[10] But if in fact this was the case, the effect would have been small.

When it comes to climate change, causes and effects are not easily separated. Orbital cycles are certainly a major cause, but as they appear everywhere in the Earth's climate record—far back into the Paleozoic—they cannot have acted alone in initiating glacial cycles, nor do they have the power to force them. Perhaps they operate something like the escapement mechanism of a grandfather clock, pacing the swing of the pendulum but not providing the power behind the swing. Such swings would be considerably amplified if they initiated changes in threshold mechanisms, especially by altering heat transfer between the Northern and Southern hemispheres through changes in the path of the Gulf Stream. This may occur regularly in some sort of seesaw balance with El Niño currents of the tropical Pacific,[11] the seesaw being a frequent phenomenon that just occasionally triggers a change in the Gulf Stream, freezing the Arctic perimeter. Whether or not this is the trigger, once initiated, such a change clearly starts a relentless feedback mechanism. Ice reflects solar energy back into space in what is known as the albedo effect: the more ice, the greater the levels of albedo and subsequent cooling and, conversely, the less ice, the less albedo and the greater the warming.

Climate Flips and Events

Greenhouse gases, orbital forcing, changes in the Earth's albedo, and changes in ocean dynamics go a long way toward explaining Pleistocene climate cycles. However, as suggested by the couplet at the beginning of this chapter, smaller cycles ride on the backs of bigger ones. These are usually irregular enough to stretch the word "cycle" to the limit, so for these I now switch to the word "event," following preferred usage in the scientific literature, although the reality is usually some sort of hybrid of these two terms.

One obvious fact about Pleistocene climates is that they were erratic, characterized by sudden transitions from one state to another. This strongly suggests that the Earth's climate system depends on the existence of unstable climate thresholds; that is, it can readily flip between two (or more) control systems. Two such thresholds have been clearly identified: changes to the ocean's thermohaline circulation (see Figure 7.5) and changes to tropical atmosphere-ocean dynamics. Full explanations of both thresholds thus far remain elusive,[12] for they must account not only for the major glacial cycles themselves but also for sudden events *within* these cycles.[13]

Two categories of abrupt climate change dominate glacial intervals: Dansgaard-Oeschger events and Heinrich events. Dansgaard-Oeschger events are repeated every 3,000–4,500 years, as recorded in Greenland ice cores and elsewhere.[14] They typically start with a rapid atmospheric warming of 5°–10°C (or an adjacent sea *surface* temperature increase of 2°–4°C) over a few decades, followed by a brief warm plateau, then cooling over a few centuries. Explanations for these excursions are mostly centered on changes to the thermohaline circulation, although alternatively they may be caused by oscillations in tropical ocean temperature, given that the oceans have the Earth's greatest capacity for heat transport.

Heinrich events are largely responsible for periods of almost instantaneous sea-level rise. They are very brief intervals of cooling followed by rapid warming, at least in the North Atlantic. These events are recorded in layers of sediment left by vast armadas of icebergs entering the North Atlantic from Baffin Bay (the western arm of the North Atlantic between Canada and Greenland) as a result of periodic collapses of the Laurentian ice shelf, a vast area of Canada. As ice accumulates on land, bottom layers start to melt, at rates that depend on the weight and temperature of the upper layers. This causes immense ice sheets to collapse—to slide into the ocean as fast-moving glaciers—raising the sea level if they are extensive enough. This in turn destabilizes ice sheets elsewhere by helping them float free of any seafloor on which they rest. And so a domino effect is produced, simultaneously affecting grounded ice everywhere around the world.

Small Events That Matter

Of course there are yet smaller events—climate "flickers" for want of a better word. Some are created by changes in the intensity of thermohaline forcing.[15] Others are abrupt warming intervals that appear to have El Niño–like origins,[16] or perhaps oscillations initiated by El Niño cycles and exported via atmospheric connections (teleconnections) toward the poles in coordination with orbital forcing.[17] There are also events with even shorter (decadal to century-long) periodicities that, if created in one part of the world, may have time-lagged or scant relevance in other parts. Such events have no direct influence on reefs, but they must be taken into account if we seek to separate human-induced climate change from background changes.

Rapid Temperature Increases Occur
Only during Glacial Intervals

Observations that rapid temperature increases have often occurred in the past wrongly imply that any rapid changes taking place today are normal rather than human induced. It *is* true that rapid rates of climate change have occurred many times in the past—in fact they are commonplace—but they occur only during glacial intervals.

Some past interglacial intervals have lasted much longer than the entire Holocene—at least four times as long—and probably exhibited all the climate variability that we have seen so far during the Holocene, and more. The best known of these short-term events occurred during the last interglacial, when intervals of extreme cold (seen in Greenland ice cores) appear to have lasted for as little as a decade during otherwise warm climes.[18]

However, it is intervals of abrupt warming in an already warm world that concern us today. Has today's climate change happened before? Antarctica's temperature has frequently gone higher than present norms as a result of natural oscillations in our climate, but these oscillations are not the same phenomena as the warming we are currently experiencing and are destined to experience over the coming century as atmospheric greenhouse gas levels rise. Pleistocene icehouse Earth has temperature oscillations, primarily at high latitudes; pre-Pleistocene Earth was much more stable, the only upward instability being occasional sudden sea-level rises, presumably resulting from the collapse of ice shelves. I stress that I am referring only to *abrupt* (in human terms) warming. As I discussed in Chapter 7, there were many instances in the past in which increased warming occurred in an already warm world (notably during the Late Oligocene, 27 mya, and the Pliocene, 5.3–2.6 mya). But these had orbital periodicities and the process took thousands of years—although in geological time they are considered "abrupt." Today's rate of warming of an already warm world appears to be a unique event in all known Earth history.

Sea Levels When They *Really* Mattered to Coral Reefs

Sea-level changes relative to land, as we have seen many times, have several very different causes—including regional land movements, seafloor spreading, and glacial cycles—that greatly affect both the rate and the degree of

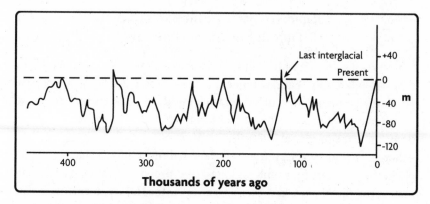

Figure 9.4   Sea-level changes (in meters) at the end of the Pleistocene as determined from the Vostok Antarctic ice cores. It is likely that sea level on the GBR was 5–7 meters above present during several of these interglacial intervals.

change. When considering the Ice Ages, we are concerned with rapid rates of change (over thousands of years) that are caused by glacial cycles, not slow changes (over many millions of years) caused by land movements.

Sea levels do not normally respond as rapidly as any measurement of atmospheric climate changes described above, but the two may be closely connected, depending on the nature of the change. Dansgaard-Oeschger events may have little influence on sea level because of the lag time of ocean temperature change, whereas Heinrich events, although primarily an atmospheric phenomenon, cause the sudden increases in sea level I mentioned earlier in response to the collapse of ice shelves.

Throughout the Ice Ages, sea-level changes were of overwhelming importance to coral reefs, and it is not difficult to see why. In conditions of relatively stable sea level, such as we have today, coral reefs can grow vertically to mid- to high-tide levels. Thereafter they can expand only horizontally. If the sea level falls, the reef will either be planed off or become aerially exposed as a slab of terrestrial limestone. This limestone will then either persist or not, depending on whether it is thick enough or resistant enough to endure subsequent aerial erosion. If the sea level rises, reefs will grow vertically, provided that the rate of rise is slow enough or the degree of rise small enough for sufficient sunlight to penetrate to allow coral and coralline algal growth. Otherwise the living veneer will "drown" as light attenuation through the water column progressively increases.

What matters is the relative height of sea and land, for vertical movements of either will have the same effect. Changes in the absolute height of the sea (such as might be measured by a satellite) on scales relevant to coral reefs are the same everywhere, so different rates of contemporaneous change between one region and another are due entirely to vertical movements of land. Thus sea-level curves determined in one part of the world have scant relevance to other parts if vertical land movements are not factored in.

The combination of changing heights of land and sea in different parts of the world and in different time frames leads to an almost endless array of different types of reef remnants. For example, reef limestone is found from moderately deep oceans to mountaintops, and the thickness of limestone beneath living reefs, irrespective of how long they have taken to form, can vary from several kilometers to almost nothing. The best example of thick reef limestone is seen in the vast Calcareous Alps of Austria or the Dolomite ranges of Italy, built on sinking shorelines of the constantly changing Tethys (see Chapter 5). The other extreme occurs where reefs have grown as far as they can vertically on a stable substrate. Such reefs may preserve some record of sea-level change if they are able to grow horizontally (prograde), but these records will always be thin and vulnerable to obliteration the next time the sea level falls. To illustrate this point, if there had been no subsidence allowing reefs to grow upward and thicker, neither the carbonate mountains of Austria and Italy nor the atolls of Micronesia would now exist, because any limestone that originally formed would only have been a thin layer and would have readily eroded away. Furthermore, without the uplift that occurred after they formed, there would probably be no evidence that the Calcareous Alps—among the most massive reefs of all time—had *ever* existed. It is therefore reasonable to suppose that many reefs as large as the GBR have existed in the past, but are now gone without having left a trace.

Ice Age sea-level changes occurred in response to polar glaciation, but these were not necessarily linked to polar temperatures. Sea ice, which accumulates in vast quantities around Antarctica and in the North Atlantic as the ocean freezes with the onset of their respective winters, influences the thermohaline circulation directly, yet it cannot influence sea level because (like ice cubes in a glass of water) the weight of ice displaces an equal weight of the ocean on which it floats. It is only when ice accumulates on land (and that principally means Antarctica today) as snow that water is actually extracted from the oceans. Therefore, for the sea level to be low it is necessary to have both low polar temperatures and adequate quantities of atmos-

·pheric water, as are normally found in the warm tropics. It is then also necessary to have an atmospheric circulation that transports water from the
tropics to polar landmasses. Optimal conditions for glacial sea-level changes
are therefore warm humid tropics and cold dry poles, with good atmospheric circulation between the two—low temperatures at the poles do not
act alone in creating low sea levels. Clearly the thermal inertia of the oceans
and the strength of ocean circulation pathways play a big part in this, and
there are several seemingly unlikely feedback mechanisms (and no doubt
others yet to be discovered) that affect it. For example, the strength of the
Ocean Conveyor is influenced by the speed of rotation of the Earth. This
speed changes with polar ice volume in order to maintain the Earth's angu-
lar momentum—just as a spinning ballerina alters her rate of spin by moving her arms and legs to redistribute her weight.

Was It Too Cold?

Unlike sea levels, temperature changes over glacial cycles vary in different
parts of the world. There are hundreds of published estimates of ocean temperatures over geological time derived from oxygen isotope studies of

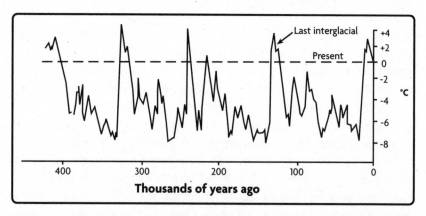

Figure 9.5   Temperature cycles at the end of the Pleistocene as determined from
the Vostok Antarctic ice cores. The last interglacial probably had two or three
peaks, although average temperatures were similar to those of today. These
measurements have uncertain relevance to other parts of the world, especially
the tropics, for they are not global means. They are, however, the most detailed
records of atmospheric temperature in existence.

bottom-dwelling microfossils (usually Foraminifera), and comparing them with their modern analogues. These can only be crude estimates when applied to extensive reef areas because of the complexities of reef currents. In principle, local temperature varies according to tides, upwelling, weather, and exposure to oceanic currents. To see what impacts low temperatures might have had on the GBR, we can limit ourselves in both space and time and go directly to northeast Australia and the last glacial cycle.

An expensive and much-cited international project, CLIMAP, indicated that minimum sea surface temperatures in the region of the GBR at the last glacial maximum were 4°C *higher* than they are today,[19] a finding that started the myth that the tropics were not affected by Ice Age cycles. Subsequent studies contradicted CLIMAP, finding that temperatures were 1°–2°C lower.[20] We need not go into the qualifications and questions that surround these results. For a convincing array of reasons, it seems that the tropical Pacific as a whole was probably no more than 3°–4°C cooler over the last glacial cycle than it is at present,[21] although it could have been up to 5°C cooler during earlier glacial maxima.[22] That is probably as cold as it has ever been on the GBR throughout the entire time of its existence.

There is one detail in this scenario that is especially relevant to the GBR. Ever since the CLIMAP results were published there have been conflicting views on the extent of cooling of the whole Western Pacific Warm Pool at the last glacial maximum—a time when temperature impacts would presumably have been the greatest. It now seems likely that at that time El Niño events would have been different from those of today, with substantially lower sea surface temperatures dominating in the eastern Pacific and cold, dry atmospheric conditions prevailing across Greater Australia and Southeast Asia. However, sea surface temperatures of the western Pacific were probably no lower than 2°C below present norms, and the Western Pacific Warm Pool itself would have remained much as it is today, although less mobile.[23] A sophisticated global computer simulation model produces predictions that agree with this synopsis of the geological data.[24]

There is no evidence that the GBR as a whole was ever subjected to low temperatures that would have been lethal to corals (prolonged lows of less than 14°C) during the Pleistocene (since 2.6 mya). Windchill may have taken its toll during glacial maxima, yet it would not have had as great an impact on reef flats as might be supposed: with repeated changes in sea level, there would seldom have been any reef flats to chill. Cold may occasionally have taken its toll on reef-building corals at greater depths, and perhaps on other reef-dwelling animals, but compared to the havoc created by sea-level changes, such instances would have been of minor importance and of only local significance.

The GBR in Kangaroo Country and
Coral Reef Modes

I conclude this chapter by returning to the beginning. Over the past 2.6 million years, the province we call the GBR dramatically changed its appearance many times—and did so radically. For 10–20 percent of the Pleistocene it would have looked something like it does today. For 50 percent of the time it would have looked and felt something like an inland cattle station does today, with semidesert scrub and cold nights and hot days. For the remainder it would have been a changing mixture of islands and reefs. The

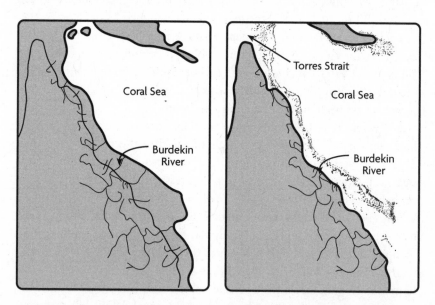

Figure 9.6   The GBR province in kangaroo country mode (left, where the entire region would have looked much like an inland cattle station today) and today's coral reef mode (right). Even within a single glacial cycle (discussed in Chapter 10), much of the GBR oscillated several times between these modes (illustrated in Figure 10.2).

islands, which would have formed as the sea invaded the land, would probably have been well forested, as rainfall at these times was relatively high. The reefs would have been of the fringing variety or wave-washed ridges of older limestone, some submerged and others not. It is hard to imagine this weird, mutable place. We now turn to the last glacial cycle, for it is here that we can explore these changes in fascinating detail.

— 10 —

The Last Glacial Cycle

From the last interglacial to the present time, sea-level changes and the environments that accompanied them are understood in some detail. This allows the history of GBR corals to be examined closely. Dramatic changes to the reefs of the GBR during the last glacial cycle are largely responsible for their modern appearance; the reefs we see today have a living veneer less than 6,000 years old.

In this chapter we watch as changing sea levels expose and reflood the coastline, altering the region we now call the GBR from reef mode to kangaroo country mode and back again in less time than it takes a small hill to erode or a scrubland to become a rainforest. Although we are still looking at climatic events from a geological perspective, we can now see the direct effects of a major climate change on reef life today. Both modes are still called "the GBR" as I defined it in the last chapter, but we see that biological reefs—those with a living veneer—are far more transitory than their limestone geological counterparts.

The last glacial cycle, which spanned only about 5 percent of the full duration of the Ice Ages, is the most important single event in the history of all reef-dwelling organisms alive today. We tend to think about this cycle in terms of the geological changes it created and the climatic mechanisms that drove it. However, as far as reef life is concerned, we also see that evolutionary, biogeographic, and genetic adjustments do not end with the stabilizing of sea levels; they are still taking place and are indeed unlikely to end because the evolutionary goalposts are shifting as climates are once again on the move.

As in other parts of this book, factual information has to be spiked here and there with a little imagination. This time we have to conjure up a strange

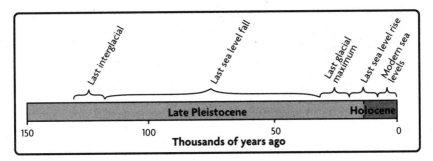

Figure 10.1 Geological setting of events described in this chapter.

countryside precisely where the GBR is now, where extensive scrubland, mangroves, and forested islands take the place of reefs; rivers snake through scrub where fishermen now drive their boats; and shorelines have cliffs and surfing beaches where there is now deep ocean. Where are the corals in this world that was? That is a question I believe we can answer.

To put this chapter into a human perspective, the start of the last glacial cycle (140,000 years ago) is about the time of the origin of the earliest totally modern humans. The origin of the GBR as we now know it (6,000 years ago) was about the time that humans built their first substantial houses.

The GBR we enjoy today—the living veneer—is indeed a very recent phenomenon, for it was only 20,000 years ago that the sea reached one of its lowest points in the entire Cenozoic, about 130 meters below present level. As more than 99 percent of all of the GBR's coral communities are shallower than 130 meters, all of them must be younger than 20,000 years—much younger—for the sea took over 10,000 years to return to its present level and it took thousands more for fully developed reef ecosystems to reshape a seascape that had not been theirs for 80,000 years.

Today the causes and effects of sea-level change have become matters of heightened interest, for the sea never remains peaceful for long, and further changes are on the way. Although this is not a subject most reef biologists think about, what we actually see when we look at a reef—its appearance and much of its biology—is largely a product of the last glacial cycle. Many of the physiological and genetic adaptations that we see today are evolutionary outcomes of environments that no longer exist. Even the colorful aerial photographs of today's reefs, such as those included in this book, are temporary artifacts of an unusually long period of sea-level stability. Reefs did not "normally" look as they do now, and when the sea level starts rising again they will no longer look as they do now. Sea level has seldom been as stable as it has been during the latter half of the Holocene; whatever the future holds, the level of the sea is certain to change.

The Onset of the Last Glacial Cycle

The sea-level rise at the end of the penultimate glacial interval (at the left of the accompanying diagram) started 140,000 years ago and was very rapid—similar to the most recent rise resulting in today's level. This was followed by an interglacial that lasted a little longer than our Holocene has so far. At that time the Earth was mostly as warm as, or warmer than, it is today, and global sea levels peaked 5–7 meters higher, as polar ice melted back into the oceans.[1]

Sea level started decreasing from the last interglacial high around 120,000 years ago, not as a smooth decrease, but rather with an initial plunge fol-

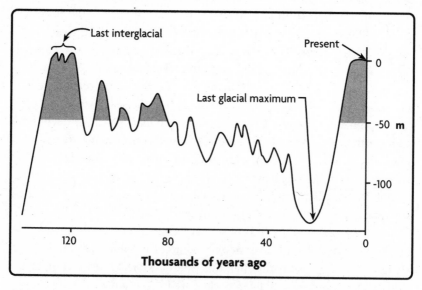

Figure 10.2   Sea-level change over the last glacial cycle. Depths are in meters below present. The shaded area indicates the time intervals when at least some part of the outer GBR lagoon would have been flooded enough for reef growth. Thus, even within this single glacial cycle, the GBR oscillated between coral reef and kangaroo country modes. There would always have been fringing reefs on the continental shelf edge, but at different positions depending on the sea level.

lowed by a string of major reversals, as shown in the illustration. (Accounts of sea levels over this time differ widely; the illustration given here is derived from studies of the fossil reefs of the Huon Peninsula of Papua New Guinea,[2] backed up by a more recent and detailed study in the Red Sea.[3]) These curves are corrected to show ice volume rather than sea level to remove the effects of local land movements. At any one point in time the sea level is almost the same everywhere. It leaves marks on land at precisely the same height, like the rings in a bathtub. It is subsequent land movements that disrupt these rings and create apparent disparities in sea-level reconstructions between one geographic area and another. The Huon reefs, which comfortably span the time we are now looking at, show that during the last decline sea levels fluctuated considerably. Heinrich events accounted for much of this fluctuation, or at least they amplified it.

Overall the sea level decreased 130 meters in about 100,000 years, an average rate of 13 cm per century. However, this overall decrease obscures a much more rapid decrease, for 30,000 years ago the sea plunged 70 meters in less than 5,000 years, at a peak rate of perhaps 1.5 meters per century,[4] creating the biggest impact on coral reefs of the whole glacial cycle. This did not happen to reefs such as we see today; the GBR at that time would have been a mixture of limestone islands left from previous high sea-level stands (later to become some of the reefs we have today), interspersed with deeper reefs already planed off by earlier low sea levels.

A century is a long time for a coral community, and a sea-level decrease of even 1.5 meters (1.5 centimeters per year) is of little consequence. Except for reef flats, even this rate of decrease would have been too slow to be the singular cause of coral extinctions, although it would have created some pressure on other organisms dependent upon the reef structure. There are plenty of coral species that grow only in shallow water (such as *Acropora papillare*, illustrated in Plate 21), but they all reach reproductive maturity in less than a decade, over which time the sea would have dropped only 15 centimeters. Sea-level decrease throughout the whole onset of glaciation was slow enough for extinction rates of coral species to remain unaffected. In short, coral communities of all types grew, changed, and disappeared independently of anything the sea level did. Moreover, although many reef microhabitats would have decreased in number as the reef became less well developed and consolidated, the range of microhabitat types at coral colony scales would generally have persisted.[5] Nevertheless, as the rate of sea-level decrease picked up and lagoonal habitats became increasingly scarce, corals (and the life that depended on them) that normally lived exclusively in shallow lagoons would have had to adapt to the relatively exposed conditions of reef edges or be locally extinguished. Repeated rapid sea-level changes may therefore be the reason why there are no long-lived coral species on the GBR today that are restricted to very shallow water.

Changing Shorelines as Sea Level Decreased

The position of the outer shoreline of the GBR would have oscillated back and forth as the last glacial cycle progressed, yet overall it crept eastward toward the edge of the continental shelf. The rate would have depended on local water depths: it would have been up to 1 kilometer per century in the south, decreasing to 100 meters per century or less in the central north, where the shelf is narrow. A mass of islands, beaches, estuaries, promontories, and mangrove forests would have continued to mark the coastline throughout most of this time—much as they do now—until most of today's GBR became land. Temporary fringing reefs may have formed in some places, although these would seldom have developed to the present extent. When the sea level reached −70 meters, most of what we now know as the lagoon area would have been exposed. As a result, the shoreline would have become less complex and the diversity of habitats would have declined sharply, especially in the north, where no inter-reef areas reach this depth and the outer reef face, as described for Tijou Reef in Chapter 1, forms a straight line that plunges down the side of the Queensland Trough.

Although the Australian continent became increasingly arid as the glacial cycle deepened, rivers still flowed, and their mouths would have nurtured a range of habitats similar to those of today, except that most would have been at the edge of the continental shelf as shown in Figure 9.6. The whole coastal zone would have become highly eroded, with rivers moving sediments of both marine and terrestrial origin eastward toward the outer reefs, to be either sequestered on the outer shelf or discharged directly into deep ocean.

Torres Strait dried out several times during the early sea-level lows, after which it formed a long-term land bridge between Australia and Papua New Guinea—a bridge that has been present to some extent throughout most of the existence of Greater Australia. For most of the glacial cycle, the Torres Land Bridge (when it was not Torres Strait) would have been vegetated by tropical savannah, enabling all manner of marsupials and other terrestrial plants and animals to cross. However, the crossings during the latter part of the glacial cycle were not like those of earlier cycles—the later crossings, unfortunately for Australia's megafauna, included humans.

Ribbon reefs would have become limestone walls with very steep cliffs formed by waves undercutting vulnerable surfaces (such as the face illustrated in Plate 37). Savannah scrub would have grown behind these walls, in some places less than a kilometer from the sea. The walls themselves would have been covered by sharp karst-eroded limestone, perhaps with pockets of spiky *Spinifex* grass growing where there was enough soil and water for them to eke out a living. Lower down the outer slope, wave action would have been heavy as the waves broke onto, rather than over, reef surfaces. Presumably coralline algae formed a protective shield against wave erosion and, as wave turbulence would have been strong for most of the year, the algal zone would have been wide and thick, as seen around exposed Pacific atolls today.

The sea level was −100 meters both 30,000 and 14,000 years ago, the former point in time when it receded and the latter when it reflooded. Over this 16,000-year interval, coral communities initially at a depth of 50 meters would have changed their species composition as the sea level fell. However, for the first time in many thousands of years, they would not have changed their actual geographic location; that is, they would not have had to move, because they would have remained within the depth that sunlight could penetrate sufficiently for coral growth. Thus for some coral communities, rather than being a time of great disturbance as has been supposed, this is likely to have been a period of relative stability, time enough for consolidated reefs to develop, albeit ones without the zones that we see today. Such reef development would have depended largely on local environmental conditions, especially the amount and composition of sediment being transported to the reef edge by rivers. In the far north these impacts would have been relatively small, for such rivers as there were would have discharged their sediment loads directly into the depths of the Queensland Trough.

Corals at the Last Glacial Maximum

Several authors have speculated about the fate of corals during the last glacial maximum. Was there a refuge? Did they return from what are now deeper reefs of the Marion Plateau?[6] The answer is actually quite simple once a few points about coral habitat requirements are reiterated: (1) A sea-level drop of 70 meters in 5,000 years would not cause regional extinctions because corals are capable of relocating quickly enough to cope with even this rate of change thanks to their mobile larvae. (2) Corals do not need reefs to survive. (3) Increases in turbidity, if there were any, would not have done much harm. As we have seen, fringing reefs associated with partly turbid water have more species than blue-water oceanic reefs. (4) Even the worst-case scenario for decrease in sea surface temperature is unlikely to have had widespread lethal consequences for any corals. The inescapable conclusion is that the last sea-level decrease had little long-term impact on the large-scale distribution of most corals. They would simply have relocated, and they had plenty of time and capacity to do so. They may not have had time to build wave-resistant reefs such as we see today in what are now well-submerged locations, but they had time enough to build fringing reefs and all manner of nonreef communities.

The Last Great Sea-Level Rise

Around 20,000 years ago the Earth went into an orbital configuration that triggered massive warming despite the sunlight-reflecting (albedo) effect of the ice that covered nearly a third of all the land. These ice sheets were enormously thick, typically 2–3 kilometers, and their retreat involved the melting of a staggering 60 million cubic kilometers of ice,[7] mostly from the vast Arctic perimeter of the time. The release of this weight of ice from landmasses and the addition of the weight of water flooding onto continental margins caused the height of land areas to change everywhere. Earth tremors and tsunamis would have been frequent events along many shorelines, although the effect on the GBR was probably small.

Just how long the sea remained at the lowest level of the last glacial maximum is debatable even though much is known about its rise since that time—like new footprints in sand, the record has not been overwritten by later events. Once the turnaround started it was rapid, similar to that of the previous glacial rise.[8] In any event, the rise was a continuous process, with occasional surges of up to 1.5 meters per century, presumably as a result of Heinrich events.

Up to about 14,000 years ago, with the sea level at −100 meters, the coastline would have been relatively straight, especially in the north. The ribbon reefs may have looked much as they did when the sea level decreased, except for the effects of an additional 16,000 years' worth of erosion (as illustrated in Plate 37). Most of the gaps between them would have remained above sea

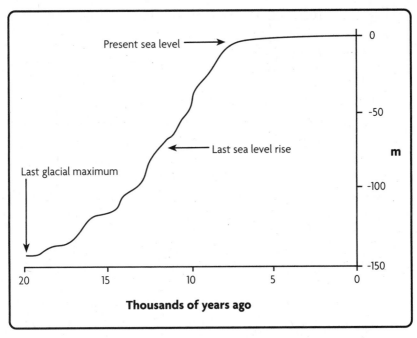

Figure 10.3 The last great sea-level rise. Depths are in meters below present. If it were shown in more detail, much of this curve would have a sawtooth appearance, reflecting sea-level surges. The effects of this flooding on the GBR would have varied geographically, as the outer shelf, depending on width, would have tilted down a few meters under the weight of overlying water.

level, except at river openings. However, all river mouths would probably have been too deep for cascades or waterfalls to form, and their openings would have been at sea level, much as they are today.

Ten thousand years ago, once the sea had risen to −50 meters, the coastline started to change, especially in the central and southern regions, where it again became a line of headlands, beaches, estuaries, promontories, and islands (illustrated in Plate 38). The atmospheric temperature by this time had become warmer than today, and there was more rainfall. The coastline would have had mangroves, rainforests, and/or eucalypt forests growing near the reefs, just as they now do along the Daintree coast of northern Queensland. The greatest difference between then and now is that for much of the GBR these would have been the outermost reefs. There would have been no extensive reef area farther seaward of the nearshore coastline and the landscape farther inland would have been flat scrubland, except where it was studded with limestone hills, many of which underlie lagoonal platform reefs today. Strong waves driven by the now-reestablished seasonal monsoons as well as occasional cyclones would have pounded unprotected parts of the coast. When the sea level reached –30 meters, the outermost lines of forests would have been reduced to large caylike islands where reefs are today. Much of the northern region and finally Torres Strait reflooded, once again separating Australia from New Guinea.

Sediment discharge from rivers, especially rivers crossing the central and southern sectors, would have greatly affected the fate of reefs at that time. The largest river in the central region, the Burdekin, still leaves its mark as a channel, now largely infilled with sediment, extending for about 160 kilometers from its present mouth almost to the outermost reefs.[9] At low sea levels, sediment from the land would have reached the outer shelf, to be discharged into deep ocean, not sequestered onto the inshore part of the GBR as it is today.

The sea reached its present level around 6,000 years ago (estimates vary by as much as ±1,500 years) and is unlikely to have gone higher than present, as once believed. As the GBR flooded, inshore reefs were slightly uplifted, while most of the shelf tilted downward, deceptively suggesting that the sea level went higher than it actually did.

The Return of the Corals

How did corals cope with these changes? As I mentioned in Chapter 3, the normal rate of reef growth (not to be confused with the faster rates of growth of coral colonies) is about 0.6 meters per century. Even so, reef growth could not have kept pace with intervals of rapid sea-level rise. Reefs that began growing at times of very low sea levels would have gradually begun to grow more slowly as the water above them became deeper and light levels decreased, until they stopped growing altogether. These reefs would have drowned or become banks of the calcareous green alga *Halimeda*, containing only a few corals that are tolerant of deep water. However, coral species themselves would have been little affected: those limited to shallow water would simply have moved up, via their larvae, colonizing available substrates as they flooded. As more depth-tolerant corals moved in behind them, all reef faces would have had zones similar to those of today, but they would have been mobile, moving up at the same pace as the sea level. At any particular spot on a reef face there would have been a progression over time of ecological changes mimicking those we now see when diving down a reef face. Again, the greatest impact would have been on species restricted to shallow water. However, as none of these form colonies anywhere near 100 years old, no species alive today would have been affected by depth changes resulting from sea-level rise. That may not always have been the case throughout the Ice Ages, for a comparison between the pre–Ice Age corals of the Era Beds and those of today shows that some species went extinct.

Ghosts of the Past

I will not describe the massive distribution changes glacial cycles must have inflicted on all high-latitude fauna and flora on land as well as in the ocean.[10] Range shifts in the Atlantic, especially for molluscs, have attracted attention primarily because the fossil record for them is so good. However, the fossil record of corals offers little insight into Pleistocene changes in coral reefs other than in the sorts of range shifts I have already mentioned. With or without fossil evidence, changes in distribution patterns we observe today show that latitudinal movements of most reef fauna could have occurred over time intervals as short as a few decades.

If we imagine the Earth viewed through a time-lapse camera mounted on a satellite, we would see reefs gradually come and go in response to sea levels rising and falling in time with the formation and retreat of the polar ice caps. Within these great cycles we would see the many smaller cycles and events I have already described, some of which would cause relatively minor changes in reef distribution, with a few having a greater effect. If we then focused on what the corals were doing, we would see a barrage of rapid flickers—each flicker being a major distribution change—at intervals of a century or less. If our satellite technology were up to it, we would also see a kaleidoscope of rapidly changing gene pools forever interacting with one another—fusing here, breaking there, and forming thousands of temporarily isolated patches.

Considering the physical devastation of the last glacial cycle, compounded by the many similar cycles that came before, the diversity of life we see on reefs today bears testimony to the capacity of reef fauna to accommodate this kind of change. At least it seems so at first glance. But appearances can be deceptive. Ghosts of the past are everywhere—genetic ghosts concealed in living bodies. This goes to the heart of the concept of reticulate evolution (see Chapter 3), in which species are not seen as genetically isolated "natural units," but rather where species, subspecies, hybrids, and the like all link up genetically and are essentially different combinations of the same thing. What we have today is a world in which species units are so genetically unstable that they maintain their separate identities only by the flimsiest of mechanisms.

Clearly, changing sea levels, currents, and local environmental conditions have kept genetic ghosts (sometimes known as chimeras) of all descriptions alive because the genetic pot has been stirred so frequently. A particular phenotype (what a "species" looks like) may disguise many genotypes (their genetic composition), and conversely a particular genotype may have many different phenotypes, depending on the environment in which it grows. (See the discussion of growth forms in Chapter 3.)

Corals—and no doubt a wealth of other plant and animal taxa—are still coming to terms with the world in which they now live, and it seems that they are sometimes ill equipped to do so, because they arose in environments that no longer exist. The symbiosis between corals and their algae is a case in point. Corals appear to have been able to tolerate the ravages of the Ice Ages amazingly well because they evolved to tolerate an icehouse world. Just how far that tolerance will extend into the world of the future is something we have good reason to question. Before pursuing this subject, we must first turn back to address a long-standing controversy—just how old is the GBR?

Many Origins

Scientific interest in the geological origins of reefs has a long history in which the GBR figures prominently. Interpretation of results from reef coring is in conflict with paleoclimatic, geographic, and biogeographic reconstructions. It is concluded that the GBR has existed far longer than the Middle Pleistocene reefs we have today, probably because earlier reefs were greatly eroded during Early Pleistocene low sea-level stands. The GBR, in one guise or another, is at least 25 million years old.

There is a great difference between my understanding of the antiquity of the GBR (at least 25 million years) and that of most reef geologists (less than 1 million years). We have to look at the future of the GBR through a combination of sciences, not just geology, and that is also how we can best understand its past. Certainly reefs are geological structures, yet they are made by living organisms and, as such, are subject to the biological and environmental tolerances of those organisms.

Original Ideas about Reef Building

How old, many have asked, is the GBR? The question itself is not a new one, for coral reefs have attracted the attention of scientists—and demanded scientific explanation of their existence—since the earliest voyages of discovery to the Caribbean and the tropical Pacific.

The famous Scottish geologist Charles Lyell, whose three-volume treatise *Principles of Geology* (1830–1833) dominated geological thought throughout much of his century, realized the importance of uplift and subsidence for reef growth. However, he believed that corals themselves played but a small part in reef building; he thought they simply grew atop submerged mountains. Atolls, he concluded, were coral-encrusted rims of volcanoes, and archipelagos were the products of vertical movements of the Earth's crust. This, he proposed, explained both the proliferation of low islands in the western Pacific and the remains of marine life now found high on mountain slopes the world over. Lyell himself never saw a reef; he based his ideas about them on the descriptions of explorers and, in effect, supported what many mariners had originally proposed. Twenty years later, Charles Darwin came up with a different view—that reefs are built by corals growing on sinking seafloors and that atolls are all that remain of mountains that have sunk far below the sea surface over vastly long periods of time.[1] How right he was.

The many accounts of Darwin's famous theory of atoll formation (and illustrations of it such as the one here) tend to give the impression that the oceans are full of mountains that conveniently subside to allow atolls to form. This is, of course, not the case. Most of the world's reefs that existed in times past were victims of seafloor spreading: they slid under plate margins, were submerged in the ocean depths and dissolved, or were uplifted so that at least their remains can still be found. Others, including most surviving reefs of the Mesozoic Tethys (see Figure 7.2) have had a sort of Darwinian history, for they grew (on and off, as and when environments allowed) on substrates that usually subsided slowly enough to allow reefs to grow, yet

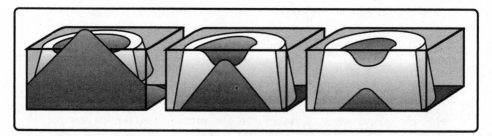

Figure 11.1   Darwin's theory of atoll formation. Reefs grow around a volcanic island (left). When that mountain subsides below sea level, the reef continues to grow and maintain its position relative to sea level (center). The atoll that results is a wall of coral, often with islands around its circular rim (right). Reefs with this type of origin are not restricted to atolls; they occur in any area where the substrate subsides. There are no atolls as such on the GBR proper, although reefs in the far north have atoll-like origins. Elizabeth and Middleton reefs south of the GBR (see Figure 11.3) may actually be atolls.

not so fast that they drowned. No matter that these were mostly barrier reefs rather than atolls. On the other hand, there are reefs that once grew, or now grow, on relatively stable substrates, including those generally associated with continental margins. These include most of today's barrier reefs, as well as many that formed when epicontinental seas flooded Europe and North Africa. The best-known and largest barrier reef today is the GBR, and Darwin's theory of atolls comes up continually in accounts of its history.[2] The association seems indelible, despite the fact that the GBR grows on one of the most stable continental margins in the world, one that may not have flexed or moved vertically by more than 100 meters or so over the past 40 million years.

There were, however, rivals to Darwin's theory. In two papers published in 1910 and 1915, the Canadian geologist Reginald Daly expounded the now largely forgotten glacial control theory of reef development, in which he proposed that decreasing sea levels during Pleistocene glaciations (at his time a fairly novel idea) would cause reefs to be planed off.[3] They would then grow afresh when the sea rose again. No fewer than 20 theories—or rather variations on the themes of Darwin and Daly—were put forward by geologists in the century after Darwin's book appeared.

Darwin himself, although rather more preoccupied with human evolution than with reefs, took some further part in this early debate.[4] Just before he died, he wrote to Alexander Agassiz of the Museum of Comparative Zoology at Harvard University: "If I am wrong, the sooner I am knocked on the head and annihilated so much the better . . . I wish that some doubly rich millionaire would take it into his head to have borings made in some of the Pacific and Indian atolls."[5] In 1896 an exploratory bore, specifically intended to test Darwin's theory, was sunk on a Tuvalu reef by the Royal Society. It reached a depth of 340 meters, vindicating Darwin, although the extract was inconclusive and the project was abandoned before the drill struck bedrock.

Darwin's wish finally came true in its entirety 56 years later—his "millionaire" being the U.S. Atomic Energy Commission. In preparation for nuclear testing, the commission sunk a series of deep boreholes at Enewetak Atoll in the northern Marshall Islands. If the reef limestone had not formed a thick layer, Lyell's views and Daly's theory would be upheld. If it *was* thick, Darwin would finally triumph. There was immense public interest in this issue: Darwin had predicted that atolls might be 5,000 feet (1,525 meters) thick—an extraordinarily prophetic guess. The first two boreholes reached volcanic foundations at 1,267 and 1,405 meters.[6]

How could Darwin have been so accurate? He might have had some idea as to how thick the Calcareous Alps of Austria were, or he might have estimated subsidence rates of volcanoes and looked at what was known at that time about the depths of the ocean in which they occur. The maximum amount of ocean seafloor subsidence in the Pacific, from surface to seafloor, is about 3,500 meters—this, in theory, is the greatest thickness any Pacific reef could attain. The greatest thickness of any reef produced by subsidence anywhere in the world is that of the Bahama Banks, which reaches 4,235 meters.

A total of 11 authors, in addition to those just mentioned, had something to say about this topic during the nineteenth century.[7] This number of publications is not many by today's standards, yet at that time they dominated scientific interest in reef geology. I do not propose to delve into the various hypotheses, because they are of only historical interest: every major geographic region on Earth has its own unique geological history, which, when combined with the effects of sea-level changes and temperature, makes the history of any reef a highly individual matter and one not readily accounted for by any general theory.

Ideas about the Origin of the GBR

Interest in the origins of the GBR arose in those early days and has never slackened. By the mid-1980s, some hundred articles offering opinions about its age had been published.[8] The following is a brief summary of the evolving views on the antiquity and present morphology of the GBR; each is followed by a comment (in italics) based on views presented in this book:

- By the mid-1960s: "Most authorities consider the whole thickness of the coral-bearing material to be of 'Recent' age."[9] *These observations had to be supposition as there was no evidence to support or refute them.*
- By the early 1970s: "The Queensland shelf did not support a reef province of any magnitude until post-Pleistocene time." In any event, any preexisting reefs had been removed by erosion.[10] *Post-Pleistocene means Holocene today, but this distinction was vague at the time.*
- During the mid-1970s (with Edward Purdy's hypothesis in mind): A pre-Holocene basement underlies the modern GBR to a depth of about 200 meters.[11] (Purdy's antecedent karst hypothesis is one of the more widely accepted concepts of reef accretion. From work in the Caribbean, Purdy proposed that reefs are composed of successive

layers of limestone, each layer overlying an earlier layer in response to a sea-level rise. Not only does this create the layered internal morphology of reefs seen in seismic profiles, it also controls their modern shape and position.) *A well-supported concept; however, there are so many exceptions to this theory in different parts of the world that its general applicability must now be questioned.*

- By the late 1970s: Many authors agree that the reefs of the GBR had an antecedent pre-Holocene basement on which reefs formed according to Maxwell's original (1968) idea of changing reef morphologies, and that the GBR is thickest at the shelf edge.[12] (Maxwell proposed that reefs evolve into new shapes because corals grow best in shallow tidal currents and ultimately choke off lagoons.) *This view correctly implies that modern reefs do not simply mimic the shape of their predecessors.*

- By the early 1980s: Reefs may have first appeared as fringing reefs as early as the Eocene (ca. 40 mya), but did not fully develop until the Pleistocene.[13] The GBR may have been initiated in the Miocene (ca. 15 mya), growing in short bursts interspersed with aerial exposure.[14] *These ideas largely predate most concepts of the Cenozoic roller coaster as outlined in Chapter 7; however, they do attempt to accommodate the emerging recognition of continental drift (Chapter 8). By this time some 30 shallow boreholes had been drilled, so there was good information about the uppermost layers of GBR reefs.*

- By the late 1980s: The GBR formed as Australia drifted into the tropics and consequently is wedge shaped: thickest in the north and thinnest in the south.[15] *These ideas are widely accepted today yet are unsupportable, as discussed below.*

- By the early 1990s: Outer reefs are less than 500,000 years old.[16] A study of Foraminifera suggests that reefs existed throughout the Pleistocene.[17] Climatic conditions indicate that coral reefs may first have appeared at the end of the Oligocene or the Early Miocene (24–20 mya).[18] *This is a discrepancy of 50:1 (25,000,000 versus 500,000 years). I discuss this below in the light of modern paleoclimatic reconstructions.*

Drilling and Seismic Profiling

The first actual attempt to find out how thick and how old the GBR is (and also to test the relevance of Darwin's hypothesis for the region) was conducted at Michaelmas Reef in the central GBR in 1926. The simple drill used reached a depth of 183 meters before the project was abandoned. The results were disappointing, as neither continuous reef limestone nor bedrock was reached; instead the drill encountered only mixed rubble. A second attempt was made in the southern GBR on the reef of Heron Island in 1937.[19] The drill reached 223 meters, yet for a second time the results were inconclusive because once again the final extract was neither limestone nor bedrock.[20] In hindsight this may have been fortunate, for there was no lack of public interest in these bores; had they struck bedrock, newspapers at the

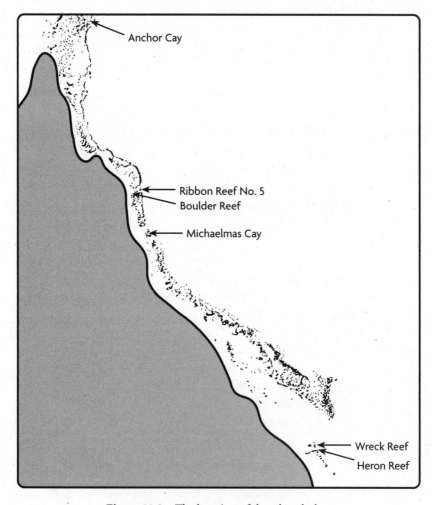

Figure 11.2   The location of deep boreholes.

time would doubtless have proclaimed Darwin wrong about reefs and therefore probably wrong about evolution.

The next drillings were a series of oil exploration "wells" sunk on Anchor Cay on the reef line just north of the deltaic reefs (see the accompanying figure), as well as in the Gulf of Papua and on Wreck Reef in the south and in inter-reef areas in the same region, all in the late 1960s. As these bores were made specifically for oil exploration and not as part of reef studies, recovery of the extract was incomplete, and the depth and age correlations were uncertain.[21] Nevertheless they, together with subsequent seismic profiling, showed extensive reef development since the Early Miocene (20 mya) in the northern GBR and northern Gulf of Papua.[22] There were conflicting interpretations of the results of the southern bores, mainly because of poor logging of the extracts, but the results were broadly in agreement with those of the old Heron Island bore, such as they were.

In the 1970s, two independent groups of scientists started shallow-coring the GBR using drills that penetrated up to 30 meters. There is considerable difference between this work and the deep boreholes that are largely dependent on petroleum exploration technology and a commensurate level of funding. Although only deep bores can potentially reveal the age of the GBR, shallow bores reveal details of the morphology of reefs and what happened to them over the last glacial cycle. This project was a major undertaking: 161 cores were taken from 48 reefs spanning the length and width of the GBR.[23] Carbon isotope analyses from the extracts showed that the thickness of Holocene reef ranged from 0 meters (living corals growing directly on Pleistocene limestone) to 29 meters, with depths of 10–20 meters being the norm. This puts the whole region into perspective because the seismic profiling that accompanied the drilling showed that most of the limestone of the GBR is less than 200 meters thick—paltry by comparison with reefs that have been studied in other parts of the world. Just how old the pre-Holocene limestone was remained unknown at that time, as only modern instruments can determine age from seismic profiles.

It was not until 1995 that two boreholes comparable to the old Heron Island bore were made, this time by an international consortium using a 50-ton drilling platform moved into place on a barge. One of these bores, 210 meters deep, was made on Ribbon Reef 5 (at the southern end of the ribbon reef line), where the substrate on which the reef rests was expected to be deep relative to the inner reefs of that region. The deepest coral recovered was from 155 meters, yet this, and much of the core up to about 36 meters, was mostly cemented rubble, not consolidated reef limestone.[24] There could be many reasons why deep limestone was not recovered here when it was present at Anchor Cay in the far north. One was the specific position of this bore site, which may have been inadvertently located over an old rubble slope, a lagoon, or an embayment, rather than the reef proper. Many times during low sea levels, this reef would have looked much like those illustrated in Plate 37. If this reef grew on a stable substrate, neither its thickness nor the age of any extract from a bore hole would be indicative of the reef's age if the older limestone on which it once rested had been eroded away. (I expand on this view below.)

The Age of the GBR: Geological Assumptions

Having assumed intellectual ownership of the question, reef geologists have continued to be more forthright than biologists on the subject of the age of the GBR. It is now widely believed that the GBR formed when Australia drifted into the tropics (meaning the tropics of today), the northernmost reefs forming first and the rest following as Australia progressed on her northward journey. A proposed extension of this notion is that the limestone platform of the GBR would be relatively thick in the north and would thin progressively toward the south because reefs had more time to develop in the north as Australia drifted steadily in that direction.[25]

In 2001 the international drilling consortium announced that the central GBR had started growing 600,000 ± 280,000 years ago.[26] The brief explanation provided then was that reef development appears to be correlated with the Mid-Pleistocene Transition from the 40,000-year to the 100,000-year orbital cycles, as described in Chapter 9.[27] This is indeed a curious conclusion, especially as it was endorsed by so many specialist geologists. It leaves me wondering what was there before this time. Was there a "Corals Keep Out" sign hanging on the gatepost of that kangaroo fence for 25,000,000 years or so? I suggest that the underlying notion—"if pre-Middle Pleistocene limestone isn't there now, it never was there"—is not a good one.

The Age of the GBR in a Wider Perspective

I have offered many observations about the age of the GBR in these pages, most of which argue against a Middle Pleistocene origin, and some of them bear repeating here. We know that over all this time there is no evidence that temperature has been low enough (lower than 18°C) to preclude reef development. It was only during the Oligocene (38–24 mya), when Australia was nearer to Antarctica than to its present position, that temperature *may* have been limiting. Ever since the Early Miocene (20 mya) or earlier, the Indo-West Pacific has been the global center of coral diversity (see Figure 8.2). Corals have been dispersing from this center for over 25 million years, occupying all the areas that their long-traveling larvae can reach, including all of northern Greater Australia. As the region of the GBR has an extensive rocky coastline not dominated by river discharge and a stable continental shelf adjacent to deep ocean, there would have to have been some environmental condition unknown in the modern world to *prevent* reefs from growing.

Extensive reef limestone of Miocene age occurs in the northern Coral Sea, including the far northern GBR, and outcrops of reef limestone of all Cenozoic epochs from Late Eocene (40 mya) onward occur in Papua New Guinea. It is hard to imagine how reefs, especially those of Papua New Guinea, could have existed—for perhaps 40 million years—without reefs forming in the region of the GBR just to the south (see the accompanying map). We also know that reefs extended as far south as New Zealand in the Miocene (at that time around latitude 45° S; see Figure 7.6), and that therefore conditions for reef growth were *better* at these higher latitudes than they are today.

The Early Pleistocene Era Beds of Papua New Guinea (see Chapter 8, and refer to the map below) had the most diverse coral community of any fossil reef on Earth, proof that there were diverse coral communities at that time in the region, which was only 300 kilometers east of the GBR. Moreover, during the Pleistocene, reefs grew far down Australia's eastern coast. Today, Elizabeth and Middleton reefs, 1,300 kilometers southeast of the southernmost reefs of today's GBR,[28] and the reefs and extensive carbonate beaches of Lord Howe Island still farther south (see Chapter 2) are likely to have a Pleistocene foundation.[29] Even the southernmost part of the GBR had reached the present latitude of Elizabeth and Middleton reefs by the Early Miocene (20 mya). It is hard to imagine how the Elizabeth and Middleton reefs could have formed anywhere near a time that precluded the formation of the GBR.

The reefs of Western Australia have a similar history. Today reefs occur south to the Houtman Abrolhos Islands, 500 kilometers farther south than the southernmost reefs of the GBR. These islands have extensive reefs, with

80 percent of the total coral diversity of all Western Australia.[30] They are probably Pleistocene in origin;[31] however, during the Late Pleistocene tropical reefs (dominated by *Acropora*) occurred around Perth, 500 kilometers farther south.[32] Again, it is hard to see how these high-latitude reefs could have formed when the GBR did not.

Australia has been drifting north at a rate of up to 6 centimeters a year. This puts the continent only about 35 kilometers south of its present position 600,000 years ago, or about 150 kilometers south of it at the beginning of the Pleistocene. This is not even 10 percent of the length of the GBR proper today, so the drift cannot conceivably be linked to the origin of the GBR over such a short time frame. During this period, the width of the tropics would not have been static; rather tropical conditions would have flickered up and down the continent, depending on glacial cycles and climatic events within those cycles. Furthermore, in the far north the Pleistocene basement is mostly only about 10 meters deep, increasing to over 20 meters

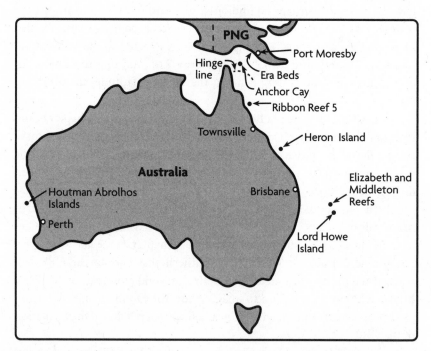

Figure 11.3   Australian and Papua New Guinean place names cited in the text. North of the hinge line there has been substantial subsidence, and the GBR has an extensive Miocene layer. South of this line the reef remains thin (200 meters or less), as there has not been enough subsidence for it to be otherwise.

in the central region. As reefs everywhere are planed off at the same level, their thickness is determined by the depth of the water in which they grow, not by the amount of time they spend growing. Minor flexures of the continental shelf have no doubt altered details of this depth pattern many times, but such movements have no relevance to the GBR's age.

I find all these observations more compelling than the age of the limestone at the bottom of a borehole, irrespective of the combined opinion of so many reef geologists. There are other explanations for their results, including the one I give below. I also suggest that the GBR is as thin as it is (mostly 150 meters or less) simply because, except in the far north, the substrate on which it rests has not subsided enough for it to be any thicker.

Antecedent Erosion

How could the Mid-Pleistocene Transition have obliterated all reef limestone before that time, yet allowed it to accumulate afterward? I suggest that Early Pleistocene reefs may have been planed off because the rate of sea-level change was slow enough to allow the forces of erosion (see Chapter 3) to keep pace with the sea levels as they fell. If they were, and if these sea-level falls, combined with bioerosion, occasionally went low enough for reefs to erode down to bedrock, all preexisting Pleistocene reefs would have been obliterated. On the other hand, increasing rates of sea-level change from the Transition onward may have been too fast for erosional processes to complete their job, leaving exposed reef limestone formed during earlier interglacial high stands behind. Over successive cycles these younger reefs would grow in increments, each increment corresponding to an interglacial sea-level high stand. A similar response of reef growth to sea-level cycles has been found in other countries, notably in the Ryukyu Islands of Japan, which were, of course, subjected to the same sea-level changes.[33]

In principle, the antecedent erosion theory presented here should be readily testable in other parts of the world, or in the far northern GBR, north of the hinge line indicated in the accompanying map. A hiatus in reef development during the Mid-Pleistocene Transition would leave a clear record in reef cores that extend down to older reef layers.

A Parsimonious History

The history of the GBR, like that of any other coral reef, is a catalogue of disasters. Sea-level changes are the main cause of those disasters, and major environmental upheavals are another. There are also reef-destroying events restricted to (geologically) narrow time frames or specific areas, including local changes in water depth and changes in surface circulation patterns. During successive time sequences, combinations of these events have stretched, perhaps many times, any notion that the GBR is a single geographically cohesive region. I have used an imaginary fence to define the area of the GBR province during the Pleistocene. Before that time we need more flexible boundaries to accommodate the up and down movements of land that occur even on the most stable of continental margins.

Northern Greater Australia probably had coral reefs in the Late Cretaceous (80 mya), for it was within warm subtropical climes at that time, and there are no compelling reasons to believe that conditions for reef growth then were unfavorable. These reefs would certainly have been devastated by K/T and the climatic upheavals of the Paleocene (65–55 mya), but no more so than other reefs. Subsequent extinction events may also have wiped out much life in the region, although again no more than in other regions. The Oligocene (38–24 mya) may have been the one epoch of the whole Cenozoic when the ocean was too cold for reef development, for we do not know if Greater Australia had left Antarctica far enough behind to have escaped the low-temperature regimes created by the formation of the Antarctic Circumpolar Current. Environment aside, the gross bathymetric and geological characters of the seafloor of the GBR region were in place by the close of the Oligocene (24 mya), and by then the region would have been within range of colonizing larvae from the north.

According to some biologists the GBR is the same age as most other reefs—9,000 to 6,000 years—because the living veneer we now see can be no older than that due to sea-level changes. For those not put off by the notion that a reef is still a reef, even when it looks like a modern-day cattle station (kangaroo country mode), we can go back at least to the Early Miocene (20 mya) and perhaps to the Middle Oligocene (30 mya). My conclusion is that the outer GBR has looked something like it does today, on and off, for at least 25 million years. During this time there may well have been intervals of little or no reef development owing to local land flexures, changing depth of sediments, sea-level changes, and terrestrial events, including volcanic activity. However, there can be no doubt that any disruptions in reef development at such times were minor compared with those brought about by the glacial cycles that completely stripped bare the living veneer of every reef we have today.

In the next chapter we go back to the time when humans first encountered the GBR, for human history, that of the GBR, and predicted climate changes have now become closely interlinked subjects. For the uninitiated, this account of the probable early human occupation of the GBR makes a bizarre story, yet it is one that best fits the information provided by the very different fields of science involved once these fields are merged.

— 12 —

Stone Age Utopia

No underwater traces of terrestrial animals have ever been found on the GBR, yet humans occupied Australia long before the last glacial maximum. Living conditions for maritime humans on the outer GBR when it was exposed at low sea levels would have been ideal. It is very likely that humans—presumably the ancestors of today's Aboriginal people—lived in caves under what are today's coral reefs, and did so long before there was human occupation of the famous caves of western Europe.

We humans are certainly changing the face of our planet—first the land and now the oceans. What is actually happening to coral reefs in general and the GBR in particular is the subject of the rest of this book. In this chapter I reflect on how humans may have first come upon the GBR, partly because this event is the start of all that follows in the remaining text, but more importantly because it finally provides a timeline that we can readily relate to— one that connects our ancestry to geological time.

The relationship between Australia's first human inhabitants and the GBR is an unwritten chronicle, yet it is no less extraordinary for that. It is undocumented because it is conjecture. Except for scraps of mangroves and some pollen, there is no direct evidence whatsoever that any terrestrial plant or animal *ever* occupied the GBR when it was exposed at low sea level. Nevertheless, it is inconceivable that it never hosted an animal population, for in its kangaroo country mode it measured 380,000 square kilometers— complete with rivers, forests, beaches, and, significantly, a vast array of habitable limestone caves.

Looking down the outer face of Tijou Reef from near the surface induces vertigo, especially if one imagines what that face would have looked like if the ocean surface were 100 meters or so lower down the slope (see the reef face in Plate 37). However, with a little imagination, the swimmer can experience much more than vertigo. A Paleolithic man might come into view, perhaps climbing down to a depth beyond sight, on a path leading to a fishing spot, or maybe climbing up to his cave with his catch in hand. Such scenes probably happened every day, at this place, for thousands of years. These people have walked in my mind's eye countless times—a bit of a worry when the effects of nitrogen narcosis bid me dive just a little deeper to find the entrance to that cave.

The Context: Famous Caves of Europe

Even the briefest glimpse of some of the Paleolithic limestone cave paintings that abound in southwest France and northern Spain provides an experience never to be forgotten. The artwork in the Lascaux caves of the Dordogne has been stunning visitors for generations, not just because of its beauty but also because of its age: some of the paintings are 17,000 years old. Nevertheless, more recent discoveries (less well known because they are

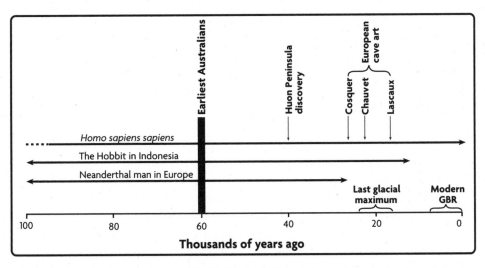

Figure 12.1 Timeline of events described in this chapter. As this book turns from geological events of the distant past to the human-controlled events of the future, there is a considerable and generally unappreciated overlap in the time of probable human occupation of the GBR and the climatic events that have shaped almost every aspect of it.

closed to the public) have eclipsed them. The paintings of Chauvet cave, discovered in the same region in 1994, are nearly twice as old—30,000 years—which makes them not only the oldest paintings ever found but among the oldest *Homo sapiens sapiens* relics in all of Europe.[1]

Setting aside considerable debate, the oldest indisputable *Homo sapiens sapiens* remains (as opposed to older forms of *H. sapiens*) are from Israel and Sub-Saharan Africa and are about 100,000 years old.[2] These numbers help to put recent archaeological findings in Australia, and Australian cave art, into proper temporal perspective.

Undersea Caves Are Well Hidden

Although cave exploring, professional and amateur, is a popular activity in southern France, the Musée National de Préhistoire tells its visitors that most likely only about half the caves of the region have yet been discovered, mainly because landslides readily close off ancient entrances. How much better hidden are Mediterranean cave entrances now submerged beneath the sea? There have been many attempts to find such entrances, and among the successes is the now famous Cosquer Cave, discovered near Marseilles in 1985.[3] Much of this cave was never flooded, and an extensive array of human artifacts, mostly works of art, remains from two widely separated intervals of occupation, 27,000 and 19,000 years ago. The only possible entrance is now 37 meters under the Mediterranean, yet when it was in use it was about 7 kilometers inland. The interesting point as far as the GBR is concerned is that this entrance remained hidden for so long, despite the fact that it is in one of the most accessible and popular diving sites in all of Mediterranean France. By contrast, the GBR challenges cave seekers with a multiplicity of ancient shorelines, spread along 2,000 kilometers of convoluted coastline—not just one coastline but many—moving according to the sea level of the time across the width of the present GBR and up and down its outer slopes.

Although no human relics have been found under any of the reefs of the GBR, I am sure that some will be uncovered one day. What relics, one might ask, could be left after at least 15,000 years of submersion in seawater? Potentially quite a few. Paleolithic flint, bones, and even charcoal have been found preserved in calcite 25 meters underwater in the large cave of Les Trémies in southern France. Paintings drawn with stenciled fingers have also been found, protected by calcite, below sea level at Cosquer, and there are many caves where the sea has left coarse engravings undamaged.

Caves of the GBR

What caves exist in the GBR region that might have been used by early humans? There are several large reef complexes in Torres Strait that look as if they were once the targets of a gigantic celestial shotgun. For example, Mary Reef in the eastern Torres Strait, if seen from the air, appears pitted with roughly circular holes, mostly less than 100 meters in diameter, known to geologists as drowned dolines and to everybody else as blue holes. They look interesting from the air but are disappointingly ordinary under water—just basin-shaped holes in patches of reef flat or lagoon. Most have rims of reef flat limestone with sloping sides and floors of soft carbonate sand and rubble. These holes are smaller and far less spectacular than the two much-photographed blue holes of the deltaic reefs of the Pompey Complex in the southern GBR (illustrated in Plate 4). The latter are circular in shape, 240 to 295 meters in diameter, and 30 to 40 meters deep. They are much deeper than the surrounding lagoon floor, which is mostly less than 10 meters deep, although not as deep as the vertical-sided deltaic channels nearby, which commonly reach 90 meters. The holes have steeply sloping coral and rubble sides that now lead to rubble floors—all that remains of caverns of cathedral-like proportions that were once beneath them.[4] There is, however, a third—less photogenic and thus little known—blue hole in the Pompey Complex that still has the original cavern, 90 meters deep at its base. The cavern appears to have caves leading out from it, but these have yet to be explored.

Apart from blue holes, there is little else to indicate the existence of reef caves from boats or aerial photographs. Not so under water, although, as demonstrated by Cosquer Cave, entrances are easily obscured, especially those deep enough to be inaccessible using scuba equipment. One of the most interesting of all the caves discovered so far occurs in the 55-meter-deep southern lagoon of Tijou Reef (see the aerial photograph in Figure 1.1). The western wall of this lagoon has a series of caves (Walker's Caves) with floor depths around 24 meters. Some entrances are large (up to 7 meters high), making the cave look like an undercut ledge; others are partially obscured by coral, whereas still others are almost totally closed off (as illustrated in Plate 42), accessible only through small openings or from other caves. There may be more caves extending back into the reef, which have not yet been explored. The length of the entire reef wall is 1.5 kilometers and the longest cave explored so far measures about 30 meters.[5]

It is easy to imagine how reef caves would have looked during periods of low sea level because they would have been much like the limestone caves we see today. Entrances like those at Tijou Reef would mostly have been wave cut when they were at sea level, but many would have been the exit paths of underground streams. The caves themselves would have been mostly horizontal, as they would have been formed between high and low Pleistocene sea levels. They may be tens to hundreds of thousands of years old, certainly old enough to be adorned with stalactites and stalagmites, the remains of which are still visible in some GBR caves today. These caves would have provided excellent shelter for any human occupant, and they may well have done so for tens of thousands of years. Perhaps the caves were adorned with the sort of rock art found today throughout northern Australia. Some might even have been burial sites.

The First Australians

The erosion and regrowth of reefs of the GBR region over the last glacial cycle to the present time has been, as we have seen, a dramatic process, brief though it was by geological standards. It is a sobering thought that much of that cycle was watched by 3,000 generations of Australians. Who were these people?

The study of the origins of Australian Aborigines is advancing rapidly, partly because of new discoveries and partly because of the development of new dating technologies. The date for the oldest known Australians keeps going farther back in time as new discoveries are made and earlier ones are reassessed. Humans have certainly occupied Australia for 45,000 ± 9,000 years, and, based on current evidence, 53,000 to 60,000 years ago is the most probable time of original occupation.[6] The oldest human remains—those of Mungo man from Willandra Lakes in southern New South Wales, now the source of the oldest human DNA in the world—are so old that these people may have had only tenuous links with modern Aborigines.[7]

There are very few human archaeological sites in all of Asia, yet a wide diversity of human remains has been found there, as well as in Australia. Some Asian humanoids are primitive, descended from *Homo erectus,* known as Java man in Indonesia.[8] *Homo sapiens neanderthalensis* (Neanderthal man), who once occupied a vast area from Europe to western Asia as a more or less distinct species, is now known to have lived, in Europe at least, up to 27,000 years ago. Furthermore, and quite astonishingly, another much smaller hu-

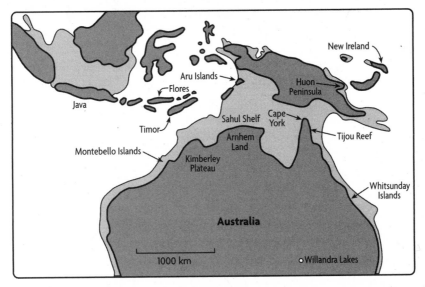

Figure 12.2 The range of sea levels of Indonesia and Greater Australia over the known time of human immigrations, with place names cited in the text. The shaded area was dry land when the sea level was −100 meters.

manoid, *Homo floresinensis* ("the Hobbit"), with characteristics reminiscent of *Australopithecus,* was discovered recently. This species is thought to have occupied the Indonesian island of Flores as recently as 13,000 years ago.[9]

For three-quarters of the time of human occupation of Australia, the present GBR was part of Greater Australia and was dry land. We may never know in detail the nature of those who may have lived in the caves under the GBR, yet there is good reason to suppose that any species or races of humans that did so were as varied temporally as we are now varied geographically. They may not have been closely related to modern Aboriginal people. It is even remotely possible that *Homo erectus* or *Homo floresinensis* reached Australia, perhaps during an earlier low-sea-level stand. Who knows? It is like reconstructing a three-dimensional jigsaw puzzle, with the top layer representing today and successively lower layers being time slices of the past, when most of the pieces are missing.

Although the evidence for Pleistocene occupation of New Guinea is sparse, we know from finds on the Huon Peninsula that humans occupied the north coast of New Guinea as long as 40,000 years ago, living primarily in the rainforests. We also know, from cave relics on the New Ireland coast, that the earliest settlers in that region lived on seafood, including molluscs, crustaceans, and fish. At 32,000 years ago, this is the earliest known instance of marine fishing anywhere in the world.[10]

The Sahul Shelf of northwestern Australia provides better possibilities for archaeological recovery of the earliest coastal Aboriginal people than eastern Australia because some of the caves in the west, not being part of a reef, are on higher ground. Caves of the Montebello and Aru islands have yielded human remains dating back 35,000 years or more,[11] and still older remains occur in inland sites on the Kimberley Plateau.[12]

Hypotheses about the earliest Australians are dominated by the simplest approaches—the timing of the lowest sea levels, the shortest sea crossings, theories of founding populations, and the easiest dispersal routes. For this reason, every major discovery (and there have been many since the 1970s) suggests some sort of reappraisal of how and when the first humans arrived in Australia.

About 800,000 years ago, our upright but smaller-brained ancestor, *Homo erectus,* reached Java, and perhaps 100,000 years ago the Hobbit first reached Flores, crossing Wallace's Line, the main demarcation between Asian and Australian fauna and flora. Since then, human or humanoid occupation of Greater Australia has at least been a real possibility. To make that journey, even at times of lowest sea level, humans would have to have made an ocean crossing of 80 to 100 kilometers on some kind of watercraft, perhaps rafts made of bamboo. Whatever the vessel, the people who made these crossings were wanderers who were not afraid of the sea. Like many Aborigines and Torres Strait islanders today, it is very likely that they, whoever they were, lived near the sea and subsisted primarily on seafood. Fish caught in coral rubble traps as the tide went out and stored in coral rubble pens (illustrated in Plate 43) would then, as now, have been a reliable source of protein. Crustaceans and molluscs of all kinds would have abounded. Turtles and dugong would have been caught then, as they are now, with specialized barb-bladed spears, launched with spear throwers. Coconuts, if present, would have augmented all diets. This is the way of life of islanders of different races and nationalities scattered throughout the entire western Pacific; it is hard to imagine that it would not have been the way of life of the earliest coast-dwelling Australians.

When humans first ventured inland, most of Australia was wetter than it is today, and there were permanent watercourses over much of the interior, making it a more hospitable land. That changed as the last glacial maximum approached, so that at the height of the glaciation about 80 percent of the continent was uninhabitable, cold, dry desert. Over many thousands of years there would have been a gradual exodus of humans from the increasingly arid interior to the vegetated coastal regions, including Arnhem Land and Cape York in the north and the GBR in the northeast.

There has been little discussion by anthropologists concerning the role of coral reefs in early Australian prehistory,[13] perhaps because it has been assumed that reefs did not exist at that time. However, it has been speculated that the earliest Australians were specifically adapted to a lifestyle of subsistence on marine resources,[14] which would have been abundant and easily gathered by early man throughout all of Australasia. As we have seen, the coastlines of Australasia did not have the same diversity and range of reefs that we see today, but they would have had fringing reefs in abundance and much the same diversity of marine life as now. Reefs then would have provided food aplenty—rather more than they do now. Then there would have been caves of all sorts right next to the fishing grounds. The entire region would have been a Stone Age Utopia.

Of course, rising sea levels changed all that. The caves would have been progressively abandoned as the sea gradually retook possession of them, returning them once again to the corals, and Aboriginal people would gradually have lost the best fishing grounds they have ever had. There are several accounts in Aboriginal oral tradition of changing sea level.[15] If those accounts could go back far enough, it is very likely that they would include stories of the GBR far more interesting than anything the historians and scientists of today could ever imagine.

Marine archaeological work in Queensland has concentrated on coastal sites likely to be threatened by sand mining, tourism, and coastal construction,[16] and so far little is known about the human prehistory that might be associated with most of the GBR's 1,200 islands. The earliest sites known to have been occupied by Aborigines are Nara Inlet on Hook Island of the Whitsunday Island group, with its well-known rock art, and Border Island with its lesser-known art remains.[17] Occupation of these sites occurred 8,150 and 7,200 years ago, respectively—ancient by archaeological standards, yet postdating most of the last sea-level rise.

Aborigines in a Fragile Land

I will soon leave the past and turn to the future, for the concluding chapters of this book touch on the prospect of a human-created mass extinction event. The start of this extinction process as far as Australia is concerned goes a long way back, perhaps to the continent's first human occupants. There has been much debate about whether ancient Australians were responsible for the extinction of the country's megafauna. It has become an emotionally charged subject, especially after the appearance of Tim Flannery's book *The Future Eaters*.[18] At the time of the last glacial cycle, Australia's terrestrial megafauna consisted of about 50 species of very large animals, the most famous being the wombat-like marsupial (*Diprotodon*), which was the size of a rhinoceros. There was also a monstrous goanna-like lizard 7 meters long and over a ton in weight, a 100-kilogram emu-like bird, a huge python-like snake, and a 3-meter-long land crocodile. Of this group of animals, only two species (the kangaroos) now survive. The main (and, to my mind, convincing) evidence that humans may have been responsible for the extinctions is the fact that this fauna survived all the glacial cycles except the last—the one that occurred after humans arrived.

The use of fire by the early Australian Aborigines may well have played a role. Fire sticks were so widely used that virtually every early Australian explorer commented on them.[19] Just what effect fire might have had on Australian flora may never be discerned, but it undoubtedly reduced the area and diversity of the forests.[20] The alternative explanation—that increasing aridity and cold as the last glacial maximum approached were primarily responsible for both deforestation and megafauna extinctions—is supported by the fact that Australia is just too vast an area to be burned by such a small number of people (about 320,000 before European settlement). Nevertheless, with or without fire, the megafauna of the country, kangaroos excepted, would have been easy prey for skilled hunters.

Whatever the cause, it is likely that it was the combination of the fire-induced changes in Australian flora and the long-standing effects of both El Niño and low soil fertility that produced the most ecologically fragile continent on Earth. Australia, as her present inhabitants are still discovering, is a continent that will never be amenable to widespread human exploitation without serious and often unpredictable consequences.

We now leave Ice Age kangaroo country behind. The humans that once occupied it, presumably the ancestors of today's Aboriginal people, departed the reflooded GBR without leaving a trace—a tantalizing gap in Australian prehistory. Today's world, to which we now turn, is a very different place. We describe the sea-level and climatic changes early Australians witnessed as being rapid, yet they are nothing compared with the changes that are about to be unleashed on the Earth we all now occupy.

— 13 —

An Enhanced Greenhouse World

The enhanced greenhouse world of today is viewed against the background of historical discovery and then described in terms of climate changes we are currently experiencing. Ocean temperatures are increasing as thermal peaks, mediated by El Niño cycles, are superimposed on greenhouse gas–induced increases in atmospheric and ocean temperatures. Broader climatic repercussions of anthropogenic CO_2 potentially affecting the future of the GBR include changes in sea level, the thermohaline circulation, tropical cyclones, and acidification.

We are now clearly in human time. The time frame of this chapter has shrunk to just a couple of centuries from the many tens of thousands of years covered in the last chapter. Indeed a couple of centuries is all the time it will take for us to change the future of our planet. In this and the following two chapters, I examine what is happening in the present and how we can use our knowledge of the past to predict what may happen in the future.

Here I explain what the expression "enhanced greenhouse" actually means in general terms and what has sparked current concerns. New discoveries about our climate are being made so frequently that the radar screen of climate change needs to be refreshed every few years. Some of the old science is being superseded, but the new science replacing it is not giving any cause for optimism.[1] Considering what is at stake, I find that scary, and I continually wonder why increasingly persuasive warnings about what the future holds are not taken more seriously by political leaders and the general public.

CO_2: The Story So Far

We all learn in childhood that CO_2 is one of life's necessities, enabling green plants to make sugars from the simplest and most abundant of ingredients:

air, water, and sunlight. However, as we have seen, CO_2 has another, more complex role to play. The small amount in the atmosphere forms a blanket around the Earth, absorbing long-wave radiation and stopping some of it from escaping into space.

On the whole the Earth manages to control the amount of CO_2 in the atmosphere by a variety of mechanisms associated with the carbon cycle—the Big Daddy of all Earthly regulators (see Chapter 6). When something goes wrong and there is a mass extinction "event," the finger of blame should not always point up to the heavens—the "blame-a-bolide" approach in a denial of Earthly responsibility. Rather it should be pointed downward at Earth's own control mechanisms, particularly the carbon cycle.

In the course of our forays through time we have seen that extinction events can generally be associated with upheavals that have multiple origins: volcanic belts created by seafloor spreading, supervolcanoes, traps, sudden releases of methane—and, yes, bolides as well. These causes have time frames ranging from minutes to millions of years. Some are direct, whereas some are themselves the result of other mechanisms. However, the major causes of extinction events all ultimately come under the umbrella of the carbon cycle.

If the carbon cycle is the big player, CO_2 is its fast-moving currency—at least the fast way of getting carbon out of the atmosphere and into the Earth's great storage vault, the ocean. Once in the ocean, carbon can be locked up almost indefinitely as carbonate rock or even returned to the mantle, whence it came originally.

There are many steps in the carbon cycle as far as CO_2 is concerned. One of these is particularly important for coral reefs: the short journey from the atmosphere to the upper layers of the ocean. This is important because, unlike most of the other steps of the cycle's control mechanisms, this one is rate limited. If it is pushed too hard, the upper ocean fails to do its job properly and CO_2 remains in the atmosphere, where, if production continues unchecked, it continues to build up indefinitely. This has two outcomes in today's world: it increases the greenhouse effect and it creates ocean acidification. I stress the emphasis on rate: over geological intervals of time the ocean is able to preserve some sort of balance with the atmosphere. It is only when CO_2 accumulates rapidly (over a few decades as opposed to many millennia) that the mechanism becomes overloaded.

Should We Be Concerned?

We have seen immense climatic changes over geological time, upheavals that have repeatedly destroyed all coral reefs and inflicted havoc on just about every other ecosystem that leaves a trail we can follow. With this background, how do we interpret today's changes? Should scientists *really* endeavor to curb our fossil fuel–powered prosperity in order to counter the effects of a gas so rare that it is measured in parts per million or of temperature changes so small that they hide behind a decimal point? Could these tiny changes seriously herald the ominous message that so many scientists are sending to the global community? The answer lies, as we have so often seen in these pages, in the understanding of time scales. Changes that appear minuscule over our paltry lifetimes are, in fact, immense when translated into a geological perspective and compared with Nature's normal perturbations. The worry is not about the amount of change to date, but about the speed at which it is taking place and the mechanisms that are driving it.

In this chapter I compare the climatic history of the Holocene (the past 11,800 years of general climate stability) with that of the twentieth century. The evidence supports the view that the world is indeed warming abnormally—but, perhaps surprisingly, not yet at the high rate that might be predicted from today's CO_2 levels. I offer some background on this issue—dealing in particular with the thermal inertia of both the oceans and Antarctica—and on international efforts to address concerns about climate change.

Since the Last Glacial Cycle

First we have to backtrack a bit, just enough to find that irascible giant called Climate drifting off into a tranquil sleep 11,800 years ago at the beginning of the Holocene (see Chapter 10). Now it seems that our greenhouse gas emissions may be disturbing his slumber. This is exceedingly unwise, for the last time he awoke he sent sea temperatures plunging in the anomalous event called the Younger Dryas. Fortunately for coral reefs, he went back to sleep again before he lowered sea levels enough to wreak his usual havoc. It is the giant's sleep pattern since the Younger Dryas that is now of interest. Occasionally, as the Holocene has progressed, he has stirred—just a little, yet enough to move the global thermometer by half a degree or so. Over the past few decades it has seemed that he is stirring again. Until recently, this might have been (and often was) attributable to his natural restlessness while asleep. But it has now become clear beyond doubt that he really is waking up again. Argue as we might about most of this projection, one thing is certain: when he does wake up, the Earth will rapidly become a very different place.

Around 14,600 years ago, while the Earth was still deglaciating, it went through the last and one of the biggest Dansgaard-Oeschger cycles of all—the Bølling Warming Event. This in turn set the stage, 1,800 years later, for the best known of all snap freezes—the Younger Dryas, so named because the original studies focused on the replacement of the forests of northern Europe by an Arctic flora that included the tiny, roselike, flowering plant *Dryas octopetala*. The Younger Dryas event has now been detected in almost all ice cores, in corals, and in many marine sequences, so broad details about it are known with unusual precision.

We know that, when the Younger Dryas ended 11,800 years ago, the average atmospheric temperature rose as much as 8°C in less than a century. Ocean temperatures, of course, lagged far behind, actually cooling a little, then rising to peak around 6,000 years ago. This works out to an average warming rate, since the last glacial maximum, of about 0.03°C per century. The collapse of ice sheets during the last sea-level rise as well as eruptions of supervolcanoes may well have produced more rapid changes, but these were short-term occurrences from point sources with limited influence. On millennial time scales there have been clearer climatic oscillations, notably swings of 5–6°C in the North Atlantic (perhaps 0.3–0.6°C per century), although nothing like this amount globally averaged, especially as the Southern Hemisphere usually counterbalances the Northern Hemisphere. Nevertheless Antarctic waters became relatively warm after the Younger Dryas, about 1°C warmer than today, and the perimeter was largely ice free. This lack of ice was a matter of considerable consequence for the thermohaline ocean circulation, which, as we have seen (Figure 7.5), depends on ice formation at both poles for its power.

Between this post–Younger Dryas peak, up until the end of the Little Ice Age (the name given to a cool interval from the fifteenth to the nineteenth centuries that was limited to the Northern Hemisphere), the Earth's mean temperature cooled, but at an average rate of about 0.02°C per century. This is a small enough number to be readily accounted for by all sorts of geographic variations and short-term anomalies. When last century's mean increase of 0.7°C (an amount almost universally agreed on by climatologists) is compared with the mean warming rate of 0.03°C per century since the last glacial maximum, the warning bells start sounding. When it is further considered that the Earth's mean temperature at the last glacial maximum, 20,000 years ago, was only 6°C colder than the present interglacial maximum, the warning bells become all pervading.

In the absence of any alternative explanation, it seems that the only way *that* amount of warming could take place naturally is through a complete flip in the Earth's climate system. The rapid warming at the end of the Younger Dryas oscillation may have been just such a flip, but this kind of climatic behavior is restricted to glacial conditions, and, given the array of uncertainties about the numbers involved, thousand-year oscillations are unlikely to have altered the mean global temperature by more than 0.2°C over the previous thousand years.[2] These numbers leave little doubt that the Earth is indeed warming rapidly. For a few years the sunspot cycle was a popular nonanthropogenic explanation for twentieth-century warming.[3] Debate about the role of changing solar radiation in creating global warming continues to this day; however, it is now being constrained by satellite measurements, the broad conclusion being that such changes are unlikely to account for more than 10 percent of any observed warming.[4]

Nevertheless, 0.6°C per century is much less than the future rates predicted for a doubling of CO_2, first because of the thermal inertia of the deep oceans and Antarctica, which creates a long lag time, but mainly because the greenhouse effect is, unfortunately, still in its infancy. This leads us to uncharted waters: the mechanisms and timeline of heat redistribution in the deep oceans still require much elucidation.

The sensitivity of the Earth to greenhouse gases is now broadly understood in general terms, but it is not yet known if our climate can actually flip from one state of equilibrium to another. To address this and the many other issues of climate science, a number of groups have developed general circulation models—numerical models that have the capacity to forecast the future and, as a measure of accuracy, hindcast the past. Such models attempt to define the contribution made by all factors that affect climate and to gradually apply increasing constraints on the model parameters to narrow the variability of the resulting predictions without sacrificing their reliability. Modifications to the models continually improve the integration of environmental variables such as the cooling effect of sulfur dioxide industrial effluent (a subject recently recognized to be of great importance),[5] short-term changes in the sun's energy (the sunspot cycle), and the role of clouds in modifying greenhouse effects.[6] Nevertheless, however well constrained models become,[7] they cannot predict future human behavior or the impact of future technologies, which remain a Pandora's Box for all modelers. What the models *can* do is make the most of the existing scientific knowledge, a major undertaking by any standards.

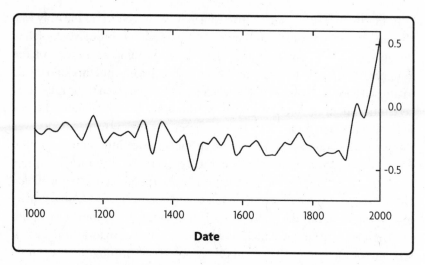

Figure 13.1 Mean global temperature over the past thousand years, showing the recent upward spike in context. This pattern is slightly different for the Northern and Southern hemispheres, which tend to balance each other, and thus the figure does not show the Little Ice Age.

On the whole, there is little accord between long-term historical temperature records (as illustrated above) and the hindcasts of general circulation models, but there are well-understood reasons why this is so. Deep oceans and ice caps do not respond to atmospheric temperature changes on hundred-year time scales; they are holding the long-term effects of CO_2 increase in check—delaying the impacts of the phenomena we are now observing. Even if CO_2 were to be held at current levels, the oceans would not reach equilibrium for a thousand years or more—leaving the problems we are creating today for future generations to deal with.

A Brief History of the Greenhouse Debate

Like many great scientific revelations, the subject of future environmental change has a history steeped in controversy. As recently as the early 1980s opinion was still divided: Was the Earth headed for an unprecedented interval of global warming? Or was it on the brink of another Ice Age? Or did the "balance of Nature" reign supreme, trivializing the efforts of humans to alter the grand scheme of things? There was good reason to trust in the balance of Nature: Didn't the top few meters of the ocean hold more of the Earth's heat than the entire atmosphere? Didn't the ocean absorb greenhouse gases within a few years after they were produced? And didn't our thermohaline circulation consign all such waste to the ocean depths within a century or so? Surely the oceans would take care of any serious threat from climate change.

By the close of the 1970s a wide spectrum of theories, many seemingly idiosyncratic, had accumulated. Maybe climate change was under some form of extraterrestrial control, the result of variations in the amount of heat coming from the sun, orbital forcing, or some other cyclical process. The forecasts based on such causes suggested that the Earth was heading for a new ice age. Or did the Earth control its own climate? Future dilution of saltwater by melting polar ice could gradually disrupt the thermohaline powering of the Ocean Conveyor, which in turn would affect the distribution of heat through the oceans and cause northern Europe to freeze. Perhaps worse, there seemed to be (and remains) a possibility that the west Antarctic ice sheet, the Earth's largest mobile ice mass, could collapse during the next millennium or sooner, much as happened repeatedly to the Laurentian ice shelf in the Northern Hemisphere during Ice Age glacial cycles. Such a collapse would have enormous consequences for both the Ocean Conveyor and sea-level rise.

For decades, climatologists have known that predictions such as these, unlikely though they are to be realized within this century, raise the fundamentally important question of stability. Is our Earth inevitably committed to another glacial cycle in defiance of any anthropogenic influence, or is our climate balanced on a knife edge, ready to topple, perhaps chaotically, one way or another at the slightest push? Or, for that matter, is what we are looking at simply the natural end of the Ice Ages and the beginning of a new era of long-term greenhouse stability? Knife-edge and chaos theories offer a myriad of possibilities—even volcanic eruptions might trigger change. Certainly these are all speculations, but they are neither remote nor idle.

GENERAL CIRCULATION MODELS. By the 1980s international bodies had joined with scientific groups in warning that the Earth's climate was changing abruptly. The Intergovernmental Panel on Climate Change (IPCC) was formed in 1988 and quickly established itself as the principal source of scientific advice to governments. This advice and the ensuing governmental responses have captured public interest and occasioned considerable debate.

The following points are offered to clarify some of the confusion I have come across regarding the use of general circulation models in IPCC reports and other publications[8]:

- General circulation models are not beauty contests; that is, they do not compete with each other. On the contrary, there has been a history of collaboration rather than competition among the scientists who build them.
- General circulation models depend on the state of computer technology, because they take a long time to run at meaningfully detailed resolutions. Rapid increases in the speed of supercomputers allow the models of today to do what could only be dreamed of before the 2001 IPCC report. That does not necessarily make the latest models right, but it does make them better. The results of general circulation models published in the 2007 IPCC report further constrain all major fields of unknowns, giving increased certainty (in a pessimistic direction) to future predictions.[9] They also test the accuracy of the 2001 predictions: one model in particular being astonishingly accurate. However, all the 2001 predictions underestimated the rate of sea-level rise now recorded by satellites.
- IPCC reports do not themselves review the models whose predictions they contain, but these models are subject to stringent review in scientific journals. (They are *not* meaningfully reviewed in popular magazines, novels, newspapers, and political statements, although these sources sometimes appear to have greater public impact.)
- Almost any process with multiple variables can be modeled, for computers can undertake cognitive operations that are far beyond human capability. As in so many areas of science, there are no better alternatives.
- The primary differences among models are a result of the assumptions they make about human population growth and resource consumption, and their mathematical protocols. However, all models indicate that the Earth is warming rapidly.
- The most difficult of all variables to quantify and constrain is the effect of atmospheric water, especially that of clouds.

Today a small and rapidly diminishing number of scientists still deny the existence of global warming, just as others deny the concept of evolution. Some skeptics have been motivated by a need to attract attention to themselves, others are swayed by religious beliefs or the prospect of financial gain, and still others are responsive to political persuasion. There are also a few scientists, especially those who view change in a geological perspective, who remain genuinely unconvinced of the value of IPCC predictions. The most common rationale is the now outdated notion that the climate changes we are currently observing are too small to reliably separate anthropogenic influences from natural fluctuations.

Genuinely skeptical scientists have an essential role to play,[10] but the same cannot be said of others who seek to bypass the process of peer review for personal reasons or political ends. There are checks and balances here: plenty of junk gets published in the best scientific journals, but very few worthwhile points ultimately escape them. Weart's *History of Global Warming* takes us to a well-argued position: "Of course climate science is full of uncertainties, and nobody claims to know exactly what the climate will do. That very uncertainty is part of what, I am confident, is known beyond doubt: our planet's climate can change, tremendously and unpredictably.... the few who contest these facts are either ignorant or so committed to their viewpoint that they will seize on any excuse to deny the danger."[11]

After twenty years of increasingly vocal warnings from the scientific community and other enlightened campaigners, political understanding is now changing and most leaders have pledged remedial actions of some sort. The current need is to mold those remedial actions into something drastic enough to tackle the problem effectively.

The Enhanced Greenhouse Effect

In the broadest context, the Earth's climate, despite the ravages it has endured, has been extraordinarily stable during the entire time that multicellular life has existed on the planet. Throughout this unimaginably long period, our oceans have covered much of the Earth's surface and our atmosphere has remained thick. Currently the Earth's atmosphere is made up of 78 percent nitrogen, 21 percent oxygen, and just under 1 percent argon. If these were the only ingredients in the atmosphere (or if the Earth had no atmosphere at all), the average temperature of the planet's surface would, in theory, be about −18°C (excluding albedo effects), and it would be an ice ball. In fact the actual average temperature is 15.5°C. This difference (33.5°C or 60°F) is largely due to the tiny amount of CO_2 that resides in our atmosphere, around 0.0375 percent or 375 ppm as I write this book. There are also traces of other greenhouse gases, notably methane (derived largely from geological sources, plant respiration, and animal life, particularly livestock and termites), nitrous oxide (largely from fertilizers), and chlorofluorocarbons (from aerosol cans and refrigerants), together with even rarer artificial gases (produced by industry).

Nitrogen, oxygen, and argon are transparent to radiation of all wavelengths. Not so CO_2 and the trace gases just mentioned. These are transparent to solar radiation (which is largely in the near infrared, visible, and ultraviolet parts of the spectrum), but they absorb outgoing radiation (which is in the far infrared). They thus create a one-way filter, allowing solar radiation in, but stopping the outward radiation of warmth (from both sunlight and natural nuclear decay), just as (for a different reason) the glass of a greenhouse does. The filtering capacities of the different gases differ considerably: CO_2 is the most important because of its quantity, yet it is only a partial filter of some wavelengths. The rarer gases are all far more opaque (methane is about 22 times more so than CO_2), leading some scientists to speculate that they could contribute almost as much to greenhouse warming as CO_2.

The mechanism of the natural greenhouse effect—why these gases are so important—is well understood in principle, although not in detail. If the mechanism were simple, the relationship between enhanced greenhouse gas levels and temperature would be a mere pocket calculator equation. The main reason why it is not, and why supercomputers and complex general circulation models are needed at all, is atmospheric water. The water content of our atmosphere varies from 0.0001 percent in the Antarctic winter to 4 percent in the humid summer tropics, the average being around 1 percent. Atmospheric water also exists in many forms. The effect of clouds on warming is one of the most significant unknowns in the models.

Many of us know that a clear sky at night leads to a crisp (perhaps frosty) morning, whereas a cloudy night will trap the day's warmth. However, the longer-term effects connected with clouds are much more complex. Clouds both trap radiated heat (a warming effect) and reflect solar insolation (a cooling effect). Different types of clouds are better at one process or the other, so that some have a net warming effect and some the opposite. Clouds are both mobile and temporary, and, unfortunately, predicting which types of clouds will occur where and when and for how long is still a challenge—yet clouds are among the most important of our climate feedback controls.

There are several important aspects of the greenhouse mechanism. Earlier reports from the IPCC predicted that an increase in atmospheric temperature of between 1.5° and 5.8°C would occur in response to a doubling of CO_2.[12] This wide range of variation is the main source of the public doubt concerning the usefulness of general circulation models. Since those early reports, the range of estimates has narrowed, with current predictions moving toward the upper end of the range. The main reasons for this are our improved understanding of the effects of clouds and of the cooling effects of sulfur dioxide, as well as the incorporation into the models of predictions about the future energy needs of rapidly developing countries.

The present level of atmospheric CO_2 (375 ppm) is about 35 percent higher than the preindustrial level (277 ppm), and CO_2 is predicted to reach double preindustrial levels some time around the middle of this century. Moreover, if no effective remedial action is taken, CO_2 is now widely (and conservatively, according to most industry specialists) predicted to reach about 970 ppm by 2100—a level over three times that of the preindustrial era. A quadrupled level will be reached some time early in the next century, which will result in roughly twice the amount of atmospheric warming we see today. Despite moves to curb them, the rate of anthropogenic greenhouse gas emissions is currently increasing at 2.5 ppm or 0.6 percent a year. Given that the rate of construction of power stations in China and India has been underestimated in the past (see Chapter 16), this issue must become a focal point for the IPCC.

On another front, the IPCC's 2001 report underestimated the effect of industrial aerosols such as sulfur dioxide in contributing to global cooling, and some studies have indicated that, were it not for these aerosols, average atmospheric temperatures would exceed the IPCC's worst-case predictions. Ironically, because they have been identified as a primary source of acid rain, they are now being scrubbed from industrial smokestack emissions—thus removing whatever protection they afford.

To put these numbers into a contemporary perspective, since instrumental record keeping began in 1861, the warmest decade has been that of the 1990s, 1998 and 2005 were the two warmest years ever recorded, and five of the six warmest years occurred between 2001 and 2005.[13] These temperatures are higher than any indicated by ice cores, tree rings, or isotopes in corals during the past thousand years,[14] and they are higher than those in any measurable interval of the Holocene.[15] Do these records show what is to come or are they part of an as yet unrecognized low-frequency variability? One study published in 1997 suggested that the decade of the 1990s could indeed be an unusual one within the long-term progress of natural greenhouse warming.[16] However the twenty-first century, with its succession of record-breaking temperatures and other climate anomalies, has not borne this out.

Future Consequences

If CO_2 emissions are not controlled, 2,000–4,000 gigatons of carbon (or more than three times that weight in terms of CO_2) will be added to the atmosphere from anthropogenic sources. The consequences of midrange and worst-case scenarios are illustrated in the accompanying figure. Either case will be an event without precedent in our era—or, for that matter, in any other known time in all Earth history.

WARMING THE OCEANS.   Until recently, much less was known about future warming of the oceans than about greenhouse warming of the atmosphere. This is partly due to time lag; it is also because events such as El Niño and changes in thermohaline circulations have been, and still are, largely unpredictable. Nevertheless ocean temperature can now be estimated from a combination of satellite data, measurements of sea-level rise, and historical ocean records. Ocean-atmosphere general circulation models have long shown that observed increases in ocean heat content are linked to atmospheric warming.[17] Now at least one model that can accurately track and predict ocean temperatures shows that the heat content of the oceans has been increasing steadily for 50 years, although this has occurred at different rates in the different oceans.[18] The mean ocean temperature has increased between 0.3°C (in the tropics) and 0.7°C over the past century,[19] and by the same reckoning it will rise as much as 2–3°C in this century. As the oceans warm they will have ever more stratified depth layers, so the all-important surface layer will become increasingly isolated from the deep-ocean buffers that help constrain ocean acidity.

SEA-LEVEL RISE.   Sea level is currently rising just over 0.3 cm per year,[20] and the rate is accelerating, leading to a predicted increase of over 90 cm by the end of this century. While this may seem small, it is only the beginning of a much larger rise to which the Earth is now committed, one that has dire long-term consequences. Thermal expansion accounts for about half of the

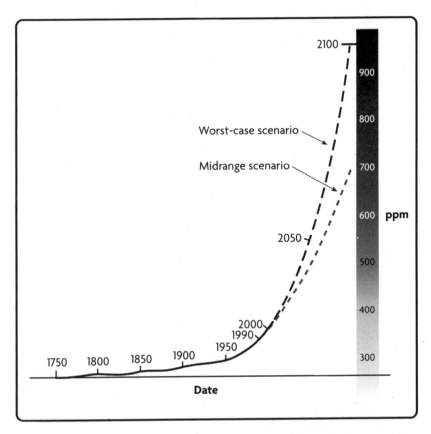

Figure 13.2 Current rate of atmospheric CO_2 increase (in ppm) from
instrumental records of the past and computer model projections of the future.
The midrange scenario assumes that most of the remedial actions now being
proposed are put into effect within a decade. The worst-case scenario (which is an
optimistic position according to some energy industry scientists) assumes that
these remedial actions are not implemented or are ineffective. Both scenarios in
this diagram undervalue the opposing influences of sulfur dioxide in dampening
the greenhouse effect and the plans of developing countries to build extensive
coal-fired power stations, which will enhance it.

rise, with the other half being caused by melting glaciers—principally those
of Greenland, which are currently melting at around 50 cubic kilometers a
year. The Greenland ice sheet is the most vulnerable to climate change; a
2°–3°C increase in mean ocean temperature, if sustained over several centuries, would melt all of Greenland's ice, causing a 6-meter increase in sea

level. If the ice sheets of Greenland and Antarctica both melted, the sea would rise a massive 70 meters. Both of these catastrophes are theoretically possible, although the probabilities are very different. Based on current predictions, Greenland's ice cap is likely to melt; that of Antarctica, at least of eastern Antarctica, will very likely persist for the current millennium at least, even with a quadrupled level of atmospheric CO_2.

Thermal expansion of the ocean is an independent dynamic; a quadruple increase in greenhouse gases would ultimately lead to a 3-meter sea-level rise from this cause alone. A combination of the effects of the melting of Greenland's ice, thermal expansion, and consequent domino effects will cause sea level to rise well over 9 meters sometime in this millennium.

Few if any coral reefs (as opposed to individual corals) would be able to grow fast enough to keep pace with this rate of sea-level rise (see Chapters 3 and 10). However, as all of today's coral species clearly survived a similar or greater rate of sea-level change after the last glacial cycle, the impact would be limited to changes in community composition, especially of the colorful reef zones and intertidal reef flat communities we see today. I use the conditional tense "would," not the predictive "will," because the combined impacts of temperature and acidification (discussed in Chapters 14 and 15, respectively) will have long made any impact of sea-level change irrelevant as far as corals are concerned.

Many coral cays as we know them will cease to exist during this century because they are only a couple of meters above high-tide level and do not have enough reef to generate sufficient sand to keep pace with erosion. Among cays likely to be affected are Raine Island (the beach illustrated in Plate 30), those of Torres Strait, and virtually all those of the southern GBR, including popular resort islands like Heron Island. Apart from its effect on human populations that live or depend on these islands, a rise in sea level will force profound distribution and population changes on a wide range of island biota, including turtles, birds, and vegetation. Other cays surrounded by shallow water and extensive reefs in the northern GBR may keep pace with sea-level rise, and some may even increase in size if sufficient coral rubble is locally available.

CHANGES TO THE OCEAN CONVEYOR.   The Ocean Conveyor dominates circulation in the Atlantic today by delivering tropical heat to the northern Atlantic, warming Europe during the cold winter months. The Conveyor is unstable where it sinks into the deep ocean and can be turned on or off by a small change in temperature or salinity in the far northern Atlantic.[21] These changes during the Pleistocene were correlated with orbital cycles asserting themselves in an icehouse world. Most general circulation models now predict that thermohaline-powered circulations will collapse as the formation of sea ice fails, first in the Northern and then in the Southern Hemisphere.[22] This could result in the freezing of northern Europe, although such an outcome is likely to be partially or totally overridden by atmospheric warming.

Failure of thermohaline circulations will also reduce the mixing of ocean layers that occurs at high latitudes. This in turn will reduce the capacity of deep-ocean buffers to control acidification. The full biological consequences of failure of the thermohaline circulation are currently matters of conjecture because we do not fully understand the downstream effects. Nevertheless, we know that they will be serious and fraught with unwelcome surprises.

CYCLONES.   Cyclones are predicted to become more severe (and presumably the cyclone season will last longer) as a result of increasing ocean temperatures. This will lead to another pressure on the GBR as wider regions of reef are damaged more frequently. Cyclonic rain can also cause lowered salinity around inshore reefs and result in loss of corals within the low-salinity layer. Mechanical cyclone damage and lowered salinity may well work synergistically with mass bleaching to reduce resilience. At present, cyclones usually strike at low tides, as they move slowly enough to be influenced by atmospheric pressure changes induced by tidal movements, and faster-moving cyclones usually weaken as they move. This is likely to change in the future: cyclones will move more quickly without being diminished and will thus strike the coast independently of the tides, which in turn will increase the likelihood of storm surges (abnormally high sea levels caused by a cyclone's low central pressure) occurring at high tides. The impact of this scenario is potentially disastrous for coastal communities, and it will be exacerbated by sea-level rise.[23] Both of these effects will diminish the role coral reefs currently play in mitigating cyclone damage. A change in the cyclone season will have further impacts if it starts to overlap with the annual mass spawning event of corals (see Chapter 3) because rainwater is lethal to coral larvae floating on the ocean surface.

ACIDIFICATION.   This is the most serious and least well known of all the currently predicted outcomes of CO_2 buildup. It is the subject of Chapter 15.

Can Anthropogenic CO_2 End the Ice Ages?

The present rate of anthropogenic CO_2 emissions into the atmosphere cannot be sustained forever, irrespective of political will. Sometime between 2100 and 2300, fossil fuel reserves (those known and even remotely predicted) will run out; but this will not translate into a proportional decline in CO_2 in the atmosphere because there is a long-term residence effect (described in Chapter 15).

The additive effects of anthropogenic methane release are a major additional intangible, one whose effects are still being determined.

The Earth now has an atmospheric CO_2 content that has probably not been equaled since the beginning of the Oligocene (38 mya) or earlier, yet this would not be apparent to a human living 10,000 years ago, or (we will have to imagine) 145,000 years ago, or for that matter at any other interglacial interval of the Pleistocene. The Earth's weather (as opposed to its long-term climate) would even have appeared much as it does today during the Miocene. Yet these similarities would all be illusions, the illusion being the vulnerability of the Earth's climate to change. Low levels of greenhouse gases made the Ice Ages possible by destabilizing the climate, allowing it to flip readily from cold glacial periods to warm interglacial periods at the bidding of orbital cycles. Today's higher CO_2 levels have changed this by making the climate less susceptible to orbital forcing. Thus, if a glacial cycle were now due—which we know is not the case and will not be so for another 30,000 years—today's CO_2 levels would probably prevent this from occurring.

However, on a geological time scale, we are looking at a spike in an otherwise low-CO_2 background. Provided that the world's plant life is allowed to recover from human abuses so that it can draw down atmospheric CO_2 once fossil reserves have been exhausted, atmospheric CO_2 will probably return to its normal Ice Age levels and Ice Age cycles will resume, albeit only after many thousands of years. In the atmosphere, the CO_2 spike will probably remain just that, a spike. Meanwhile, unfortunately, that same atmospheric spike may have caused long-lasting and fundamental changes in the ocean. The damage done to the Earth's coral reefs and other marine ecosystems and foodwebs is likely to continue into much more extended geological time, as previous extinctions have clearly demonstrated.

Coral reefs are exceptionally vulnerable to both temperature and acidity, which means that they are vulnerable to climate spikes and to the consequences of a spike that will persist far beyond the brief period of the spike itself. In the next chapters I review the Earth's history to find conditions comparable to those of today that indicate the nature of changes that lie ahead. We have already changed the Earth's climate from one that can best be described in terms of cycles to one that can be better described in terms of events. One aspect of any future scenario is clear: fast-responding elements of our climate (the atmosphere and surface ocean waters) will be out of phase with slow-responding elements (ice sheets and deep oceans) to an extent that has seldom, if ever, been the case before. This likens our tampering with the Earth's climate to a game of Russian roulette, with every chamber of the cylinder loaded. We must take the bullets out—all of them, quickly and at any cost—for this particular gun has a hair trigger and devastating firepower.

— 14 —

Temperature and Mass Bleaching

Mass bleaching in corals is a recent global phenomenon that has already caused extensive damage to coral communities and is certain to have an increasingly devastating impact as this century progresses. Bleaching is now occurring with sufficient frequency that extensive areas of coral reefs worldwide are becoming algae-dominated rubble. El Niño events are natural phenomena that pulse warmed oceanic water onto reefs of the GBR and, at the present time, determine the onset of mass bleaching events. However, this role of El Niño is temporary, and it will come to an end once the thermally capped Western Pacific Warm Pool broadens enough to cause mass bleaching in non–El Niño years.

We have seen that the average temperature of the oceans has risen by 0.7°C (0.3°C in the tropics) over the past century. Surely corals cannot be so attuned to temperature that such a trivial increase can cause mass bleaching of entire reef tracts? Clearly not directly, but indirectly—yes. These temperatures are global averages that disguise seasonal and spatial variations that are crucial for marine life.

Temperature Affects Different Organisms in Different Ways

Understanding why and how temperature changes are more critical for some species than for others requires us to take a closer look at the effect of temperature on their physiology and evolutionary history.

Compared with terrestrial organisms, marine species have evolved in habitats with highly predictable temperature regimes. Air has very little thermal inertia. Although this has the disadvantage of leading to wide temporal and spatial temperature fluctuations, it has given terrestrial organisms strong evolutionary incentives to manage temperature extremes, both behaviorally and physiologically. Water is the opposite; its far greater thermal inertia dictates that only warm-blooded mammals and some large fish can maintain a body temperature that is significantly different from that of their environment. Furthermore, the ocean's relatively constant and predictable temperature has led to far fewer evolutionary mechanisms to deal with any abnormal regimes, should these arise. Marine invertebrates (with the exception of some intertidal species such as crabs) have no temperature sensors; they have no use for them. Most have no control over their body temperatures and so cannot use temperature to regulate the rate of their biochemical processes, notably the rate of enzyme-catalyzed reactions. No matter—the ocean does this for them. The stability of ocean temperature compared with air temperature is a great gift, for it makes the rate of physiological functions predictable without any need for evolutionary invention or metabolic cost.

Most terrestrial animals become stressed if their body temperatures go over a certain limit, and they employ an assortment of physiological and behavioral mechanisms to prevent this from happening. Not so with most marine animals—there is seldom any need to escape, nor anywhere to go. Intertidal animals are the exception. They have developed avoidance strategies—they burrow in mud, tough it out, or move to a place where they are sheltered from direct sunlight. Such options do not exist for corals, especially those that are exposed at low tide (illustrated in Plate 24).

As we have seen, all reef corals live in a zone close to the air-ocean interface, one of the most physiologically challenging of all environments. Having committed themselves to building reefs in the shallowest waters, they must maintain the health of their symbioses to continue to exist. More to the point, this appears to be why they are closely attuned to the upper temperature limit of the ocean, as I discussed in Chapter 3. Throughout their evolutionary history, that upper limit has been one of the unfailing physical constants of our planet. Like the change of seasons, the brightness of the sun, or the viscosity of air, ocean temperature is one of the attributes of the Earth that has shaped evolutionary design.

For corals, the rate of photosynthesis and thus the rate of both calcification and growth are dependent on temperature, yet at the same time they must avoid heat stress. This has led to a temperature optimum of around 27°C, although this can vary by a few degrees depending on the local environment. Moreover, GBR corals have a margin of tolerance of around 4°C above the optimum; this is normally all they need, unless they live on reef flats that are exposed at low tide. However, as we saw in Chapter 4, this puts them at risk of heat stress if the upper temperature threshold is exceeded. At that point, zooxanthellae become more than just food and oxygen producers—they may also become producers of toxic free oxygen radicals.

Links between Mass Bleaching and Enhanced Greenhouse Warming

The linking of mass bleaching to abnormally high ocean temperatures is one thing; the linking of these temperatures to enhanced greenhouse warming—warming from anthropogenic CO_2—is quite another. A key question is: Is mass bleaching a recent phenomenon or did it occur before the rise of anthropogenic CO_2?

The first mass bleaching of corals in the summer of 1981/1982, on the GBR and elsewhere, was not initially attributed to climate change; however, once climate change was implicated as a possible cause, the event sounded the first alarm that global warming could seriously affect marine life. That alarm has now been ringing, ever more stridently, for more than 20 years. Marine biologists have been quick to respond: more than five hundred research papers have been published on the causes and mechanisms of bleaching, and these in turn have stimulated increasingly rigorous studies of the physical environments with which they are associated. Such environmental studies are themselves nested within the wider science of climate change, as a stand-alone investigation into what is clearly a major environmental tragedy. A multitude of questions have now been raised: Has it happened before? What is the prognosis? What can be done about it?[1]

DID MASS BLEACHING OCCUR DURING PAST INTERGLACIALS OR EARLIER? If we look back into evolutionary time there have been many peaks in ocean temperature, as seen in ice core records (illustrated in Figure 9.5). This observation is often made by skeptics to argue that today's rises have been seen frequently in the past and are part of a natural climate cycle. However, ice core temperature peaks have doubtful relevance to tropical oceans, although they do show that polar ice volumes were periodically smaller than they are today, as a result of higher polar temperatures, longer interglacial intervals, or both.

Unfortunately, fossil reefs do not provide us with any information on bleaching in the geological past, nor is it known what zooxanthellae existed during the early Cenozoic, when CO_2 levels were far above those of today. Perhaps the zooxanthellae in symbiosis with corals during earlier times were better partners than those of today. Certainly modern coral-zooxanthellae symbioses were selected for when CO_2 was relatively low and tropical oceans were cooler. If so, those partnerships are not as optimal as they once were, and it is time for a change, *if* change is possible. The oceans may indeed contain varieties of zooxanthellae, possibly rare ones, that would be able to take on the job in a thermally stressed world, but this is wishful thinking for it has yet to be demonstrated. If such varieties exist, swapping of types may have happened many times—perhaps continuously—in the past. However, the evidence now emerging is somewhat to the contrary, for the phylogeny (genetic history) of corals and that of zooxanthellae are closely matched, indicating that corals do not readily swap their symbionts. Moreover, even if they do, these phylogenies indicate that the swapping process would take many thousands of years to complete,[2] a period too long to offer any useful benefit in today's abruptly changing environment.

ARE OBSERVATIONS OF BLEACHING LINKED TO INCREASED SCUBA DIVING?
Could mass bleaching have been occurring continuously yet be perceived as a recent phenomenon only because of the advent of scuba diving? Examining historical records, we find that bleaching received passing mention as a minor curiosity in the scientific literature of the early twentieth century, with only one isolated observation from the GBR. In this early literature, and up to the 1960s, there is not the slightest hint of mass bleaching in any reef region of the world. However, this does not constitute proof that it never occurred, especially as scientists did not take to scuba diving until well into the second half of the century.

There is no record of any mass bleaching on the GBR until the 1980s. Before then any instance of coral mortality directly attributable to bleaching was isolated in both time and place.[3] I myself worked continually on the GBR throughout the 1970s and had many associates who studied crown-of-thorns starfish back in the 1960s, a period when concerns about the extent of starfish damage resulted in widespread surveys of whole reef systems. There was no mass bleaching throughout that time. Moreover, there is not the slightest possibility that mass bleaching went unnoticed because it was mistaken for starfish damage. The feeding scars left by starfish are bare skeletons and have only a superficial resemblance to the pale or whitened tissue caused by bleaching. Evidence of starfish feeding is almost always patchy on single large colonies, whereas a full dose of bleaching is not. Significantly, too, mass bleaching targets inshore fringing reefs, where the water is shallow and relatively turbid—reefs that are generally avoided by the starfish.

Furthermore, there is convincing evidence that severe mass bleaching did *not* occur during the past few centuries. *Porites* forms very large colonies, often 3 meters high and 5 meters in diameter. Such colonies are studied by scientists seeking historical temperature and rainfall records, which can be inferred from their growth bands (see Chapter 3). Many of these colonies are hundreds of years old. When such colonies die naturally they do so piecemeal, by breaking apart under their own weight or becoming senescent. In contrast, entire surfaces of 500-year-old colonies along whole reef tracts have died in recent mass bleaching events, a form of mortality that is very distinct. Bleaching is the only cause of such mass death ever observed on the GBR. If the current death rate from bleaching of these long-lived colonies, or anything remotely like it, had been maintained over the past millennium, there would no longer be any large *Porites* colonies alive today. Yet such colonies dominate most inshore fringing reefs.

We can be confident that there was no mass bleaching on the GBR between 1960 and the first major event in 1981 and that mass bleaching is unlikely to have been a major influence on coral mortality during the past few centuries.

Links to El Niño Events

There is no clear link between enhanced greenhouse warming and the frequency or intensity of El Niño events. Analyses of historical records and projections from general circulation models are both ambivalent on the subject. The general climatic changes accompanying El Niño development are fairly well understood (see Chapter 4), although the factors controlling their initiation, intensity, and periodicity remain obscure. The 1997/1998 El Niño event may have been the most extreme in recorded history, and it is still possible that this and the two other major events of the past two decades (1981/1982 and 2001/2002) were exacerbated by other, slower, climatic cycles that are part of the natural variability of the Earth's climate and not a direct response to greenhouse warming.[4]

Although any direct causal link between enhanced greenhouse warming and El Niño intensity and frequency is thus uncertain, it is clear beyond doubt that El Niño cycles and mass bleaching on the GBR are connected.

Mass bleaching, we now know, is not caused by an overall increase in ocean temperature—that paltry 0.3°C in the tropics I referred to earlier—but by short-term concentrations of heat in the affected areas. We saw in Chapter 4 that on the GBR these temperature increases are caused by El Niño events, which pulse oceanic water from the Western Pacific Warm Pool, perhaps 1–2°C above what was once normal, into coastal regions. If this water is then trapped in the GBR lagoon it can warm still further, exacerbating the effects of the original pulse.

Although much still remains unknown, we have garnered a great deal of information and can sketch the essential relationships among El Niño cycles, global ocean temperatures, and mass bleaching. First, we know that enhanced (anthropogenic) greenhouse warming is occurring as a result of the amount and rate of buildup of CO_2 (see Chapter 13). Moreover, the oceans are warming far more slowly than the atmosphere because of thermal inertia, and a significant proportion of this warm water is remaining in the surface layers of tropical oceans because it is being accumulated too rapidly to be adequately dispersed and mixed by natural water circulation. We have also seen that thermal energy from enhanced greenhouse warming of the oceans is concentrated in the Western Pacific Warm Pool, the world's largest mobile body of heat.

El Niño events are now pulsing warm water (via the mechanism described in Chapter 4) from the Western Pacific Warm Pool onto the GBR, where it may be further heated in the lagoon. These temperature peaks have become lethally high only during the past few decades. The events themselves are not the result of global warming, but are a natural phenomenon of geological antiquity. There is, however, continuing debate over the role of enhanced greenhouse warming in altering the frequency or intensity of the events.

The association between El Niño events and mass bleaching is likely to be a temporary one as far as the GBR is concerned. As the Western Pacific Warm Pool widens and deepens, its central core at the thermal cap temperature of 31°C will begin to bathe outer reef regions in non–El Niño years. At that point the thermal peaks currently delivered by El Niño will become less and less exceptional, until they become irrelevant. This process is probably already beginning: as we saw in Chapter 4, 2006 was not an El Niño year and yet the GBR experienced considerable mass bleaching. There were similar observations in other parts of the world in both 2005 and 2006. Finally, although El Niño oscillations will become irrelevant for the GBR, they may continue to play a role in transmitting warm water pulses to other regions of the world for some time to come as the Warm Pool deepens and widens.

The Timeline

We have already entered a time frame in which mass bleaching is occurring without El Niño enhancement. If the relationship of atmospheric CO_2 levels to the amount or frequency of bleaching continues on its present trajectory, there will be a point at which every year will be comparable to the worst El Niño events of the past, with a similar impact on corals. At the present rate of CO_2 increase this will happen by midcentury. Put another way, the frequency of bleaching events will be reduced from every 3 to 7 years to every year, and their impacts will be increasingly widespread. Once again, we are talking about only half a century—an abrupt event in human time, an *instantaneous* event by any standards of evolution, let alone geology.

Is the worst yet to come? A key study based on a comparison between the 1997/1998 and the 2001/2002 mass bleaching events indicates that an increase in temperature of 1°C from the 1997/1998 level would increase the extent of bleaching from 50 to 82 percent, that an increase of 2°C would raise that to 97 percent, and that an increase of 3°C would cause total mortality.[5] This gives a disturbingly clear measure of just how close to the upper limits of tolerance GBR corals already are. However, in one sense these numbers could be considered misleading as ocean temperatures are not likely to keep going higher; instead the summer temperature of the Western Pacific Warm Pool will remain stable at 31°C, and this pool will have enlarged sufficiently to affect the GBR every year, with or without an El Niño event.

The effect of abnormally warm water on corals is a cumulative one; it depends on both the time of exposure and the actual temperature. As we have seen, corals in other parts of the world can adapt to normal temperatures higher than 31°C. Corals are more susceptible to swift temperature change than to the absolute temperature levels, which may mean that they will be at their most vulnerable during the next few decades while temperature variability remains high and pulsing continues. Once the waters bathing the reef are close to or at the thermal cap temperature all summer, temperature *variability* may actually moderate, giving corals greater opportunity to adjust to the new regime. This again depends on time—the amount of time needed to stabilize GBR lagoon water to a new "normal" level and the time corals take to adapt to it. Unfortunately, on our present

trajectory, there may be few corals remaining to benefit from this temperature stabilization.

A Changing GBR

On the GBR, reefs affected by mass bleaching tend to recover in much the
same way as those damaged by crown-of-thorns starfish and tropical cyclones. This recovery can take place, superficially, in as short a time as a
decade, largely owing to the rapid return of Acropora and other fast-
growing weedlike corals. Rapid recoveries are, however, highly dependent
on an abundant supply of coral larvae from healthy reefs; abundant herbivorous fish in close proximity, to keep algal growth in check; good water quality; and the absence of subsequent impacts from the same or other sources.
In places where these conditions are all met, reef slopes reduced to rubble
can undergo spectacular recoveries, as is illustrated in Plate 48. In such communities, once Acropora has returned, the extraordinary wealth of other reef
biota can also reestablish, including slow-growing corals.

But what happens when there is a failure in one or more of these conditions? One aspect is beyond doubt: reefs prone to bleaching will become
increasingly patchy. Some areas will be more affected than others, but most
are likely to undergo cycles of denudation and recovery, the latter diminishing as areas of dead reef become more extensive. As this process continues, one of several scenarios may take precedence, depending on local
conditions that are perhaps more relevant to algae than to corals. In some
parts of the GBR somewhat transitory algal communities have already
established themselves; in other parts they occur naturally on a seasonal
basis. If shelter-providing corals are so extensively destroyed that there are
not sufficient numbers of herbivorous fish to control the growth of macroalgae, many reefs will look like those illustrated in Plates 51 and 52, dominated by Sargassum, Padina, or both, intermixed with more bleaching-
resistant corals.

More extensive and prolonged Sargassum-dominated communities sig-
nal the furthest extent of reef degradation on the GBR thus far, largely
because the reefs are otherwise healthy and host enough fish to allow recovery to take place. This is not the case in other parts of the world, where
fishing pressure has prevented recovery and other types of algae, especially
Padina, have taken over as the dominant and semipermanent species. Where
this does not occur, the dead corals may become covered by a dark reddish

slime (the cyanobacteria *Entophysalis*), illustrated in Plates 54 and 55. Corals that continue to grow amid extensive slime are commonly affected by white-band or black-band disease (illustrated in Plate 56). Recovery under these conditions appears to be slow or even nonexistent. Not only were the reefs illustrated here devoid of coral, they were also almost lifeless, as few reef organisms live with bacterial slime.

One exception is the green coralline alga *Halimeda,* which may invade or even replace the slime. Today *Halimeda* may offer a first step on the road to recovery for slime-covered reefs, as it creates a form of healthy, three-dimensional, shelter-providing habitat that may encourage the return of algae-eating fish. However, in a world of acidified oceans, this will be only a temporary measure, a matter to which we return in the next chapter.

Safe Havens

Mass bleaching is occurring on a time scale that is "abrupt" by any measure. The bleaching that has taken place so far has not occurred slowly enough for communities to be able to move or for any sort of evolutionary adaptation to take place. If corals are to survive, they will need safe havens.

Do such safe havens exist? Certainly they do. The best refuges will be those in deeper water, not just because these are likely to be relatively cool, but also because light levels are low. Most locations on the outer edge of the continental shelf will offer protection, as constant mixing with off-shelf ocean water will prevent the further warming that can occur in the GBR lagoon. The ultimate refuges will likely be the lower slopes of outer reefs, especially those that slope steeply and are shielded from the sun. It is ironic that these are the very same places that would have been refuges for corals during intervals of low sea level. However, because at least 25 percent of the corals alive today never occur below 40 meters, depth for them may offer no long-term solution.

Retreat to higher latitudes is frequently suggested as a possible escape. This might occur within the GBR if time allows, but not south of the GBR. As indicated in Chapter 2, the southern limit of the GBR is determined by bathymetry: there are no options for extensive reef growth farther south apart from the few reef areas mentioned. Even if there were suitably large substrates, projected increases in acidification starting at high latitudes (see Chapter 15) would shut this door.

Looking farther afield to other reef regions of the world, it is likely that some may show little mass bleaching from temperature increase. For example, many of the large reef tracts of Komodo Island, Indonesia, are continuously bathed in cold water from upwelling and may never be subjected to temperature stress. Moreover, as I noted previously, there are many reefs in the equatorial Pacific whose corals have not been damaged by the thermal cap of 31°C. As this cap is unlikely to change to any significant degree, such reefs may also remain unaffected by mass bleaching. Likewise, there are reefs in the southern Red Sea and the Persian/Arabian Gulf where surface temperatures can reach 36°C without harm to the corals, but they bleach with a temperature rise of only 1°C above normal, so their future must be considered doubtful.

Artificial refuges are also a possibility, bearing in mind that corals protected from strong sunlight do not bleach. This leaves open the possibility of using floating shade cloth to protect coral on submerged reef areas during times of thermal stress. Such a strategy would, of course, be a final act of desperation—akin to protecting a tract of forest from fires by installing sprinklers.

Other Escape Routes: Acclimatization and Adaptation

Acclimatization (the process through which individuals' tolerance of environmental conditions increases during their lifetime) and adaptation (an evolutionary process involving natural selection through survival of the fittest) are seemingly the only other escape routes from the warm world of the future that are open to corals.

ACCLIMATIZATION.   There is evidence, on both local and global scales, that the same or closely related coral species show different tolerances to temperature in different locations. On local scales, good examples are corals that tolerate the very high temperatures found in intertidal pools, in water around natural thermal vents, or close to the thermal outlets of power stations.[6] We also know that normal maximum water temperatures found in particular geographic areas play a significant role in determining tolerance to bleaching. Furthermore, as just mentioned and as discussed in Chapter 4, whole suites of corals can survive at 36°C in the Persian/Arabian Gulf, parts of the southern Red Sea, and sporadically elsewhere. Like most animals, corals may adapt to tolerate these temperatures by altering their biochemical pathways.[7] On local scales this process is likely to be due to acclimatization; across more widely separated geographic areas there may be an element of genetic selection, especially where tolerance to local extreme conditions is involved.

On the GBR there are cross-shelf as well as latitudinal variations in coral bleaching thresholds, suggesting that thermal tolerance can change over small (tens of kilometers) as well as large (more than hundreds of kilometers) spatial ranges.[8] This may be due to some combination of acclimatization and adaptation, although the latter process now seems more likely, given that the former offers only a narrow range of options.

ADAPTATION.   It is possible that corals were once adapted to higher temperatures in the geological past—during the early part of our era, when CO_2 levels were much higher than they are today. There is, however, little or no evidence for or against this hypothesis. As outlined in Chapter 7, the template of today's oceans is so different from those of the remote past that meaningful comparisons are questionable. The studies, referred to earlier, that show that the genetic histories of corals and zooxanthellae closely match argue against any long-term history of adaptation by the changing of symbionts.

An Uncertain Future

There has recently been a spate of suggestions as to how corals might be able to adapt and how we might be able to assist this process by culturing preadapted genetic strains or by transplanting corals from one country to another, a strategy akin to "saving" forests by introducing exotic species or genetically engineering existing indigenous species. This sort of "coral gardening" is a last resort—one more likely to create problems than solve them. We must help Nature if we can, but not by usurping her role.

There is no escaping the simple truths I have just described. Neither corals nor zooxanthellae will be able to evolve heat resistance in a time frame remotely commensurate with the projected rate of ocean temperature increase, nor one even vaguely relevant to human civilization. The future of corals in a rapidly warming world is thus unlikely to involve evolution of new genetic types of zooxanthellae or new physiological mechanisms within corals. In the time now available, acclimatization may have a significant role to play, although it must be emphasized that such processes have their limits—as does the hope that future recovery lies in new symbiotic associations with existing genetic types of zooxanthellae. The best that can be hoped for is that somewhere in the biology of corals there is something that can help them win this race against time. How much time remains cannot be determined with any certainty, but it is a matter of only a few decades. Evolutionary processes—if there are any corals left to evolve—will eventually play a role, but only over many millennia at the very least.

Regrettably, mass bleaching is not the only threat looming for coral reefs. As alluded to in earlier chapters, there is an even more serious danger from anthropogenic CO_2 hovering in the background. Those reefs that escape mass bleaching will not have the same good fortune when ocean waters become acidified. Rather the reverse: the safe havens from elevated temperatures that I have identified here (cool and deep locations) will be the first to be targeted by this frightening and insidious process—one, as we will see in the next chapter, that is about to become the central issue for marine environments the world over.

— 15 —

Ocean Acidity and
Coralline Osteoporosis

Increasing anthropogenic CO_2 is destined to acidify all the oceans of the world. The pH of the oceans will decrease at an accelerating rate during the present century. Although largely unrecognized, this is set to become the most serious of the many consequences of elevated CO_2 for corals and coral reefs. If allowed to continue unchecked, acidification could readily recreate the ocean chemistry that drastically affected all marine life at the beginning of our era.

The prospect of ocean acidification is frightening. We saw in Chapter 6 that, linked as it is to other parts of the carbon cycle, acidification was probably a major cause of mass extinctions and reef gaps in the oceans of our remote geological past, especially the K/T mass extinction (65 mya) at the close of the Mesozoic Era. Today acidification is not frightening because of any immediate impact on corals. Compared to the effects of mass bleaching, which are dramatically obvious today, the consequences of acidification are still vague, and its major effects are still a few decades away. Acidification is serious because of *commitment*—a word that will soon be used with increasing frequency in the scientific literature.

Commitment embodies the concept of unstoppable inevitability, according to which the nature and health of future environments will be determined not by our actions at some future date but by what is happening today. The oceans, including the ocean depths, respond slowly to atmospheric conditions, whether a temperature increase or a CO_2 buildup, which means that the full effects of acidification will take time to develop. Nevertheless, this is only a delay: the factors causing acidification will have irretrievably committed the Earth to the process long before its effects become anywhere near as obvious as those of mass bleaching today.

Nonspecialists who are well aware of the role played by anthropogenic CO_2 in enhancing greenhouse warming are not as conversant with its role in ocean acidification. This is partly because the effects of acidification are as yet not visible, but also because the subject has received much less coverage in both the popular and the scientific press. So far, the topic largely resides in humdrum chemical equations, in seemingly innocuous changes in ocean pH, and in computer models.

Recapping CO_2 Impacts in the Geological Past

Not all ocean chemistry catastrophes in the ancient world can be directly blamed on atmospheric CO_2 levels, but in most cases we look in vain for alternative explanations. The geological past has shown us many times over that the Earth has enormous reserves of carbon that can be converted into CO_2 gas and its chemical associates via biological and geological pathways that operate at very different rates. Whatever the process, there is one fundamental certainty: the Earth *does* have accessible carbon reserves sufficient to produce lethal levels of CO_2 one way or another. Just how past levels accumulated to the extent they apparently did is seldom clear, although there is little doubt that synergies—the compounding effects of many causes— were usually involved in the release of CO_2 or methane or both. In the past the same result has been achieved many times without extraterrestrial or, for that matter, human help.

CO_2 levels have had a massive impact on coral reefs over geological time. Before assessing their past and future influence on acidification and its consequences, let us review the main points discussed in earlier chapters:

- Mass extinctions affect reefs as much as any other ecosystem on Earth. They have brought corals to total extinction once (the end Permian mass extinction, 251 mya) and to near extinction four times (the other mass extinction events).
- Variations in the concentration of atmospheric CO_2 result in fluctuations in both ocean temperature and sea level. CO_2-induced temperature variations have occurred continuously throughout the existence of all life on Earth, whereas rapid sea-level variations occur only when the Earth has polar ice caps.
- CO_2, one way or another, is likely to have been implicated in all mass extinction events. The Ordovician mass extinction (434 mya) was

virtually a dress rehearsal for our icehouse Pleistocene past combined with our possible (short-term) greenhouse future.

- Methane is second only to CO_2 as a cause of environmental decline, but the two gases are linked: methane readily oxidizes to CO_2, a process that decreases its greenhouse effect but increases its effect on ocean acidification.
- It is likely that the ocean chemistry after K/T (65 mya) reflects what these gases are capable of doing. Broadly comparable conditions probably occurred after all the mass extinctions, as well as many background extinctions that have affected coral reefs.
- Azooxanthellate and zooxanthellate corals were equally affected by the K/T mass extinction, convincingly implicating degradation in water chemistry as a primary cause.
- Reef gaps after mass extinctions may have multiple causes, yet all seem closely linked to ocean acidity, a process that prevents corals from building skeletons and (for the last two mass extinctions) coralline algae from consolidating them.
- Paleozoic corals, which had calcite skeletons, may have been less affected by acidity than modern corals, which have aragonite skeletons.

There are other forms of degradation of ocean chemistry besides acidity, with lack of oxygen and the presence of hydrogen sulfide (which go together) being the most important. Over geological time scales all these different types of water degradation can occur together to affect whole oceans, just as they do over brief intervals of time today when atoll lagoons turn anoxic. (For example, in 1988 a brief failure of normal tidal flushing of the lagoon of Cocos [Keeling] Atoll in the Indian Ocean resulted in the death of all corals and most fish and other life. The whole lagoon first started smelling of hydrogen sulfide and then became acidified and anoxic.)

Carbonates in the Ocean: The Giant Antacid Tablet

The chemistry of CO_2 dissolved in seawater is generally understood, although it is not straightforward,[1] because the capacity of CO_2 to dissolve in the oceans is sensitive to atmospheric concentration as well as to water temperature. Increasing atmospheric concentration drives more CO_2 into the ocean, but rising ocean temperatures reduce the capacity of the ocean to absorb it. This temperature effect is significant: it reduces the capacity of the oceans to absorb CO_2, although, at least currently, not enough to counter the effect of the additional uptake that is due to increasing atmospheric concentration.

About half of all CO_2 from anthropogenic sources still remains in the atmosphere. Of the remainder, most has been taken up by the ocean,[2] a process that has now used up about one-third of the total storage capacity of the ocean surface.[3] The rest has been taken up by terrestrial life.[4]

It is clear that, without uptake of anthropogenic CO_2 by the oceans, atmospheric levels would be about 55 ppm higher than at present. The preindustrial levels of carbonate ions in seawater were about 85 percent HCO_3^- and 15 percent CO_3^{2-}; doubling atmospheric CO_2 will alter this ratio to about 90 percent HCO_3^- and 10 percent CO_3^{2-}. On time scales of decades to centuries, if dissolved ocean surface CO_2 continues to increase in proportion to atmospheric CO_2, a doubling of the latter from preindustrial levels will result in a 30 percent decrease in total carbonate ion concentration and a 60 percent increase in hydrogen ion concentration in surface waters. These changes will increasingly diminish the ocean's capacity to absorb CO_2 from the atmosphere—the proportional net rate of ocean extraction from the atmosphere declining in a self-reinforcing cycle, even though the physical rate of exchange of CO_2 between atmosphere and ocean will remain approximately constant.[5]

If CO_2 levels are allowed to increase to 650–700 ppm, as is projected to occur later this century, a return to twice the preindustrial level of 560 ppm will take disproportionately longer (hundreds of years) owing to this slowing of the rate of uptake by the oceans. It is generally unappreciated just how long it will take to bring CO_2 concentrations back down to normal levels. If we continue to produce CO_2 at the present rate, we can expect the atmosphere to retain significant effects from it for between 30,000 and 35,000 years, which, when modeled, means that 17–33 percent of the excess CO_2 currently in the atmosphere will still be there a thousand years from now.[6]

The acidification effect caused by increasing atmospheric CO_2 will initially be buffered by bicarbonate-carbonate ion exchange, but once the buffers are overwhelmed (depending on as yet unpredicted depth effects) it will change relatively abruptly. Unlike enhanced greenhouse temperature increase, the acidification effect of CO_2 will not bounce back to a benign level if atmospheric CO_2 returns to normal; the oceans will remain acidified until they are neutralized by the dissolving of marine carbonate rocks and the weathering of rocks on land, a hugely protracted process.

When CO_2 levels increase to 560 ppm, the Southern Ocean surface waters will be undersaturated with respect to aragonite,[7] and the pH will be reduced by about 0.24 units—from almost 8.2 today to a little more than 7.9. At the present rate of acidification, all reef waters will have an aragonite saturation state ($\Omega_{aragonite}$) of 3.5 or less by the middle of this century. The simulation illustrated in Plate 57 shows that when this happens only a few reefs of the Pacific will have carbonate saturation adequate for uninhibited coral growth.[8] When CO_2 levels reach 800 ppm later this century, the decrease will be 0.4 units,[9] and dissolved carbonate ion concentration will have decreased by almost 60 percent. At that point all the reefs of the world will be affected.

Dissolution of calcium carbonate begins at pH 7.9, at which stage carbonate sediments on the ocean floor become a giant antacid tablet, making it virtually impossible for the oceans to actually turn acid, yet at the same time preventing living organisms from forming carbonate skeletons. The levels of CO_2 and pH predicted by the end of this century may not have occurred since the Middle Eocene[10] (45 mya; see Figure 7.4), but the all-important *rate* of change we are currently experiencing has no known precedent. There can be no evolutionary solution for such a rate of change.

Just what the long-term outlook might be is unpredictable. The protracted recovery times (reef gaps) of the ancient world would have been greatly extended by *prolonged* high atmospheric CO_2 levels; just what happens when that CO_2 is a *short-term* spike against a background of *low* CO_2 levels is less clear because there is no known precedent in the geological record from which to draw comparisons. However, a failure of the Ocean Conveyor at the same time as a failure of the biological pump (the capacity of phytoplankton to extract CO_2 from seawater) would lead to increased isolation of warm surface waters from deep ocean buffers for prolonged periods of time (even by geological standards)—on the order of hundreds of thousands of years.

The ocean, with its larger inventory and longer residence time, is already in charge of the destiny of the Earth's climates—our human focus on the atmosphere notwithstanding.

Coral Calcification: The Future Outlook

The effect of doubling seawater CO_2 levels on coral calcification can be calculated, modeled, and experimentally tested.[11] Although there are varying opinions as to the *short-term* future effects of decreased aragonite saturation on coral calcification in a greenhouse world, there can be no doubt that the medium- and long-term consequences are likely to be dire as the buffering action of marine carbonates progressively fails.[12]

There is a roughly direct relationship between aragonite saturation and the capacity of corals to calcify[13] when temperatures are near optimum levels. In the longer term, when atmospheric CO_2 is doubled, calcification may be reduced by up to 50 percent.[14] This production rate is well below that required to offset reef breakdown from bioerosion (see Chapter 3), which means that, as this century progresses, reefs will erode, not grow.

The issue of commitment introduced at the beginning of this chapter is another matter entirely. The long-term outlook is that reefs will be committed to a path of destruction long before any effects are visible. Just what happens to corals, as opposed to reefs, under these conditions is unclear. Will they simply grow more slowly, or will they grow at the same speed and have weaker (less calcified) skeletons—a sort of coralline osteoporosis? Will they become more vulnerable to boring organisms and pathogens? The study of such details is still in its infancy.

There will no doubt be considerable species-specific variability based on the degree to which different corals can actively control the calcification process as carbonate ions become scarcer. Their tolerance to other synergistic stresses, their growth forms, and perhaps even their ability to alter the skeletal material they lay down will vary among species. A recent study indicates that some scleractinian corals can build skeletons from a form of calcite in artificially acidified experimental conditions.[15] This accords with the discovery of partly calcitic scleractinian corals of the Late Cretaceous (100 mya; Chapter 6)—even so these corals did not survive the K/T mass extinction. Even if a wide range of Scleractinia can switch to making skeletons of calcite (improbable though this is), it would be at best a short-term, stop-gap measure in maintaining corals against the forces of erosion.

There are many unknowns. Despite a considerable amount of research over many decades, much remains to be discovered about the biochemical mechanisms of coral calcification: the degree to which it is based on carbonate or bicarbonate ions and its relationships to primary productivity, temperature, light, and (particularly) details of ocean chemistry.

Today it can probably be claimed that no downturn in reef coral calcification has yet been observed in natural reef environments, although the same cannot be said of some other calcifying organisms. Changes are now being observed in the aragonite compensation depth and in the pH of surface waters of the Southern Ocean. The aragonite compensation depth has always limited the distribution of azooxanthellate corals; now, as it shallows, it has begun excluding them from the ocean depths they have inhabited for millions of years.[16] Phytoplankton, especially the aragonite coccoliths that create extensive blooms on the ocean surface and are responsible for the removal of a high proportion of carbonate derived from atmospheric CO_2, are already being adversely affected in the Southern Ocean.

The Future of Ocean Acidification

Ocean acidification is a new area of science in which data of all sorts are conspicuously wanting.[17] To date there has also been relatively little cross-fertilization among the different fields most relevant to the issue. Thus, for example, ocean carbon modelers use mild phrases like "adverse biological consequences" to describe environmental conditions that would, in the long term, be absolutely catastrophic for reefs. There is also a general lack of awareness of the role of CO_2 in determining the fortunes (or rather the misfortunes) of marine life in the remote past. These are not criticisms; I am merely drawing attention to the fact that the subject of ocean acidification, despite its importance, does not come surrounded by a wealth of iron-clad science.[18] Rather it is based on a small number of sound scientific studies that must be heeded every bit as carefully as we heed those dealing with global warming today.

Fortunately acidification does not have anything like the number of variables that must be taken into account in dealing with global warming. Future trends in ocean pH and aragonite saturation are becoming predictable, at least in relation to atmospheric CO_2 levels. The general, far-reaching negative consequences of reduced calcification on marine ecosystems are also predictable. What is still far from clear is exactly how these effects will manifest themselves: which will come first, which species will be most susceptible, and what second-order effects there will be for other dependent components of affected marine food webs. The overall scenario is now grounded in sound science; these are details still to be filled in.

The first widespread biological impact of acidification, already under way, is on the phytoplankton of the Southern Ocean, potentially affecting the food source of krill, small shrimplike animals that are the linchpin of virtually all Southern Ocean food webs. Deep-sea (azooxanthellate) corals are likely to be next in line, with 70 percent of the area they now occupy becoming undersaturated with respect to aragonite by the middle of this century.[19] As acidification spreads to the tropics, the first organisms to be affected will be those that deposit magnesium calcite skeletons, especially reef-consolidating coralline algae. Corals and other reef organisms with aragonitic skeletons will be next, followed by a wide range of reef-dependent biota as the complexity of the reef structure begins to break down. These impacts, like those of temperature, will at first be patchy in time as well as space because of the vagaries of the ocean currents and short-term cycles to which they are linked.[20]

Ultimately—and here we are looking at centuries rather than millennia—the ocean pH will drop to a point at which a host of other chemical changes, including a lack of oxygen, may kick in. If this happens, the description I gave of the oceans at the end of K/T, or something like it, will become a reality. We have set the stage for the sixth great mass extinction, and another few decades like our last century will see the Earth committed to a trajectory from which there will be no escape.

This account of acidification may seem like a science-fiction horror story, but there is little evidence of fiction either in the science on which it is based or in the simplified interpretation I have given here. A continued business-as-usual scenario of CO_2 production will ultimately result in destruction of marine life on a colossal scale. It has happened before and it can happen again.

Furthermore, as I explained earlier, CO_2 is far from the only source of carbon that gives cause for concern. If some of the Earth's reserves of terrestrial methane are also released through mining, or via melting of the permafrost and the draining of tropical marshlands (both of which are already occurring), undersaturation of both aragonite and calcite will ensue in all of the Earth's oceans, in an even shorter time frame.[21] The amount of marine methane sequestered on continental shelves is over 5,000 gigatons, perhaps more carbon than is stored as fossil fuel and far more than was released during the Late Paleocene Thermal Maximum (55 mya). If a small fraction of this methane were to be released—through buoyancy changes, allowing ice-like slurries to float free of the substrate, or simply through melting, resulting from any regional temperature increase—it would accelerate both greenhouse warming and ocean acidification.[22] Nothing comparable to this has occurred so rapidly at any time in the known geological record, the only imaginable exception being the time of the end Permian mass extinction (251 mya), about which we know so little (see Chapter 5).

Coral reefs will not respond to acidification as rapidly, or as visibly, as they will to temperature stress. However, their response will occur throughout all of the oceans, and it will be permanent as far as humans are concerned. When both temperature stress and acidification are taken together the prognosis for corals is bleak indeed. The predicted rate of change is so great that there is no possibility that corals will be able to rely on genetic adaptation to respond to bleaching stress or reduced pH. Any adaptive advantage must already be present in today's gene pool for it to be effective. Even if temperature-tolerant symbiotic zooxanthellae are available, the species that might survive in an acidified ocean would be relatively vulnerable, certainly more so than during previous extinction events when CO_2 buildup was more gradual, allowing time for adaptive change.

Surviving reef corals will probably be only nonbranching species, for they will have weakened skeletons and will grow only where they are protected from wave action. The myriad of grazing fish seen on healthy reefs today will, in consequence, be gone. Likewise, the wonderful diversity of life we enjoy on reefs will be replaced by algal and bacterial communities growing on rock (illustrated in Plates 54 and 55), awash from a higher sea level and pounded by waves from more frequent tropical storms.

Ocean acidification *must* be taken seriously and as a matter of great urgency if the world's oceans are not to be committed to a future of unbridled destruction. It has happened before and it not only *can* happen again, it *will* happen again unless adequate intergovernmental action is taken on CO_2 emissions now. This is one of the most serious (if least well understood) of all predicted environmental changes on Earth, yet so far it has attracted only the most superficial publicity and, to date, only the beginnings of intergovernmental recognition. Preventative action is the same as for global warming and coral bleaching, but the time frame and severity of acidification, as well as its long-term consequences, have no equal. For those few scientists who understand what looms ahead, the Earth might seem like a neglected car—continually being driven past the mechanic's shop to a car wash for a quick touch-up, when what is really needed is urgent mechanical repair.

— 16 —

The Ocean's Canary

The predicted demise of the GBR and most other coral reefs, first from mass bleaching and then from irreversible acidification will occur in this century if anthropogenic greenhouse gas emissions are not drastically curbed within a decade. Although this is one of several such predictions grounded in a wide array of solid science, a lack of international willingness to confront core issues will soon lead to unstoppable processes that could bring on an extinction event the likes of which the world has not seen for 65 million years.

Tijou Reef is an awesome place, especially when huge ocean rollers build up over the outer face and break on the reef flat with a roar loud enough to strike fear into the heart of any mariner. When I first dived on that face on a calm day more than thirty years ago, I reflected on how bizarre it was that the tiny coral polyps that built this massive fortress should be so pathetically vulnerable to the vagaries of the climate of the distant, frozen poles—places as different from a coral reef as any on Earth. When the northern continents freeze and the oceans recede, the corals of the GBR are forced to abandon their self-made limestone homes and live somewhere else—in places that are not reefs as we know them. At such times corals, along with most other reef species, are clearly able to sustain their existence; however, the abundance of this life, which makes reefs unique, must inevitably be forfeited.

Today, as I imagine these tiny polyps going about their daily lives, the same thoughts return, but this time they are even more bizarre. Now the lives of these simple creatures are being threatened by human policy decisions, perhaps made in Beijing or Washington, D.C. This is not chaos theory, according to which the beating wings of a butterfly might create the turbulence that ultimately becomes a tornado. It is a much better understood cause-and-effect relationship, the cause being greenhouse gases of our own making and the effect being changes to our environment. What scientists are only now coming to appreciate is the unprecedented speed with which this is happening. Although this book is not specifically about climate change, the magnitude and the predicted acceleration of adverse effects make it inevitable that this subject has become its central concern. Argue as we might about the details of computer models, temperature, pH, ocean circulations, and the rest, the GBR, the ocean's canary, has given us an unequivocal warning. The consequences of ignoring that warning will be dire.

Abrupt Change in a Human-Controlled World

Of all the negative impacts humans have had on global environments, over half have occurred within my lifetime—since the end of World War II. In that infinitesimally brief interval, environmental impacts have gone from something that few people even noticed to levels that we now know are not remotely sustainable. In that time most of the world's major ecosystems have deteriorated to the point that they no longer have any pristine components left, where even the future existence of many of them may be shrouded in doubt. In that time much of the world's vulnerable megafauna, both marine and terrestrial, has become dependent on some form of human intervention for its continued existence—protection by us from us. In most cases this protection offers our most valued fauna an essential respite, but it can also set in motion conditions for its demise, perhaps not in the world we currently live in, but in one that could well come into being should our capricious First World economies falter under the impact of a (human-scale) global catastrophe. Such a catastrophe might be of human origin (runaway climate change clearly topping the list, but also including such events as a viral pandemic or a nuclear war) or a natural event (such as a supervolcano, bolide, or giant tsunami). Whatever the cause, the global stability we have long enjoyed will not last indefinitely—it never has before and it certainly will not now.

Should First World economies go into a major recession, it is hardly likely that it will be business as usual for today's conservation practices in whatever political arenas ultimately emerge. Conservation is expensive, and in the wake of such a catastrophe it will have to compete with other priorities— if indeed humans are still masters of their own destiny. After all, conservation to preserve biodiversity is about surviving millennia, not centuries. We myopic humans plan and act in terms of decades, not even centuries.

In the unlikely event that I live for another forty years, I will see the world's human population double before its predicted leveling off. Can it realistically be assumed that such an increase will "only" have double the present environmental impact? No. Many developing countries aspire to the living standards of the industrialized world, which roughly translates into First World per capita environmental impacts.

China, with about one-fifth of the Earth's total population, has the fastest-growing economy of all, at nearly 10 percent a year. China derives three-quarters of her energy requirements from coal (one-quarter of the global total), generating 12 percent of the world's anthropogenic CO_2. China's achievement of First World living standards alone would approximately double the entire world's human resource needs and environmental impacts.[1]

Although mitigating strategies are being put in place, such as transferring energy dependency from fossil fuels to renewable resources and the invention of more energy-efficient means of transport (transport currently generates 30 percent of anthropogenic CO_2), the world's primary energy demand is expected to climb 1.7 percent annually over the next forty years. Moves to reduce energy use may have already produced tangible results, although only on scales relevant to present consumption. Over those next forty years, my instant of time on this planet will have seen it change from one where conservation needs went almost unnoticed to one where even our physical environment will depend on human management.

Climates to Come

The two preceding chapters are depressingly devoid of optimism. The Kyoto Protocol is now a decade old, and the criteria on which it was based are out of date. The most recent census of atmospheric CO_2 concentration shows that its rate of increase is now at an all-time maximum—6.3 billion tons per year—and is increasing annually by 0.3 percent. Augmented at this rate, CO_2 emissions will reach 12 billion tons a year by 2030 and 20 billion tons by 2100, resulting in an atmospheric concentration of 1,100 ppm at the end of this century—exceeding all current IPCC forecasts.[2]

Throughout the pages of this book, I have illustrated change in the concentration of atmospheric CO_2 over three different intervals of time: the time of the existence of reefs (hundreds of millions of years; Figure 5.8), during our own era (tens of millions of years; Figure 7.4), and during gla-

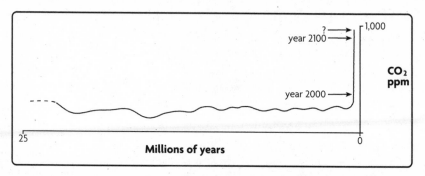

Figure 16.1 Change in CO_2 levels from the GBR's most likely time of origin to its foreseeable future. At this scale, the increase in the anthropogenic CO_2 spike is a vertical line. If this diagram were redrawn with a horizontal axis 250 meters long, the spike would *still* be a vertical line.

cial cycles (hundreds of thousands of years; Figure 9.3). In the accompanying illustration I show a fourth—change over the longevity of the GBR, incorporating the latest forecasts. At this scale the rate of increase since industrial times is starkly obvious. We are dealing with a geological-scale event that is taking place so rapidly that it can be studied in just a few human lifetimes. There are even children alive today who may have the dubious privilege of observing the whole process almost from beginning to end.

The potential to recreate the conditions of a mass extinction, at least as far as marine life is concerned, is very real and the event will be under way long before it is clearly visible, by which time it will be absolutely unstoppable.

Whether one is inclined to pessimism or just rational judgment, we have on record the views of numerous farsighted scientists to suggest what the future may hold for our species in view of its impact on the environment. The alarm is sounded on every side, and in no uncertain terms:

> Now it's too late to change and we cannot organise ourselves to stop. I speculate that our system is in free fall, out of control.
>
> —*Michael Boulter*[3]

> Our species, then, is on the brink of causing, single-handedly, the worst mass extinction in 65 million years.
>
> —*David Jablonski*[4]

> On a geological timescale . . . the wheel is spinning at a
> blurring rate, and the disappearance of species amounts
> to a virtually instantaneous mass extinction.
>
> —*Les Kaufman*[5]

> One cannot reasonably compare the K/T extinction with
> the current human destruction of the biosphere. The first
> was a relatively minor setback.
>
> —*"Jack" Briggs*[6]

I do not seek to be emotive; I have selected these particular messages because I believe they are all, in their individual ways, fundamentally true. They are not specifically relevant to climate change; the focus is on human destruction of the biosphere, and in any event these quotes predate current recognition of approaching ocean acidification. I select another, from among many, which is of current relevance:

> Scientists estimate that if habitat conversion and other
> destructive human activities continue at their present rates,
> half the species of plants and animals on Earth could be
> either gone or at least fated for early extinction by the end
> of this century. A full quarter will drop to this level during
> the next half century as a result of climate change alone.
>
> —*E. O. Wilson*[7]

And one with a personal human perspective:

> Ours are the most fortunate generations that have ever
> lived. Ours might also be the most fortunate generations
> that ever will. We inhabit a brief historical interlude between ecological constraint and ecological catastrophe.
>
> —*George Monbiot*[8]

It cannot rationally be doubted that we are now at the start of an event that has the potential to become the Earth's sixth mass extinction. This time there are no bolides, no supervolcanoes, and no significant sea-level changes. Our seas are not yet dangerously acidified, and our reefs and forests, damaged though many may be, are still wondrous places. This is not an extinction event being driven by an environmental upheaval with a geological cause and a geological time frame. For the first time in the history of the Earth, the cause is unquestionably biological. Bolides aside, this means that it is a far more rapid process than any extinction of the past. Until recently it has also meant that it has primarily targeted terrestrial rather than marine species. But our extinction event is no longer just a matter of humans displacing other species; it is now a case of humans changing the environment. Moreover, let us be clear about the scope of such human influence. This book has focused on reefs and corals, but as we saw in Chapter 6, changes in climate and acidification together have the power to disrupt many, if not all, marine food webs. A collapse of similar dimensions today would be catastrophic for marine life, and for the millions of humans dependent upon it. Land environments will not suffer from acidification, but from our study of past climate changes we know that terrestrial ecosystems will suffer similar fates, albeit via different mechanisms.

Human impacts and global environments were, until recently, very different subjects. That has now changed.

Awareness

We are now facing the inescapable conclusion that the GBR, along with all the other coral reefs in the world, will be diminished beyond anything we have ever considered "normal" as a direct result of human-induced climate change—and that this will happen during the present century. I have laid out the evidence as objectively as possible, my primary purpose being to heighten awareness of the rate at which the changes are happening. It is hard to know for certain just what sort of awareness exists outside the scientific arena—that is, in government and among the general public. On the one hand, a conference is held somewhere in the world every week or so on some aspect of enhanced greenhouse warming, and it has been *the* central issue at virtually all international meetings of reef scientists. On the other hand, most of the general public remains blissfully unaware of the seriousness of its consequences.

A decade ago the effects or even the existence of climate change could reasonably be debated, but this is no longer the case. Today virtually all the articles published in respected scientific journals accept climate change as an established fact. The debates are no longer about *if* our climate is changing, but about the mechanisms, consequences, and speed—the science—of the process.

Nevertheless, at times Australian and international media have played a negative role in the public awareness of human-induced climate change. Many of the popular media have seen it as their function to offer a "balanced" approach, giving equal coverage to climate change science and climate change skeptics, even though the those in the latter category have long been a small and rapidly vanishing minority. This has resulted in a distorted view of scientific consensus that keeps the public in a perpetual state of indecision—no small matter when the subject is as important as the future of the Earth's climate. Such public uncertainty, in combination with pressure from groups with vested interests, has prolonged government inaction in some democratic countries (notably the United States and Australia), and this delay is already having far-reaching consequences. The GBR will be among the first in a long line of dominoes to fall, because mass bleaching will precede acidification; others will follow quickly if warnings from climate science go unheeded.

A Matter of Time

A look back at the fossil record of marine life offers a chilling reminder that there is an intrinsic period for biodiversity to recover from extinctions. That timeline for reefs can be measured in hundreds of thousands to millions of years.[9] Whatever is happening to biodiversity now is, as far as humans are concerned, for keeps if effective action is not taken. Of that there can be no doubt.

The prospect that anything possessing the grandeur of the GBR could be decimated within a century seems preposterous, especially in the light of all that the GBR has been through in the past. There is always uncertainty in predicting the future, and no doubt this story will still take many unforeseen turns. But with the planet's health at stake, how many of us, I wonder, are prepared to gamble that there has been a miraculous miscalculation on the part of thousands of scientists in a dozen disciplines? Personally, I believe that the evidence is increasingly unequivocal. In a CO_2-belching, business-as-usual world, acidification will soon rival and then surpass mass bleaching as the foremost marine management issue. If drastic action is not taken *now,* by 2030–2050 temperature increases will have led to widespread degradation of the GBR. The frequency and perhaps the severity of El Niño events may be little changed, but they will be largely irrelevant. The thermal cap of 31°C will remain in place, but the oceans will continue to absorb more and more heat. As the Western Pacific Warm Pool broadens and deepens, the kinds of impacts once restricted to El Niño years will eventually become annual—effectively normal—events. By that time, mass bleaching will have blighted the entire GBR many times. There will be intervals of recovery, but they will be increasingly brief.

Also by 2030–2050 the more insidious process of acidification will have spread to equatorial regions and will be exerting its influence throughout the tropics, including the GBR. Increased temperatures will have delayed its impact on surface waters, but by then corals will not be growing as they used to because the entire reef ecosystem will have lost its current resilience.

What will the GBR look like by the end of this century if we take no decisive action? This cannot be predicted with certainty, as the changes will be nonlinear; that is, they will occur in steps as short-term climate cycles interact and as ocean buffers fail. It is certain, however, that reefs will have none of the rich diversity and spectacular beauty that they have today. Plate 54 illustrates a would-be reef of the future.

Of course there can be no end to the GBR as a geological structure, except in the broadest geological time. However, let us not confuse its capacity to recover from kangaroo country mode with its ability to recover from acidification. The former involves reef life abandoning reef habitats as the sea level falls, then returning to them as it rises—something it is clearly able to do. The latter involves a hugely prolonged alteration in ocean chemistry that will be permanent as far as humans are concerned. Unlike sea-level change, this change *does* have the capacity to destroy life on a global scale. If the corals of one reef can be killed off, then the same can happen to any other reef: size offers no protection. Pockets of shallow-water coral communities may persist in lagoons where there is good protection from wave action, peak temperatures, and direct sunlight. There may also be remnant coral communities deep down outer reef faces—places we know little about—that are bathed in upwelled water containing reserves of carbonate buffers. But these survivors will be a small minority. There can be no doubt that, if we humans continue on our present course, these consequences will ensue. Our goal *must* now be to alter that path to ensure that they do not.

Buying time has become *the* central issue. Over the past century an explosion of energy-consuming technologies has changed our world beyond recognition and kept us on a track of resource consumption and pollution far greater than the Earth can tolerate. The question now is whether industrialized countries are prepared to make the investment necessary for new technologies to replace old ones before the latter are due for replacement. So far, apparently not: since 1985, with the exception of a few very recent initiatives, governmental funding for energy research and development has fallen in every industrialized country except Japan. Democracy, however desirable for human peace and stability, is not a form of government that sacrifices economic progress for any reason, certainly not something as nebulous as climate change—at least not until it is far too late.

This century will be by far the most challenging that humans have ever faced. At the top of the agenda for the governments and citizens of the industrialized nations is consideration of the extent to which they are prepared to protect the environment at the expense of economic progress. Time is running out, and the longer we rely on fossil fuels the costlier it will become to kick the addiction and the closer we will come to being unable to do so. The necessity to separate what is economically best for humanity from what is best for the environment has become critical. If there is no concerted action, humans, at least those in the industrialized countries, may be able to party on for a few more decades using fossil fuel—protected as they are from major inconvenience by technology—before the crisis overtakes them. However, the same cannot be said for the other species that share our planet as well as for most humans in developing countries. They cannot escape the environments that the energy-hungry are creating.

We may liken our biosphere to a bank. Our ancestors started making minor withdrawals soon after they earned the name *Homo sapiens.* No matter—this was a bank of unimaginable wealth. It survived many ups and downs well enough for thousands of years until just recently, when industrialization and the population explosion it unleashed created the conditions for a "run." Now we are forcing that bank to make unsecured loans, and we are also making repeated withdrawals in unprecedented amounts. I cannot say with certainty what will happen when this bank fails, but I believe that the youth of today are likely to find out.

The Choice

The prognosis for the GBR and other coral reefs of the world does indeed seem bleak, but it is not yet hopeless. The future well-being of the environment, terrestrial as well as marine, depends on cutting anthropogenic green-house gas emissions, and that will require intergovernmental cooperation and investment on an unprecedented scale. These reductions will eventually be forced on humanity, although if this step is delayed until we reach a no-option-but-to-act stage, it will long have been too late. If we as individuals want to preserve any degree of ecological stability, we must be vocal in bringing about government action. Time is critical: the point of no return—the tipping point—is probably within a decade.

In a world where scientists have made space travel possible and have mapped out the human genome, there is indeed hope. A raft of alternative low-emission energy and power-saving technologies is now emerging, some innovations showing great promise. Unfortunately many cannot be adequately developed and implemented in the time left to us. We must buy them more time—by taking individual action and by pressuring governments to radically refocus their efforts on reducing CO_2 emissions. Right now the most pressing need is to understand the urgency of the situation and to keep our priorities straight.[10] Space exploration can wait. Energy-saving breakthroughs to protect our environment cannot.

We have at our disposal the technological means to slow CO_2 buildup. In the short term, sequestering liquid CO_2 deep underground[11] or extracting it using crushed limestone (a relatively temporary measure because of the volume required) show the most promise. There are also ideas—although they are little more than ideas at this stage—about how CO_2 might be removed from the atmosphere with less energy than it took to put it there in the first place.

We must look imaginatively and creatively at all possibilities, including the contentious option of nuclear power. Of course power from nuclear fusion, clean and unlimited, would be a panacea—unfortunately little more than a happy dream at this point. Hydrogen fuel cells, the harnessing of solar and wind energy, and biological fuels from sugar plantations will all help, although with such limited time, less energy-consuming lifestyles remain the only realistic option. The reality is that the longer we remain dependent on fossil fuel, the more expensive the alternatives become.

We are now entering a world where political leaders may not live to see the consequences of their actions—or lack of action—but their children and grandchildren certainly will. Are we to consign all our descendants to see reef life only in giant aquaria, where all aspects of water quality are artificially controlled. Personally I do not find this prospect engaging. I pity these future generations, who will not experience the boundless beauty of a world that I have taken for granted for most of my life.

Of course the burning question as far as the GBR is concerned is what can be done now to protect it. The first, and ultimately only effective, step is to stop polluting our Earth with greenhouse gases. Individuals *can* make a difference, by changing their personal lifestyles to reduce their own energy consumption and by pressuring governments into action to reduce consumption in public arenas. The second is to minimize other stresses affecting reef biota in order to maximize the reef's resilience to the adversities of the future. We must also keep hope for the future alive. There may come a time during this century when most reefs the world over will look like the worst of them do today—so degraded that people who remember what a healthy reef looks like might come to feel that reefs are no longer worth bothering with. Whatever the future holds, we must never entertain such thoughts about the greatest marine World Heritage region on Earth. The need now is to keep the GBR in as good a state as possible, by whatever management techniques are at hand, and to help herbivores, especially fish, keep algae at bay.

This decade represents a window of choice, a period of crisis during which we must do whatever is necessary to prevent our century from becoming a transition to disaster. If we do not act, or do not act fast enough, marine and coastal ecosystems will be set on an irretrievable path of extermination that will eventually see a meltdown in coastal economies with devastating cost to natural environments and human societies. When this is combined with terrestrial effects of climate change, the combination is catastrophic. The cause may have been a spike, but the effect will, at least in the case of ocean acidification, last for a minimum of hundreds of thousands of years. The GBR will have become but a reef of the past for this vast stretch of time.

This cannot be allowed to happen. The proactive alternative is the only alternative that can be accepted. With immediate global action now to drastically reduce CO_2 emissions there will come a time when the crisis has passed. The GBR, although scarred, will come through whatever lies ahead and once again be the place it is now. Ironically, even then, it is destined to remain so only briefly—for about 30,000 years. For, as long as Antarctica is still frozen and greenhouse gas levels have returned to something like normal, the configuration of the Earth's orbit around the sun will once again throw that mysterious switch and send the Earth plunging into another ice age—and the GBR back into kangaroo country mode.

Whether any humans will be around at that time to climb down the face of Tijou Reef as their ancestors probably once did remains an unanswerable question. The options are ours. For if we do not change our ways, Gaia, her forests denuded and her oceans acidified, will have taken just revenge.

> The planet we live on has merely to shrug to take some frac-
> tion of a million people to their death. But this is nothing
> compared with what may soon happen; we are now abusing
> the Earth that it may rise and move back to the hot state it
> was in fifty-five million years ago, and if it does most of us,
> and our descendants, will die.
>
> —*James Lovelock*[12]

Notes

Glossary

Acknowledgments

Index

Notes

1. The Big Picture

1. J. Diamond, *Guns, Germs, and Steel* (New York: W.W. Norton, 1997).
2. V. Courtillot, *Evolutionary Catastrophes: The Science of Mass Extinction* (Cambridge, U.K.: Cambridge University Press, 1999).
3. S. A. Earle, *Sea Change: A Message of the Oceans* (New York: G. P. Putnam's Sons, 1995)

2. The Great Barrier Reef: An Overview

1. M. D. Spalding, C. Ravillious, and E. P. Green, *World Atlas of Coral Reefs* (London: University of California Press, 2001).
2. L. M. DeVantier, G. De'ath, E. Turak, T. J. Done, and K. E. Fabricius, "Species Richness and Community Structure of Reef-Building Corals on the Nearshore Great Barrier Reef," *Coral Reefs* 25 (2006): 329–340.
3. T. J. Done, "Patterns in the Distribution of Coral Communities across the Central Great Barrier Reef," *Coral Reefs* 1 (1982): 95–107.
4. D. Hopley, S. G. Smithers, and K. E. Parnell, *The Geomorphology of the Great Barrier Reef: Development, Diversity and Change* (Cambridge, U.K.: Cambridge University Press (2007).
5. J. E. N. Veron, "Deltaic and Dissected Reefs of the Northern Region," *Philosophical Transactions of the Royal Society of London B: Biological Sciences* 284 (1978): 23–27.
6. W. G. H. Maxwell, "Deltaic Patterns in Reefs," *Deep-Sea Research* 17 (1970): 1005–1018.
7. R. H. Richmond, "Energetics, Competency, and Long-Distance Dispersal of Planula Larvae of the Coral *Pocillopora damicornis*," *Marine Biology* 93 (1987): 527–533.

8. The principal subject of J. E. N. Veron, *Corals in Space and Time: The Biogeography and Evolution of the Scleractinia* (Sydney, N.S.W.: University of New South Wales Press, 1995).

9. The original study at the generic level is given in J. W. Wells, "A Survey of the Distribution of Reef Coral Genera in the Great Barrier Reef Region," *Report of the Great Barrier Reef Committee* 6 (1955): 1–9. Species details are in J. E. N. Veron, *Corals in Space and Time: The Biogeography and Evolution of the Scleractinia* (Sydney, N.S.W.: University of New South Wales Press, 1995).

10. D. Hopley, *The Geomorphology of the Great Barrier Reef: Quaternary Development of Coral Reefs* (New York: John Wiley and Sons, 1982); J. E. N. Veron, *Corals in Space and Time: The Biogeography and Evolution of the Scleractinia* (Sydney, N.S.W.: University of New South Wales Press, 1995).

11. Reviewed and updated from original studies by the author and his colleagues by V. J. Harriott and S. A. Banks, "Latitudinal Variation in Coral Communities in Eastern Australia: A Qualitative Biophysical Model of Factors Regulating Coral Reefs," *Coral Reefs* 21 (2002): 83–94.

12. J. W. Wells, "A Survey of the Distribution of Reef Coral Genera in the Great Barrier Reef Region," *Report of the Great Barrier Reef Committee* 6 (1955): 1–9; J. Pickett, "A Late Pleistocene Coral Fauna from Evans Head, N.S.W.," *Alcheringa* 5(1–2) (1981): 71–83.

13. J. E. N. Veron and T. J. Done, "Corals and Coral Communities of Lord Howe Island," *Australian Journal of Marine and Freshwater Research* 30 (1979): 203–236; V. J. Harriott, P. L. Harrison, and S. A. Banks, "The Coral Communities of Lord Howe Island," *Marine and Freshwater Research* 46 (1995): 457–465.

14. C. D. Woodroffe, D. M. Kennedy, B. G. Jones, and C. V. G. Phipps, "Geomorphology and Late Quaternary Development of Middleton and Elizabeth Reefs," *Coral Reefs* 23 (2004): 249–262.

15. J. E. N. Veron, "A Biogeographic Database of Hermatypic Corals: Species of the Central Indo-Pacific, Genera of the World," *Australian Institute of Marine Science Monograph Series 10* (Townsville, Qld.: Australian Institute of Marine Science, 1993).

3.   Corals and Reefs: Controls and Processes

1. This concept, in the context of this chapter, is discussed by D. R. Bellwood, T. P. Hughes, C. Folke, and M. Nyström, "Confronting the Coral Reef Crisis," *Nature* 429 (2004): 827–833.

2. R. K. Trench, "The Cell Biology of Plant-Animal Symbosis," *Annual Reviews of Plant Physiology* 30 (1979): 485–531; R. Rowan and D. A. Powers, "Ribosomal

RNA Sequences and the Diversity of Symbiotic Dinoflagellates (Zooxanthel-lae)," *Proceedings of the National Academy of Science USA* 89 (1992): 3639–3643.

3. L. Muscatine, "Nutrition of Corals," in O. A. Jones and R. Endean, eds., *Biology and Geology of Coral Reefs*, Vol. 2: *Biology 1* (New York: Academic Press, 1973), pp. 77–115.

4. Articles cited in this paragraph postdate the primary review of O. Hoegh-Guldberg, "Climate Change, Coral Bleaching and the Future of the World's Coral Reefs," *Marine and Freshwater Research* 50 (1999): 839–866.

5. K. E. Ulstrup and M. J. H. van Oppen, "Geographic and Habitat Partitioning of Genetically Distinct Zooxanthellae (*Symbiodinium*) in *Acropora* Corals on the Great Barrier Reef," *Molecular Ecology* 12 (2003): 3477–3484.

6. A. F. Little, M. J. H. van Oppen, and B. L. Willis, "Flexibility in Algal Endo-symbioses Shapes Growth in Reef Corals," *Science* 304 (2004): 1492–1494.

7. C. J. Crossland, "Latitudinal Comparisons of Coral Reef Structure and Func-tion," *Proceedings of the Sixth International Coral Reef Symposium* 1 (1988): 221–226, and many subsequent authors.

8. J. E. N. Veron and P. R. Minchin, "Correlations between Sea Surface Tempera-ture, Circulation Patterns and the Distribution of Hermatypic Corals of Japan," *Continental Shelf Research* 12 (1992): 835–857.

9. P. W. Glynn, J. E. N. Veron and G. M. Wellington, "Clipperton Atoll (Eastern Pa-cific): Oceanography, Geomorphology, Reef-Building Coral Ecology and Bio-geography," *Coral Reefs* 15 (1996): 71–99.

10. Assessments of reef carbonate production are reviewed by A. Vecsei, "A New Es-timate of Global Reefal Carbonate Production Including the Fore-Reefs," *Global and Planetary Change* 43 (2004): 1–18.

11. S. V. Smith, "Coral Reef Calcification," in D. J. Barnes, ed., *Perspectives in Coral Reefs* (Townsville, Qld.: Australian Institute of Marine Science, 1983), pp. 240–247, and several subsequent studies.

12. Reviewed by L. F. Montaggioni, "History of Indo-Pacific Coral Reef Systems since the Last Glaciation: Development Patterns and Controlling Factors," *Earth-Science Reviews* 71 (2005): 1–75; D. Hopley, S. G. Smithers, and K. E. Par-nell, *The Geomorphology of the Great Barrier Reef: Development, Diversity and Change* (Cambridge, U.K.: Cambridge University Press, 2007).

13. A review of this extraordinary discovery, which continues to shed light on many previously unknown aspects of coral reproduction, is given in P. L. Harrison, "Sexual Characteristics of Scleractinian Corals: Systematic and Evolutionary Implications," *Proceedings of the Fifth International Coral Reef Congress (Tahiti)* 2 (1985): 337–342.

14. The arguments are presented in J. E. N. Veron, "Reticulate Evolution in Corals," *Proceedings of the Ninth International Coral Reef Symposium (Bali)* 1 (2002): 43–48.

4.   The State of the Great Barrier Reef

1. A highly informative review of threats to coral reefs prior to the full realization of the impact of global warming is given in C. Birkeland, ed., *Life and Death of Coral Reefs* (New York: Chapman and Hall, 1997).

2. Global Coral Reef Monitoring Network, *Status of Coral Reefs of the World* (Townsville, Qld: Australian Institute of Marine Science (biannual reports), 1998, 2000, 2002, 2004). Published electronically: www.aims.gov.au.

3. Gerry Allen, personal communication.

4. Records of Emre Turak and the author.

5. This is a difficult subject to quantify; see J. M. Pandolfi, R. H. Bradbury, E. Sala, T. P. Hughes, K. A. Bjorndal, R. G. Cooke, D. McArdle, L. McClenachan, M. J. H. Newman, G. Paredes, R. R. Warner, and J. B. C. Jackson, "Global Trajectories of the Long-Term Decline of Coral Reef Ecosystems," *Science* 301(5635) (2003): 955–958.

6. C. Birkeland, "Ratcheting Down the Coral Reefs," *Bioscience* 54(11) (2004): 1021–1027; www.coralreef.org.

7. P. Clare, *The Struggle for the Great Barrier Reef* (Sydney, N.S.W.: Collins, 1971); T. Brown, *Crown of Thorns: The Death of the Great Barrier Reef?* (Sydney, N.S.W.: Angus and Robertson, 1972); P. James, *Requiem for the Reef* (Brisbane: Foundation Press, 1976); J. A. Wright, *The Coral Battleground* (Melbourne: Thomas Nelson, 1977).

8. D. Haynes, J. Brodie, J. Waterhouse, Z. Bainbridge, D. Bass, and B. Hart, "Assessment of the Water Quality and Ecosystem Health of the Great Barrier Reef (Australia), Part 1: Conceptual Models," *Environmental Management* (in press).

9. A comprehensive review is given in L. Burke, E. Selig, and M. Spalding, *Reefs at Risk in Southeast Asia* (Washington, D.C.: World Resources Institute, 2002).

10. Personal observations and Global Coral Reef Monitoring Network, *Status of Coral Reefs of the World* (Townsville, Qld: Australian Institute of Marine Science (biannual reports) 1998, 2000, 2002, 2004). Published electronically: www.aims.gov.au.

11. An extensive array of data on these subjects is given in M. Furnas, *Catchments and Corals: Terrestrial Runoff to the Great Barrier Reef* (Townsville, Qld.: Australian Institute of Marine Science, 2003).

12. An excellent synthesis is given by K. E. Fabricius, "Effects of Terrestrial Runoff on the Ecology of Corals and Coral Reefs: Review and Synthesis," *Marine Pollution Bulletin* 50 (2005): 125–146.

13. K. E. Fabricius and E. Wolanski, "Rapid Smothering of Coral Reef Organisms by Muddy Marine Snow," *Estuarine, Coastal and Shelf Science* 50 (2000): 115–120.

14. GBRMPA website, www.gbrmpa.gov.au.

15. This case, for a wide range of biota from microbes to commercially harvested species, is made by S. R. Palumbi, "Humans as the World's Greatest Evolutionary Force," *Science* 293 (2001): 1786–1790. Evidence for the world's best-studied fish species is in E. M. Olsen, M. Heino, G. R. Lilly, M. J. Morgan, J. Brattey, B. Ernande, and U. Dieckmann, "Maturation Trends Indicative of Rapid Evolution Preceded the Collapse of Northern Cod," *Nature* 428 (2004): 932–935.

16. O. Hoegh-Guldberg, "Climate Change, Coral Bleaching and the Future of the World's Coral Reefs," *Marine and Freshwater Research* 50 (1999): 839–866.

17. O. Hoegh-Guldberg and R. J. Jones, "Diurnal Patterns of Photoinhibition and Photoprotection," *Marine Ecology Progress Series* 183 (1999): 73–86; R. J. Jones and O. Hoegh-Guldberg, "Diurnal Changes in the Photochemical Efficiency of the Symbiotic Dinoflagellates (Dinophyceae) of Corals: Photoprotection, Photoinactivation and the Relationship to Coral Bleaching," *Plant, Cell and Environment* 24 (2001): 89–99.

18. Summarized by B. E. Brown, "Adaptations of Reef Corals to Physical Environmental Stress," *Advances in Marine Biology* 31 (1997): 221–299.

19. Historical accounts are given in B. E. Brown, "Disturbances to Reefs in Recent Times," in C. Birkeland, ed., *Life and Death of Coral Reefs* (New York: Chapman and Hall, 1997), pp. 354–378; B. E. Brown, R. P. Dunne, M. S. Goodson, and A. E. Douglas, "Marine Ecology: Bleaching Patterns in Reef Corals," *Nature* 404 (2000): 142–143; and R. Berkelmans and J. K. Oliver, "Large-Scale Bleaching of Corals on the Great Barrier Reef," *Coral Reefs* 18 (1999): 55–60.

20. P. W. Glynn, "Widespread Coral Mortality and the 1982–83 El Niño Warming Event," *Environmental Conservation* 11(2) (1984): 133–146; P. W. Glynn, "Coral Mortality and Disturbances to Coral Reefs in the Tropical Eastern Pacific," in P. W. Glynn, ed., *Global Ecological Consequences of the 1982–83 El Niño-Southern Oscillation* (Amsterdam: Elsevier Oceanography Series, 1990), pp. 55–126; and P. W. Glynn, "Coral Reef Bleaching in the 1980's and Possible Connections with Global Warming," *Trends in Ecology and Evolution* 6 (1991): 175–179, pioneered this work. Reviewed by P. W. Glynn, "Coral Reef Bleaching: Ecological Perspectives," *Coral Reefs* 12 (1993): 1–17; B. E. Brown, "Disturbances to Reefs in Recent Times," in C. Birkeland, ed., *Life and Death of Coral Reefs* (New York: Chapman and Hall, 1997), pp. 354–378; B. E. Brown, R. P. Dunne, M. S. Goodson, and A. E. Douglas, "Marine Ecology: Bleaching Patterns in Reef Corals," *Nature* 404 (2000): 142–143; O. Hoegh-Guldberg, "Climate Change, Coral Bleaching and the Future of the World's Coral Reefs," *Marine and Freshwater Research* 50 (1999): 839–866.

21. Details of these surveys are given in R. Berkelmans and J. K. Oliver, "Large-Scale Bleaching of Corals on the Great Barrier Reef," *Coral Reefs* 18 (1999): 55–60.

22. J. M. Lough, "1997–98: Unprecedented Thermal Stress to Coral Reefs?" *Geophysical Research Letters* 27(23) (2000): 3901–3904.

23. An informative review specifically relevant to the GBR is given in R. Berkelmans, "Time-Integrated Thermal Bleaching Thresholds of Reefs and Their Variation on the Great Barrier Reef," *Marine Ecology Progress Series* 229 (2002): 73–82.

24. Good reviews are given in P. L. Jokiel and S. L. Coles, "Response of Hawaiian and Other Indo-Pacific Reef Corals to Elevated Temperatures," *Coral Reefs* 8 (1990): 155–162; and S. L. Coles and B. E. Brown, "Coral Bleaching: Capacity for Acclimatization and Adaptation," *Advances in Marine Biology* 46 (2003): 183–223.

25. C. B. Cook, A. Logan, J. Ward, B. Luckhurst, and C. J. Berg, Jr., "Elevated Temperatures and Bleaching on a High Latitude Coral Reef: The 1988 Bermuda Event," *Coral Reefs* 9 (1990): 45–49; G. S. Aeby, J. C. Kenyon, J. E. Maragos, and D. C. Potts, "First Record of Mass Coral Bleaching in the Northwestern Hawaiian Islands," *Coral Reefs* 22 (2003): 256.

26. R. Berkelmans and M. J. H. van Oppen, "The Role of Zooxanthellae in the Thermal Tolerance of Corals: A Nugget of Hope for Coral Reefs in an Era of Climate Change," *Proceedings of the Royal Society B: Biological Sciences* 273(1599) (2006): 2305–2312.

27. B. E. Brown, "Disturbances to Reefs in Recent Times," in C. Birkeland, ed., *Life and Death of Coral Reefs* (New York: Chapman and Hall, 1997), pp. 354–378; B. E. Brown, R. P. Dunne, M. S. Goodson, and A. E. Douglas, "Marine Ecology: Bleaching Patterns in Reef Corals," *Nature* 404 (2000): 142–143; B. E. Brown, R. P. Dunne, M. S. Goodson, and A. E. Douglas, "Experience Shapes the Susceptibility of a Reef Coral to Bleaching," *Coral Reefs* 21 (2002): 119–126.

28. K. E. Ulstrup and M. J. H. van Oppen, "Geographic and Habitat Partitioning of Genetically Distinct Zooxanthellae (*Symbiodinium*) in *Acropora* Corals on the Great Barrier Reef," *Molecular Ecology* 12 (2003): 3477–3484; K. E. Fabricius, "Effects of Terrestrial Runoff on the Ecology of Corals and Coral Reefs: Review and Synthesis," *Marine Pollution Bulletin* 50 (2005): 125–146; R. Berkelmans and M. J. H. van Oppen, "The Role of Zooxanthellae in the Thermal Tolerance of Corals: A Nugget of Hope for Coral Reefs in an Era of Climate Change," *Proceedings of the Royal Society B: Biological Sciences* 273(1599) (2006): 2305–2312.

29. T. Li, T. F. Hoga, and C.-P. Chang, "Dynamic and Thermodynamic Regulation of Ocean Warming," *Journal of the Atmospheric Sciences* 57(20) (2000): 3353–3365, and many earlier publications.

30. H. F. Diaz and V. Markgraf, *El Niño and the Southern Oscillation: Multiscale Variability and Global and Regional Impacts* (Cambridge, U.K.: Cambridge University Press, 2000); J. M. Lough, "Sea Surface Temperature Variations on Coral Reefs: 1903–1998," *AIMS Report No. 31* (Townsville, Qld.: Australian Institute of Marine Science, 2000). An excellent account of the 2002–03 El Niño is given

by M. J. McPhaden, "Evolution of the 2002/03 El Niño," *American Meteorological Society* 85(5) (2004): 677–695.

5. Mass Extinctions and Reef Gaps

1. Comprehensive compilations of the causes of mass extinctions and the subsequent recovery of reefs are given by J. J. Sepkoski Jr., "Patterns of Phanerozoic Extinction: A Perspective from Global Databases," in O. H. Walliser, ed., *Global Events and Event Stratigraphy* (Berlin: Springer-Verlag, 1995), pp. 35–51, and R. Wood, *Reef Evolution* (Oxford, U.K.: Oxford University Press, 1999). A summary of the main points is in G. D. Stanley Jr., "Introduction to Reef Ecosystems and Their Evolution," in G. D. Stanley Jr., ed., *The History and Sedimentology of Ancient Reef Systems* (New York: Kluwer Academic/Plenum, 2001), pp. 1–39.

2. Dates for the appearance and disappearance of several thousand families and several tens of thousands of genera of marine invertebrates have been compiled by D. M. Raup and J. J. Sepkoski Jr., "Periodic Extinction of Families and Genera," *Science* 231 (1986): 833–836, and J. J. Sepkoski Jr., "Patterns of Phanerozoic Extinction: A Perspective from Global Databases," in O. H. Walliser, ed., *Global Events and Event Stratigraphy* (Berlin: Springer-Verlag, 1995), pp. 35–51. Their analyses are very informative, especially as there is broad agreement between the two taxonomic levels.

3. J. E. N. Veron, *Corals of the World* (3 volumes) (Townsville, Qld.: Australian Institute of Marine Science, 2000).

4. R. A. Berner, "GEOCARB II: A Revised Model of Atmospheric CO_2 Over Phanerozoic Time," *American Journal of Science* 294 (1994): 56–91; R. A. Berner, "The Rise of Plants and Their Effect on Weathering and Atmospheric CO_2," *Science* 276 (1997): 544–546. Reviewed by T. J. Crowley and R. A. Berner, "CO_2 and Climate Change," *Science* 292 (2001): 870–872.

5. Reviewed by A. Hallam and P. B. Wignall, *Mass Extinctions and Their Aftermath* (Oxford, U.K.: Oxford University Press, 1997).

6. B. D. Webby, "Global Biogeography of Ordovician Corals and Stromatoporoids," in B. Webby and J. R. Laurie, eds., *Global Perspectives on Ordovician Geology 2* (Rotterdam, Netherlands: Balkema, 1992), pp. 261–276; P. Copper, "Evolution, Radiations, and Extinctions in Proterozoic to Mid-Paleozoic Reefs," in G. D. Stanley Jr., ed., *The History and Sedimentology of Ancient Reef Systems* (New York: Kluwer Academic/Plenum, 2001), pp. 89–119.

7. P. Copper, "Silurian and Devonian Reefs: 80 Million Years of Global Greenhouse between Two Ice Ages," in W. Kiessling, E. Flügel, and J. Galonka, eds., *Phanerozoic Reef Patterns. SEPM Special Publication* 72 (Tulsa, Okla.: Society for Sedimentary Geology, 2002), pp. 181–238.

8. P. Copper, "Ancient Reef Ecosystem Expansion and Collapse," *Coral Reefs* 13 (1994): 3–11.

9. A. G. Cook, "Sedimentology and Depositional Environments of the Middle Devonian Lower Fanning River Group (Big Bend Arkose and Burdekin Formation), Burdekin Subprovince, North Queensland, Australia," *Memoirs of the Queensland Museum* 38(1) (1995): 53–91.

10. P. E. Playford, "Devonian 'Great Barrier Reef' of Canning Basin, Western Australia," *American Association of Petroleum Geologists Bulletin* 64(6) (1980): 814–840.

11. P. Copper, "Ancient Reef Ecosystem Expansion and Collapse," *Coral Reefs* 13 (1994): 3–11.

12. D. J. McLaren and W. D. Goodfellow, "Geological and Biological Consequences of Giant Impacts," *Annual Review of Earth and Planetary Science* 18 (1990): 123–171.

13. Reviewed by P. Copper, "Evolution, Radiations, and Extinctions in Proterozoic to Mid-Paleozoic Reefs," in G. D. Stanley Jr., ed., *The History and Sedimentology of Ancient Reef Systems* (New York: Kluwer Academic/Plenum, 2001), pp. 89–119.

14. D. H. Erwin, *The Great Paleozoic Crisis: Life and Death in the Permian* (New York: Columbia University Press, 1993); D. H. Erwin, "The Permo-Triassic Extinction," *Nature* 367 (1994): 231–236; J. J. Sepkoski Jr., "Patterns of Phanerozoic Extinction: A Perspective from Global Databases," in O. H. Walliser, ed., *Global Events and Event Stratigraphy* (Berlin: Springer-Verlag, 1995), pp. 35–51.

15. R. Wood, *Reef Evolution* (Oxford, U.K.: Oxford University Press, 1999); M. Boulter, *Extinction: Evolution and the End of Man* (London: Fourth Estate, 2002).

16. G. Ryskin, "Methane-Driven Oceanic Eruptions and Mass Extinctions," *Geology* 31(9) (2003): 741–744.

17. W. Kiessling, "Phanerozoic Reef Trends Based on the Paleoreef Database," in G. D. Stanley Jr., ed., *The History and Sedimentology of Ancient Reef Systems* (New York: Kluwer Academic/Plenum, 2001), pp. 41–88; E. Flügel and B. Senowbari-Daryan, "Triassic Reefs of the Tethys," in G. D. Stanley Jr., ed., *The History and Sedimentology of Ancient Reef Systems* (New York: Kluwer Academic/Plenum, 2001), pp. 217–249.

18. G. D. Stanley Jr., "The History of Early Mesozoic Reef Communities: A Three-Step Process," *PALAIOS* 3 (1988): 170–183; G. D. Stanley Jr., "Introduction to Reef Ecosystems and Their Evolution," in G. D. Stanley Jr., ed., *The History and Sedimentology of Ancient Reef Systems* (New York: Kluwer Academic/Plenum, 2001), pp. 1–39; J. J. Sepkoski Jr., "Patterns of Phanerozoic Extinction: A Perspective from Global Databases," in O. H. Walliser, ed., *Global Events and Event Stratigraphy* (Berlin: Springer-Verlag, 1995), pp. 35–51.

19. L. Beauvais, "Evolution and Diversification of Jurassic Scleractinia," *Palaeontographica Americana* 54 (1984): 219–224; George Stanley, personal communication.

20. R. Wood, *Reef Evolution* (Oxford, U.K.: Oxford University Press, 1999); E. Flügel and B. Senowbari-Daryan, "Triassic Reefs of the Tethys," in G. D. Stanley Jr., ed., *The History and Sedimentology of Ancient Reef Systems* (New York: Kluwer Academic/Plenum, 2001), pp. 217–249.

21. T. J. Crowley and R. A. Berner, "CO_2 and Climate Change," *Science* 292 (2001): 870–872, updated and reviewed by M. Hautmann, "Effect of End-Triassic CO_2 Maximum on Carbonate Sedimentation and Marine Mass Extinction," *Facies* 50 (2004): 257–261.

22. G. D. Stanley Jr., "The History of Early Mesozoic Reef Communities: A Three-Step Process," *PALAIOS* 3 (1988): 170–183; G. D. Stanley Jr., "Introduction to Reef Ecosystems and Their Evolution," in G. D. Stanley Jr., ed., *The History and Sedimentology of Ancient Reef Systems* (New York: Kluwer Academic/Plenum, 2001), pp. 1–39.

23. Different aspects of this view are given by L. Beauvais, "Jurassic Corals from the Circum-Pacific Area," *Memoirs of the Association of Australasian Palaeontologists* 8 (1989): 291–302; W. Kiessling, "Phanerozoic Reef Trends Based on the Paleoreef Database," in G. D. Stanley Jr., ed., *The History and Sedimentology of Ancient Reef Systems* (New York: Kluwer Academic/Plenum Publishers, 2001), pp. 41–88; and R. R. Leinfelder, "Jurassic Reef Ecosystems," in G. D. Stanley Jr., ed., *The History and Sedimentology of Ancient Reef Systems* (New York: Kluwer Academic/Plenum, 2001), pp. 251–309.

24. Different points of view, but similar conclusions, are given by B. R. Rosen and D. Turnšek, "Extinction Patterns and Biogeography of Scleractinian Corals across the Cretaceous/Tertiary Boundary," *Memoir of the Association of Australasian Palaeontologists* 8 (1989): 355–370; J. E. N. Veron, *Corals in Space and Time: The Biogeography and Evolution of the Scleractinia* (Sydney, N.S.W.: University of New South Wales Press, 1995); and W. Kiessling, "Phanerozoic Reef Trends Based on the Paleoreef Database," in G. D. Stanley Jr., ed., *The History and Sedimentology of Ancient Reef Systems* (New York: Kluwer Academic/Plenum, 2001), pp. 41–88.

25. J. E. N. Veron, *Corals in Space and Time: The Biogeography and Evolution of the Scleractinia* (Sydney, N.S.W.: University of New South Wales Press, 1995).

26. E. Gili, J.-P. Masse, and P. W. Skelton, "Rudists as Gregarious Sediment-Dwellers, Not Reef-Builders, on Cretaceous Carbonate Platforms," *Palaeogeography, Palaeoclimatology, Palaeoecology* 118 (1995): 245–267.

27. R. W. Scott, "Evolution of Late Jurassic and Early Cretaceous Reef Biotas," *PALAIOS* 3 (1988): 184–193.

28. J. M. Philip and C. Airaud-Crumière, "The Demise of the Rudist-Bearing Carbonate Platforms at the Cenomanian-Turonian Boundary: A Global Control," *Coral Reefs* 10 (1991): 115–125.

29. E. J. Barron, "A Warm, Equable Cretaceous: The Nature of the Problem," *Earth-Science Reviews* 19 (1983): 305–338.

30. E. J. Barron and W. M. Washington, "Warm Cretaceous Climates: High Atmospheric CO_2 as a Plausible Mechanism," in E. T. Sundquist and W. S. Broecker, eds., *Geophysical Monograph*, Vol. 32: *The Carbon Cycle and Atmospheric CO_2: Natural Variations, Archaean to Present* (Washington, D. C.: American Geophysical Union, 1985), pp. 546–553.

31. R. A. Berner, "GEOCARB II: A Revised Model of Atmospheric CO_2 over Phanerozoic Time," *American Journal of Science* 294 (1994): 56–91; E. Tajika, "Climate Change during the Last 150 Million Years: Reconstruction from a Carbon Cycle Model," *Earth and Planetary Science Letters* 160 (1998): 695–707; E. Tajika, "Carbon Cycle and Climate Change during the Cretaceous Inferred from a Biogeochemical Carbon Cycle Model," *The Island Arc* 8 (1999): 293–303. Reviewed by A. Gale, "The Cretaceous World," in S. J. Culver and P. F. Rawson, eds., *Biotic Response to Global Change: The Last 145 Million Years* (Cambridge, U.K.: Cambridge University Press, 2000), pp. 4–19; C. C. Johnson, D. Sanders, E. G. Kauffman, and W. W. Hay, "Patterns and Processes Influencing Upper Cretaceous Reefs," W. Kiessling, E. Flügel, and J. Galonka, eds., *Phanerozoic Reef Patterns. SEPM Special Publication* 72 (Tulsa, Okla.: Society for Sedimentary Geology, 2002), pp. 549–585.

32. L. Alvarez, W. Alvarez, F. Asaro, and H. V. Michel, "Extraterrestrial Cause for the Cretaceous-Tertiary Extinction: Experimental Results and Theoretical Interpretation," *Science* 208 (1980): 1095–1108.

33. W. Glen, "What Killed the Dinosaurs?" *American Scientist* 78 (1990): 354–370.

34. A broad review is given by N. MacLeod, P. F. Rawson, P. L. Forey, F. T. Banner, M. K. Boudagher-Fadel, P. R. Brown, J. A. Burnett, P. Chambers, S. Culver, S. E. Evans, C. Jeffery, M. A. Kaminski, A. R. Lord, A. C. Milner, A. R. Milner, N. Morris, E. Owen, B. R. Rosen, A. B. Smith, P. D. Taylor, E. Urquhart, and J. R. Young, "The Cretaceous-Tertiary Biotic Transition," *Journal of the Geological Society of London* 154 (1997): 265–292.

35. V. Courtillot, *Evolutionary Catastrophes: The Science of Mass Extinction* (Cambridge, U.K.: Cambridge University Press, 1999), revised from the original 1995 French edition.

36. J. C. Briggs, "A Cretaceous-Tertiary Mass Extinction? Were Most of the Earth's Species Killed Off?" *Bioscience* 41 (1991): 619–624.

37. B. R. Rosen, "Algal Symbiosis and the Collapse and Recovery of Reef Communities: Lazarus Corals across the Cretaceous/Tertiary Boundary," in S. J. Culver and P. F. Rawson, eds., *Biotic Response to Global Change: The Last 145 Million Years* (Cambridge, U.K.: Cambridge University Press, 2000), pp. 164–180; B. R.

Rosen and D. Turnšek, "Extinction Patterns and Biogeography of Scleractinian Corals across the Cretaceous/Tertiary Boundary," *Memoir of the Association of Australasian Palaeontologists* 8 (1989): 355–370.

6.   Messages from Deep Time

1. O. B. Toon, K. Zahnle, D. Morrison, R. P. Turco, and C. Covey, "Environmental Perturbations Caused by the Impacts of Asteroids and Comets," *Reviews of Geophysics* 35 (1997): 41–78. Imaginary descriptions of bolide impacts and resulting tsunamis are in I. Plimer, *A Short History of Planet Earth* (Sydney, N.S.W.: Australian Broadcasting Commission, 2001).
2. D. Jablonski, "Mass Extinctions: New Answers, New Questions," in L. Kaufman and K. Mallory, eds., *The Last Extinction* (Cambridge, Mass.: MIT Press, 1986), pp. 43–61.
3. L. J. Rothschild and A. M. Lister, eds., *Evolution on Planet Earth: The Impact of the Physical Environment* (London: Academic Press, 2003).
4. Reviewed by D. Jablonski, "Mass Extinctions: New Answers, New Questions," in L. Kaufman and K. Mallory, eds., *The Last Extinction* (Cambridge, Mass.: MIT Press, 1986), pp. 43–61.
5. D. M. Raup and J. J. Sepkoski Jr., "Periodic Extinction of Families and Genera," *Science* 231 (1986): 833–836.
6. Explanatory accounts are given by J. A. Kleypas and C. Langdon, "Overview of CO_2-Induced Changes in Seawater Chemistry," *Proceedings of the Ninth International Coral Reef Symposium (Bali)* 2 (2002): 1085–1089; J. A. Kleypas and C. Langdon, "Coral Reefs and Changing Seawater Carbonate Chemistry," in J. T. Phinney, O.Hoegh-Guldberg, J. A. Kleypas, W. Skirving and A. Strong, eds., *Coral Reefs and Climate Change: Science and Management: American Geophysical Union Coastal and Estuarine Studies* 61 (2006): 73–110. ; and R. W. Buddemeier, J. A. Kleypas, and R. B. Aronson, *Coral Reefs and Global Climate Change: Potential Contributions of Climate Change to Stresses on Coral Reef Ecosystems* (Arlington, Va.: Pew Center on Global Climate Change, 2004).
7. C. Pelejero, E. Calvo, M. T. McCulloch, J. F. Marshall, M. K. Gagan, J. M. Lough, and B. N. Opdyke, "Preindustrial to Modern Interdecadal Variability in Coral Reef pH," *Science* 309 (2005): 2204–2207.
8. M. Fine and D. Tchernov, "Scleractinian Coral Species Survive and Recover from Decalcification" *Science* 315 (2007): 1811.

7.   The Cenozoic Roller Coaster

1. S. I. D'Hondt, J. King, and C. Gibson, "Oscillatory Marine Response to the Cretaceous-Tertiary Impact," *Geology* 24(7) (1996): 611–614; S. I. D'Hondt, P.

Donaghay, J. C. Zachos, D. Luttenberg, and M. Lindinger, "Organic Carbon Fluxes and Ecological Recovery from the Cretaceous-Tertiary Mass Extinction," *Science* 282 (1998): 276–279. Reviewed by P. N. Pearson, P. W. Ditchfield, J. Singano, K. G. Harcourt-Brown, C. J. Nicholas, R. K. Olsson, N. J. Shackleton, and M. A. Hall, "Warm Tropical Sea Surface Temperatures in the Late Cretaceous and Eocene Epochs," *Nature* 413 (2001): 481–487.

2. S. Bains, R. M. Corfield, and R. D. Norris, "Mechanisms of Climate Warming at the End of the Paleocene," *Science* 285 (1999): 724–726.

3. G. R. Dickens, "The Blast in the Past," *Nature* 401 (1999): 752–755.

4. J. Zachos, M. Pagani, L. Sloan, E. Thomas, and K. Billups, "Trends, Rhythms, and Aberrations in Global Climate 65 Ma to Present," *Science* 292 (2001): 686–693; D. Thomas, J. C. Zachos, T. J. Bralower, E. Thomas, and S. Bohaty, "Warming the Fuel for the Fire: Evidence for the Thermal Dissociation of Methane Hydrate During the Paleocene-Eocene Thermal Maximum," *Geology* 30(12) (2002): 1067–1070.

5. J. W. Wells, "Scleractinia," in R. C. Moore, ed., *Treatise on Invertebrate Paleontology, Coelenterata* (Lawrence, Kan.: Geological Society of America, 1956), among others.

6. P. N. Pearson, P. W. Ditchfield, J. Singano, K. G. Harcourt-Brown, C. J. Nicholas, R. K. Olsson, N. J. Shackleton, and M. A. Hall, "Warm Tropical Sea Surface Temperatures in the Late Cretaceous and Eocene Epochs," *Nature* 413 (2001): 481–487.

7. P. N. Pearson and M. R. Palmer, "Middle Eocene Seawater pH and Atmospheric Carbon Dioxide Concentrations," *Science* 284 (1999): 1824–1826.

8. These temperature regimes are discussed by E. J. Barron, "Eocene Equator-to-Pole Surface Ocean Temperatures: A Significant Climate Problem?" *Palaeoceanography* 2 (1987): 729–739; C. G. Adams, D. E. Lee, and B. R. Rosen, "Conflicting Isotopic and Biotic Evidence for Tropical Sea-Surface Temperatures During the Tertiary," *Palaeogeography, Palaeoclimatology, Palaeoecology* 77(3–4) (1990): 289–313; and L. A. Frakes, J. E. Francis, and J. I. Syktus, *Climate Modes of the Phanerozoic* (Cambridge, U.K.: Cambridge University Press, 1992).

9. A good review is P. N. Pearson and M. R. Palmer, "Atmospheric Carbon Dioxide Concentrations over the Past 60 Million Years," *Nature* 406 (2000): 695–699.

10. D. M. Raup and J. J. Sepkoski Jr., "Periodic Extinction of Families and Genera," *Science* 231 (1986): 833–836.

11. The literature is summarized by J. C. Zachos, M. W. Wara, S. Bohaty, M. L. Delaney, M. R. Petrizzo, A. Brill, T. J. Bralower, and I. Premoli-Silva, "A Transient Rise in Tropical Sea Surface Temperature during the Paleocene-Eocene Thermal Maximum," *Science* 302 (2003): 1551–1554.

12. A. F. Budd, "Diversity and Extinction in the Cenozoic History of Caribbean Reefs," *Coral Reefs* 19 (2000): 25–35.

13. M. E. Raymo and W. F. Ruddiman, "Tectonic Forcing of Late Cenozoic Climate," *Nature* 359 (1992): 117–122.

14. E. M. Truswell, "Vegetation Changes in the Australian Tertiary in Response to Climatic and Phytogeographic Forcing Factors," *Australian Systematic Botany* 6 (1993): 533–557.

15. D. A. Feary, P. J. Davies, C. J. Pigram, and P. A. Symonds, "Climatic Evolution and Control on Carbonate Deposition in Northeast Australia," *Palaeogeography, Palaeoclimatology, Palaeoecology* 89 (1991): 341–361.

16. J. Zachos, M. Pagani, L. Sloan, E. Thomas, and K. Billups, "Trends, Rhythms, and Aberrations in Global Climate 65 Ma to Present," *Science* 292 (2001): 686–693.

17. The many references are cited by E. N. Edinger and M. J. Risk, "Oligocene-Miocene Extinction and Geographic Restriction of Caribbean Corals: Roles of Turbidity, Temperature, and Nutrients," *PALAIOS* 9 (1994): 576.

18. N. J. Shackleton and J. P. Kennett, "Paleotemperature History of the Cenozoic and the Initiation of Antarctic Glaciation: Oxygen and Carbon Analyses of DSDP Sites 277, 279, 281," in J. P. Kennett and R. E. Houtz, eds., *Initial Reports of the Deep Sea Drilling Project 29* (Washington, D.C.: U.S. Government Printing Office, 1975), pp. 743–755.

19. Reviewed by L. A. Frakes, J. E. Francis, and J. I. Syktus, *Climate Modes of the Phanerozoic* (Cambridge, U.K.: Cambridge University Press, 1992).

20. C. G. Adams, "An Outline of Tertiary Paleogeography," in L. R. M. Cocks, ed., *The Evolving Earth*, Vol. 14 (Cambridge, U.K.: British Museum [Natural History], Cambridge University Press, 1981), pp. 221–235.

21. Good summaries are given in W. J. Schmitz Jr., "On the Interbasin-Scale Thermohaline Circulation," *Reviews of Geophysics* 33 (1995): 151–173, and M. Williams, D. Dunkerley, P. De Deckker, P. Kershaw, and J. Chappell, *Quaternary Environments*, 2nd edn. (Sydney, N.S.W.: Arnold, 1998).

22. K. Romine and G. Lombari, "Evolution of Pacific Circulation in the Miocene: Radiolarian Evidence from DSDP Site 289," in J. P. Kennett, ed., *The Miocene Ocean: Paleoceanography and Biogeography, Geological Society of America Memoir 163* (1985): 273–290, and many subsequent accounts.

23. N. J. Shackleton and J. P. Kennett, "Paleotemperature History of the Cenozoic and the Initiation of Antarctic Glaciation: Oxygen and Carbon Analyses of DSDP Sites 277, 279, 281," in J. P. Kennett and R. E. Houtz, eds., *Initial Reports of the Deep Sea Drilling Project 29* (Washington, D.C.: U.S. Government Printing Office, 1975), pp. 743–755.

24. L. A. Frakes, J. E. Francis, and J. I. Syktus, *Climate Modes of the Phanerozoic* (Cambridge, U.K.: Cambridge University Press, 1992).

25. B. P. Flower, "Warming without High CO_2," *Nature* 399 (1999): 313–314.

26. J. P. Kennett, *Marine Geology* (Englewood Cliffs, N. J.: Prentice-Hall, 1982); M. B. Cita and J. A. McKenzie, "The Terminal Miocene Event," in K. J. Hsu, ed.,

Mesozoic and Cenozoic Oceans: American Geophysical Union Geodynamics Series 15 (1986): 123–140; and many later studies.

27. B. W. Hayward, "Lower Miocene Corals from the Waitakere Ranges, North Auckland, New Zealand," *Journal of the Royal Society of New Zealand* 7 (1977): 99–111; B. W. Hayward and F. J. Brook, "Fossil Reef Corals in Situ," *Newsletter of the Geological Society of New Zealand* 54 (1981): 43.

28. A. G. Coates, J. B. C. Jackson, L. S. Collins, T. M. Cronin, H. J. Dowsett, L. M. Bybell, P. Jung, and J. A. Obando, "Closure of the Isthmus of Panama: The Near-Shore Marine Record of Costa Rica and Western Panama," *Geological Society of America Bulletin* 104(7) (1992): 814–828.

29. K. W. Burton, H.-F. Ling, and R. K. O'Nions, "Closure of the Central American Isthmus and its Effect on Deep-Water Formation in the North Atlantic," *Nature* 386 (1997): 382–385.

30. M. Esteban, "Significance of the Upper Miocene Coral Reefs of the Western Mediterranean," *Palaeogeography, Palaeoclimatology, Palaeoecology* 29 (1980): 169–188.

8.   Australia Adrift

1. A highly informative account of the life of Gondwana is given by P. Vickers-Rich and T. Hewett Rich, *Wildlife of Gondwana: Dinosaurs and Other Vertebrates from the Ancient Supercontinent* (Bloomington: Indiana University Press, 1999).

2. An unsurpassed review of this subject is given by E. M. Truswell, "Vegetation Changes in the Australian Tertiary in Response to Climatic and Phytogeographic Forcing Factors," *Australian Systematic Botany* 6 (1993): 533–557. A beautifully illustrated account is given by M. E. White, *The Greening of Gondwana* (East Roseville, N.S.W.: Kangaroo Press, 1998).

3. A detailed if dated account is given by J. J. Veevers, ed., *Oxford Monographs on Geology and Geophysics,* No. 2: *Phanerozoic Earth History of Australia* (Oxford, U.K.: Clarendon Press, 1984).

4. P. J. Davies, P. A. Symonds, D. A. Feary, and C. J. Pigram, "The Evolution of the Carbonate Platforms of Northeast Australia," *Controls on Carbonate Platform and Basin Development, Society of Economic Paleontologists and Mineralogists Special Publication* 44 (1989): 233–258; Z. Wang and C. A. Stein, "Subsidence of the Gulf of Papua in the Cenozoic," *Tectonophysics* 205 (1992): 409–426.

5. A synopsis is given in R. D. Müller, V. S. L. Lim, and A. R. Isern, "Late Tertiary Tectonic Subsidence on the Northeast Australian Passive Margin: Response to Dynamic Topography?" *Marine Geology* 162 (2000): 337–352.

6. L. B. Collins, "Tertiary Foundations and Quaternary Evolution of Coral Reef Systems of Australia's North West Shelf," in M. Keep and S. J. Moss, eds., *The Sedimentary Basins of Western Australia 3: Proceedings of the Petroleum Explo-*

ration Society of Australia Symposium, Perth, Western Australia (Perth,W.A.: Petroleum Exploration Society of Australia, 2002), pp. 129–152.

7. The living reefs are described by A. Heyward, E. Pinceratto, and L. Smith, eds., *Big Bank Shoals of the Timor Sea: An Environmental Resource Atlas* (Townsville, Qld.: Australian Institute of Marine Science, 1997).

8. F. G. Stehli and J. W. Wells, "Diversity and Age Patterns in Hermatypic Corals," *Systematic Zoology* 20 (1971): 115–126, revised by J. E. N. Veron, *Corals in Space and Time: The Biogeography and Evolution of the Scleractinia* (Sydney, N.S.W.: University of New South Wales Press, 1995).

9. J. E. N. Veron, *Corals in Space and Time: The Biogeography and Evolution of the Scleractinia* (Sydney, N.S.W.: University of New South Wales Press, 1995).

10. J. E. N. Veron and R. Kelley, "Species Stability in Reef Corals of Papua New Guinea and the Indo-Pacific," *Memoirs of the Association of Australasian Palaeontologists* 6 (1988):1–69.

9.   The Ice Ages

1. An excellent review is given by K. Lambeck, T. M. Esat, and E.-K. Potter, "Links between Climate and Sea Levels for the Past Three Million Years," *Nature* 419 (2002): 199–205.

2. M. E. Raymo, "Global Climate Change: A Three Million Year Perspective," in G. J. Kukla and E. Went, eds., *Start of a Glacial* (Berlin: Springer-Verlag, 1992), pp. 207–223, updated and expanded by EPICA Community Members, "Eight Glacial Cycles from an Antarctic Ice Core," *Nature* 429 (2004): 623–628.

3. W. H. Berger and E. Jansen, "Mid-Pleistocene Climate Shift: The Nansen Connection," in O. M. Johannessen, R. D. Muensch, and J. E. Overland, eds., *The Role of the Polar Oceans in Shaping the Global Environments. Geophysical Monographs* 84 (1994): 295–311, revised and updated by EPICA Community Members, "Eight Glacial Cycles from an Antarctic Ice Core," *Nature* 429 (2004): 623–628.

4. D. Paillard, "The Timing of Pleistocene Glaciations from a Simple Multiple-State Climate Model," *Nature* 391 (1998): 378–381.

5. N. J. Shackleton, "The 100,000-Year Ice-Age Cycle Identified and Found to Lag Temperature, Carbon Dioxide, and Orbital Eccentricity," *Science* 289 (2000): 1897–1902.

6. J. R. Petit, J. Jouzel, D. Raynaud, N. I. Barkov, J.-M. Barnola, I. Basile, M. Bender, J. Chappellaz, M. Davis, G. Delaygue, M. Delmotte, V. M. Kotlyakov, M. Legrand, V. Y. Lipenkov, C. Lorius, L. Pepin, C. Ritz, E. Saltzman, and M. Stievenard, "Climate and Atmospheric History of the Past 420,000 Years from the Vostok Ice Core, Antarctica," *Nature* 399 (1999): 429–436; H. Fischer, M. Whalen, J. Smith, D. Mastroianni, and B. Deck, "Ice Core Records of Atmospheric CO_2 around the Last Three Glacial Terminations," *Science* 283 (1999): 1712–1714.

7. The issue is reviewed by A. Vecsei and W. H. Berger, "Increase of Atmospheric CO_2 during Deglaciation: Constraints on the Coral Reef Hypothesis from Patterns of Deposition," *Global Biogeochemical Cycles* 18 (2004): GB1035, doi: 10.1029/2003GB002147.

8. B. N. Opdyke and J. C. G. Walker, "The Return of the Coral Reef Hypothesis: Basin to Shelf Partitioning of $CaCO_3$ and its Effect on Atmospheric CO_2," *Geology* 20 (1992): 733–736; A. Vecsei and W. H. Berger, "Increase of Atmospheric CO_2 during Deglaciation: Constraints on the Coral Reef Hypothesis from Patterns of Deposition," *Global Biogeochemical Cycles* 18 (2004): GB1035, doi: 10.1029/2003GB002147.

9. A useful summary of the role of orbital cycles in greenhouse gases emissions is given by W. F. Ruddiman, "The Role of Greenhouse Gases in Orbital-Scale Climatic Changes," *EOS Transactions, American Geophysical Union* 85(1) (2004): 1–7.

10. W. F. Ruddiman, "The Anthropogenic Greenhouse Era Began Thousands of Years Ago," *Climatic Change* 61 (2003): 261–293.

11. This case is made by M. A. Cane, "A Role for the Tropical Pacific," *Science* 282 (1998): 59–61, and A. C. Clement, R. Seager, and M. A. Cane, "Orbital Controls on the El Niño/Southern Oscillation and the Tropical Climate," *Paleoceanography* 14(4) (1999): 441–456.

12. The issues are discussed in W. S. Broecker, "Does the Trigger for Abrupt Climate Change Reside in the Ocean or in the Atmosphere?" *Science* 300 (2003): 1519–1522.

13. The literature is reviewed in J. P. Bluemle, J. M. Sabel, and W. Karlén, "Rate and Magnitude of Past Global Climate Changes," in L. C. Gerhard, W. E. Harrison, and B. M. Hanson, eds., *Geological Perspectives of Global Climate Change. AAPG Studies in Geology* 47 (Tulsa, Okla.: American Association of Petroleum Geologists, 2001), pp. 193–211.

14. Well reviewed for the nonspecialist by S. Rahmstorf, "Ocean Circulation and Climate during the Past 120,000 Years," *Nature* 419 (2002): 207–214.

15. T. M. Dokken and E. Jansen, "Rapid Changes in the Mechanism of Ocean Convection during the Last Glacial Period," *Nature* 401 (1999): 458–461.

16. C. Charles, "The Ends of an Era," *Nature* 394 (1998): 422–423.

17. D. A. Hodell, S. L. Kanfoush, A. Shemesh, X. Crosta, C. D. Charles, and T. P. Guilderson, "Abrupt Cooling of Antarctic Surface Waters and Sea Ice Expansion in the South Atlantic Sector of the Southern Ocean at 5000 cal yr. B.P.," *Quaternary Research* 56 (2001): 191–198.

18. K. T. Pickering, "The Cenozoic World," in S. J. Culver and P. F. Rawson, eds., *Biotic Response to Global Change: The Last 145 Million Years* (Cambridge, U.K.: Cambridge University Press, 2000), pp. 20–34.

19. CLIMAP Members, "Seasonal Reconstructions of the Earth's Surface at the Last Glacial Maximum," *Geological Society of America Map Chart Series* 36 (1981);

W. F. Ruddiman, "The Last Interglacial Ocean," *Quaternary Research* 21 (1984): 123–224.

20. D. Rind and D. Peteet, "Terrestrial Conditions at the Last Glacial Maximum and CLIMAP Sea Surface Temperature Estimates: Are They Consistent?" *Quaternary Research* 24 (1985): 1–22; R. Thunell, D. Anderson, D. Gellar, and Q. Miao, "Sea-Surface Temperature Estimates for the Tropical Western Pacific during the Last Glaciation and Their Implications for the Pacific Warm Pool," *Quaternary Research* 41 (1994): 255–264; T. T. Barrows, S. Juggins, P. De Deckker, J. Thiede, and J. I. Martinez, "Sea-Surface Temperatures of the Southwest Pacific Ocean during the Last Glacial Maximum," *Paleoceanography* 15(1) (2000): 95–109; and others.

21. R. A. Kerr, "The Tropics Return to the Climate System," *Science* 292 (2001): 660–661; M. K. Gagan, E. J. Hendy, S. G. Haberle, and W. Hantoro, "Post-Glacial Evolution of the Indo-Pacific Warm Pool and El Niño–Southern Oscillation," *Quaternary International* 118–119 (2004): 127–143.

22. D. W. Lea, D. K. Pak, and H. J. Spero, "Climate Impact of Late Quaternary Equatorial Pacific Sea-Surface Temperature Variations," *Science* 289 (2000): 1719–1724.

23. For a good review see P. De Deckker, N. J. Tapper, and S. Van De Kaars, "The Status of the Indo-Pacific Warm Pool and Adjacent Land at the Last Glacial Maximum," *Global and Planetary Change* 35 (2002): 25–35.

24. Z. Liu, S. I. Shin, B. Otto-Bliesner, J. E. Kutzbach, E. C. Brady, and D. E. Lee, "Tropical Cooling at the Last Glacial Maximum and Extratropical Ocean Ventilation," *Geophysical Research Letters* 29 (2002): 481–484.

10.   The Last Glacial Cycle

1. M. T. McCulloch and T. Esat, "The Coral Record of Last Interglacial Sea Levels and Sea Surface Temperatures," in D. Weis and D. J. DePaolo, eds., *Isotope Tracers in Geochemistry and Cosmochemistry* (Amsterdam: Elsevier, 2000), pp. 107–129.

2. K. Lambeck and J. Chappell, "Sea Level Change through the Last Glacial Cycle," *Science* 292 (2001): 679–686.

3. M. Siddall, E. J. Rohling, A. Almogi-Labin, C. Hemleben, D. Meischner, I. Schmelzer, and D. A. Smeed, "Sea-Level Fluctuations during the Last Glacial Cycle," *Nature* 423 (2003): 853–858.

4. A wealth of detail is given by K. Lambeck and J. Chappell, "Sea Level Change through the Last Glacial Cycle," *Science* 292 (2001): 679–686, and Y. Yokoyama, T. M. Esat, and K. Lambeck, "Coupled Climate and Sea-Level Changes Deduced from Huon Peninsula Coral Terraces of the Last Ice Age," *Earth and Planetary Science Letters* 193 (2001): 579–587.

5. An account of molluscs given by J. B. C. Jackson, "Pleistocene Perspectives on Coral Reef Community Structure," *American Zoologist* 32 (1992): 719–731, makes a similar point, as do J. W. Valentine and D. Jablonski, "Biotic Effects of Sea Level Change: The Pleistocene Test," *Journal of Geophysical Research* 96 (1991): 6873–6878.

6. An imaginative suggestion by P. J. Davies and J. A. McKenzie, "Controls of the Pliocene-Pleistocene Evolution of the Northeastern Australian Continental Margin," *Proceedings of the Ocean Drilling Program* 133 (1993): 755–762.

7. M. Williams, D. Dunkerley, P. De Deckker, P. Kershaw, and J. Chappell, *Quaternary Environments*, 2nd edn. (Sydney, N.S.W.: Arnold, 1998), revised upward by K. Lambeck and J. Chappell, "Sea Level Change through the Last Glacial Cycle," *Science* 292 (2001): 679–686.

8. M. T. McCulloch and T. Esat, "The Coral Record of Last Interglacial Sea Levels and Sea Surface Temperatures," in D. Weis and D. J. DePaolo, eds., *Isotope Tracers in Geochemistry and Cosmochemistry* (Amsterdam: Elsevier, 2000), pp. 107–129.

9. C. R. Fielding, J. D. Trueman, G. R. Dickens, and M. Page, "Anatomy of the Buried Burdekin River Channel across the Great Barrier Reef Shelf: How Does a Major River Operate on a Tropical Mixed Siliciclastic/Carbonate Margin during Sea Level Lowstand?" *Sedimentary Geology* 157 (2003): 291–301.

10. Marine impacts are reviewed by K. Roy and J. M. Pandolfi, "Responses of Marine Species and Ecosystems to Past Climate Change," in T. E. Lovejoy and L. Hannah, eds., *Climate Change and Biodiversity* (New Haven, Conn.: Yale University Press, 2006), pp. 160–172.

11. Many Origins

1. C. R. Darwin, *The Structure and Distribution of Coral Reefs. Being the First Part of the Geology of the Voyage of the Beagle, Under the Command of Capt. Fitzroy, R.N. During the Years 1832 to 1836* (London: Smith Elder and Co., 1842).

2. N. Harvey, "A Century of Ideas Since Darwin: Evolution of the Great Barrier Reef," *Proceedings of the Royal Geographical Society of South Australia* 81 (1984): 1–21. Darwin himself repeatedly refers to the GBR in this context in C. R. Darwin, *The Structure and Distribution of Coral Reefs. Being the First Part of the Geology of the Voyage of the Beagle, Under the Command of Capt. Fitzroy, R.N. During the Years 1832 to 1836* (London: Smith Elder and Co., 1842).

3. R. A. Daly, "Pleistocene Glaciation and the Coral Reef Problem," *American Journal of Science* 30 (1910): 297–308; R. A. Daly, "The Glacial Control Theory of Coral Reefs," *Proceedings of the American Academy of Arts and Sciences* 51 (1915): 155–251.

4. Good accounts of Darwin's studies of coral reefs are given by D. R. Stoddart, "Darwin, Lyell, and the Geological Significance of Coral Reefs," *British Journal*

for the History of Science 9 (1976): 199–218, and B. R. Rosen, "Darwin, Coral Reefs and Global Geology," *BioScience* 32 (1982): 519–525.

5. F. Darwin, *The Life and Letters of Charles Darwin* (London: John Murray, 1887). (Francis Darwin was Charles Darwin's son.)

6. H. S. Ladd, E. Ingerson, R. C. Townend, M. Russell, and H. K. Stephenson, "Drilling on Eniwetok Atoll, Marshall Islands," *American Association of Petroleum Geologists Bulletin* 37 (1953): 2257–2280.

7. N. Harvey, "A Century of Ideas Since Darwin: Evolution of the Great Barrier Reef," *Proceedings of the Royal Geographical Society of South Australia* 81 (1984): 1–21.

8. A good account of this history is given by N. Harvey, "A Century of Ideas since Darwin: Evolution of the Great Barrier Reef," *Proceedings of the Royal Geographical Society of South Australia* 81 (1984): 1–21.

9. O. A. Jones, "Geological Questions Posed by the Reef," *Australian Natural History* 15 (1966): 245–249.

10. O. A. Jones, "Great Barrier Reefs," in R. W. Fairbridge, ed., *Encyclopaedia of Geomorphology* (New York: Reinhold, 1968), pp. 492–499; E. D. Gill, "Coast and Continental Shelf of Australia," *Quaternaria* 12 (1970): 115–127.

11. P. J. Davies, "The Geological Structure of the Great Barrier Reef," *Habitat* 3 (1975): 3–8, following E. G. Purdy, "Reef Configurations: Cause and Effect," in L. F. Laporte, ed., *Society of Economic Palaeontologists and Mineralogists, Special Publication* 18 (1974): 9–76. This idea is reviewed by D. Hopley, *The Geomorphology of the Great Barrier Reef: Quaternary Development of Coral Reefs* (New York: John Wiley and Sons, 1982).

12. G. R. Orme and P. G. Flood, "The Geological History of the Great Barrier Reef: Aspects in the Light of New Evidence," *Proceedings of the Third International Coral Reef Symposium* 2 (1977): 37–43, and others, following W. G. H. Maxwell, *Atlas of the Great Barrier Reef* (Amsterdam: Elsevier, 1968).

13. P. A. Symonds, P. J. Davies, and A. Parisi, "Structure and Stratigraphy of the Central Great Barrier Reef," *Journal of Australian Geology and Geophysics* 8 (1983): 277–291.

14. J. F. Marshall, "The Pleistocene Foundations of the Great Barrier Reef," *Proceedings of the Great Barrier Reef Conference 1983*, J. T. Baker, R. M Carter, P. W. Sammarco, and K. P. Stark, eds., pp. 123–128.

15. P. J. Davies, P. A. Symonds, D. A. Feary, and C. J. Pigram, "Horizontal Plate Motion: A Key Allocyclic Factor in the Evolution of the Great Barrier Reef," *Science* 238 (1987): 1697–1700; P. J. Davies, P. A. Symonds, D. A. Feary, and C. J. Pigram, "The Evolution of the Carbonate Platforms of Northeast Australia," in *Controls on Carbonate Platform and Basin Development, Society of Economic Paleontologists and Mineralogists Special Publication* 44 (1989): 233–258.

16. P. J. Davies, "Origins of the Great Barrier Reef," *Search* 23 (1991): 193–196; P. J. Davies and J. A. McKenzie, "Controls of the Pliocene-Pleistocene Evolution of

the Northeastern Australian Continental Margin," *Proceedings of the Ocean Drilling Program* 133 (1993): 755–762.

17. L. F. Montaggioni and M.-T. Verec-Peyré, "Shallow Water Foraminiferal Taphocoenoses at Site 821: Implications for the Evolution of the Central Great Barrier Reef, Northeast Australia," *Proceedings of the Ocean Drilling Program, Scientific Results* 113 (1993): 365–378.

18. D. A. Feary, P. J. Davies, C. J. Pigram, and P. A. Symonds, "Climatic Evolution and Control on Carbonate Deposition in Northeast Australia," *Palaeogeography, Palaeoclimatology, Palaeoecology* 89 (1991): 341–361.

19. H. C. Richards and D. Hill, "Great Barrier Reef Bores, 1926 and 1937: Descriptions, Analyses and Interpretations," *Report of the Great Barrier Reef Committee* 5 (1942): 1–122.

20. D. Hill, "An Introduction to the Great Barrier Reef," *Proceedings of the Second International Symposium on Coral Reefs* 2 (1973): 723–731. A historical perspective is given by J. Bowen and M. Bowen, *The Great Barrier Reef: History, Science, Heritage* (Cambridge, U.K.: Cambridge University Press, 2002).

21. W. G. H. Maxwell, "Geomorphology of Eastern Queensland in Relation to the Great Barrier Reef," in O. A. Jones and R. Endean, eds., *Biology and Geology of Coral Reefs*, Vol. 1: *Geology 1* (New York: Academic Press, 1973), pp. 233–272; personal communications in the 1980s with Graham Maxwell.

22. J. J. Veevers, ed., *Oxford Monographs on Geology and Geophysics*, No. 2: *Phanerozoic Earth History of Australia* (Oxford, U.K.: Clarendon Press, 1984). An overview is given by P. J. Davies, P. A. Symonds, D. A. Feary, and C. J. Pigram, "The Evolution of the Carbonate Platforms of Northeast Australia," in *Controls on Carbonate Platform and Basin Development, Society of Economic Paleontologists and Mineralogists Special Publication* 44 (1989): 233–258.

23. Reviewed by D. Hopley, S. G. Smithers, and K. E. Parnell, *The Geomorphology of the Great Barrier Reef: Development, Diversity and Change* (Cambridge, U.K.: Cambridge University Press, 2007).

24. C. J. R. Braithwaite, H. Dalmasso, M. A. Gilmour, D. D. Harkness, G. M. Henderson, R. L. F. Kay, D. Kroon, L. F. Montaggioni, and P. A. Wilson, "The Great Barrier Reef: The Chronological Record from a New Borehole," *Journal of Sedimentary Research* 74(2) (2004): 298–310.

25. P. J. Davies, P. A. Symonds, D. A. Feary, and C. J. Pigram, "Horizontal Plate Motion: A Key Allocyclic Factor in the Evolution of the Great Barrier Reef," *Science* 238 (1987): 1697–1700; P. J. Davies, P. A. Symonds, D. A. Feary, and C. J. Pigram, "The Evolution of the Carbonate Platforms of Northeast Australia," in *Controls on Carbonate Platform and Basin Development, Society of Economic Paleontologists and Mineralogists Special Publication* 44 (1989): 233–258.

26. International Consortium for Great Barrier Reef Drilling, "New Constraints on the Origin of the Australian Great Barrier Reef: Results from an International

Project of Deep Coring," *Geology* 29 (2001): 483–486; C. J. R. Braithwaite, H. Dalmasso, M. A. Gilmour, D. D. Harkness, G. M. Henderson, R. L. F. Kay, D. Kroon, L. F. Montaggioni, and P. A. Wilson, "The Great Barrier Reef: The Chronological Record from a New Borehole," *Journal of Sedimentary Research* 74(2) (2004): 298–310.

27. A concept that originates from P. J. Davies and J. A. McKenzie, "Controls of the Pliocene-Pleistocene Evolution of the Northeastern Australian Continental Margin," *Proceedings of the Ocean Drilling Program* 133 (1993): 755–762.

28. C. D. Woodroffe, D. M. Kennedy, B. G. Jones, and C. V. G. Phipps, "Geomorphology and Late Quaternary Development of Middleton and Elizabeth Reefs," *Coral Reefs* 23 (2004): 249–262.

29. C. D. Woodroffe, M. E. Dickson, B. P. Brooke, and D. M. Kennedy, "Episodes of Reef Growth at Lord Howe Island, the Southernmost Reef in the Southwest Pacific," *Global and Planetary Change* 49 (2005): 222–237.

30. J. E. N. Veron and L. M. Marsh, "Hermatypic Corals of Western Australia: Records and Annotated Species List," *Records of the Western Australian Museum, Supplement No. 29* (Perth: Western Australian Museum, 1988), pp. 1–136.

31. Lindsay Collins, personal communications.

32. G. W. Kendrick, K.-H. Wyrwoll, and B. J. Szabo, "Pliocene-Pleistocene Coastal Events and History Along the Western Margin of Australia," *Quaternary Science Reviews* 10 (1991): 419–439.

33. N. Sagawa, T. Nakamori, and Y. Iryu, "Pleistocene Reef Development in the Southwest Ryukyu Islands, Japan," *Palaeogeography, Palaeoclimatology, Palaeoecology* 175 (2001): 303–323; K. Yamamoto, Y. Iryu, T. Sato, S. Chiyonobu, K. Sagae, and E. Abe, "Responses of Coral Reefs to Increased Amplitude of Sea-Level Changes at the Mid-Pleistocene Climate Transition," *Palaeogeography, Palaeoclimatology, Palaeoecology* 241 (2006): 160–175.

12.   Stone Age Utopia

1. J.-M. E. Chauvet, E. B. Deschamps, and C. Hellaire, *Chauvet Cave: The Discovery of the World's Oldest Paintings* (London: Thames and Hudson, 1996); this is an account by the cave's discoverers.

2. An extraordinary account of this subject is given by D. Lewis-Williams, *The Mind in the Cave: Consciousness and the Origins of Art* (London: Thames and Hudson, 2002).

3. J. Clottes and J. Courtin, *The Cave beneath the Sea: Paleolithic Images at Cosquer,* trans. M. Garner (New York: Harry N. Abrams, 1994); this is an account by the cave's discoverers.

4. D. G. Backshall, J. Barnett, P. J. Davies, D. C. Duncan, N. Harvey, D. Hopley, P. J. Isdale, J. N. Jennings, and R. Moss, "Drowned Dolines: The Blue Holes of the

Pompey Reefs, Great Barrier Reef," *BMR Journal of Australian Geology and Geophysics* 4 (1979): 99–109, give a detailed discussion. D. Hopley, *The Geomorphology of the Great Barrier Reef: Quaternary Development of Coral Reefs* (New York: John Wiley and Sons, 1982), illustrates how dolines can develop from caves.

5. L. Zell (2004), at www.lenzell.com/research_tijou.htm, and personal communications with Len Zell.

6. Carefully argued reviews of an extensive literature are given by J. Allen, "When Did Humans First Colonize Australia?" *Search* 20(5) (1989): 149–154.

7. This much debated idea is presented by J. Flood, *Archaeology of the Dreamtime: The Story of Prehistoric Australia and Its People* (Sydney, N.S.W.: Angus and Robertson, 1999) and many others.

8. These issues are discussed in a broad context by J. Mulvaney and J. Kamminga, *Prehistory of Australia* (Washington, D. C.: Smithsonian Institute Press, 1999), who review the evidence, and S. Mithen, *After the Ice: A Global Human History 20,000–5000 BC* (London: Weidenfeld and Nicholson, 2003).

9. M. Morwood and P. van Oosterzee, *The Discovery of the Hobbit* (Sydney, N.S.W.: Random House, 2007).

10. J. Allen, "When Did Humans First Colonize Australia?" *Search* 20(5) (1989): 149–154, reprinted in T. Murray, ed., *Archaeology of Aboriginal Australia* (St. Leonards, N.S.W.: Allen and Unwin, 1998).

11. S. O'Connor, M. Spriggs, and P. Veth, eds., *The Archaeology of the Aru Islands, Maluku Province, Terra Australis* (Canberra, Australia: Research School of Pacific and Asian Studies, Australian National University, 2005).

12. A comprehensive account of the Aboriginal archaeology of northern Australia is given by P. Veth, M. Smith, and P. Hiscock, *Desert Peoples* (Oxford, U.K.: Blackwell, 2005).

13. A. J. Barham and D. R. Harris, "Prehistory and Palaeoecology of Torres Strait," in P. M. Masters and N. C. Fleming, eds., *Quaternary Coastlines and Marine Archaeology: Towards A Prehistory of Land Bridges and Continental Shelves* (London: Academic Press, 1983), pp. 529–557.

14. J. Kingdon, *Self-Made Man and His Undoing* (London: Simon and Schuster, 1993).

15. Many such instances, most from southern Australia, are recorded by J. Flood, *Archaeology of the Dreamtime: The Story of Prehistoric Australia and Its People* (Sydney, N.S.W.: Angus and Robertson, 1999).

16. Reviewed by J. Hall and I. J. McNiven, *Australian Coastal Archaeology. Research Papers in Archaeology and Natural History 31* (Canberra: ANH Publications, Australian National University, 1999).

17. A comprehensive review of the maritime life of Whitsunday islanders is given by B. Barker, *The Sea People: Late Holocene Maritime Specialisation in the Whitsunday Islands, Central Queensland* (Canberra: Pandanus Books, 2004).

18. The "Stop Press" (New Light on Megafaunal Extinction) in J. Flood, *Archaeology of the Dreamtime: The Story of Prehistoric Australia and Its People* (Sydney, N.S.W.: Angus and Robertson, 1999), summarizes the public reaction to T. Flannery, *The Future Eaters: An Ecological History of the Australasian Lands and People* (Chatswood, N.S.W.: Reed Books, 1994).

19. Historical details are given by T. Flannery, *The Future Eaters: An Ecological History of the Australasian Lands and People* (Chatswood, N.S.W.: Reed Books, 1994).

20. A. P. Kershaw, "Late Cenozoic Plant Extinctions in Australia," in P. S. Martin and R. G. Klein, eds., *Quaternary Extinctions: A Prehistoric Revolution* (Tucson: University of Arizona Press, 1984), pp. 601–709.

13.   An Enhanced Greenhouse World

1. Intergovernmental Panel on Climate Change (IPCC), *IPCC Fourth Assessment Report: Climate Change 2007: The Physical Science Basis, Summary for Policymakers*, eds., R. Alley and 32 others (Geneva, Switzerland: IPCC. www.ipcc .ch/pub/pub.htm).

2. An excellent discussion is given by W. F. Ruddiman, *Earth's Climate: Past and Future* (New York: W. H. Freeman, 2001).

3. E. N. Parker, "Sunny Side of Global Warming," *Nature* 399 (1999): 416–417.

4. A recent account is given by R. T. Pinker, B. Zhang, and E. G. Dutton, "Do Satellites Detect Trends in Surface Solar Radiation?" *Science* 308(5723) (2005): 850–854.

5. M. Wild, H. Gilgen, A. Roesch, A. Ohmura, C. N. Long, E. G. Dutton, B. Forgan, A. Kallis, V. Russak, and A. Tsvetkov, "From Dimming to Brightening: Decadal Changes in Solar Radiation at Earth's Surface," *Science* 308(5723) (2005): 847–850.

6. This issue is discussed by L. R. Kump, "Reducing Uncertainty about Carbon Dioxide as a Climate Driver," *Nature* 419 (2002): 188–190.

7. Reviewed by S. C. B. Raper and F. Giorgi, "Climate Change Projections and Models," in T. E. Lovejoy and L. Hannah, eds., *Climate Change and Biodiversity* (New Haven, Conn.: Yale University Press, 2005), pp. 199–210.

8. A. B. Pittock, "Coral Reefs and Environmental Change: Adaptation to What?," *American Zoologist* 39(1) (1999): 10–29. An expert account of general circulation models particularly relevant to Australia is given by A. B. Pittock, *Climate Change: Turning Up the Heat* (Collingwood, Victoria: CSIRO, 2005).

9. Intergovernmental Panel on Climate Change (IPCC), *IPCC Fourth Assessment Report: Climate Change 2007: The Physical Science Basis, Summary for Policymakers*, eds. R. Alley and 32 others (Geneva, Switzerland: IPCC. www.ipcc .ch/pub/pub.htm).

10. An insightful view of this intractable subject is given by A. B. Pittock, *Climate Change: Turning Up the Heat* (Collingwood, Victoria: CSIRO, 2005).

11. S. R. Weart, *The Discovery of Global Warming* (Cambridge, Mass.: Harvard University Press, 2003), p. 199.

12. Intergovernmental Panel on Climate Change (IPCC), *IPCC Third Assessment Report: Climate Change 2001*, Synthesis Report, eds. R. T. Watson and the Core Writing Team (Geneva, Switzerland: IPCC), with subsequent updates, www .ipcc.ch/pub/pub.htm; T. J. Crowley and R. A. Berner, "CO_2 and Climate Change," *Science* 292 (2001): 870–872; other expert reports also describe how greenhouse gases and atmospheric temperatures are linked.

13. Intergovernmental Panel on Climate Change (IPCC), *IPCC Third Assessment Report: Climate Change 2001*, Synthesis Report, eds. R. T. Watson and the Core Writing Team (Geneva, Switzerland: IPCC), with subsequent updates, www .ipcc.ch/pub/pub.htm.

14. R. S. Bradley, *Paleoclimatology: Reconstructing Climates of the Quaternary,* 2nd Ed. (New York: Academic Press, 1999).

15. Intergovernmental Panel on Climate Change (IPCC), *IPCC Third Assessment Report: Climate Change 2001*, Synthesis Report, ed. R. T. Watson and the Core Writing Team (Geneva, Switzerland: IPCC), with subsequent updates, www .ipcc.ch/pub/pub.htm.

16. M. Latif, R. Kleemam, and C. Eckert, "Greenhouse Warming, Decadal Variability, or El Niño?: An Attempt to Understand the Anomalous 1990's," *Journal of Climate* 10 (1997): 2221–2239.

17. S. Levitus, J. I. Antonov, J. Wang, T. L. Delworth, K. W. Dixon, and A. J. Broccoli, "Anthropogenic Warming of Earth's Climate System," *Science* 292 (2001): 267–270.

18. S. Levitus, J. I. Antonov, T. P. Boyer, and C. Stephens, "Warming of the World Ocean," *Science* 287 (2000): 2225–2229; T. M. Barnett, D. W. Pierce, and R. Schnur, "Detection of Anthropogenic Climate Change in the World's Oceans," *Science* 292 (2001): 270–274.

19. A. B. Pittock, "Coral Reefs and Environmental Change: Adaptation to What?" *American Zoologist* 39(1) (1999): 10–29, and others.

20. Concise reviews are given by J. Hansen, "Defusing the Global Warming Time Bomb," *Scientific American* 290(3) (2004): 68–77 and J.A. Church and N.J. White, "A 20th Century Acceleration in Global Sea-Level Rise," *Geophysical Research Letters* 33(1) (2006): L01602 pp. 1–4.

21. R. A. Kerr, "Big El Niños Ride the Back of Slower Climate Change," *Science* 283 (1999): 1108.

22. W. S. Broecker, "Thermohaline Circulation, the Achilles Heel of Our Climate System: Will Man-Made CO_2 Upset the Current Balance?" *Science* 278 (1997): 1582–1588; W. S. Broecker, S. Sutherland, and T.-H. Peng, "A Possible 20th-Century Slowdown of Southern Ocean Deep Water Formation," *Science* 286 (1999): 1132–1135.

23. These data are reviewed by J. Nott and M. Hayne, "High Frequency of 'Super-Cyclones' along the Great Barrier Reef over the Past 5,000 Years," *Nature* 413 (2001): 508–512.

14. Temperature and Mass Bleaching

1. A useful review of such questions is given by R. W. Buddemeier, J. A. Kleypas, and R. B. Aronson, *Coral Reefs and Global Climate Change: Potential Contributions of Climate Change to Stresses on Coral Reef Ecosystems* (Arlington, Va.: Pew Center on Global Climate Change, 2004).
2. Ove Hoegh-Guldberg, personal communication of an as yet unpublished study.
3. P. W. Glynn, "Coral Reef Bleaching: Ecological Perspectives," *Coral Reefs* 12 (1993): 1–17, summarizes the history of observations. Details of sightings on the GBR are given in R. Berkelmans, G. De'ath, S. Kininmonth, and W. J. Skirving, "A Comparison of the 1998 and 2002 Coral Bleaching Events on the Great Barrier Reef: Spatial Correlation, Patterns and Predictions," *Coral Reefs* 23 (2004): 74–83.
4. R. A. Kerr, "Big El Niños Ride the Back of Slower Climate Change," *Science* 283 (1999): 1108.
5. R. Berkelmans, G. De'ath, S. Kininmonth, and W. J. Skirving, "A Comparison of the 1998 and 2002 Coral Bleaching Events on the Great Barrier Reef: Spatial Correlation, Patterns and Predictions," *Coral Reefs* 23 (2004): 74–83.
6. S. L. Coles and B. E. Brown, "Coral Bleaching: Capacity for Acclimatization and Adaptation," *Advances in Marine Biology* 46 (2003): 183–223.
7. K. Fitt, B. E. Brown, M. E. Warner, and R. P. Dunne, "Coral Bleaching: Interpretation of Thermal Tolerance Limits and Thermal Thresholds in Tropical Corals," *Coral Reefs* 20 (2001): 51–65.
8. R. Berkelmans, "Time-Integrated Thermal Bleaching Thresholds of Reefs and Their Variation on the Great Barrier Reef," *Marine Ecology Progress Series* 229 (2002): 73–82.

15. Ocean Acidity and Coralline Osteoporosis

1. Details of ocean chemistry involving the carbon cycle are in M. Follows and T. Oguz, *The Ocean Carbon Cycle and Climate* (London: Kluwer Academic Publishers, 2004).
2. J. Raven (Chair), *Ocean Acidification Due to Increasing Atmospheric Carbon Dioxide* (London: The Royal Society, 2005), a major review.
3. The results of two major efforts to inventory carbon in the oceans, the World Ocean Circulation Experiment and the Joint Global Ocean Flux Study, are given

by C. L. Sabine, R. A. Feely, N. Gruber, R. M. Key, K. Lee, J. L. Bullister, R. Wanninkhof, C. S. Wong, D. W. R. Wallace, B. Tilbrook, F. J. Millero, T.-H. Peng, A. Kozyr, T. Ono, and A. F. Rios, "The Oceanic Sink for Anthropogenic CO_2," *Science* 305 (2004): 367–371.

4. An exceptionally informative review is given by R. A. Feely, C. L. Sabine, K. Lee, W. Berelson, J. Kleypas, V. J. Fabry, and F. J. Millero, "Impact of Anthropogenic CO_2 on the $CaCO_3$ System in the Oceans," *Science* 305 (2004): 362–366.

5. C. L. Sabine, R. A. Feely, N. Gruber, R. M. Key, K. Lee, J. L. Bullister, R. Wanninkhof, C. S. Wong, D. W. R. Wallace, B. Tilbrook, F. J. Millero, T.-H. Peng, A. Kozyr, T. Ono, and A. F. Rios, "The Oceanic Sink for Anthropogenic CO_2," *Science* 305 (2004): 367–371.

6. J. Raven (Chair), *Ocean Acidification Due to Increasing Atmospheric Carbon Dioxide* (London: The Royal Society, 2005).

7. J. M. Guinotte, R. W. Buddemeier, and J. A. Kleypas, "Future Coral Reef Habitat Marginality: Temporal and Spatial Effects of Climate Change in the Pacific Basin," *Coral Reefs* 22 (2003): 551–558, and personal communications with these authors.

8. J. M. Guinotte, R. W. Buddemeier, and J. A. Kleypas, "Future Coral Reef Habitat Marginality: Temporal and Spatial Effects of Climate Change in the Pacific Basin," *Coral Reefs* 22 (2003): 551–558.

9. U. Riebesell, I. Zondervan, B. Rost, P. D. Tortell, R. E. Zeebe, and F. M. M. Morel, "Reduced Calcification of Marine Plankton in Response to Increased Atmospheric CO_2," *Nature* 407 (2000): 364–367; K. Caldeira and M. E. Wickett, "Anthropogenic Carbon and Ocean pH," *Nature* 425 (2003): 365; J. C. Orr, S. Pantoja, and H.-O. Pörtner, "Introduction to Special Section: The Ocean in a High-CO_2 World," *Journal of Geophysical Research* 110(C9) (2005): C09S01, 3 pp.

10. K. Caldeira and M. E. Wickett, "Anthropogenic Carbon and Ocean pH," *Nature* 425 (2003): 365.

11. C. Langdon, "Review of Experimental Evidence for Effects of CO_2 on Calcification of Reef Builders," *Proceedings of the Ninth International Coral Reef Symposium (Bali)* 2 (2002): 1091–1098.

12. J.-P. Gattuso, D. Allemande, and M. Frankignoulle, "Photosynthesis and Calcification at Cellular, Organismal and Community Levels in Coral Reefs: A Review of Interactions and Control by Carbonate Chemistry," *American Zoologist* 39(1) (1999): 160–183; J.-P. Gattuso, M. Frankignoulle, I. Bourge, S. Romaine, and R. W. Buddemeier, "Effect of Calcium Carbonate Saturation of Seawater on Coral Calcification," *Global and Planetary Change* 18 (1998): 37–47; J. A. Kleypas, R. W. Buddemeier, D. Archer, J.-P. Gattuso, C. Langdon, and B. N. Opdyke, "Geochemical Consequences of Increased Atmospheric Carbon Dioxide on Coral Reefs," *Science* 284 (1999): 118–120; C. Langdon, T.

Takahashi, C. Sweeney, D. Chipman, and J. Goddard, "Effect of Calcium Carbonate Saturation State on the Calcification Rate of an Experimental Coral Reef," *Global Biogeochemical Cycles* 14(2) (2000): 639–654; N. Leclercq, J.-P. Gattuso, and J. Jaubert, "CO_2 Partial Pressure Controls the Calcification Rate of a Coral Community," *Global Change Biology* 6 (2000): 329–334; C. Langdon and M. J. Atkinson, "Effect of Elevated pCO_2 on Photosynthesis and Calcification of Corals and Interactions with Seasonal Change in Temperature/Irradiance and Nutrient Enrichment," *Journal of Geophysical Research* 110(C9) (2005): C09S07, 16 pp.

13. C. Langdon, T. Takahashi, C. Sweeney, D. Chipman, and J. Goddard, "Effect of Calcium Carbonate Saturation State on the Calcification Rate of an Experimental Coral Reef," *Global Biogeochemical Cycles* 14(2) (2000): 639–654; S. Barker and H. Elderfield, "Foramaniferal Calcification Response to Glacial-Interglacial Changes in Atmospheric CO_2," *Science* 297 (2002): 833–835; R. A. Feely, C. L. Sabine, K. Lee, W. Berelson, J. Kleypas, V. J. Fabry, and F. J. Millero, "Impact of Anthropogenic CO_2 on the $CaCO_3$ System in the Oceans," *Science* 305 (2004): 362–366; many earlier publications.

14. Lucid accounts are given by J. A. Kleypas, R. W. Buddemeier, D. Archer, J.-P. Gattuso, C. Langdon, and B. N. Opdyke, "Geochemical Consequences of Increased Atmospheric Carbon Dioxide on Coral Reefs," *Science* 284 (1999): 118–120; and J. M. Guinotte, R. W. Buddemeier, and J. A. Kleypas, "Future Coral Reef Habitat Marginality: Temporal and Spatial Effects of Climate Change in the Pacific Basin," *Coral Reefs* 22 (2003): 551–558.

15. J. B. Ries, S. M. Stanley, and L. A. Hardie, "Scleractinian Corals Produce Calcite, and Grow More Slowly, in Artificial Cretaceous Seawater," *Geology* 34(7) (2006): 525–528.

16. J. M. Guinotte, R. W. Buddemeier, and J. A. Kleypas, "Future Coral Reef Habitat Marginality: Temporal and Spatial Effects of Climate Change in the Pacific Basin," *Coral Reefs* 22 (2003): 551–558.

17. Information gaps are reviewed in detail by J. A. Kleypas, R. A. Feely, V. J. Fabry, C. Langdon, C. L. Sabine, and L. L. Robbins, "Impacts of Ocean Acidification on Coral Reefs and Other Marine Calcifiers: A Guide for Future Research," in *Report of a Workshop Held 18–20 April 2005, St. Petersburg, FL, Sponsored by NSF, NOAA and the U.S. Geological Survey* (2006).

18. A brief history is given by J. C. Orr, S. Pantoja, and H.-O. Pörtner, "Introduction to Special Section: The Ocean in a High-CO_2 World," *Journal of Geophysical Research* 110(C9) (2005): C09S01, 3 pp. A glance at the publication dates of the references listed here attests to the fact that the study of ocean acidification is a recently emerging science.

19. J. M. Guinotte, J. Orr, S. Cairns, A. Freiwald, L. Morgan, and R. George, "Will Human-Induced Changes in Seawater Chemistry Alter the Distribution of

Deep-Sea Scleractinian Corals?," *Frontiers in Ecology and the Environment* 4(3) (2006): 141–146.

20. C. Pelejero, E. Calvo, M. T. McCulloch, J. F. Marshall, M. K. Gagan, J. M. Lough, and B. N. Opdyke, "Preindustrial to Modern Interdecadal Variability in Coral Reef pH," *Science* 309 (2005): 2204–2207.

21. K. Caldeira and M. E. Wickett, "Anthropogenic Carbon and Ocean pH," *Nature* 425 (2003): 365.

22. For a pertinent, chilling review, see D. Archer, "Fate of Fossil Fuel CO_2 in Geologic Time," *Journal of Geophysical Research* 110(C9) (2005): C09S05, 6 pp.

16. The Ocean's Canary

1. J. Diamond, *Collapse: How Societies Choose to Fail or Survive* (London: Viking, 2005). I refer here to Chapter 12, about China.

2. A balanced review of current energy issues and their political settings is given by P. Roberts, *The End of Oil: The Decline of the Petroleum Economy and the Rise of a New Energy Order* (London: Bloomsbury, 2004).

3. M. Boulter, *Extinction: Evolution and the End of Man* (London: Fourth Estate, 2002). The author is a professor of paleobiology at the University of East London.

4. D. Jablonski, "Mass Extinctions: New Answers, New Questions," in L. Kaufman and K. Mallory, eds., *The Last Extinction* (Cambridge, Mass.: MIT Press, 1986), pp. 43–61. The author is a professor of paleontology at the University of Chicago.

5. L. Kaufman, "Why the Ark Is Sinking," in L. Kaufman and K. Mallory, eds., *The Last Extinction* (Cambridge, Mass: MIT Press, 1986), pp. 1–41. The author has written many insightful works on extinctions.

6. J. C. Briggs, "A Cretaceous-Tertiary Mass Extinction? Were Most of the Earth's Species Killed Off?" *Bioscience* 41 (1991): 619–624. The author is one of the world's foremost historical biogeographers.

7. E. O. Wilson, *The Creation* (New York: W.W. Norton, 2006). The author is one of the foremost biologists of our time.

8. G. Monbiot, *Heat: How to Stop the Planet Burning* (London: Penguin Books, 2006). A grass-roots insight into how climate change might be managed.

9. This message is elaborated by J. W. Kirchner and A. Weil, "Delayed Biological Recovery from Extinctions throughout the Fossil Record," *Nature* 404 (2000): 177–180.

10. N. Stern, *The Economics of Climate Change: The Stern Review* (Cambridge: Cambridge University Press, 2006). This is a crucial study of the impacts of climate change on human economies. However, its focus on stabilizing atmos-

pheric CO_2 at 450–550 ppm does not set the level low enough to protect coral reefs and a wide range of other marine and terrestrial ecosystems.

11. J. Bradshaw and T. Dance, "Mapping Geological Storage Prospectivity of CO_2 for the World's Sedimentary Basins and Regional Source to Sink Matching," in *Proceedings of the Seventh International Conference on Greenhouse Gas Control Technologies*, Vol. 1: *Peer-Reviewed Papers and Plenary Presentations, Vancouver, Canada, September 5–9, 2004*; Intergovernmental Panel on Climate Change (IPCC), *IPCC Third Assessment Report: Climate Change 2001*, Synthesis Report, ed. R. T. Watson and the Core Writing Team (Geneva, Switzerland: IPCC); www.ipcc.ch/pub/pub.htm; John Bradshaw, personal communications.

12. Whether or not one agrees with his stance on nuclear energy, Lovelock is one of the great holistic thinkers of our age. The reader who can spare a thought for the Earth's future is urged to read J. Lovelock, *The Revenge of Gaia: Why the Earth Is Fighting Back—and How We Can Still Save Humanity* (London: Allen Lane, 2006).

Glossary

$\Omega_{aragonite}$. Aragonite is the form of calcium carbonate that corals use to build skeletons. The solubility of calcium carbonate in seawater, which varies depending on its composition, is described as the saturation state of $CaCO_3$ (known by the symbol Ω), which is the product of the concentrations of the two ions (Ca^{2+} and CO_3^{2-}). At the point where $CaCO_3$ either precipitates or dissolves $\Omega_{aragonite}$ equals 1.

Acidification of the ocean.   A reduction in pH, where the ocean becomes more acidic, meaning less alkaline. Even acidified oceans remain alkaline; oceans never become acidic.

Adaptation.   An evolutionary process in which species or groups of individuals are genetically altered by natural selection. This usually occurs in response to changes in their physical or biological environment.

Ammonites.   Extinct molluscs of the Class Cephalopoda (which includes squids and octopuses). Ammonites are important fossils, which first appeared in the Paleozoic Era and persisted until the K/T mass extinction. They had an external shell coiled into a plane spiral, with septa dividing it into chambers.

Anoxia.   Lack of oxygen.

Aragonite.   A form of calcium carbonate with an orthorhombic crystal structure used by scleractinian corals, many molluscs and phytoplankton, and some coralline algae to build skeletons. Aragonite is unstable over geological time and recrystallizes to calcite.

Azooxanthellate corals.   Corals of any taxonomic group that do not have symbiotic algae in their tissues and thus have no need of sunlight. They are commonly found under overhangs or in caves in shallow tropical waters. However, most live as solitary individuals in the ocean depths, limited only by the aragonite compensation depth and their tolerance of the freezing temperatures found below thermoclines.

Belemnites.   Extinct molluscs of the Class Cephalopoda (which includes squids and octopuses). Belemnites are important fossils of the Mesozoic Era that persisted until the K/T mass extinction. They had a bullet-shaped internal shell with septa dividing it into chambers.

Bolides.   Huge asteroids that have periodically hit the Earth with a far greater force than anything else in its history, sending shock waves around the globe, triggering chains of volcanic eruptions, and creating tsunamis of vast size. The most famous of all bolides hit the Earth at the close of the Mesozoic Era (K/T), sending up a dust cloud that enveloped the planet and left minute traces of iridium, a very rare heavy metal almost entirely derived from extra-terrestrial sources, on all the continents. The bolide's effect is also seen in occurrences of shocked quartz—quartz that has been microscopically restructured by the passage of shock waves.

Calcite.   A form of calcium carbonate with a hexagonal crystal structure, used by Paleozoic corals and a wide variety of molluscs and other marine life to build skeletons. Calcite is the most stable form of calcium carbonate over geological time; the high-magnesium calcite that encrusting coralline algae produce is the least stable.

Carbonate compensation depth.   A term usually applied to the depth at which calcite becomes soluble. Reef organisms build their skeletons out of three forms of calcium carbonate: high-magnesium calcite (the most soluble), aragonite, and calcite (the least soluble). Descending from the ocean surface there is a point (or horizon) at which high-magnesium calcite becomes soluble (that is, where $\Omega_{\text{high-magnesium calcite}} = 1$), a deeper horizon where aragonite becomes soluble ($\Omega_{\text{aragonite}} = 1$), followed by a still deeper one where calcite becomes soluble ($\Omega_{\text{calcite}} = 1$).

Central American Seaway.   The seaway between North and South America that was closed by the emergence of the Isthmus of Panama, 3.4 million years ago.

Cnidaria.   The phylum to which all corals and many related taxa belong. It is classified as follows:

Class Hydrozoa
    Order Hydroidea (hydroids)
    Order **Milleporina** (including Genus *Millepora*)
    Order **Stylasterina** (including Genera *Distichopora* and *Stylaster*)
Class Scyphozoa (jellyfishes)
Class Cubozoa (sea wasps)
Class Anthozoa
  Subclass Octocorallia
    Order **Helioporacea** (*Heliopora coerulea*)
    Order **Alcyonacea** (soft corals, *Tubipora,* sea fans and relatives)
    Order Pennatulacea (sea pens)
  Subclass Hexacorallia

Order Actiniaria (simple sea anemones)
Order Zoanthidia (colonial anemones)
Order Corallimorpharia (corallimorpharians)
Order **Scleractinia** (true stony corals)
Order **Rugosa** (Paleozoic corals)
Order **Tabulata** (Paleozoic corals)
Subclass Ceriantipatharia
Order Antipatharia (black corals)
Order Ceriantharia (tube anemones)

Groups having some or all species with stony skeletons are indicated in bold.

Coccoliths. Phytoplankton that secrete platelets or rings of calcium carbonate in enormous quantities. These have accumulated as a major component of carbonate oozes of the ocean floor since the Cambrian.

Conodonts. Tiny fishlike primitive vertebrates that went completely extinct at the end Triassic mass extinction. Their fossil remains are toothlike structures up to 2 millimeters long composed of calcium phosphate. Although conodonts are useful indicators of the age of the rocks in which they occur, because they are widespread, abundant, and were probably pelagic, little is known of their biological affinities.

Corals. A general term used in reference to any large Cnidaria that is neither free-swimming nor an anemone or anemone-like. The name corals commonly refers to "hard" and "soft" corals, depending on whether or not the taxon has a skeleton. In this book, the term refers to Scleractinia (now living) and two extinct groups, Rugosa and Tabulata, all of which have calcium carbonate skeletons.

Corallimorpharians. Anemone-like solitary or colonial Cnidaria forming flat discs with short, club-tipped tentacles arranged in rings around the mouth, found all around the world.

Coralline algae. Algae with calcium carbonate skeletons, including *Halimeda* and encrusting coralline algae. The latter are an essential component in reef building, as they bind coral rubble.

Diagenesis. Processes such as cementation, compaction, replacement, and crystallization that are the means by which unconsolidated sediments are turned into hard stone. With corals, diagenesis is the nemesis of paleontologists because the term refers to the alteration of fossil skeletons of aragonite (an orthorhombic crystal structure) to calcite (a hexagonal structure), or, on shorter time scales, to aragonite from other sources. These processes not only obliterate the original structure of the skeleton but also render it undatable.

El Niño event. Part of the El Niño Southern Oscillation (see Figure 4.1).

Foraminifera.   Protozoa that are abundant in the plankton and on the seafloor of all oceans. They typically have calcareous tests ranging in size from microscopic to 50 millimeters in diameter and are used extensively in the dating of geological marine sedimentary strata. They form calcareous oozes found in vast quantities the world over.

Gaia hypothesis.   A view of the Earth as a self-regulating system. Organisms, atmosphere, surface rocks, and oceans interact in a complex of feedback mechanisms to create a system that makes the Earth habitable for contemporary life. The Gaia hypothesis proposes that there are self-regulating feedback mechanisms that keep the Earth's physical environment in a stable nonequilibrium state that allows for the continued existence of complex life forms.

General circulation models.   Coupled ocean and atmosphere numerical models designed to forecast and hindcast the Earth's climate. General circulation models are the main tool used for predicting future trends in climate, both atmospheric and marine.

Greenhouse effect.   A natural function of the atmosphere that maintains the Earth's surface temperature at levels that allow the biosphere as we know it to exist. Anthropogenic CO_2 increases atmospheric warming, hence the term "enhanced greenhouse effect."

Halimeda.   Large green algae composed of circular discs with aragonite skeletons linked together into a chain. Commonly called neptune's necklace.

Ice Ages.   The Pleistocene Epoch, 2.6 million to 11,800 years ago.

Indo-West Pacific.   A term used by biogeographers to refer to the Indian Ocean plus the western Pacific.

La Niña events.   Part of the El Niño Southern Oscillation (see Chapter 4).

Little Ice Age.   A Northern Hemisphere cool interval that lasted from the fifteenth to the nineteenth centuries.

Mass bleaching.   Simultaneous widespread whitening of corals owing to expulsion or death of zooxanthellae.

Mass spawning.   An annual event on the GBR in which a high proportion of corals release egg and sperm bundles almost simultaneously.

Methane (CH_4).   The main component of natural gas, methane is 22 times as potent as CO_2 as a greenhouse gas. Very large quantities of methane, known as methane clathrates or hydrates, exist naturally as icelike slurries on continental slopes.

Milankovitch cycles.   An alternative name for orbital forcing.

Orbital forcing.   Variations in the Earth's orbit in terms of eccentricity, the tilt of the rotational axis, and the wobble of the Earth's axis of rotation (see Figure 9.2).

pH.   A measure of acidity, pH is a negative logarithmic scale, so a decrease of 1 pH unit means a tenfold increase in the concentration of H^+ ions. The oceans are always alkaline (with a pH higher than 7).

Photosynthesis. The synthesis of carbohydrate by green plants (including the zooxanthellae of corals) in chloroplasts from CO_2 as a carbon source and water as a hydrogen donor, with the release of oxygen as a waste product, requiring sunlight as an energy source.

Radiocarbon dating. All living matter contains the carbon isotope ^{14}C, which is formed in the atmosphere at a constant rate and ingested by all life with food and air. This isotope decays to ^{12}C at a constant rate; thus the time of death of an organism can be calculated by measuring the ratio of ^{14}C to ^{12}C in its body. The technique starts to fail in remains older than about 40,000 years and cannot be used to reliably date the oldest human remains.

Radiolaria. Protozoa found in the plankton of all oceans and on the seafloor. They have tests made of silica that are up to a few millimeters in diameter and form siliceous (or radiolarian) oozes found in vast quantities the world over.

Reefs and coral reefs. These terms have different meanings. Paleozoic reefs are often dominated by calcifying sponges and other reef-building organisms and are therefore not coral reefs. The corals themselves belong to two distinct orders, Rugosa and Tabulata, which form skeletons of calcite. Modern reefs are mostly built by scleractinian corals, which form skeletons of aragonite, although there are exceptions and qualifications to the use of this term.

Rudists. A group of bivalve molluscs that differ from most other bivalves in having a right valve that is conical, cylindrical, or coiled and a left valve that is a flattened lid. During the Cretaceous (141–65 mya) they came to dominate reefs, especially fringing reefs, where they formed meadows that were more extensive than coral communities. Some rudists also formed true wave-resistant reefs. They were reduced in abundance toward the end of the Cretaceous and did not survive the K/T mass extinction.

Rugose corals. One of the two orders of corals of the Paleozoic. It is likely that Rugosa had symbiotic algae, that is, they were zooxanthellate.

Sargassum. A very common group of macroalgae.

Scleractinia. The dominant group of corals of the Mesozoic and Cenozoic eras, generally divisible into reef-building groups that have symbiotic zooxanthellae and non-reef-building (mostly deep-water) groups that do not.

Sea-level changes. Not necessarily a result of the accumulation or melting of polar ice, as is popularly believed, sea-level change is caused primarily by seafloor spreading, which creates changes in the actual volume of an ocean basin. Glaciation is the second most important cause, but there are others, including thermal expansion, plastic (isostatic) deformation of landmasses (as a direct result of changes in the weight of water or ice on the land), and changes in the amount of water in the atmosphere.

Sequestration of CO_2. Approximately 50 percent of all anthropogenic CO_2 comes from stationary sources, which can, in theory, be sequestered. It is possible to sequester this CO_2 under sedimentary strata—effectively returning it to the geological formations from which oil and gas were originally extracted.

Stromatoporoid sponges. Very large coralline sponges of the Paleozoic Era that were often major reef builders.

Subduction zone. The region where the margin of one continental plate slides under another.

Sulfur dioxide (SO_2). Sulfur dioxide emissions from industrial smokestacks have increased at the same exponential rate as those of CO_2, and sulfate aerosols derived from sulfur dioxide have long been believed to cause climate cooling by forming minute particles that become the nuclei of water droplets, thence clouds, which reflect heat. If these sulfates are in fact countering the effects of greenhouse gases, future global temperatures may accord more with the upper end of general circulation model predictions as smokestack emissions are cleaned up.

Sunspot cycles. Once a prime candidate for a nonanthropogenic explanation of twentieth-century warming, with some climate models suggesting that increasing solar radiation could explain between 20 and 50 percent of the warming observed. It could thus be argued that the doubling of CO_2 over the past century may have caused a temperature increase of perhaps 0.4°C. Debate about the role of changing solar radiation in global warming is gradually being brought to an end by satellite measurements, and it is now believed that sunspot cycles are unlikely to account for more than 10 percent of observed warming.

Super-Tethys Sea. An extension of the Tethys Sea that covered much of Europe during periods of high sea levels in the Mesozoic Era.

Symbiosis. The close and commonly obligatory association of two types of organisms living together, frequently but not necessarily for mutual benefit. The term covers the association between zooxanthellae (an alga) and corals.

Tabulate corals. One of the two orders of corals of the Paleozoic, Tabulata probably had symbiotic algae, that is, they were zooxanthellate.

Taxon. A taxonomic unit of any level.

Tethys Sea. A major ocean area of the Paleozoic and Mesozoic eras. The shape of the Tethys changed greatly over this time, progressively diminishing during the early Cenozoic Era until it closed up completely in the late Miocene.

Thermocline. A layer of ocean water in which temperature decreases rapidly with increasing depth. A widespread permanent thermocline exists beneath the warm, relatively well-mixed surface layer at typical depths of 200–1,000 meters. Water temperature beneath the thermocline decreases relatively slowly. During tropical summers, the thermocline is generally close to the ocean surface, whereas at higher latitudes, where there is considerable mixing, it is relatively deep.

Traps.   Massive basalt floods, the largest volcanic products on Earth. Traps typically form plates thousands of meters thick, with terraced or stairlike margins.

Western Pacific Thermal Cap.   A thermal cap is the highest temperature that a
very large expanse of ocean can theoretically reach. For the western Pacific this
temperature is 31°C.

Western Pacific Warm Pool.   The area of highest temperature of the western
Pacific Ocean, and the world's largest mobile body of heat.

Zooxanthellae.   Single-celled algae that have a symbiotic relationship with reef-
building corals. Zooxanthellae are of many types (clades) and are a major
energy source for their host corals.

Zooxanthellate corals.   Almost all scleractinian reef corals as well as some non-
scleractinian corals have symbiotic algae in their tissues. All zooxanthellate
corals must live in sunlight and normally do not tolerate temperatures below
14°C. A few species, found mostly in the western Atlantic, are both zooxanthellate and azooxanthellate.

Acknowledgments

The views and opinions expressed in this book are my own, and I take sole responsibility for them. That said, this volume would never have come to completion were it not for the efforts of Mary Stafford-Smith, who criticized, scrutinized, and questioned every aspect of it, repeatedly coming up with unique insights and following them with such persistence and determination that I consider this book hers as much as mine.

This text crosses a wide array of scientific fields, some of which I understood at the outset, for I have spent most of my working life as a coral reef scientist. However, it also delves into areas of science with which I originally had no detailed familiarity. Thus, small though it may be, this book took many years to research, for I found it necessary to follow its main themes to their ultimate conclusions. In all I have drawn on over 3,000 books and articles, all of which *should* be cited but are not, for reasons of space. So my second heartfelt acknowledgment goes to the scientists who made this book possible—those who are cited and the many more who are not.

Yet I soon discovered that reading a host of references, essential though that may be, does little to build syntheses, let alone syntheses for a broad readership. That required help, not only with the facts, but in linking facts together in ways that were both accurate and meaningful. So I sent drafts of chapters, and in many cases the whole book, to friends and colleagues; I asked them to find any fault of fact in their own fields and to let me know about anything they found questionable or difficult to follow in others. The responses I received were extraordinarily detailed and thoughtful. This may not have been for any personal reason, for I have probably worn out my colleagues on that account long ago. Rather it illustrates their obvious desire to help promote this book's message among the general public. Theirs was the response of people who have a sense of concern for the future of the Great Barrier Reef and for coral reefs in general—the same concern that motivated me to undertake this project in the first place.

These acknowledgments would go on for many more pages if I were to include all those who have talked to me, or emailed me, about questions I have had. They know who they are, and I am grateful to them. Here I name only those whom I pestered the most and who made special efforts—all busy people who gave their time willingly.

This book contains much discussion of climates: I am sure Janice Lough, a climatologist only a thirty-second walk from my office at the Australian Institute of Marine Science (AIMS) is happy to see it finished. Little farther away, Gregg Brunskill, a biogeochemist, was a mine of information and a wonderful colleague. The geomorphologist David Hopley (James Cook University of North Queensland; JCU) has been working on the GBR as long as I have, and so I particularly appreciated his detailed scrutiny of the whole text. On the vexing subject of mass bleaching in corals, I thank Ove Hoegh-Guldberg (University of Queensland) and Madeleine van Oppen (AIMS) for their help and time. Reef acidification is a particularly difficult subject, partly because it is so new, but also because it is so important. I needed help, and Bob Buddemeier (University of Kansas) gave it, not only on that subject, but for most of the book. My thanks also go to others who have helped me understand acidification, especially John Guinotte (Institute of Marine Conservation Biology), Joanie Kleypas (National Centre for Atmospheric Research), Chris Langdon (Rosenstiel School of Marine and Atmospheric Science; RSMAS), and Bradley Opdyke (Australian National University; ANU). Special thanks also go to John Guinotte for his computer simulation of future acidification and to several members of the staff of the National Oceanic and Atmospheric Administration (NOAA) for the computer imagery of ocean temperatures, both prepared especially for this book.

I discussed the issue of Aboriginal occupation of the GBR with many anthropologists, and I particularly thank Peter Veth (Australian Institute of Aboriginal and Torres Strait Islander Studies) for his help. George Stanley (University of Montana), a specialist in Mesozoic corals, provided many helpful comments, as did other geologists, notably Ian Macintyre (Smithsonian Institution). I thank Jim Bowen (University of New England) for help with GBR history and Richard Kenchington, along with several members of the staff of the Great Barrier Reef Marine Park Authority (GBRMPA), for their comments. Len Zell knows the GBR as well as anybody—thanks for everything, Len.

I am always thanking John Chappell (ANU) for something, this time for going down many meandering paths with me. John Bradshaw (Geoscience Australia) helped me through the details of the future of carbon dioxide; I was fortunate to have met him. I thank Hugh Davies (University of Papua New Guinea) for help with the difficult subject of the geology of that country. I also appreciate discussions with those who offered information, literature, or advice that I found helpful: Gerry Allen, Peter Bell, Ray Berkelmans, Colin Braithwaite, Bob Carter, Lindsay Collins, Alex Cook, Terry Done, Sylvia Earle, Katharina Fabricius, Peter Glynn, Peter Harrison, John Jackson, Marjaana Kokkonen, David Lewis-Williams, Yossi Loya, Lucien Montaggioni, Christina Phelan, Bill Precht, William Skirving, Craig Steinberg, Liz Truswell, Jody Webster, and Colin Woodroffe. I am grateful to various staff members at the Hadley Centre (U.K.), the Centre for Climate Change Research (U.K.), the Musée National de Préhistoire (France), and NOAA (U.S.A.).

Big-picture reviewers have been, for me, invaluable. I single out Lyndon DeVantier (who has worked on corals in many countries), Russ Reichelt (Reef and Rainforest Research Centre), and Mark Stafford Smith (Commonwealth Scientific and Industrial Research Organisation), for they not only reviewed the whole book in detail but also offered excellent thoughts on its scope and about how problematic issues might best be dealt with. Their voices echo through these pages.

I am grateful for the comments of two anonymous referees.

I have much respect for the views of field experts; Lyndon DeVantier and Emre Turak, as well as many other companions on dozens of field trips, have played an important role in shaping this book.

Information comes from many sources, including the colleagues I have mentioned and others that I have not. However, at the end of the day it is often unlocked only through the efforts of willing librarians, and I particularly thank Mary-Anne Temby and Jo Tasker (AIMS) and Susie Davies (GBRMPA). Liz Howlett (AIMS) worked on the long task of organizing references, and Tim Simmonds helped with photographs. I thank Fiona Alongi for the diagrams and for putting up with my endless stream of little "edits." The photographs I have selected are among many hundreds offered and freely given, several of them taken by Emre Turak specifically for this book. Geoff Kelly's artwork is wonderful, again given freely for earlier publications. Once again, thanks, Geoff.

When all is said and done this book will be useful only if it is readable: I thank Liz Tynan (JCU), with her expertise in science journalism, and Princeton Editorial Associates for helping Mary and me toward that goal.

Finally I thank AIMS and my many friends and colleagues there for help and support in so many ways.

Index

Aboriginal people: ancestry of, 52, 179–180; and fire, 182, Plate 43; fish traps of, 180; and megafauna extinction, 182

Abrupt climate change, 56, 79–80, 107, 118, 141–143, 189, 206, 208, 222–223

Acanthaster planci. See Crown-of-thorns starfish

Acclimatization, 209–210

Acidification, 104–112, 212–220, 265, Plate 57; and anoxia, 101–102, 108, 111; and azooxanthellate coral, 104, 106; and biodiversity, 219–220; and bioerosion, 134, 219; and calcification, 105, 107, 219; and carbon dioxide, 111; and coral, 104–107; and extinctions, 214; future of, 112, 212, 215, 218–221, 227, 231, Plate 57; and the Great Barrier Reef, 224, 226–229, 231; inertia of, 110; and mass extinctions, 105–112; and the Ocean Conveyor, 197; and oxygen, 102–105; rate of increase, 110–112, 183–184, 212, 219–221, 227; and reef gaps, 106–109, 212; and skeleton growth, 107, 212–220; of the Southern Ocean, 208, 218. *See also* Carbonates; Carbon cycle; Carbon dioxide; pH

Acid rain: and K/T, 84; and mass extinctions, 84, 101–111, 193; Permian, 77

Acropora, 37, 58, 96, 153, Plates 15, 19, 21; growth rate, 40; as habitat builders, 106, 207; past distribution of, 170

Acropora papillare, 153, Plate 21

Adaptation, 37, 43, 95, 110, 151, 208–210, 220, 265

Aerial reef erosion, 43, 144, 165

Agassiz, Alexander, 163

Albedo effect, 141

Algae: calcareous algae, 105; *Padina,* 207; *Sargassum;* 207. *See also* Algal symbiosis; Coralline algae; Macroalgae; Zooxanthellae

Alvarez and the K/T bolide, 84

Alveopora, 13, 54, Plate 16

Ammonites, 79, 82, 265

Anemones, 1, 30, 267

Anoxia, 101–102, 214, 265; and acidification, 108; and hydrogen sulfide, 37, 77, 101–102; and mass extinctions, 102, 111; and oil formation, 102; and oxygen, 101–102

Anoxic events: and extinctions, 101–102, 111; of the Mesozoic, 86, 101–103; of the Permian, 77

Antarctica: climates, 33, 114, 117–119, 123, 126–128, 138, 143, 185–187; forests, 118, 122, 127–128; glaciers, 114, 118; ice core records, 136, 138–140, 143–144, 146; ice sheets, 138–139, 189, 196, 231. *See also* Gondwana

Antarctic Circumpolar Current, 118–120, 126, 131, 137, 172

Antecedent erosion, theory of, 165, 167, 171

Anthropogenic impacts, 47–62, 222–231. *See also* Acidification; Bleaching; Carbon dioxide; Climate change; Extinction; Fishing; Great Barrier Reef; Greenhouse effect; Temperature; Tourism impacts

Anthropogenic spike in carbon dioxide, 188, 198–199, 216, 224, 231

Aragonite: and diagenesis, 69, 75, 82; fossils, 82; saturation, 102, 104; saturation depth, 102, 104–105, 218, 266; saturation states, 104–105, 214–216, 218, 265, Plate 57. *See also* Aragonite skeletons; Carbonates

Aragonite skeletons, 104, 214; of algae, 218; of coral, 69, 75, 82, 104, 214–217; of Foraminifera, 28, 71, 147, 165; of rudists, 82, 108–109

Archaeological sites, 176, 178–181

Arctic Perimeter, 138, 141, 156, 186

Arnhem Land, 21, 39, 181

Asia: coral, 21; reefs, 47, 50, 181

Askeletal coral, 109, Plate 6

Atmosphere: and climate regulation, 62, 64, 71, 99–105, 114–115, 137–138, 141, 184, 191; composition of, 99–104, 184, 191, 215; inertia of, 71, 100, 115, 119, 184, 194, 199, 205; stability of, 100, 138, 141, 198, 215; teleconnections, 142; water in, 100, 192, 194. *See also* Carbon dioxide; ENSO; Walker Circulation

Atolls, 16–17, 23, 39, 101, 145, 155, 162–163, 214

Australia: drift of, 9, 115, 126–128, 130, 133, 154, 165, 168–170; isolation of, 129–133; marine immigrations to, 127, 131; megafauna, 47, 155; Miocene collision, 121, 127, 129–133; paleoenvironments, 131, 168–171, 179–181; rift from Gondwana, 127–129. *See also* Aborigines; Archaeological sites; Cave art; Coral; Great Barrier Reef; Reefs

Azooxanthellate coral, 30, 70, 82, 265; and acidification, 102, 104; Cretaceous, 82; depth of, 104–106, 214, 218; extinction of, 70, 82, 90–93, 95–98, 102; habitats of, 94, 102, 104, 218

Bacterial slime, 36, 53, 208, 220

Barrier reefs, 16, 163. *See also* Great Barrier Reef

Belemnites, 82, 265–266

Bermuda reefs, 27, 59

Big Bend reefs, 74–75

Biodiversity: centers of, 132; conservation of, 39, 222; coral, 19, 32, 35, 39, 48; of the

Coral Triangle, 14, 19–20, 131, 132, 169; and depth, 32; of fossil reefs, 81–86; of the future, 120, 122, 228; gradients, 12, 63, 95, 113, 118–120, 123; of the Great Barrier Reef, 19, 48; and habitat, 32, 35, 39, 54; and latitude, 19, 23, 39; and mass extinctions, 67, 70, 78, 81–83, 86–87, 95; and reef gaps, 95, 127; of reefs, 1, 23, 48, 78; of soft bottom communities, 14, 54; of the Tethys Sea, 113, 122, 131

Bioerosion, 42, 165, 167, 171, 217, Plates 39, 40

Biogeographic gradients, 12, 63, 95, 113, 118–120, 123

Biogeography, 17, 19–20, 81, 126–127, 161

Bleaching of coral: causes of, 33, 56–62, 64, 97, 107, 200–209; effects of, 6, 56–62, 97, 197, 200–209, 212, 220–221, 227; and light, 33, 56–60, 111. *See also* Mass bleaching; Temperature

Blue holes, 177, Plate 4

Bolides, 76, 83–85, 87, 91–92, 98, 100, 103, 107–108, 111–112, 184, 266

Bølling Warming Event, 186

Bore holes, 116, 130, 163, 165–168, 171

Boron isotope signatures, 71, 116

Bottom trawling, 15, 46, 49, 54–55, Plate 28

Buffers: and acidification, 104–107, 112, 117, 194, 197; carbonate, 37, 101, 103–107, 112, 117, 215–216, 228; and depth, 105, 110; and the Ocean Conveyor, 197; and temperature, 105. *See also* Acidification; Anoxia; Carbon dioxide; Carbonates; pH

Bycatch, 54–55, Plate 28

Calcareous algae, 105, 158

Calcareous Alps, 28, 79, 145, 164

Calcification: and acidification, 103–107; and carbon dioxide, 99, 103; of the future, 105–106, 216–218; and light, 93, 140; rates of, 28, 32, 35, 91, 105; and skeleton building, 42, 91, 93; and temperature, 33, 93, 96, 107, 201

Calcite, 266; and diagenesis, 69, 75; fossils, 69, 75, 109, 214; saturation depth, 266; saturation state, 266; and temperature, 139. *See also* Calcite skeletons; High-magnesium calcite

Calcite skeletons: of molluscs, 27, 77; of rudists, 109; of rugose coral, 77; of Scleractinia, 217; of tabulate coral, 77

Calcium carbonate. *See* Carbonates

Canning Basin reefs, 74, 76

Carbonate Compensation Depth, 218

Carbonates, 28, 99, 214–216; buffers, 103, 107, 112, 214–217; and carbon dioxide, 99–100, 103, 117; compensation depth, 266; deep water, 216; dissolution of, 91, 215–217; forms of, 28, 69, 215–216; and ocean chemistry, 89, 99, 103–105, 110, 183–184, 214–217; and pH, 103–105, 107, 218–219; reefs, 28, 34, 40, 42, 91, 104, 145, 169, 177, 184; saturation of, 215–216. *See also* Aragonite saturation depth; Calcite saturation depth

Carbon cycle, 98–100; and carbon dioxide, 10, 64, 99–112, 184–185; and mass extinctions, 10, 100–112, 212. *See also* Acidification; Carbonates

Carbon dioxide, 71, 99–100, 213–214; and acidification, 10, 77, 89, 101–102, 104, 184, 197, 212, 214–216; and anthropogenic influences, 183–198, 218–224; anthropogenic spike in, 184, 193–194, 198, 215–216, 224, 231; and calcification, 35, 102–105, 140, 183, 216–218; and carbonates, 99–100, 103, 117; and carbon cycle, 10, 64, 99–112, 184–185; and climate change, 183–198, 210–215; future predictions of, 193–194, 198, 214–216, 223–224; and glacial cycles, 113, 135, 139–140, 198; and the Great Barrier Reef, 135–136; and greenhouse effects, 103, 191–192, 198, 213–214; in ice cores, 71, 139–140; and mass extinctions, 10, 103–108, 111–112, 183–185, 214–215, 219; measurement of, 109–110, 117, 125, 139–140, 195, 213, 215, 224; and methane, 9, 100, 103, 116, 124, 219; ocean/atmosphere balance, 71, 76, 100–101, 103, 184, 214–216; and ocean chemistry, 89, 99, 103–105, 110, 183–184, 214–216, 218; ocean uptake of, 64, 71, 104–107, 115, 188, 214–216; and paleoclimates, 76–77, 79–80, 83–85, 87, 89, 106–110, 113, 116–118, 120–125, 140, 198, 210; and pH, 103–105, 112, 116; and photosynthesis, 101–102, 183–184; rate of increase, 191, 195–198, 223; and seafloor spreading, 107; and sea level, 125, 135, 196, 213; sequestration of, 230; solubility of, 64, 140, 212–213; spikes, 107–108, 184, 193–194, 198, 215–216, 219, 224, 231; and temperature, 117, 123, 125, 139, 187–188, 203–206, 213, 216. *See also* Cenozoic, carbon dixoide

Carbonic acid, 101, 104, 121

Carboniferous, 68, 77, 96

Carbon mass modeling, 71

Caribbean: coral, 19–20, 39, 58–60, 114, 124, 131; of the Miocene, 122; of the Oligocene, 118; reefs, 27, 50

Caryophylliidae, 82, Plate 8

Caves: of the Great Barrier Reef, 4, 174–175, 177–179; human occupation of, 4, 174–177, 181; submerged, 4, 10, 178

Cays, 13–14, 47, 166–168, 170, 196

Cenozoic: carbon dioxide, 84–86, 103–110, 114–118, 120–125, 130, 135, 139–140; coral, 107, 113–114, 116, 118, 122, 124, 126, 128, 130–134, 155–156, 158–162, 168–169; environments, 113–125; events, 107, 115, 119, 123–125, 131, 141; greenhouse, 114–118; plate tectonics, 115, 118–122, 126–130; reefs, 113–118, 122–132; temperatures, 113, 116–120, 123–125

Centers of biodiversity, 12, 19, 48, 113, 124, 126, 131, 132, 169

Central American Seaway, 83, 113, 115–116, 118, 122, 124, 131, 266. *See also* Isthmus of Panama

Charonia tritonis, 51

Chimeras, 160

China, 193, 223

Chlorofluorocarbons, 192

Clades of zooxanthellae, 31–32, 38, 60, 210

Clams, 30–31, 108

CLIMAP, 147

Climate models, 116, 139, 147, 187–190, 192–195, 197, 204, 213, 215–216, 218, 222. *See also* General circulation models

Clipperton Atoll, 39, Plate 17

Clouds: dust, 84, 92; greenhouse effect of, 187, 190, 192–193; water, 187, 190, 192–193

Cnidaria, 28–30, 266

Coccoliths, 28, 218, 267

Coevolution, 29

Colonization, 17, 21, 36, 44, 53–54, 67, 95, 131–133, 158, 172, 207

Colony formation, 29, 40, 43, 57, 59, 70, 153, Plate 15

Competition, 30, 37–38, 106

Conodonts, 79, 267

Conservation: future, 39, 49–51, 54–55, 222–223; on the Great Barrier Reef, 5, 47–51, 54–55, Plate 27; of megafauna, 47–49, 222; of sharks, 47, 49–50. See also Anthropogenic impacts

Continental positions, 73–76, 78, 83–86, 115, 126–130

Cook Islands, 64

Coral, 267; and acidification, 104–107; askeletal, 109, Plate 6; biodiversity, 19, 32, 35, 39, 48; biodiversity gradients, 12, 63, 95, 113, 118–120, 123; cleaning, 36; communities, 22–23, 32–33, 36, 51, 59–60, 95, 98, 135, 151, 153, 156, 200, 228, Plates 22, 24, 25, 48; and continental drift, 130–133; drop-out sequence, 21–22; evolution, 19, 29, 43–44, 55, 67–70, 95, 106, 121, 132, 150–151, 201, 208–211, 216; family tree, 69, Plate 8; feeding, 13, 54, 93; fossil record, 22, 66–70, 72, 75, 82, 85–88, 90, 107, 116, 131–133, 159, 169, 202; growth rates, 34–35, 41, 44, 60, 90, 155, 216; habitats, 21, 32, 34–36, 38–40, 82, 97, 104, 106–107, 128, 133, 153–155, 208, 225, Plate 19; high latitude, 34, 64, 96–97, 104–105, 120, 170, 208; mass spawning, 53–54, 197; and reefs, 28–30; reproduction, 43, 53–54, 60, 153, 197, Plates 10, 11; soft, 2, 20; structure, 26, 37, 75, 96, 105, Plates 5, 15; tabulate, 29, 67, 69, 72, 77, 108–109, 267, 270; taxonomy, 44, 70; and temperature, 33–35; of Western Australia, 21, 34, 169–170. See also Azooxanthellate coral; Biodiversity; Biogeography; Bleaching of coral; Calcification; Centers of biodiversity; Colonization; Colony formation; Depth of coral; Dispersal; Environments; Extinction; Great Barrier Reef, coral; Larvae of coral; Mass bleaching; Nutrients; Paleontology of coral; Reefs; Rugose coral; Scleractinia; Skeletons; Zooxanthellate coral

Corallimorpharia, 78, 267

Coralline algae, 13, 15, 27, 29, 37–39, 42, 109, 111, 144, 155, 208, 214, 219, 267

Coral reefs. See Reefs

Coral Sea: basin, 24–25, 128; bathymetry, 24; formation of, 128–129, 132; reefs, 25

Coral Triangle, 19–20; age of, 132; biodiversity of, 19–20, 48; formation of, 20

Coring of reefs. See Reef drilling

Cosmic rays, 98

Cretaceous: azooxanthellate coral, 82, 90–91, 93; coral, 82–83, 93, 95, 97, 107, 217; events, 82–83; marine life, 82–83; reefs, 82, 85–86, 129; sea levels, 83; temperature, 83–84, 96–97, 172. See also K/T mass extinction

Cross-shelf gradients, 12, 35, 52

Crown-of-thorns starfish, 5, 14, 46, 48, 50–51, 53–54, 64, 106, 203, Plate 29

Currents: and evolution, 43–44, 70; and reef erosion, 17–18, 42; surface, 21, 63, 118–119, 172; tidal, 2, 15–18, 42, 61–62, 165, 214. See also Antarctic Circumpolar Current; Dispersal; East Australia Current; Leeuwin Current

Cyanobacteria, 36, 53, 208, 220

Cycles of climate change. See Glaciation; Ice Ages; Last glacial cycle; Milankovitch cycles; Orbital forcing

Cyclones, 15, 54, 158, 197, Plate 31

Cynarina lacrymalis, Plates 6, 7

Daintree reefs, 53, 157

Daly, Reginald, theory of reef formation, 163

Dansgaard Oeschger events, 141, 144, 186

Darwin, Charles, theory of atoll formation, 16, 162–165

Darwinian evolution, 29, 43, 55

Deccan traps, 85, 92, 107

Degraded reefs, 36, 97, 231, Plates 49–52, 54–55. See also Acidification; Cyanobacteria; Fishing; Mass bleaching

Deltaic reefs, 15–18, 42, 167, 177

Depth of coral, 27, 32, 94, 158

Detritus feeders, 13, 54, 93

Devonian: carbon dioxide, 71, 80, 87, 108; climates, 73; coral, 74–75; events, 73; mass extinction, 73–76, 108, 111; reefs, 73–75, Plate 34; sea levels, 73

Diagenesis, 40, 90, 133, 267

Dinosaurs, extinction of, 81, 85, 112, 127–128

Disease, 56, 60, 97–98, 106, 208, Plate 56

Dispersal, 12, 17, 19–20, 43–44, 81, 94–95, 132–133, 169, 180

Diversity. See Biodiversity

Dolines, 177

Dolomite Ranges, 145

Drake Passage, 114–115, 119, 122–123, 131

Drilling of reefs. See Reef, drilling

Drop-out sequence, 21–22

Drowning of reefs, 16, 94, 130, 144, 158, 163

Dryas octopetala, 186

Duncanopsammia axifuga, 132, Plate 13

Dust clouds, 84, 92

East Australian Current, 21

Ecosystem evolution, 28–29

Elizabeth Reef, 21, 23, 162, 169–170

El Niño, 267. See also ENSO

Encrusting algae, 39

Enhanced greenhouse warming. See Greenhouse effect

ENSO, 62–65, Plate 53; age of, 204–205; frequency of, 64–65; future of, 58–59, 200, 205–206, 227; and greenhouse effects, 183, 200, 204–206, 223; and mass bleaching, 59, 62, 65, 202–206; mechanism of, 63–64, 205; teleconnections, 142; and temperature, 62, 147, 200, 205–206. See also Walker Circulation

Entophysalis, 36, 53, 208, 220

Environmental gradients, 12, 52, 63, 95, 113, 118–120, 123

Environment: cross-shelf variation in, 12, 52, 210; and depth, 39, 62, 91, 93, 104–105, 152, 154–159, 164, 171–172, 194, 208, 218; estuarine, 13, 53; latitudinal variation in, 32–33, 95–97, 104–105, 119–120, 169–170, 197; and turbidity, 32, 35, 52, 156; and turbulence, 3, 15, 23, 30, 35–39, 61, 106; and wave energy, 12–13,

15, 29–30, 36–37, 42, 86, 106, 155–156. See also Azooxanthellate coral; Coral; Greenhouse effect; Greenhouse gases; Ice Ages; Icehouse climates; Light; Sediment; Temperature

Eocene: of Australia, 129; climates,118–120; coral, 131; extinction, 131; reefs, 125, 131, 169; temperatures, 125

Epicontinental seas, 73–74, 83, 86, 97, 163

Era Beds, 132–133, 159, 169–170

Erosion: aerial, 144; antecedent, 165,167, 171–172; biological, 42, 171, 217, Plates 39, 40; of cays, 196; chemical, 91; of reefs, 41–42, 91–92, 105, 111; by sea-level change, 171–172

Estuarine environments, 53

Evolution: and coevolution, 29; of coral, 19, 29, 43–44, 68, 131, 201–202, 208–211; and currents, 43–44, 70; Darwinian, 29, 43, 55; of ecosystems, 35; of humans, 175–176, 178–180; and reef gaps, 95, 106; reticulate, 43–44, 70; of Scleractinia, 19–20, 28, 78, 121–122, 132–133, 160; of species, 19, 44, 55, 135, 200–201. See also Centers of biodiversity; Extinction; Mass extinction

Evolutionary time, 43, 94, 202, 206, 208–211

Extinction: of azooxanthellate coral, 70, 82, 90–93, 95–98, 102–106, 214, 218; background, 68, 70, 79, 89, 94, 97–98, 103, 108, 113, 116–118, 131, 214; causes of, 84–85, 89–112; of coral, 72, 75, 77, 91, 93–97, 106–107, 111, 131, 153, 217; of Foraminifera, 82; of the future, 221; human induced, 181, 221, 224–227; of marine reptiles, 108, 127; of megafauna, 182; Pleistocene, 155; rate of, 66, 85, 87, 220; regional, 155; See also Carbon cycle; Carbon dioxide; Mass extinction

Extraterrestrial cycles, 84, 98, 189. See also Orbital forcing

Family tree, of Scleractinia, 69, Plate 8

Far eastern Pacific, 19–20, 39, 57, 124

Faulting, 16

Faunal gradients, 12, 63, 95, 113, 118–120, 123

Faviidae, 82, 93, 107, Plate 8

Fish, 14, 40, 42, 48–49, 55, 86, 130, 201; herbivorous, 34, 40, 54, 82, 207–208, 220,
231, Plate 18; sharks, 49–50, 108
Fishing, 47–50, 54–55, 180–181, 207
Fish traps, 180, Plate 43
Flatworms, 30
Flinders Reef, 21–22
Fly River, 20–21, 25
Foraminifera, 28, 267; as environmental
indicators, 71, 116, 138–139, 147, 165;
extinctions of, 82
Fossil fuel, 102, 198, 219, 229–230
Fossil record: of carbon dioxide, 71; of
coral, 67–70, 72, 77, 90, 107; interpretation of, 68–70, 75, 87–88; of reefs, 66, 70,
87–88, 116, 153, 159, 169; sequences in,
68–69; of soils, 71, 103, 107; value of, 69,
77, 82, 85–86, 131–132, 159, 227
Fringing reefs, 14, 16, 149, 152, 154, 156,
165, 181, 204
Fungiid coral, 34

Gaia hypothesis, 231, 267
Gastrodermal cells, 31, 57
General circulation models, 187–190,
192–194, 204, 267
Generic ages of coral, 132
Genetic dwarfing, 55
Genotypes, of coral, 29, 43–44, 70, 95,
150–151, 159–160, 210; selection of, 210,
220; of zooxanthellae, 31–32, 60, 203,
210. See also Reticulate evolution
Geographic variation: of coral, 59, 186; of
zooxanthellae, 59
Geological intervals, 7–8
Geological time, 28, 184
Glacial cycles, 68, 71, 94, 96, 100, 118, 133,
136–160, 185–186, 189
Glaciation: Antarctic, 113–114, 117–119,
123, 126, 128, 134, 137–138; and carbon
dioxide, 113, 135, 139–140, 198; cycles of,
68, 71–72, 94, 96, 118, 136–141, 144,
150–155; and extinctions, 96, 159; Ice
Age, 136–141, 150–155; Miocene, 123;
Pleistocene, 135–141, 189–199, 231. See
also Heinrich events
Glaciers: of Antarctica, 114, 118; melting of,
142, 152, 195–196

Global center of biodiversity, 131, 132. See
also Centers of biodiversity
Global warming, 183–199. See also Carbon
dioxide; Greenhouse effect; Greenhouse
gases; Temperature
Gondwana, 73–74, 118–119, 127–130
Goniopora, 13
Gradients: biogeographic, 12, 63, 95, 113,
118–120, 123; cross-shelf, 12, 35, 52;
drop-out, 21–22; See also Environmental
gradients; Latitudinal gradients
Great Barrier Reef: and acidification, 224,
226–229, 231; age of, 10, 167–173; antecedent erosion, 171; area of, 12; biodiversity, 19, 48; boreholes, 165–168;
and carbon dioxide, 135–136; caves, 4,
174–175, 177–179; changes in, 49–50;
comparisons with other regions, 47–49;
conservation of, 5, 47–51, 54–55, Plate
27; coral, 20–23, 33, 96, 201, 206; definitions of, 135, 172; and earliest humans,
174, 178–181; future of, 209–210,
212–213, 218, 220, 227–231; and greenhouse effect, 202–206; habitat diversity,
12, 21, 35, 39–40, 154–155; hingeline,
170–171; lagoon, 14–16, 62, 135,
152–154, 205–206, 208; and the last
glacial maximum, 155–157, 174–175,
180, 182, 186; and the Mid-Pleistocene
Transition, 139, 168, 171; Miocene limestone, 169; oil exploration, 50, 167; and
oil spills, 46; origins, 10, 121–123,
130–133, 167–173; Pleistocene reefs, 161,
167–172; reefs, 2–5, 9–10, 12–23; size, 1,
12; soft bottom communities, 14, 54;
southern limit, 12; species diversity, 1, 22,
32, 48; temperature, 21, 33–35, 147;
thickness, 165, 167–168; threats to,
46–47, 51, 189, 211, 220, 229–231; zonation, 13–15, 151, 155, 158, 196. See also
Anthropogenic impacts; ENSO; Reefs
Greater Australia, 127–130, 154, 169, 172,
179–180
Greenhouse effect, 191–194, 268; anthropogenic, 10, 58, 115, 140, 183, 187,
193–194, 198, 202–205, 211–213, 215, 221,
223–225; and clouds, 187, 190, 192–193;
debate about, 187–189, 205, 226–227; fu-

ture of, 194–199, 223–231; and sulfur dioxide, 101, 187, 193, 195, 270. *See also* Carbon dioxide; Cenozoic, greenhouse; ENSO; Methane; Temperature
Greenhouse gases, 125, 139, 187, 192–193, 221, 230–231; mechanism of, 189, 192–193
Greenland: ice core records, 139, 142–143; ice sheets, 195–196
Growth rates: of coral, 40–41, 107; of reefs, 40
Guilds, 29, 34
Gulf Stream, 141

Habitats. *See* Environments
Halimeda, 158, 208, 268, Plates 50, 55
Health of reefs, 2, 36, 45, 60, 201, 207–208, 220, 231
Heat transport, 61, 63, 72, 119, 121, 138, 141–142, 187, 189, 194, 205, 227
Heinrich events, 141–142, 144, 153, 156
Heliofungia actiniformis, 13, Plate 20
Heliopora, 27, 266
Herbivorous fish. *See* Fish
Heron Island: borehole, 166–167; and sea-level rise, 196
High islands, 13–14, 22
High latitude, coral, 34, 96–97, 105, 208; reefs, 96, 169–170
High-magnesium calcite, 105, 109, 111, 219, 266. *See also* Calcite
Hinchinbrook Island, 13
Hingeline of the Great Barrier Reef, 170–171
Holocene: climates, 143, 152, 185–187, 193–194; events, 136–137; reefs, 167
Homo, species of, 175–176
Houtman Abrolhos Islands, 34, 169–170
Humans: ancestry, 175–181; earliest fishing, 180; and extinctions, 182; immigrations, 178–179; impacts on reefs, 47–50, 54–55, 207; maritime archaeological sites, 176, 178–181; occupation of caves, 4, 174–177, 181; population increase, 48, 50, 52, 190, 196, 223; resource consumption, 190, 223, 228. *See also* Anthropogenic impacts; Last Glacial Cycle, Tourism impacts
Huon Peninsula, 153, 175, 179
Hybridization, 43–44, 160

Hydrogen sulfide: and anoxia, 37; and mass extinctions, 77, 86, 101–102, 214

Ice Ages, 134–160, 268; carbon dioxide, 71, 117, 139–140; causes, 136–141; climates, 141–148; coral, 133–135, 147, 151–160, 164–172; cycles, 136–141, 150–155; events, 141–142; extinctions, 133–135, 155–156; glaciations, 136–149; sea-levels, 135–139, 142–148, 150–158; temperatures, 138–147, 156–157, 169–172, 185–186
Ice core records, 139–144, 146, 186, 193, 202
Icehouse climates, 113, 121, 160, 197. *See also* Ice Ages
Ice sheets, 142, 156, 186, 189, 195–196, 199
Ice shelf collapses, 142–144, 186, 189
Ice volume, 128, 139, 146, 153, 202
Impacts. *See* Anthropogenic impacts
Indian Ocean: coral, 19–20, 58; reefs, 47
Indonesia: coral, 20, 48, 131; humanoid fossils, 178–179; reefs, 12, 19, 48, 94, 127
Indo-West Pacific, 268
Inertia: and acidification, 99, 112, 212, 217; of Antarctica, 138, 185; of the atmosphere, 71, 99, 138, 199; of ice sheets, 71, 138; of the ocean, 71, 99, 120, 138, 144, 187, 194, 199
Inorganic nutrients, 53
Intergovernmental Panel on Climate Change (IPCC): function of, 189; predictions of, 190–193, 223
International Consortium for Great Barrier Reef Drilling, 167–168
Inter-reef habitats, 46, 54, 154
Iridium, 184
Islands, 13–15, 19, 22–23, 34, 39, 94–95, 196
Isostatic rebound, 156–157
Isthmus of Panama, 57, 124, 266. *See also* Central American Seaway

Japan, coral, 19, 21, 96; reefs, 34, 47, 171
Jurassic, carbon dioxide, 85, 102; coral, 82; reefs, 67, 80–81

K/T mass extinction, 81–86, 90, 96–97; and acidification, 102, 106–107; and azooxanthellate coral, 90–91, 93, 97–98;

K/T mass extinction (*continued*)
    and carbon dioxide, 83–84, 107; causes
    of, 83–85, 93, 102–103, 106–108, 112; and
    reefs, 85; timing of, 84–85
Kyoto Protocol, 223

Lagoons, 23, 34–37, 86, 101, 153–154, 177,
    205, 214, 228. *See also* Great Barrier Reef
    lagoon
Lag-time. *See* Inertia
La Niña events, 268. *See also* ENSO
Larvae of coral, 17, 20–21, 32, 36, 44, 51,
    53–54, 131–133, 156, 158, 169, 172, 197,
    207, Plate 11
Last glacial cycle, 150–160; aftermath of,
    185–187; carbon dioxide of, 139–140;
    and corals, 158–160; and the Great Bar-
    rier Reef, 94, 154–160; and humans, 174,
    178, 181–182; onset, 152–154; sea levels
    of, 72, 151–156; shorelines, 154–158;
    temperatures of, 72, 147
Last glacial maximum: age of, 151; coral,
    155; and the Great Barrier Reef, 155–
    160; sea levels, 156; temperatures,
    147
Last interglacial: climates, 143–144, 146; sea
    levels, 145–146
Last sea level rise, 52, 151, 156–159
Late Paleocene Thermal Maximum, 103,
    115, 125, 130, 219
Latitudinal gradients, 32–33, 95, 118–119,
    123
Leeuwin Current, 21, 119
Leptoseris, 32
Light: and bleaching, 33, 56–60; and coral,
    2, 30–39, 52–53, 92–93, 96, 107; latitudi-
    nal gradients in, 32–33, 95–96; limita-
    tions, 14–15, 32–33; and mass extinc-
    tions, 92–93; and sediment, 14, 32, 36, 52,
    56; and zooxanthellae, 13, 15, 30–33
Limestone: composition, 144–145; weather-
    ing, 40, 42–43, 90, 94, 144, 155, 168. *See
    also* Reefs, erosion
Little Ice Age, 186, 188, 268
Lophelia, 27
Lord Howe Island, 22–23, 34, 169–170,
    Plates 2, 19
Lyell, Charles, 161–163

Macroalgae, 29, 34, 40, 97, 106, 207, Plates
    19. 52
Madagascar, 52, 127
Management interventions, 51, 54–55, 65,
    223, 231
Mangroves, 14, 37–38, 151, 154, 157, 174
Marine sediments. *See* Sediment
Marine snow, 53
Marion Plateau, 24, 128, 155
Maritime archaeology, 180–181
Mass bleaching, 56–65, 202–211, 268, Plates
    44–47; causes, 56–62, 202–206; and ENSO,
    59, 62, 65, 204–206; future developments,
    205–211; geographic variation in, 57–60;
    and greenhouse effect, 202–204; history
    of, 56–59, 203–204; and light, 33, 56–60,
    111; of *Porites,* 204, Plate 47; surveys of,
    58, 203; and temperature, 56–62, 64, 97,
    200–202, 208–209; temporal variation in,
    203–205; and ultraviolet light, 59, 98
Mass extinction, 66–112; causes of, 6,
    67–69, 72, 76–77, 79–81, 91–98, 100–112;
    Devonian, 73–76; future, 65, 112,
    216–220, 222–229, 231; Ordovician,
    72–73; Permian, 77; Triassic, 79. *See also*
    Carbon cycle; Extinction; K/T mass
    extinction; Reefs, gaps
Mass spawning, 53–54, 197, 268
Maxwell's concept of reef evolution, 165
Media, 227
Mediterranean Sea, 97, 123, 176
Megafauna: Australian, 155; marine, 47–49,
    122; terrestrial, 122, 155, 182
Mesozoic reefs: and anoxic events, 86,
    101–102, 108, 111; and carbon dioxide,
    80, 83–85, 99–111; and sea levels, 80,
    82–85, 87–88, 94–95
Methane, 102–103, 268; and climate change,
    84, 100; conversion to carbon dioxide,
    100, 103, 115–116, 214; cycles, 140; future
    release of, 140, 198, 219; as a greenhouse
    gas, 103, 124; ice, 102–103, 112; and the
    Late Paleocene Thermal Maximum, 115,
    125; and mass extinction events, 77, 84,
    100, 103, 213–214; quantity of, 103, 219
Michaelmas Cay deep bore, 165–166
Microatolls, 128, Plate 41
Micronesian atolls, 145

Middleton Reef, 21, 23, 162, 169–170, Plate 3

Mid-Pleistocene Transition, 139, 141, 168, 171

Milankovitch cycles, 268. *See also* Orbital forcing

Millepora, 27, 59, 266

Miocene: of Australia, 129–133, 169–170; carbon dioxide, 117–118, 121, 123, 125; climates, 121–125; Climatic Optimum, 123–124; coral, 124, 131–133; environments, 121–124, 198; events, 121–124, 129; glaciations, 123; limestone, 122, 131, 169; pH, 123; reefs, 116, 122–123; temperatures, 125; of the Tethys Sea, 122–123

Models, of climate change, 139, 147, 187–190, 192–195, 204, 218, 222; of ocean chemistry, 215–216

Molluscs, 27, 30, 77, 82, 109, 159, 180

Morphological variation, 38, 43

New Caledonia, 48

New Guinea. *See* Indonesia; Papua New Guinea

New Zealand fossil reefs, 123, 169

Nitrogen, 84, 101, 191–192

Nitrous oxide, 101, 192

Northwest Shelf, 130, 180

Nuclear power, 230

Nuclear winter, 84, 92

Nutrients, 15, 52–53

Ocean: depth layers, 32, 62–64, 102, 104–105, 120, 194, 218; thermal expansion, 194, 196; thermocline, 63–64, 270. *See also* Acidification; Buffers; Carbonates; Carbon dioxide; Currents; Inertia of the Ocean; Ocean chemistry; pH; Temperature

Ocean chemistry, future, 216–220, 228; present, 214–216. *See also* Acidification; Carbonates; Carbon dioxide; General circulation models; pH

Ocean Conveyor, 120–121, 124, 146, 189, 196–197, 216. *See also* Thermohaline convection

Oil: exploration, 50, 130, 167; formation of, 102; spills, 46

Oligocene: climates, 118–119, 121, 131, 143; events, 119, 121; extinctions, 118, 131; of Australia, 118, 128, 131, 169, 172; reefs, 131, 169, 172, 198

Orbital forcing, 99, 136–139, 141–143, 156, 168, 189, 197–198, 231

Ordovician: climates, 72; coral, 67; events in, 72–73; mass extinction, 72–73, 87; reefs, 72–73

Organic nutrients, 53

Origins of the Great Barrier Reef. *See* Great Barrier Reef, origins

Orpheus Island, 58

Oxygen: and acidification, 86, 101, 130, 214; and extinction events, 77, 84, 86, 101–102, 108, 130, 219; free radicals, 57, 202; isotopes, 138–139, 146; toxicity, 33, 35, 56–57, 101. *See also* Anoxia

Ozone layer, 98

Pachyseris, 13

Padina, 207, Plate 51

Paleocene climates, 115, 117, 125, 130, 172

Paleocene Thermal Maximum, 103, 115, 125, 130, 219

Paleolithic humans, 174–182; art, 175–176, 180–181; relics, 176, 178, 180

Paleontology of coral, 69–70, 72, 77, 82, 85, 90, 107, 116, 159, 169, 227

Paleosols, 71, 103, 107

Paleotemperatures. *See* Temperature

Paleozoic: carbon dioxide, 71, 76–77, 80; coral, 29, 69, 72, 75, 77–78, 108–109; events, 68, 72–74, 76–77; reefs, 66–70, 72–77; sea levels, 68–69, 71–73, 76–77, 80; temperatures, 71–73, 76–77, 79

Palm Island coral, 58, 95

Panthalassa Ocean, 73–74, 76, 78, 81, 97

Papua New Guinea, coral, 20, 131–132; limestone, 25, 129, 131; reefs, 25, 115, 153, 169–170

Parrot fish, 42

Pavona maldivensis, 70

Peat bogs, 86

Permafrost, 102, 219

Permian: coral, 90, 111; events, 77, 108; marine life, 77; mass extinction, 77–78, 92, 98, 102, 219; ocean chemistry, 77; reefs, 77

pH, 268; and acidification, 103–105; and carbonate saturation, 103–104; and carbon dioxide, 100, 103–104; of the future, 212, 216–219; measurement of, 104; of the present, 104, 107, 116, 216, 218; rate of change, 104, 112, 212, 216–217
Philippines, 19, 94
Photosynthesis, 269; and carbon dioxide, 30, 99–102, 107, 140; and coral, 13, 15, 27, 30, 201; and light, 30, 59, 93; and oxygen, 56–57, 111; and temperature, 33, 95
Phytoplankton, 28, 53, 99–100, 102, 105, 139, 216, 218
Planing off of reefs, 4, 144, 153, 163, 171
Plankton. See Phytoplankton; Zooplankton
Plate tectonics: and carbon dioxide, 99–100, 107, 110, 125; and continental drift, 87, 100, 115; and sea levels, 71, 94. See also Seafloor spreading; Traps; Volcanism
Platform reefs, 16, 23, 158
Pleistocene, 134–149; carbon dioxide, 135, 140–141, 198; coral, 124, 131–133, 158–160; extinctions, 94, 133; glacial cycles, 135–141, 189–199, 231; orbital forcing, 136–137, 139, 141, 168, 171, 197, 231; reefs, 23, 161–173; sea levels, 52, 94, 139, 143–144, 148–149, 171; temperatures, 116, 143–144, 146–148. See also Last glacial cycle
Pliocene climates, 122–123, 136, 143
Pocillopora damicornis, 36, 38, 69
Pollen indicators of environments, 81, 139
Pompey complex, 16–18, 41, 177
Porites, 34, 40–41, 107, 123, 128, 204, Plate 41
Poritidae, 60, 93, Plate 8
Protists, 30
Purdy's antecedent karst hypothesis, 164

Queensland Plateau, 24–25
Queensland Trough, 3, 16, 128, 154–155

Radiocarbon dating, 269
Radiolaria, 82, 269
Raine Island, 196, Plate 30
Rainwater dissolution, 142
Range shifts, 159. See also Dispersal
Red Sea: coral, 19, 32, 44, 58; reefs, 44, 48; salinity crisis, 97, 123; sea level changes, 97, 153; temperature, 209

Reefs, 26–27; area loss, 95; barrier, 16, 163; building, 26–30, 33–34, 37, 39, 77–78, 83, 89–97, 109–111, 161–164; and carbon dioxide production, 140; channels, 17–18, 42, 177, Plate 23; classification, 16; and corals, 39–40; definitions of, 269; degradation, 36, 50, 53, 100–112, 118, 207, 214, 227; deltaic, 15–18, 42, 167, 177; drilling, 165–168; erosion, 41–42, 91–92, 105, 111; gaps, 67, 80, 87–91, 95–96, 98, 106–108, 111, 212, 214, 216; growth, 27–28, 30, 33–35, 39–41, 67, 94–96, 109–110, 128, 152, 158, 161–164, 169, 171–172, 208; growth rates, 40; habitats, planing off, 4, 144, 153, 163, 171; platform, 16, 23, 158; progradation, 145; research history, 161–168; structure, 16, 72, 161–168; types of, 16; zonation, 23, 155, 158, 196, 201. See also Azooxanthellate coral; Biodiversity; Carbonates; Caves; Cenozoic reefs; Drowning of reefs; Environments; Extinction; Fringing reefs; Glacial cycles; Great Barrier Reef, Health of reefs; Holocene, Mass extinction; Mesozoic reefs; Paleozoic reefs; Platform reefs; Refugia; Ribbon reefs; Sea level changes; Temperature, Tethys Sea; Zooxanthellate coral
Refugia, 135, 155, 208–209
Reproduction of coral, 43–44. See also Larvae of coral; Spawning of coral
Reticulate evolution, 43–44, 70, 160, Plate 9
Ribbon reefs, 3–4, 15–17, 128, 155–156, 165, 167, 170, Plates 1, 22, 37
Ribbon Reef borehole, 166–167
Rill weathering, 42
Rivers, 13–15, 19–21, 36, 47–48, 51–53, 169
Rivers and sea level, 148, 151, 154–155, 157–158, 174
Rudists, 82–83, 108–109, 130, 269
Rugose coral, 29, 69, 72, 75, 77, 108–109, 267, 269
Ryukyu Islands, 34, 171

Safe havens. See Refugia
Salinity, 14, 36, 41, 53, 56, 59, 86, 97, 106, 197
Salinity crises, 86, 97
Sand, calcareous, 15, 23, 36, 52

Sargassum, 207, 269, Plate 52
Saturation state. *See* Aragonite; Calcite;
    Carbonates; High-magnesium calcite
Scientific methodology, 190–191, 226
Scleractinia, 267, 269; family tree, 69, Plate
    8; origins of, 77–78; skeletons of, 26,
    28–30, 36, 54, 69, 82, 90, 104–105,
    108–109, 214, 217–220. *See also* Azooxan-
    thellate coral; Coral; Coral, evolution of;
    Diagenesis; Extinction; Mass extinction;
    Rugose coral; Soft coral; Tabulate coral;
    Zooxanthellate coral
Seabed communities. *See* Soft bottom com-
    munities
Sea floor spreading, 85, 99–100, 117, 125,
    127–128, 134, 162, 184
Sea level changes, 269; Cenozoic, 117;
    curves, 80, 156–158; and erosion,
    171–172; and extinctions, 69–70, 94–95;
    future, 194–196; and greenhouse effects,
    194–196; Ice Age, 134–135, 138, 143–146,
    151–158, 171–172; and ice volume, 128,
    139, 146, 153, 202; the last great rise,
    156–158; and mass extinctions, 69–70,
    94–95; Paleozoic and Mesozoic, 71,
    94–95, 117; and plate tectonics, 71, 94;
    present rate of increase, 194–196; and
    reef growth, 94–96, 110, 128, 152, 158,
    161–164, 171–172, Plates 37, 38; and
    shorelines, 148, 154–156, 176. *See also*
    Carbon dioxide; Caves; Drowning of
    reefs; Paleontology of coral; Rivers and
    sea level; Seafloor spreading
Sediment: composition, 14, 52; cores, 125,
    139, 142; distribution, 52; and light, 36;
    and rivers, 53–54, 155, 158; sequestration,
    52, 154, 158; suspension, 52–53; toler-
    ance, 12, 36, 52; and turbulence, 3, 15, 23,
    30, 35–39, 61, 106
Seismic profiling, 130, 165, 167
Sequestration, 269; of carbon dioxide, 230;
    of sediment, 52, 154, 158
Sharks, 2–3, 47, 49–50, 108
Ships, grounding of, 46
Shocked quartz, 84
Shoreline changes with sea level, 154–156,
    176
Siberian traps, 76, 92, 108

Silurian reefs, 73, Plate 33
Sintering of ice, 139
Sixth mass extinction, characteristics of,
    225–226; rate of approach, 219
Skeletal architecture, 37–38
Skeletal plasticity, 38–39
Skeleton: absence of, 109; and acidification,
    107, 212–220; and aragonite saturation,
    102, 104; building density, 36, 40, 105;
    and diagenesis, 90, 133; environmental
    records in, 40–41, 71, 116, 128, 138–139,
    146; X-rays of, 40–41. *See also* Aragonite
    skeletons; Calcification; Calcite skeletons;
    Colony formation; Skeletal plasticity
Skeptics of climate change, 66, 112,
    190–191, 202, 227
Soft-bottom communities, 14, 54
Soft coral, 2, 30, 266
Solitary Islands, 21–22
Solomon Islands, 21, 43, 48
South Equatorial Current, 63
Southern Ocean acidification, 216, 218
South Pacific Convergence Zone, 64
Spawning of coral, 53–54, 197. *See also*
    Reproduction of coral
Spear fishing, 49, 180, Plate 27
Species: changes within, 38, 43–44, 69–70;
    concepts of, 43–44, 160; evolution, 19–20,
    29, 43–44, 55, 67, 69–70, 95, 200–202,
    208–211. *See also* Biodiversity; Fossil
    record
Spike: carbon dioxide, 107–108, 198, 216,
    224; climate, 188, 198–199, 231
Sponges: calcifying, 79; Paleozoic, 27;
    stromatoporoid, 72, 76, Plate 32; zooxan-
    thellate, 30
Spur and groove formations, 42, Plate 23
Stone Age humans. *See* Paleolithic humans
Storms, 54, 85, 158, 197, 220
Stromatoporoid sponges, 72, 76, 270,
    Plate 32
Structure: of coral, 26, 37, 75, 96, 105; of
    reefs, 27–29, 42, 77–78, 82, 110, 132,
    165–168, 219
Subduction zones, 88, 99, 129, 270
Substrate composition, 14–15, 21, 23, 30,
    32, 36, 52–53, 145
Sulfur dioxide, 101, 187, 193, 195, 270

Sunscreens, 33, 57
Sunspot cycles, 187, 270
Super Tethys Sea, 83, 97, 270
Supervolcanoes, 92, 100, 184
Supranoxic events, 101
Surface currents, 21, 63, 118–119, 172; and
    evolution, 43–44, 70. *See also* Currents
Symbiosis, 29–30, 32, 34, 96, 203, 270. *See
    also* Zooxanthellae
Symbiotic coral. *See* Zooxanthellate coral
Synergies, 35, 91, 100–101, 106–107, 111,
    197, 213

Tabulate coral, 29, 67, 69, 72, 77, 108–109,
    267, 270
Taxonomy of coral, 70
Teleconnections, 142
Temperature, 33–35, 60–62; acclimatization
    to, 209–210; and acidification, 100, 105,
    217, 220; adaptation to, 95–97, 110, 151,
    206, 208–210; and carbon dioxide solu-
    bility, 64, 140, 212–213; control of,
    191–192, 194; effects on marine life,
    200–202; and extinctions, 64, 140,
    212–213; and geological records, 71–72;
    and growth rates, 34–35; Ice Age,
    146–147; and ice cores, 71, 142–144,
    146–147; latitudinal gradients, 34, 95–97,
    118–120, 123; limits for coral, 34, 62, 95,
    209; limits for reefs, 33–34; and mass
    bleaching, 203–205; and mass extinc-
    tions, 95–97; measurement of, 61–62,
    Plate 53; and photosynthesis, 33, 95; and
    reef growth, 33–35; sea surface, 61–62;
    stratification, 194; stress, 56, 59, 97,
    201–202, 209; tolerance, 201–202, 209.
    See also Bleaching of coral; Buffers;
    Cenozoic; Cretaceous; ENSO; Eocene;
    Greenhouse gases; Icehouse climates; Last
    glacial cycle; Late Paleocene Thermal
    Maximum; Miocene; Paleozoic; Pleis-
    tocene; Thermal Cap
Tethys Sea, 270; biodiversity of, 118,
    121–123, 131; closure of, 121, 123; coral
    of, 122–123, 132; currents of, 118; geo-
    graphic positions of, 73–74, 76, 78, 83,
    115, 122
Thermal Cap, 35, 62, 97, 205–206, 209, 227

Thermal expansion of the oceans, 194, 196
Thermal inertia. *See* Inertia
Thermocline, 63–64, 270
Thermohaline convection, 120–121,
    141–142, 145, 186, 194, 197. *See also*
    Ocean Conveyor
Tidal regimes, 15, 61. *See also* Currents
Tijou Reef, 3–4, 16, 24, 49, 154, 174,
    177–178, 221, 231, Plate 42
Time, biological, 7; concepts of, 7–8; evolu-
    tionary, 7, 43, 202, 206; geological, 7–8,
    35, 79, 143, 198; human, 7, 183, 198, 206,
    222–231
Time lags. *See* Inertia
Torres Strait, 39, 148, 154, 158, 177, 180,
    196
Tourism impacts, 47–49, 55, 181
Townsville Trough, 24
Toxins, 97–98
Traps, lava, 76, 83, 85, 87, 92, 101, 107–108,
    184, 270
Trawling, 15, 46, 49, 54–55
Triassic: coral, 70, 77–79, 81, 90, Plate 35;
    mass extinction, 79, 81; reefs, 78, Plate 35
Triton, giant, 51
Tsunamis, 84, 91–62, 156, 222
Tubastrea, 30, Plate 14
Turbidity, 14, 30, 32, 36, 39, 47, 52, 156, 204
Turbulence, 3, 15, 23, 30, 35–39, 61, 106
Turtles, 47, 82, 108, 180, 196, Plate 30

Ultraviolet light, 59, 98, 192

Vanuatu, 20–21
Vermetid worms, 27
Volcanism, 84–85, 92, 99–101, 111, 121,
    125, 172, 184, 186, 189
Vostok ice records, 136, 139–140, 144, 146

Walker Circulation, 63–64
Walker's Caves, 4, 177, Plate 42
Warming. *See* Temperature
Water quality, 36–37, 51–54. *See also* Health
    of reefs; Nutrients; Sediment; Turbidity
Wave energy, 15, 37; and turbulence, 3, 15,
    23, 30, 35–39, 61, 106
Weathering of rock, 42, 94, 99, 106, 215
West Antarctic Ice Sheet, 189

Western Australia, archaeological sites, 180; coral, 34, 170; currents, 21, 119; reefs, 51, 60, 130, 169–170

Western Pacific Thermal Cap, 35, 62–63, 97, 205–206, 209, 227, 271

Western Pacific Warm Pool, 62–65, 147, 200, 205–206, 227, 271

Whales, 2, Plate 26

Whale sharks, 2

White band disease, 208, Plate 56

Whitsunday Islands: archaeological sites, 181; coral diversity, 95

X-rays of coral, 40–41

Younger Dryas event, 185–187

Zonation of reefs, 13–15, 151, 155, 158, 196

Zooplankton, 31, 54, 57

Zooxanthellae, 30–32, 271, Plate 12; concentration in coral, 31; extracellular, 108–109; genetic history, 202–203, 210, 220; genetic modifications, 210; geographic variations in, 32, 59; intracellular, 108–109; and light, 30, 33, 56–57, 60, 93; and oxygen, 33, 35, 57, 202; and photosynthesis, 30, 33, 35, 38; size of, 31; symbiosis, 30–32, 35, 56; and temperature, 35, 57, 60; temporal variation in, 202–203, 210, 220; uptake by coral, 32. *See also* Bleaching of coral; Clades of zooxanthellae; Mass bleaching

Zooxanthellate coral, 30, 32, 70, 82, 91, 93–96, 98, 104–107, 214, 271. *See also* Coral; Scleractinia